ALSO BY TODD S. PURDUM

A Time of Our Choosing: America's War in Iraq
(with the staff of *The New York Times*)

AN IDEA
WHOSE TIME
HAS COME

AN IDEA
WHOSE TIME
HAS COME

TWO PRESIDENTS, TWO PARTIES,

AND THE BATTLE FOR

THE CIVIL RIGHTS ACT OF 1964

TODD S. PURDUM

Henry Holt and Company
New York

Henry Holt and Company, LLC
Publishers since 1866
175 Fifth Avenue
New York, New York 10010
www.henryholt.com

Henry Holt® and 🅗® are registered trademarks of
Henry Holt and Company, LLC.

Library of Congress Cataloging-in-Publication Data

Purdum, Todd S., author.
   An idea whose time has come : two presidents, two parties,
and the battle for the Civil Rights Act of 1964 / Todd S. Purdum.
      pages cm
   Includes bibliographical references and index.
   ISBN 978-0-8050-9672-9 (hardback)—ISBN 978-0-8050-9673-6 (electronic book)
1. United States. Civil Rights Act of 1964.   2. Civil rights—United States—
History—20th century.   3. United States—Politics and government—1961–1963.
4. United States—Politics and government—1963–1969.   I. Title.
   KF4744.5151964.P87 2014
   342.7308'5—dc23   2013038545

First Edition 2014

Designed by Meryl Sussman Levavi

Printed in the United States of America

1   3   5   7   9   10   8   6   4   2

For Dee Dee, of course

"Stronger than all the armies is an idea whose time has come."

—Senator Everett McKinley Dirksen,
June 10, 1964

Contents

Part Three
THE SENATE

AN IDEA
WHOSE TIME
HAS COME

Prologue

JUST AFTER 1:30 P.M., in the near-empty chamber of the United States Senate, a handsome, dark-haired freshman was taking his back-bencher's turn at a thankless task: presiding over a desultory debate on the need for federal library services. Edward M. Kennedy, thirty-one years old, had been the junior senator from Massachusetts for barely a year and had yet to make a speech from the floor. Suddenly, Richard Riedel, a Senate press liaison who had first come to the Capitol a half century earlier as a nine-year-old page, came running onto the Senate floor, in a breach of all decorum. He rushed for the rostrum and told the presiding officer, "The most horrible thing has happened! It's terrible, terrible!"

Kennedy, who had been signing letters and autographing photographs, paused to ask, "What is it?"

"Your brother," Riedel began, before remembering that the senator had two brothers. "Your brother the president. He's been shot." Riedel had seen the news on the Associated Press ticker in the Senators' Lobby, the long corridor behind the chamber, and immediately began spreading the news. Kennedy leaped up and ran toward his own office, followed by

David Schoumacher, a young CBS News reporter who had started work that very week. "I don't know anything," Kennedy told him. "I just heard."

A few blocks down Massachusetts Avenue, at the Chilean embassy, Senator Hubert H. Humphrey of Minnesota, who had lost the 1960 Democratic nomination to John F. Kennedy after hard-fought primaries in Wisconsin and West Virginia, was sitting down with his wife, Muriel, at a luncheon in honor of the ambassador of Australia. The other guests included Ralph Dungan, a special assistant to President Kennedy, and Edward P. Morgan, a veteran broadcast reporter working for ABC News. An urgent telephone call summoned Morgan away from the table with the same bulletin from Dallas. He returned and told Humphrey, and together they called Dungan into a space outside the dining room. After what seemed an interminable delay, Dungan confirmed the news with the Secret Service and left for the White House. Humphrey remained, heading to his car parked in front of the embassy to listen for updates on the radio.

Across the Potomac River in McLean, Virginia, Attorney General Robert F. Kennedy, who two days earlier had turned thirty-eight years old, was at home taking a break from a daylong conference on organized crime. He was having lunch with his friend Robert Morgenthau, the United States attorney in Manhattan, eating a tuna fish sandwich, when the telephone rang by his backyard pool. At the other end of the line was the formidable director of the Federal Bureau of Investigation, J. Edgar Hoover, already in his fortieth year as head of the nation's most powerful law enforcement agency. His voice was cold, his manner curt. "I have news for you," he said. "The president's been shot."

The attorney general struggled to understand. "What? Oh—I—is it serious?" he stammered.

"I think it is serious," Hoover replied. "I am endeavoring to get details. I'll call you back when I find out more."

In Atlanta, Martin Luther King Jr., the thirty-four-year-old preacher who for nearly a decade had been leading his nonviolent campaign for civil rights in cities across the South, was under the weather and watching television at home in bed. He had special reason to be grateful to President Kennedy, whose intercession and dramatic phone call to his wife, Coretta, during the 1960 campaign had helped secure King's release from jail after he was arrested at a lunch counter sit-in at an Atlanta department store and sentenced to hard labor. Now, King called out to his wife, who was on the phone downstairs, "Corrie, I just heard that Kennedy has been shot, maybe killed." And then he told her, "Oh, I hope that he will live, this is just terrible. I think that if he lives, if he pulls through this, it will help him to understand better what we go through."

* * *

As the minutes ticked by toward 2:00 p.m. Washington time, and then 2:30, Ted Kennedy raced on foot through the streets of his Georgetown neighborhood with his aide Milt Gwirtzman, trying in vain to find a working phone. A mass of sudden midday calls to share the news from Texas had overwhelmed the Chesapeake & Potomac Telephone Company's entire system.

At 2:35, United Press International moved its definitive flash from Dallas: PRESIDENT KENNEDY DEAD. In McLean, Bob Kennedy heard the news in a phone call from Taz Shepard, the president's naval aide, and then in another abrupt call from Director Hoover, who simply said, "The president's dead," and hung up. (Robert Kennedy would later say that Hoover had seemed "not quite as excited as if he were reporting the fact that he had found a Communist on the faculty of Howard University.")

At the Chilean embassy, Hubert Humphrey received confirmation from Ralph Dungan at the White House and announced the news to the luncheon guests. Then he broke down in tears. Unsure of what else to do, he headed to the Northwest Gate of the White House and into Dungan's office in the West Wing, where a group including a young assistant secretary of labor named Daniel Patrick Moynihan had gathered. "What have they done to us?" Humphrey cried out. Later he would recall, "For most of us who gathered there, there was nothing, really, to do. The fact of his death was so overwhelming; yet in this house where he worked, ate, slept, played with his kids, it was impossible to think of him in the past tense. The reality was so horrendous that the whole atmosphere, paradoxically, took on an unreal quality."

In the Senate, it was the Republican minority leader, Everett McKinley

Dirksen, a sixty-seven-year-old small-town boy from Pekin, Illinois, who had to make a motion for adjournment because the Democratic majority leader, Mike Mansfield of Montana, was too overcome. The scene was so chaotic that the journal of official proceedings does not even mention the reason for the break. Dirksen, who had once practiced before his family's cows the florid oratory that would make him known as "the Wizard of Ooze," had engaged President Kennedy, his former Senate colleague, with affectionate badinage, and just that fall he had helped the president gain the Senate's assent to the Nuclear Test Ban Treaty. Now he was a visage of melancholy, his jowly face contorted and gray with grief. He told reporters, "Only someone suffering from aberrations of personality and motivated by insane passion would be guilty of the assassination of the great leader of the greatest country on earth."

In the Senators' Lobby, with its big leather chairs and racks of out-of-town newspapers, a knot of members clustered around the Associated Press wire ticker. In the center was sixty-six-year-old Richard Brevard Russell Jr. of Georgia, a stern bachelor who was the master of the chamber's rules, the mentor to younger Democrats, the leader of the conservative southern caucus—and no great booster of John Fitzgerald Kennedy. As the bulletins came in from Dallas, Russell read them aloud, and his voice began to waver with each new bit of bad news, until finally the tears ran down his face.

The crusty House Republican leader, Charles A. Halleck of Indiana, a self-described "gut-fighter" who only the day before had excoriated the president's legislative record, now insisted: "The world should know that in this hour of national tragedy Americans stand together as one—shocked and grieved at this incredible news. Political differences had no part in the personal affection I felt for President Kennedy—an affection I have reason to believe the president felt for me."

In Atlanta, Martin King told his wife, "This is what's going to happen to me. This is such a sick society."

King was especially crushed, because he felt that John Kennedy was finally coming around on civil rights. The previous June, on the same night that Governor George C. Wallace had sought unsuccessfully to block the integration of the University of Alabama, Kennedy had made a nationally televised speech, at last pledging his administration's support for the kind of comprehensive civil rights bill that King and others had been demanding for years. Three months later, after the murder of four little girls in a bombing at the Sixteenth Street Baptist Church in Birmingham, King thought that Kennedy had showed renewed resolve to see the bill enacted.

The next month, on October 29, the civil rights bill, H.R. 7152, passed the House Judiciary Committee, with crucial help from its ranking Republican member, Representative William M. McCulloch of Ohio, who called Kennedy's assassination "a tragic death, especially for one so young, who had so much to do and, for the doing, he had so little time."

But on this November afternoon, the bill lay bottled up in the House Rules Committee, whose chairman, eighty-year-old Representative Howard W. Smith of Virginia, an ardent segregationist, had announced his intention to keep it there indefinitely. Now, King thought, the world would never get to see what history might have had in store had Kennedy lived.

Clarence Mitchell, the chief Washington lobbyist for the National Association for the Advancement of Colored People, the nation's oldest and largest civil rights group, had been working tirelessly on behalf of H.R. 7152, and his organization issued a statement saying that President Kennedy's "consistent commitment to and espousal of basic human rights for all earned the undying enmity of frantic and loathsome bigots," and adding, "We have no doubt that the assassin was motivated by a hatred of the president's ideals."

That night, when Jacqueline Kennedy had returned from Texas and was grieving at Bethesda Naval Hospital as doctors conducted an autopsy on her murdered husband, she also thought of civil rights, but she was brought up short when Bob Kennedy explained that the president's presumed assassin was a pro-Cuban Communist sympathizer, not a right-winger. "He didn't even have the satisfaction of being killed for civil rights," the First Lady told her mother, Janet Auchincloss. "It's—it had to be some silly little Communist."

But Martin King and Jackie Kennedy weren't counting on another figure in that day's drama, another man in the motorcade in Dallas, who had just become the nation's thirty-sixth president: Lyndon Baines Johnson of

Texas. Together with the crucial, indispensable support of King, Mitch-ell, Bob Kennedy, Humphrey, Halleck, McCulloch, and Dirksen—and over the relentless opposition of Russell—Johnson was about to make some history of his own. And the civil rights bill would be at its very heart.

This is the story of the legislative and political battle to pass that bill. As such, it is largely the story of the words and actions of white men, who, with rare exceptions in 1963 and 1964, possessed the sole official agency to enact—or block—any such law, at a time when just five of the 535 members of Congress were black. The American civil rights move-ment was a massive grassroots effort, involving tens of thousands of black and white citizens, whose labors over many decades had aroused the nation's conscience and spurred demands for legal change that made the Civil Rights Act of 1964 possible. But paradoxically, the bill itself was pro-posed and passed mostly by men whose personal acquaintance with black Americans was limited to their own domestic servants and the leaders of the movement who had provided the moral impetus and historical argu-ment for its fierce necessity. Its passage was, in that sense, all the more remarkable.

* * *

TWO DAYS AFTER KENNEDY'S funeral, President Johnson addressed a joint session of Congress in the Capitol that had been his professional home for thirty-two years. "All I have I would have given gladly not to be standing here today," he told his former colleagues and the noontime national television audience tuning in for its first extended look at the new president. "The greatest leader of our time has been struck down by the foulest deed of our time." He invoked the passage in the martyred president's inaugural address in which Kennedy had acknowledged that his agenda would not be finished "in the first thousand days, nor in the life of this administration, nor even perhaps in our lifetime on this planet," but had nevertheless insisted, "Let us begin." Johnson now said, "Let us continue."

The new president went on to add, "No memorial oration or eulogy could more eloquently honor President Kennedy's memory than the earliest possible passage of the civil rights bill for which he fought so long. We have talked long enough in this country about equal rights. We have talked for a hundred years or more. It is time now to write the next chapter, and to write it in the books of law."

Johnson was a most unlikely tribune for the cause he now espoused. A southerner born just eight years into the twentieth century, he still talked in private about "Nigras," in terms that would not have pleased Martin Luther King or the NAACP, or the editorial board of the *New York Times*, for that matter. As Senate majority leader, he had helped pass the first serious civil rights legislation of modern times in 1957, but to gain its passage he had arranged for it to be so watered down as to make it all but unenforceable in actual practice across the South. For Johnson's whole time in the Senate, Richard Russell had been his particular teacher and cherished friend, and Russell was perhaps the Senate's single most influential supporter of segregation and its most skilled opponent of civil rights legislation.

But in fact, Johnson's views on civil rights had been evolving for years. Now they had hardened into certitude that the time had come for change. Within days of the assassination, he was telling friends, "I'm going to be the president who finishes what Lincoln began." And he summoned Russell to the White House for a blunt talking-to. "Dick," Johnson said, "you've got to get out of my way. I'm going to run over you. I don't intend to cavil or compromise."

"Well, Mr. President, you may well do that," Russell replied. "But if you do, you'll not only lose this election, you will lose the South forever."

Johnson did not disagree with Russell's political analysis. He also knew that because of Russell's stance, passing a civil rights bill would depend on strong Republican support, support that was far from assured. But he thought that the passage of comprehensive civil rights legislation was vital precisely because it might act as a balm for the climate of hate and extremism that was then being widely blamed for the Kennedy assassination—and because it was a key to establishing his own credibility to pursue his other ambitious goals. He could not know that the assassination marked just the latest twist in a period of civic unrest and political tumult unrivaled since the Civil War itself. Or that some aspects of the proposed civil rights bill would still be debated in national politics nearly fifty years into the future. Or that a child in Hawaii named Barack Hussein Obama, who was two years, three months, and eighteen days old on November 22, would one day be president of the United States.

Johnson could not even know that over the next seven months, H.R. 7152—"An act to enforce the constitutional right to vote, to confer jurisdiction upon the district courts of the United States of America to provide relief against discrimination in public accommodations, to authorize the Attorney General to institute suits to protect constitutional rights in public facilities and public education," among other things—would consume the country. He could not know that it would prompt the longest debate in the history of his beloved Senate, lasting not quite two minutes more than 534 hours. He could not know that the debate would contribute to one of the great, early running stories in television news, or that the bill's final passage would coincide with the brutal murder of three young civil rights workers in Philadelphia, Mississippi.

All Johnson could know for certain that grim November was that after three decades in politics—three decades of arm twisting and nose counting and vote seeking, compromise and guile—he had at last reached the top of the heap and was his own man, no longer a congressman from the Hill Country of Texas or even a senator from the Lone Star Republic, but the president of all these United States. And he was determined to see what he could do with the job.

"The endless abrasions of delay, neglect and indifference have rubbed raw the national conscience," Johnson told a group of labor leaders days after the assassination. "We have talked too long, we have done too little. And all of it has come too late. You must help me make civil rights in America a reality."

At a meeting that December, when Roy Wilkins, the executive secretary of the NAACP, asked him why he was supporting civil rights legislation after so many years of comparative indifference, Johnson paused before replying, in phrases made famous by Martin Luther King himself: "You will recognize the words I'm about to repeat," the president said, " 'Free at last, free at last, thank God almighty, I'm free at last.' "

PART ONE

THE
ADMINISTRATION

1

A Century's Unfinished Business

TUESDAY, FEBRUARY 12, 1963

IT WAS A PARADOX not lost on John F. Kennedy that even as the United States undertook to celebrate the centennial of the Civil War, it often seemed on the verge of a second one. In many ways, Kennedy's America, like Abraham Lincoln's, was two countries—North and South, black and white, still separate and unequal. In January 1961, Georgia's Democratic governor, Ernest Vandiver, had avoided the awkwardness of having to attend the festivities marking the anniversary of his state's secession from the union only by arranging to be in Washington for Kennedy's own inauguration.

Now, two years later, peaceful protests—and the violent backlash against them—had spread across the South, from lunch counter sit-ins and "Freedom Rides" aimed at desegregating public places and interstate buses, to firebombing mobs and defiant public school boards that had closed their districts' doors rather than mix black and white students. Rigid racial segregation remained a fact of law and life in the states of the Old Confederacy nearly a century after the War Between the States had ended. And the federal government in Washington seemed just as unable—or at least as unwilling—to resolve the growing conflict over civil rights as it had been to grapple with the uproar over slavery in the 1850s.

Nothing better exemplified Kennedy's deep and abiding ambivalence about how to handle the uncomfortable politics of the issue than his indecision over how to mark the centennial of Lincoln's signing of the Emancipation Proclamation on January 1, 1863. In September 1962, Kennedy had declined to attend a ceremony at the Lincoln Memorial commemorating the centenary of the proclamation's first draft, instead sending a six-paragraph recorded statement to be broadcast over the public address system while he himself watched the America's Cup yacht races off Newport, Rhode Island. "The best commemoration lies not in what we say today," Kennedy had said, "but in what we do in the days and months ahead to complete the work begun by Abraham Lincoln a century ago."

Just what Kennedy himself would do was the dominant question of the day. The president may have been willing to skip the commemoration ceremony, but he was nevertheless chagrined to see that Nelson Rockefeller, the Republican governor of New York and a potential rival for the White House in 1964, *had* appeared at it, armed with one of the Empire State's most precious archival possessions: the draft proclamation in Lincoln's own hand. In his speech that day, Rockefeller urged the nation to rededicate itself to the "basic belief in the worth and dignity of the individual and the right of each to full and equal opportunity in sharing the American dream."

Rockefeller had the political standing to make such a plea. For much of the century since the Civil War, civil rights had been a Republican cause—to the degree that it had been a real cause for either major party at all. The 1960 Republican and Democratic platform planks on civil rights had been virtually identical and equally strong, if still mostly un-acted-on three years later. John Kennedy well knew that he could not take the black vote for granted, in part because of his own party's powerful southern segregationist wing, and that the prospects in Congress for meaningful civil rights legislation were fraught at best.

So the president was always on the lookout for ways to shore up black support without alienating the white legislators whose backing he needed for his administration's broader program. And now, on Lincoln's birthday, he had agreed to hold a White House reception for some eight hundred black Americans—by far the largest such assembly ever gathered under the president's roof. At the last minute, the White House had notified all the guests to arrive via the Executive Mansion's Southwest Gate (so as to avoid the press), and press secretary Pierre Salinger had assured white reporters that the gathering was only a minor social event. Some of the nation's most prominent civil rights leaders—among them A. Philip Randolph, the godfather of the movement and the longtime leader of the Brotherhood of Sleeping Car Porters, and Clarence Mitchell, of the NAACP—had declined to attend the party, in protest over Kennedy's failure to propose new civil rights legislation. Still, the evening won wide and sympathetic coverage in the black press, while drawing little notice in mainstream newspapers.

Kennedy's principal personal reaction to the party was pique. He noticed his friend Sammy Davis Jr. and his white wife, the Swedish actress May Britt, among the throng of guests, mischievously invited by Louis Martin, a black former newspaper publisher who was the Democratic Party's chief point man on civil rights. Davis's interracial relationship with Britt had made him such an anathema to segregationists that Kennedy had banned him from performing at the inaugural gala organized by their mutual friend Frank Sinatra two years earlier, and now the president was so determined to avoid photographs of the two together in the White House that he urged his wife to pull Britt aside. Jacqueline Kennedy was so angry at her husband's request that she soon left the formal reception in tears. The Davises' presence "kind of really put a pall on the whole thing," the president's civil rights adviser Lee White would recall.

On the very afternoon of the reception, the president had received a formal 246-page report from the United States Civil Rights Commission, an independent fact-finding body established by Congress in 1957, declaring that black Americans in the twentieth century had experienced "a freedom more fictional than real," and adding, "The final chapter in the struggle for equality has yet to be written." The nation's single most prominent civil rights figure, Martin Luther King Jr., offered an even sharper view. "The administration sought to demonstrate to Negroes that it has concern for them while at the same time it has striven to avoid inflaming the opposition," King would write in *The Nation*. "The most cynical view holds that it wants the vote of both and is paralyzed by the conflicting needs of each."

* * *

IN FACT, WHEN IT came to civil rights, much of America was paralyzed in 1963. For every glimmer of racial progress, there were shades of set-backs. The Supreme Court had outlawed segregation in public schools in 1954, but in much of the country, segregation was still the norm. In the South, just twelve thousand of the three million black students attended integrated schools. Martin Luther King's 1955 boycott to desegregate pub-lic buses in Montgomery, Alabama, had succeeded (thanks to a parallel lawsuit financed by the NAACP), but his subsequent direct action campaigns—including a long desegregation crusade in Albany, Georgia, in 1961 and 1962—had fizzled.

In the broader culture, the picture was also mixed. Jackie Robinson had broken Major League Baseball's color line with the Brooklyn Dodg-ers in 1947, and now black athletes such as Bill Russell in the National Basketball Association and Jim Brown of the National Football League had become stars in their own right. But not until 1959—three years after Robinson's *retirement*—had the Boston Red Sox become the last big-league franchise to open its roster to black players, and black sports stars were still the exception, not the rule.

As early as 1956, Harry Belafonte's *Calypso* had become the first million-selling long-playing record in history, because of its crossover appeal to blacks and whites alike, and the same year, Nat King Cole became the first black entertainer to host his own network television program, on NBC. But Cole's show never did manage to attract a national sponsor, so he had abandoned it after thirteen months, complaining, "Madison Avenue is afraid of the dark." Even now, the favorite TV guest gig of Lena Horne, Hollywood's first black female star and pinup girl, was appearing on Perry Como's weekly variety show on NBC, because he was one of the few hosts willing to violate the taboo against blacks and whites touching on the air. The 1962–63 television season's sixth-rated entertainment program starred Andy Griffith as a sweet-reasoned southern sheriff dispensing justice in the idyllic town of Mayberry, North Carolina, in a "situation comedy" where no black characters ever entered the situation.

The United States was already sending black troops to help the government of South Vietnam in its struggle against Communism, but it was not welcoming them home with a communitarian spirit. One black Army captain, just back from his first tour in Vietnam and stationed at Fort Benning, Georgia, was tired and hungry one day after fixing up a modest rental house for his wife and baby son. He stopped at a local drive-in in hopes of ordering a hamburger to go. He knew he could not be served inside, but thought he might get curb service. "I pulled in and after a small eternity, a waitress came to my car," he would recall.

"Are you Puerto Rican?" the waitress asked.

"No," the soldier answered.

"Are you an African student?" she wondered.

"No," the soldier replied. "I'm a Negro. I'm an American. And I'm an Army officer."

"Look, I'm from New Jersey," the waitress said, "and I don't understand any of this. But they won't let me serve you. Why don't you let me go behind the restaurant, and I'll pass you a hamburger out the back window?"

"I'm not *that* hungry," snapped the captain, whose name was Colin Powell. "As I drove away," he would recall years later, "I could see the faces of the owner and his customers in the restaurant windows enjoying this little exercise in humiliation."

Even in the highest councils of state, the segregationist South made no apologies for its defiant attitude. Indeed, many white southerners took pains to contend that it was *they* who had been humiliated. In one typically revealing exchange on the floor of the United States Senate in 1962, Paul Douglas of Illinois, one of the chamber's most enthusiastic civil rights supporters, tried to ascertain whether Richard Russell, the powerful leader of the Senate's southern caucus, actually supported the Fifteenth Amendment to the Constitution, which had prohibited denial of a citizen's right to vote, based on his "race, color or previous condition of servitude." "I am not enthusiastic about the amendment," an indignant

Russell replied. "That amendment was written in the blood of the Civil War and was inevitable after Appomattox and the South is reconciled to it, but it was written in blood . . . If the Senator is going to try to get me to apologize for the Civil War at this late date, or to get on my knees any further than was necessary at Appomattox, I shall not do it."

* * *

THE CHALLENGE OF CIVIL rights as the 1960s dawned was simple yet profound: In the century since the Civil War, the nation had neither fully accepted the consequences of the conflict's outcome nor enforced the provisions of the Thirteenth and Fourteenth Amendments passed in the war's wake, guaranteeing full citizenship and the equal protection of the laws to all Americans, regardless of race—let alone the Fifteenth Amendment's promise of voting rights. In the Reconstruction era, Congress had at least tried, passing the Civil Rights Act of 1875, which granted full and equal access to public accommodations—hotels, restaurants, trains, and so on—to blacks and whites alike. But in 1883, ruling in a group of consolidated cases, the Supreme Court of the United States had held that Congress lacked the power to outlaw discrimination by private individuals, a decision that had never been overturned. In 1896, in the case of *Plessy v. Ferguson*, the High Court had further enshrined segregation by ruling that "separate but equal" facilities for blacks and whites were compatible with the Constitution.

For six decades following the *Plessy* decision, through two world wars, rapid technological innovation, and innumerable other changes in American life, rigid separation of the races was the legal and practical fact throughout the states of the Old South, while schools, transportation, and accommodations for blacks and whites remained far from equal. No significant civil rights bill had passed Congress in all that time, and perhaps only 20 percent of eligible blacks were registered to vote.

Finally, in 1954, in *Brown v. Board of Education*, a case involving the public schools of Topeka, Kansas (consolidated with several similar cases from other jurisdictions), the Supreme Court unanimously held that "separate" was inherently *unequal*, overturning *Plessy* and creating rising public pressure to make good at last on the full promise of emancipation.

In 1957, the administration of President Dwight D. Eisenhower proposed what would become the first major civil rights law since Reconstruction, aimed at guaranteeing access to the voting booth for America's black citizens and giving the federal government sweeping powers to intervene in states and localities to force the desegregation of public schools. The bill would also create a six-member, bipartisan federal Commission on Civil Rights with power to investigate discriminatory practices, and would elevate the civil rights section of the Justice Department into a full-fledged division. Eisenhower's personal support for civil rights had been notably weak, but his attorney general, Herbert Brownell, still took seriously the Republicans' heritage as the Party of Lincoln, and he had a powerful and unlikely ally in the Democratic Senate majority leader, Lyndon Johnson. Throughout his career in Congress, Johnson had been a staunch New Deal liberal but also a loyal segregationist, voting with his southern colleagues to maintain the status quo. Now he had presidential ambitions of his own, and he knew that he could not win nationwide office on such a platform. So Johnson undertook the wheeling and dealing and watering down that made it possible to forestall a southern filibuster and pass the Civil Rights Act of 1957, stripping it of enforcement powers and provisions to desegregate public places while retaining relatively weak provisions for voting rights.

A similarly weak bill was passed by Congress in 1960 and it, too, did little to reverse the practical impacts of segregation. In Augusta, Georgia, there were five hotels and motels that would take dogs, and only one where blacks could go with confidence. A Senate Commerce Committee study found that a black family traveling from Washington, D.C., to Miami would have to drive an average distance of 141 miles between destinations to find overnight accommodations. And the United States Commission on Civil Rights judged 57 percent of housing for blacks to be substandard.

The 1960 Democratic platform had included a sweeping civil rights plank, calling for an end to discrimination in voting, education, lunch counters, housing, and employment; promising to use the "full powers" of the 1957 Civil Rights Act to secure blacks the right to vote; pledging to "take whatever action is necessary" to eliminate literacy tests and poll taxes; supporting "peaceful demonstrations for first-class citizenship"; and demanding that every school district affected by the *Brown* decision submit at least preliminary plans for compliance by 1963. The Republicans—pressured by Nelson Rockefeller and others—had taken an almost equally strong stance. Both parties were officially committed to change, and both had raised expectations of action.

Still, John Kennedy's trusted counselor and speechwriter Ted Sorensen recalled that his boss privately worried that the Democrats had embraced "too many antagonistic specifics that could not be fulfilled, raising too many unwarranted hopes and unnecessary fears." In fact, Richard Russell, the Senate's most ardent defender of segregation, gloomily concluded that Kennedy would not only work to implement the platform but would actually "advocate civil rights legislation beyond" it.

* * *

BUT IN THE FIRST two years of the Kennedy administration, no such advocacy was forthcoming. Instead, the president temporized at every turn. The plain truth was that John Kennedy believed that strong civil rights legislation would be difficult if not impossible to pass, and that it could well jeopardize the rest of his legislative program. Yes, the president enjoyed large majorities in both houses of Congress, with a three-to-two Democratic advantage in the House and a two-to-one advantage in the Senate, where there were sixty-seven Democrats compared with just thirty-three Republicans. But eighteen of those Senate Democrats were implacable segregationists, which meant that the president's party, by itself, could not muster a simple majority for civil rights legislation, much less the two-thirds vote that would be needed under the Senate's rules to cut off debate and force a vote on any bill. Indeed, the internal North-South fissures in the Democratic Party were so pervasive, and so powerful, that *Congressional Quarterly*, the authoritative chronicler of legislative action on Capitol Hill, recorded the parties' votes in those days not just two ways, as "R" and "D," but three: as "R" and "ND" and "SD." No civil rights bill could pass without substantial Republican support, and while many Republicans still liked to think of themselves as supporting civil rights, many also resisted the sort of government incursion into private property rights that they believed compulsory integration would entail.

So Kennedy saw civil rights legislation as an ideal to aspire to—perhaps in a second term—and not a hill to die on. Senator Barry Goldwater of Arizona, Kennedy's most likely Republican rival for the presidency in 1964, took note of the president's perpetual hesitation on the issue at the 1962 Gridiron Club roast. "When my administration takes office in January 1965," Goldwater teased, "I will use the full powers provided in the Civil Rights Acts of 1957 and 1960 to secure for all Americans the right to vote. But, like your administration, Mr. President, I will not set any specific date for this action."

Yet it was Kennedy himself who had done so much to raise expectations of more meaningful action. In the 1960 campaign, he had asserted that an executive order barring discrimination in federally supported housing was a simple matter of the "stroke of a pen." But he did not issue any such order until November 1962, and even then it applied only to housing built in the future. "It took a hell of a lot more struggle and examination than I think we realized, and I'm sure the candidate realized, when he uttered those famous words," his adviser Lee White would recall. "Toward the end of '61 and '62, a lot of people began sending ink and pens for the president. To the extent that you can laugh about a joke when you're the butt of it, he thought it was pretty damn funny. We sent the pens to some school for the retarded. We didn't want them to go to waste."

Earlier in 1962, Kennedy had made a comparably weak push for a bill to end the arbitrary state literacy tests that were routinely used to disenfranchise blacks in the South. He supported an effort by the Senate's Democratic leader, Mike Mansfield, to make the completion of a sixth-grade education presumptive proof of literacy. But the effort ended in two humiliating failures to break a southern filibuster.

Still, Kennedy *had* taken important symbolic steps on civil rights. At the beginning of his term, he had approved the adoption of new regulations barring discrimination by users of federal lands, as a way of pressuring George Preston Marshall, the defiantly segregationist owner of the Washington Redskins football team, to hire a black player in time for the 1962 NFL season. (The Redskins were about to move into a new stadium, built and owned by the federal government on land under jurisdiction of the National Park Service, making them subject to the new rules.)

The president was also deeply concerned that segregation was giving the United States an international black eye—and the Soviet Union a handy propaganda tool—and never more so than with regard to the embarrassing discrimination faced by diplomats from the newly independent African nations. Restaurants and motels along U.S. Route 40 in Maryland, part of the principal highway between New York and Washington, had refused to serve—and, in at least one case, had manhandled—African ambassadors traveling to and from the United Nations in Manhattan. So Kennedy ordered top State Department officials to wage a campaign to end the discrimination. But the president often seemed as irked by the diplomats as by the recalcitrant restaurateurs. "Tell these ambassadors I wouldn't think of driving from New York to Washington," he snapped to his chief of protocol, Angier Biddle Duke. "Tell them to fly!"

* * *

THE KENNEDY ADMINISTRATION COULD not avoid all substantive action on civil rights, if only because it had inherited several pending legal cases from the Eisenhower administration. The first test came in 1961, in New Orleans, where Louisiana school officials had been resisting the court-ordered integration of two public schools for a year. After efforts at negotiation failed, the Justice Department—headed by the president's brother, Attorney General Robert Kennedy—resolved to file contempt charges against the state superintendent of education, who had been withholding federal funds as a means of keeping the two schools from functioning. The superintendent quickly backed down.

Yet another case loomed in Prince Edward County, Virginia. In response to the *Brown* decision, many Virginia school districts had opted simply to close some schools rather than accede to integration. In 1959, a federal court had ruled that this practice was unconstitutional, so Prince Edward County reacted by dismantling its school system altogether, creating a private "academy" and leaving blacks with no education whatever. On May 8, 1961, again after voluntary negotiations failed, the Justice

Department filed suit to reopen the schools, enraging Virginia politicians, chief among them the state's powerful Democratic senator, Harry F. Byrd.

Bob Kennedy insisted that his department was merely "maintaining the orders of the courts," and "doing nothing more nor less," as he put it in a speech at the just-integrated University of Georgia that same week. The attorney general's ringing tone conveyed a greater sense of urgency— and outrage. Referring to the Prince Edward County case, he vowed, "I say to you that if the orders of the court are circumvented, the Department of Justice will act. We will not stand by or be aloof. We will move." He mentioned his support for "the 1954 decision," as he referred to *Brown*, but added, "My belief does not matter. It is the law. Some of you may believe the decision was wrong. That does not matter. It is the law."

But none of the new president's symbolic moves—and none of the imperatives of pending legal cases—could compete for practical impact with the actions of a determined group of travelers who had decided in that spring of 1961 to take matters into their own hands. Following in the tradition of King's bus boycott, and the widespread student sit-ins at lunch counters throughout the South, this latest wave of protesters dubbed themselves "Freedom Riders." The rides were the brainchild of James Farmer, who wanted to draw attention to his lesser-known civil rights organization, the Congress of Racial Equality. On May 4, 1961, a delegation of black and white riders piled onto Greyhound and Trailways buses in Washington, D.C., bound for New Orleans to test southern enforcement of a December 1960 Supreme Court ruling banning discrimination in facilities used in interstate transportation. CORE's press release announcing the rides had gone astray in the Justice Department, and the first the president and his administration learned of the rides was on Sunday, May 14—Mother's Day, as it happened—when a group of Freedom Riders were set upon outside Anniston, Alabama, by a mob of fifty cars full of white men carrying clubs and lead pipes, who firebombed their bus. The six riders on board were beaten, before escaping in cars driven by local blacks. Later, a second group was beaten upon its arrival in Birmingham. The president was livid, both because he was considering meeting Soviet premier Nikita Khrushchev in Vienna the following month (and the

Soviet Union delighted in using such incidents to embarrass the United States), and because he had known nothing about the intrepid riders.

The situation was all the worse because it soon became known that Birmingham police officers, under the command of the city's racist public safety commissioner, Theophilus Eugene "Bull" Connor, had given the white mob a half-hour grace period to beat up the arriving riders before belatedly showing up at the bus terminal after the damage was done. Now the riders who were not already hospitalized found themselves trapped by an angry crowd at the Birmingham airport, where they were trying to catch a plane to New Orleans. Attorney General Kennedy sent a top aide, a courtly former journalist from Tennessee named John Seigenthaler, as the president's personal emissary to rescue them. Alabama's governor, John Patterson, whose support the Kennedys had courted assiduously in the 1960 campaign and with whom they had worked to maintain good relations despite his segregationist views, at first agreed to provide protection for the riders. But then he changed his mind and went incommunicado for days.

Such drama was the last thing the administration needed or wanted, and the president asked his top civil rights adviser to get CORE to stop the rides. But another contingent of riders set out from Nashville, and by Friday, May 19, the situation grew still more explosive as police arrested some of the would-be riders and took others into protective custody. Seigenthaler received assurances from Governor Patterson, who at last agreed to meet with him, that Alabama had "the means, ability and the will to keep the peace."

Based on that promise, twenty-one riders now boarded a bus in Birmingham on Saturday, May 20, bound for New Orleans. The riders made it only as far as the state capital at Montgomery before being attacked by a crowd of a thousand angry whites at the terminal there—where, despite warnings from the FBI and the state highway patrol that the buses would be arriving, no local police were on hand. "My heart was in my throat," Seigenthaler would recall. "I knew, suddenly, betrayal." Stopping his rental car, he tried to help a young white woman rider who was being chased by the mob. "I grabbed her by the wrist, over the hood of the car, had her right at the door and she put her hands up on the door jamb and said,

'Mister, I don't want you to get hurt. I'm non-violent. I'm trained to take this. Please don't get hurt. We'll be fine.' And I said, 'Get your ass in the car, sister!' And at that moment, they wheeled me around and they hit me with a pipe." Seigenthaler was beaten unconscious and left on the pavement for twenty-five minutes before the police finally took him to a hospital.

The attorney general was outraged and sent some four hundred federal marshals, under the command of his deputy, Byron White, to stand by at Maxwell Air Force Base outside Montgomery.

The next day, Sunday, May 21, Martin Luther King arrived in town for a mass meeting at the city's First Baptist Church, only to find himself and fifteen hundred black congregants surrounded by an angry mob outside. President Kennedy sent in the marshals to control the menacing crowd, and as the situation escalated, considered calling in Army units. But before that could happen, Governor Patterson declared martial law and sent in the Alabama National Guard, which dismissed the marshals and dispersed the crowd. When the guard at first refused to let the crowd inside the church leave—ostensibly for their own protection—a frantic King called the attorney general, saying he had been betrayed. "You shouldn't have withdrawn the marshals," he said. "Patterson's National Guard won't protect us." In a tired, even tone, Bob Kennedy told him, "Now, Reverend, don't tell me that. You know just as well as I do that if it hadn't been for the United States marshals, you'd be dead as Kelsey's nuts right now."

The standoff had infuriated both John and Robert Kennedy, and it left a bitter legacy. Neither man would ever talk to Governor Patterson again. Some months later, when organizers at the Aspen Institute in Colorado asked James Farmer of CORE, who had been leading a seminar there, to change his schedule to stay an extra day to attend a speech by the attorney general, the word came back from Bob Kennedy, "If that son of a bitch Farmer is going to be there, I'm not coming," Farmer would recall. "That was the attitude the Kennedys had from the Freedom Rides on."

Indeed, the defining attitude of the Kennedy brothers in this period was that the federal government's police powers in matters of local law enforcement were severely limited—and its ability to protect independent actors such as the Freedom Riders correspondingly weak. They believed they were doing the best they could. "What we did was to outline what our authority was and we went to the maximum of what we felt we could do constitutionally," Bob Kennedy would recall. "You could argue, during that period of time it would have been much better not to have this system of government—you know, not to have a democracy. I think, at any time, you can say that it would be much better if we could have sent people—large numbers, perhaps . . . to protect" demonstrators. "But I think that it comes back to haunt you at a later time. I think that these matters should be decided over a long range of history, not on a temporary basis or under the stress of a particular crisis."

Overnight, the Freedom Rides had pushed racial integration to the top of the national agenda and had pushed John Kennedy himself to the breaking point. In the midst of the crisis, during a meeting with members of a newly created advisory council for the Peace Corps, his signature international assistance initiative, Harry Belafonte, the singer and civil rights activist, expressed admiration for Kennedy's position on civil rights but asked if the president "could say something a little more about the Freedom Riders." Another council member, Eugene Rostow, the dean of the Yale Law School, chimed in, saying, "There is a need now for moral leadership." After the group left, the president summoned an aide and exploded, "What in the world does he think I should do? Doesn't he know I've done more for civil rights than any president in American history?"

Arguably, Kennedy had. But soon enough, events would prove once again just how much more there was to do—how much more that only a new law could do.

* * *

SIXTEEN MONTHS AFTER THE Freedom Rides, in the fall of 1962, the Kennedys faced a new civil rights crisis when the federal courts ordered the admission of James Meredith, a young Air Force veteran, as the first black student in the history of the University of Mississippi. Meredith had taken his first step toward integrating Ole Miss on the day of John Kennedy's inauguration. Furious that the new president had not directly mentioned civil rights in his inaugural address, despite the pledges of the Democratic platform, he mailed a letter asking for an application for admission, in hopes of putting pressure on the Kennedy administration. After a long legal battle, backed by the NAACP, Justice Hugo Black of the Supreme Court, an Alabama native and onetime member of the Ku Klux Klan, finally ordered Meredith's admission on September 10, 1962, for that fall semester. Robert Kennedy promptly began negotiations with Mississippi's governor, Ross Barnett, to secure Meredith's peaceful admission. Barnett was more communicative than Alabama's John Patterson but no more cooperative, twice blocking Meredith's attempts to register.

"It's best for him not to go to Ole Miss," Barnett told the attorney general.

"But he *likes* Ole Miss," Bob Kennedy insisted.

At last, on September 27, the attorney general believed he had worked out a staged arrangement in which Meredith, escorted by federal marshals, would arrive on campus and Barnett himself would stand in the way until forced to move aside by U.S. marshals at gunpoint. But the deal foundered on the question of just how many guns would have to be drawn. (Barnett wanted to look helpless in the face of federal firepower.) Kennedy ordered his aides and Meredith to turn around and withdraw.

All along, John Kennedy had followed his brother's actions, determined to avoid a confrontation of the kind that had forced Dwight Eisenhower to send federal troops to Little Rock in 1957 to enforce the desegregation of Central High School. But as Barnett continued to delay, tempers rose and would-be defenders of Mississippi's honor trickled into Oxford from all over, armed and ready. Finally, on Saturday, September 29, the president decided that he himself should talk to Barnett for the first time.

"Well now, here's my problem," the president told the governor. "I don't know Mr. Meredith, and I didn't put him in the university, but on the other hand, under the Constitution, I have to carry out the order and I don't want to do it in any way that causes difficulty to you or anyone else. But I've got to do it." President Kennedy instructed Barnett to work out a new plan with the attorney general. Minutes later, on the phone with Bob Kennedy, Barnett came up with another theatrical idea: Meredith could register in Jackson while Barnett would remain in Oxford and pretend he had been fooled. The attorney general rejected that idea out of hand, so the president got back on the phone with Barnett and, in a complete about-face, now embraced the Jackson plan. But that deal, too, fell apart within hours—after Governor Barnett showed up at a raucous Ole Miss football game shouting "I love Mississippi!" and, emboldened by the fierce emotions of the crowd, telephoned the attorney general to say the Jackson idea was out.

"Why that goddamned son of bitch!" President Kennedy exploded. He now had no choice but to sign the legal papers that would allow the dispatch of federal troops to Mississippi if needed. The next day, Sunday, the attorney general once again thought he had reached an agreement with Barnett—this time by threatening to release the White House's tape recordings of their earlier discussions, which would show that Barnett had been plotting cooperation all along.

From there, the situation quickly deteriorated, as Meredith made his way onto the campus, backed by three hundred federal marshals—a motley crew of Treasury agents, border patrolmen, and prison guards under the command of Nicholas Katzenbach, who had succeeded Byron White as deputy attorney general and had been dispatched with a team from the Justice Department only hours before. A mob of a thousand students and angry local residents was gathered, held back by state troopers.

Even as the president prepared to go on national television at 10 p.m. Washington time, to announce Meredith's arrival in Oxford, the state troopers suddenly withdrew. It would never be clear just who gave the order. But the result was that President Kennedy told the country that the Constitution obliged him to "implement the orders of the court with whatever means are necessary," without knowing that a riot was already under way. The crowd charged the Lyceum, the university's main administration building, with rocks, bottles, and rifle and shotgun fire, mistakenly thinking Meredith was inside. (He was actually in a dormitory.) Two people were killed in the melee, and more than a third of the marshals—160 men—were wounded, twenty-eight of them by gunfire.

The president now ordered regular Army units to deploy from Memphis to Oxford on the double. But it took them agonizing hours to get there as the riot continued. "Where's the Army?" Kennedy fairly screamed through the telephone at his secretary of the Army, Cyrus Vance, while another aide in the Oval Office wondered if the troops could "take a cab from the airport." At one point, an infuriated president mused about the Army, "They always give you their bullshit about their instant reaction and their split-second timing, but it never works out. No wonder it's so hard to win a war."

The White House kept in touch with the team in Oxford through a pay phone that Katzenbach had commandeered with a single dime, ordering the operator to keep an open line to Washington. At the height of the battle, Bob Kennedy asked his press spokesman Ed Guthman, who was in Oxford with Katzenbach, "How's it going?" and Guthman replied, "Pretty rough. It's getting like the Alamo." After a pause, the attorney general responded, "Well, you know what happened to those guys, don't you?"

But Katzenbach's ragtag army survived, and by Monday morning, October 1, twenty-three thousand soldiers were stationed around Oxford, and Meredith attended his first class on campus—in colonial American history. With the crisis over, James McShane, the wry and battle-hardened chief of the U.S. Marshals Service, who had once been a New York City police officer and a bodyguard and driver for John Kennedy in his Senate days, felt liberated enough to taunt Governor Barnett by asking, "Meredith is in, and now do you know who No. 2 is going to be?"

"No, who?" the governor replied.

"Sonny Liston!" McShane announced, referring to the malevolent, mobbed-up black boxer who had just unseated the popular black heavyweight champion, Floyd Patterson, the week before.

Mordant humor aside, the Kennedy brothers—already under fire from liberals for their failure to propose civil rights legislation—now worried that they would take political heat in the coming midterm elections for the Ole Miss crisis and their failure to keep order. Days later, the president's pollster, Louis Harris, reported just the opposite—that Kennedy's political support had spiked all over the key northern industrial states. Harris added, "Every Democrat running for major office should put front and center that this country needs firm and resolute leadership such as the president demonstrated in the Mississippi case."

* * *

IN JANUARY 1963, ROBERT Kennedy prepared a status report on civil rights for the president, in which he argued that—grim headlines from Ole Miss notwithstanding—future historians would "find, on the contrary, that 1962 was a year of great progress in civil rights." By some benchmarks, this was true. Before the Kennedy administration took office, the Justice Department had taken action to secure voting rights—ranging from inspections to lawsuits—in just thirty counties around the country; now that number was 115. Segregation in interstate commerce—on trains and buses—had been virtually eliminated (thanks in large part, of course, to pressure from the Freedom Riders). Sixty schools had been desegregated in the past year, bringing the total to 972. Of the 350 assistant United States attorneys appointed by the Kennedy administration to date, thirty-two were black, and half of them had been appointed in 1962 alone. Of 114 federal marshals appointed since January 20, 1961, fourteen were black—eleven of them appointed in 1962.

But these measures, however real, paled in comparison with the principal demand of civil rights supporters: comprehensive new federal legislation to outlaw segregation. And on this front, John Kennedy was once again found wanting. On February 28, 1963, two weeks after the Lincoln's birthday event at the White House, he sent his first civil rights message to Congress, calling for a strengthening of voting rights provisions, abolition of literacy tests, appointment of federal voting referees, new technical and financial assistance for school desegregation, and a four-year extension of the federal Civil Rights Commission, whose mandate was set to expire.

"Let it be clear in our own hearts and minds, that it is not merely because of the Cold War, and not merely because of the economic waste of discrimination, that we are committed to achieving true equality of opportunity," the president declared. "The basic reason is because it is right."

But civil rights groups saw Kennedy's message as so disappointing—no mention of public accommodations, no real legislative follow-up—that they raised the threat of cooperation with Republican legislators, who had already introduced various civil rights measures of their own. Even though the Republicans could not pass a bill by themselves, if they were seen as seizing the initiative on civil rights, they might pry away some northern and black votes in the 1964 election and weaken Kennedy's prospects. Kennedy wanted to forestall any such effort by the opposition party, even as he insisted that the time was not ripe on Capitol Hill for a comprehensive bill. "We go up there with that and they'll piss all over us," he told his aides. It was Kennedy who had got the ball rolling, of course, with his promises in the 1960 campaign, and his resolute enforcement of the court orders at Ole Miss and in the school desegregation cases. Now he seemed frozen in place by the growing gulf between his stirring words and his cautious actions. And no less resourceful a goad than Martin Luther King himself had resolved to do something about that paralysis.

By April 1963, King had decided that the time had come for another campaign of direct action. And while his stated goal was the desegregation of Birmingham, Alabama—the nation's largest Jim Crow city—his true target was the Kennedy administration. It was no accident that he began this latest campaign at a moment of rising expectations. In March, a reform candidate, Albert Boutwell, had placed first in an election for the newly created post of mayor of Birmingham, the city having eliminated its board of commissioners. But "Bull" Connor, the belligerent public safety commissioner who had allowed the beatings of the Freedom Riders to go unchecked, ran in second place behind Boutwell in the March balloting and in a runoff on April 2, and he refused to surrender his post. So on the morning of April 3, groups of protesters sought service at the lunch counters in five stores in downtown Birmingham, four of which promptly stopped serving food altogether. In the ensuing week, some 150 demonstrators were arrested, but the protest was not generating much heat until a judge granted Connor's request for an injunction barring King from further marches. On April 12, Good Friday, the drama intensified when King was arrested with his deputy, Ralph Abernathy, and placed in solitary confinement in the Birmingham jail.

There, on scraps of paper and in the margins of newspapers, he would write his famous "Letter from Birmingham Jail." And though its words would not become public for another month, they were among the most damning ever used to sum up the status quo for American blacks. "For years now I have heard the word, 'Wait!'" King wrote. "It rings in the ear of every Negro with piercing familiarity. This 'Wait!' has almost always meant, 'Never.'" He expressed special disappointment with the "white moderate" who "is more devoted to 'order' than to justice; who prefers a negative peace which is the absence of tension to a positive peace which is the presence of justice."

King was released from jail on April 20, and almost immediately he began planning the next round of action. James Bevel, one of King's top aides at the Southern Christian Leadership Conference, had a daring, dangerous idea, a "children's crusade." Bevel had spent weeks organizing and training elementary and high school students in Birmingham in the techniques and strategies of nonviolence. King was ambivalent about using the children, but he was desperate for a display that would shock the nation's conscience and move the president to action at last. And so on Thursday, May 2, hundreds of young people marched out of Birmingham's Sixteenth Street Baptist Church to face Connor's police force, waiting across the street. By day's end, nearly a thousand protesters had been taken to jail, only a handful of them adults. The next day, as the first children again set out from the church, Connor's forces warned them to disband or face high-pressure fire hoses. King's army refused to budge, and soon hundred-pound-per-square-inch blasts of water knocked the marchers to the ground, tearing the clothing from their backs. When a group of blacks alarmed by such tactics began tossing bricks toward the police, Connor let loose five snarling German shepherds. In a flash, the resulting images—terrifying even in grainy black-and-white news film and photographs—galvanized the world. "Look at those niggers run!" Connor crowed.

* * *

THE NEXT AFTERNOON, AT a half-hour meeting in the White House with representatives of the liberal group Americans for Democratic Action, the president was exasperated at the riveting photograph in that day's *New York Times* of a police dog lunging at a protester in Birmingham. "Bull Connor just eats this up," he said. "The fact of the matter is, that's just what Connor wants." Then Kennedy launched into a discursive, defensive soliloquy, the agitation and frustration in his voice echoing into the hidden tape recorder that he had installed to preserve conversations for use in writing his anticipated memoirs. "Now, we've worked as hard as we possibly could, given the laws we have," he said at one point. "We've shoved and pushed," he went on a few minutes later, "and the Department of Justice . . . There's nothing that my brother's given more time to."

But then he added, "I quite agree if I were a Negro, I'd be awfully sore."

The president reserved special scorn for the armchair pundits in Washington who bemoaned the situation in Birmingham, while continuing to eat at the elite Metropolitan Club, around the corner from the White House. The club had recently abandoned its long-standing practice of offering honorary memberships to all members of the diplomatic corps, to avoid having to admit black ambassadors from the newly independent African nations, and several top Kennedy aides had resigned from the club in protest. "I had some newspaperman in here telling me about 'Isn't it outrageous in Birmingham?'" the president declared. "I said, 'Why are you over there eating at the Metropolitan Club every day?' You talk about Birmingham . . . Some of our distinguished columnists every day at lunch . . . They wouldn't even let Negro ambassadors in . . . He said, 'Well, we want to work from the inside.' And I said, 'Well, your one contribution is now they won't let white ambassadors in' . . . So I don't know what the difference really is . . . It's just one of degree." Kennedy then pulled back, looking at the larger picture. "I think we have worked hard on civil rights," he said. "I think it's a national crisis and the Negro leadership is divided. And it isn't because of any political reluctance. As far as I'm concerned, I doubt if the Democratic Party carries any more than perhaps two or three Southern states in 1964."

Finally, almost as if talking to himself, the president simply gave up. "I couldn't agree with you more that this is . . . ," he said, not finishing the thought, before concluding: "I'm president of the United States and that's a disastrous picture this morning."

Everything about the situation in Birmingham was disastrous. Later that day, Kennedy sent Burke Marshall, the meticulous, methodical lawyer who headed the Civil Rights Division of the Justice Department, to Alabama to try to arrange a truce. After days of shuttling back and forth between the city's white business leaders and the protesting black groups, Marshall produced a tentative agreement on gradual desegregation of Birmingham's public facilities, and a pledge by the city to hire black employees. But the effort collapsed when King and Abernathy were thrown back in jail, their bail on the earlier charges increased to $2,500 each, and the city fathers insisted on a total of $250,000 in bail money to release the more than five hundred children who were still clogging the city's lockups. Secretly, with the help of labor leaders like Walter Reuther of the United Auto Workers, and Harry Belafonte—who had arranged for a $100,000 cash loan from Nelson Rockefeller himself—the Kennedys raised the bail money. A deal was struck on Friday, May 10, and King returned to Atlanta in relief and triumph.

But the very next night, bombs exploded in Birmingham, tearing a hole through the living room of the Reverend A. D. King, Martin's brother, and blowing the front off the Gaston Motel, just below the room where Martin King himself had been staying. Within minutes, angry black rioters began pouring into the streets, throwing bricks and bottles at the police and burning and looting stores in black neighborhoods. The situation was only inflamed when Alabama's newly elected and defiantly segregationist governor, George C. Wallace, dispatched some three hundred "special deputies," swinging clubs and brandishing shotguns, just as the local authorities seemed to be getting things under control.

Once more, John Kennedy had to weigh sending federal troops into a southern state. At a tense meeting on Sunday evening, May 12, with Bob Kennedy, Burke Marshall, and others, the president asked Marshall, "This has a lot of Oxford in it, doesn't it?" and Marshall responded in a way that crystallized why the administration considered the situation so explosive: "Yes, it does, but it's different, because there we had a white mob against a Negro, a single Negro. Here we have a Negro mob . . ."

"A Negro mob." The very words meant that the slow, unfolding crisis of civil rights in the South had reached a new and even more politically dangerous stage for the president, and that he would have to act accordingly. Scrambling to defuse demonstrations or hustling to enforce piecemeal court orders would no longer suffice. It was becoming clear to both John and Robert Kennedy that the only way to end the demonstrations was to end the discrimination that prompted them. And the only way to do that, they reluctantly realized, would be with a broad new law.

In the short term, the president decided to place Army units stationed near Birmingham on alert, and to federalize the Alabama National Guard if necessary. Just before nine o'clock that Sunday night, he went on television to declare, "The Government will do whatever must be done to preserve order, to protect the lives of its citizens and to uphold the law of the land." Meantime, Martin Luther King, who had rushed back to Birmingham, toured the city's black wards, preaching calm in pool halls and social clubs. The next day, the boxer Floyd Patterson and the baseball legend Jackie Robinson appeared at a mass rally aimed at calming nerves.

A fragile peace prevailed in Birmingham. But demonstrations soon spread to more than half a dozen other cities in both North and South. John Kennedy was running out of time, and he knew it.

2

A Great Change Is at Hand

As the clocks in the White House ticked toward 8:00 p.m. at the end of a hot early summer day, the president of the United States was fretting over the draft of a speech that he was supposed to deliver on national television in just a few minutes but that was still perhaps only three-fifths done. And he was, to the surprise of his aides, "awfully damn nervous." For nervousness was by no means the natural state of John Fitzgerald Kennedy. After all, as a junior naval officer in World War II, he had swum through miles of open ocean—towing a wounded comrade by the straps of a life preserver held in his teeth, despite a chronic bad back—after a Japanese destroyer sliced his PT boat in two. He had published a Pulitzer Prize–winning book elevating Ernest Hemingway's definition of courage as "grace under pressure" into a personal and political creed. On this busy evening, Kennedy was under pressure, all right, but he was struggling to maintain grace.

Hours earlier, Nicholas Katzenbach, the deputy attorney general, had peacefully arranged the integration of the University of Alabama, securing the admission of two black students pursuant to a federal court order, over the adamant objections of Governor George Wallace, after Kennedy asserted federal control over the Alabama National Guard. When the day began, such an outcome had been far from assured, and Kennedy had asked the three television networks to reserve time that evening, in case he needed to address the nation in the wake of violence—as he had done on that grim Sunday night eight months earlier when a riot erupted during the integration of Ole Miss. Now, with the Alabama crisis successfully resolved, most of Kennedy's advisers believed a speech was unnecessary. He overruled them, instinctively knowing that the time had come at last for him to speak out on the topic that had consumed the country that spring.

The previous month's siege in Birmingham had made a huge impact on the president—and on the country at large—as civil rights demonstrations spread to Jackson, Mississippi; Cambridge, Maryland; Raleigh, North Carolina; Chicago; Philadelphia; and New Rochelle and Syracuse, New York. For days, the newspapers had been reporting that Kennedy's response to the growing crisis would be the long-awaited comprehensive civil rights bill. Events had finally forced Kennedy's hand, as he himself had implicitly acknowledged only the day before, in a commencement address at American University. The main thrust of the speech was the president's announcement that the United States would suspend atmospheric nuclear testing, coupled with a plea for a new understanding of world peace. "For in the final analysis," he had said, "our most basic common link is that we all inhabit this small planet. We all breathe the same air. We all cherish our children's futures. And we are all mortal." But then he had pointedly added: "In too many of our cities today, the peace is not secure because freedom is incomplete. It is the responsibility of the executive branch at all levels of government—local, State and National—to provide and protect that freedom for all of our citizens by all means within our authority. It is the responsibility of the legislative branch at all levels, wherever the authority is not now adequate, to make it adequate."

So now, as technicians strung lights and cable and set up their cameras in the Oval Office, a plain screen blocking the gray-green and gold drapes and the south-facing windows behind the president's desk, Kennedy found himself in the Cabinet Room next door with his brother Bob, "quietly going frantic," as one aide would recall. Almost alone among the president's top advisers, Bob Kennedy had urged him to make the speech, and now he was helping him figure out just what to say. Together, the brothers scratched notes on scraps of White House stationery. "Lesson—Committed to uphold system of law," John Kennedy wrote in his swift, spidery hand. Bob Kennedy noted, "Uphold orders of court. Live under system of law," adding, "Country as a whole must go far beyond symbols."

The president teased Burke Marshall, who was also standing by in the Cabinet Room. "Come on, now, Burke," he said. "You must have some ideas."

Down the hall in his own office, Kennedy's most trusted speechwriter, Ted Sorensen, who had been preoccupied for weeks with the American University speech, was now feverishly seizing on statistics and bits of past statements to compose yet another major address, whose pages were delivered to the president as fast as Sorensen's faithful secretary, Gloria Sitrin, could type them. In the end, time ran out, and Kennedy had at best ten minutes of material in his hands as he took his place before the cameras in the Oval Office, a pillow propped behind his back to help his posture. Andrew Hatcher, his assistant press secretary and the highest-ranking black aide in his White House—in *any* White House up to that point—stood silently to the side, just out of camera range.

"The monitor is all right, but the camera ought to be brought up," the president said, nervously fidgeting with the papers resting on a small, slanted reading stand atop his desk, a glass of water at his right hand.

All his life, Jack Kennedy had possessed an exquisite appreciation for the vagaries, frailties, and ironies of life, together with an uncanny sense of timing. At the beginning of his Senate career in 1953, Sorensen would recall, Kennedy favored civil rights legislation "as a political necessity consistent with his moral instincts." Now, Sorensen judged, he was about to commit himself to such legislation "as a moral necessity inconsistent with his political instincts." His civil rights adviser Harris Wofford would later remember that the president was fond of reciting the poetic passage from the Book of Ecclesiastes—the one proclaiming that there is a "time to keep silence, and a time to speak"—but adding his own mordant,

Kennedyesque coda: "A time to fish, and a time to cut bait." This muggy twilight was a time to fish.

"Stand by, Mr. President," a technician intoned.

"Good evening, my fellow Americans," the president began.

* * *

KENNEDY'S DECISION TO MAKE the speech may have been sudden, but the consideration behind it was anything but. By May and June 1963, the crisis in Birmingham—the dogs and hoses and bombings, the children in jail, the horrifying news footage—had combined with the experiences and instincts of a lifetime to leave the president no choice.

On May 14, Robert Kennedy had addressed a meeting of Alabama newspaper editors, warning them that if Martin Luther King's campaign of nonviolence failed, less responsible leaders would follow. By May 17, on a flight to Asheville, North Carolina, for a speech, Bob Kennedy and Burke Marshall agreed that the time had at last come for a comprehensive civil rights bill, and they directed Harold Greene, a Justice Department lawyer, to begin the work of preliminary drafting—though the bill itself was still as unfinished as the speech the president was about to deliver. Even those of Kennedy's aides most sympathetic to the civil rights cause tended to approach the problem more as a political headache than as a moral crusade. "My friends all say the Negro maids and servants are getting antagonistic," Bob Kennedy reported to the president on the morning of May 20, as they met with Marshall, Sorensen, the White House civil rights adviser Lee White, and the president's political aides Kenneth O'Donnell and Lawrence O'Brien to discuss whether and how to offer a bill. A few minutes later, when Marshall tried to explain the importance of a strong public accommodations provision—that separate restrooms and lunch counters was the "one thing that makes all Negroes, regardless of age, maddest"—the attorney general dismissed him. "They can stand at the lunch counters," he scoffed. "They don't have to eat there. They can pee before they come to the store or the supermarket."

Yet even Bob Kennedy had to acknowledge that, for blacks, the situation was grim. A review of federal employment in Birmingham by the administration's own Civil Service Commission had found, for example, that outside the Veterans Administration and the post office, just fifteen blacks were on the federal payroll in the entire city, out of a pool of two thousand jobs. Still, Larry O'Brien, the president's chief liaison to Congress, warned that the president—already struggling to pass a major tax bill, among other legislation—was "going to run smack into a straight-out draw" on Capitol Hill if he sent up a civil rights bill now.

Later in the same meeting, when Bob Kennedy suggested that the president convene meetings at the White House with both blacks and whites—including Martin Luther King and other protest leaders—to talk about the problem and build support for a bill in the coming days, the president revealed his personal ambivalence about King. "The trouble with King is everybody thinks he's our boy anyway," he said. "King is so hot these days, it's like Marx is coming to the White House. I'd like to have some southern governors or mayors or businessmen in first. And my program should have gone up to the hill first."

But events kept pressing. Just eight days later, on May 28, demonstrations again exploded, this time in Jackson, Mississippi, the state capital, where a thirty-seven-year-old former Army sergeant named Medgar Evers, now the local field secretary for the NAACP, had called for a "massive offensive." City police stood idly by for hours as a parade of whites rushed the local Woolworth's lunch counter, where some black and white students and a white sociology professor from a nearby college were seeking service, and poured ketchup, mustard, sugar, and salt over the demonstrators. When a former policeman kicked the professor to the floor, then kicked one of the students repeatedly in the face, the white counterdemonstrators poured salt into the raw wounds.

The president's top advisers met again four days later, on June 1, and Burke Marshall told Kennedy that they had passed the point of no return. "I think it's absolutely essential that you have legislation," Marshall said. (A statement drafted that same day by Ted Sorensen—apparently never issued—declared that comprehensive legislation that year, "however long it takes or however troublesome it may be is an unavoidable necessity.")

Then Kennedy made a point of soliciting the views of the person who was surely the best legislative tactician in the room: Vice President Lyndon Johnson, who tended to keep his own counsel at such meetings. "I haven't read the bill . . . I haven't seen it," Johnson demurred, later adding, in a voice so soft that the Oval Office taping system barely picked it up, "I'm not very competent to counsel you." Johnson then gave a hint of his deeper feelings, exclaiming, "We've got to go through with passing . . . We've got to bear down, very important that we get an agreement, else yours will be just another gesture."

In fact, Johnson had much more specific advice in mind, and he asked Ken O'Donnell for a meeting with the president, to discuss civil rights. Not for the first time, O'Donnell said no, so the vice president turned instead to Norbert Schlei, a senior lawyer in the Justice Department's Civil Rights Division, who promptly alerted the White House. On June 3, Ted Sorensen telephoned Johnson, who unburdened himself of some pointed advice: Kennedy needed to take far more extensive soundings of Congress, and get the rest of his legislative agenda in better shape, before submitting a civil rights bill. And he should take the fight directly to the people, by making a major speech, ideally somewhere in the South—perhaps San Antonio. "I believe he'd run some of the demagogues right in the hole," Johnson said. "This aura, this thing, this halo around the president: everybody wants to believe in the president, the commander in chief. I think he'd make the Barnetts and the Wallaces look silly. The good people, the church people, I think have to come around to him—not the majority of them, maybe, but a good many of them over the country—and it would really unify the North. He'd be looking them straight in the face."

Then in the next breath, Johnson warned of the dangers for the rest of Kennedy's legislative agenda if the civil rights bill wasn't handled just right. "I think that he'll be cut to pieces with this and I think he'll be a sacrificial lamb," he said. "I think his program will be hurt if it's not killed." But, in the end, Johnson made it clear he was fully in the fight. "We got a little pop gun, and I want to pull out the cannon," he said. "The president is the cannon."

Johnson could not have known it, but the cannon was ready to fire.

* * *

JOHN KENNEDY WON THE presidency in 1960 with more than 70 percent of the black vote. But virtually nothing in his background or breeding had prepared him for truly understanding—much less grappling with how to redress—the painful realities faced by black Americans. There is no record of his ever even having visited the Deep South states of Mississippi, Alabama, Louisiana, or Arkansas until 1956, when he was nearly forty years old. Meeting a black dentist in San Francisco during the 1960 campaign, Kennedy was asked how many black people he was friends with, and was forced to reply, "Doctor, I don't know five people of your caliber well enough to call them by their first names, but I promise to do better." As late as the 1950s, he told a British friend that he had learned—as if he had just heard it for the first time—"this marvelous expression," from the black Harlem congressman Adam Clayton Powell: "Uncle Tom." James Farmer of the Congress of Racial Equality would judge that Kennedy was "ignorant on civil rights in particular and blacks in general at the time he became president." In fact, Kennedy had once told Jackie Robinson, "I don't know any Negroes. Would you introduce me to some?"

Growing up in Brookline, Massachusetts, and Bronxville, New York, Kennedy was, as he would later put it, a child of "one of the great fortunes of the world." He had lived through the Great Depression but had no real understanding of it until he read about it at Harvard. "We had bigger houses, more servants, we traveled more," he explained. His father, Joseph P. Kennedy, a self-made multimillionaire, had felt the sting of anti-Irish prejudice in his native Boston but was nevertheless himself a vicious anti-Semite. Any blacks the younger Kennedy might have encountered held strictly servile roles. As president, he would tell Daniel Patrick Moynihan that he could never get over Harry Truman's "talking all the time about 'the niggers.'" But as a libidinous teenager he was not above bearding his boarding school friend Lem Billings about the risk of syphilis in a "nigger" brothel. At Harvard, he inherited his older brother Joe Jr.'s black "gentleman's gentleman," a valet named George Taylor, who picked up the clothes Kennedy carelessly tossed in a heap. They might banter about Kennedy's fondness for women and Taylor's for whiskey, but it was not a relationship of equals.

When Kennedy joined the Navy in October 1941, on the eve of America's entry into World War II, the service had about four thousand black sailors, but they worked strictly as mess men, peeling potatoes, making beds, and cleaning rooms. Only the previous year, fifteen black mess men aboard the USS *Philadelphia* had written to the *Pittsburgh Courier* complaining about conditions and discouraging other blacks from enlisting and winding up in the same straits. The signers were thrown in the brig, indicted for conduct prejudicial to good order, and dishonorably discharged.

After the war, when Kennedy first went to Washington as a freshman congressman from Massachusetts, he inherited yet another black valet, this one named George Thomas, as a gift from the *New York Times* columnist Arthur Krock, a family friend. Thomas would serve Kennedy all through his political career, until the last morning of his life, laying out his clothes, shining his shoes, and arranging his laundry and dry cleaning. That didn't spare Thomas from bearing the brunt of Kennedy's occasional irritation, as he did when the valet told the writer Jim Bishop, preparing an article about a day in the president's life for *Good Housekeeping*, that Kennedy owned twenty-five pairs of shoes and changed his shirt about six times a day. Later, Kennedy regaled his friend Ben Bradlee with the tale of how he upbraided Thomas for this lapse, "imitating George, hemming as he puts his eyes to the ceiling," Bradlee would recall.

"How many pairs of shoes do you own, George?" the president had asked his valet.

"One," George had replied.

"Well," Kennedy had countered, "don't you see how most of the people who own only one pair of shoes might resent my having twenty-five—even if it were true?"

Asked by Bradlee how many pairs he did have, Kennedy claimed to have no idea, but admitted that he had changed his shirt four times on the day of their conversation.

And yet. And yet Jack Kennedy, who had endured not only anti-Irish and anti-Catholic bias but a lifetime of severe gastrointestinal ailments and debilitating back pain, had just enough of a chip on his shoulder to make him sympathetic to the underdog, and just enough experience of suffering to soften his heart. "I think he felt that, as an Irishman, somewhere along the line, he'd been discriminated against," recalled George Smathers, his best friend in the Senate. Even as president, Kennedy knew that his ancestry would leave him blackballed by Boston's blue-blood Somerset Club, where he had once witnessed a speaker say that the Democrats were the party of "the help."

"Can you believe that such people can still be around?" Kennedy had fumed to a friend.

Kennedy once countermanded the skipper of the presidential yacht *Honey Fitz*, who had started to steam toward the dock of the Edgartown Yacht Club, a WASP bastion on Martha's Vineyard, without advance permission. "My God!" Kennedy exclaimed, "they'd have my hide if I just barged in there."

Another friend, the artist William Walton, believed that Kennedy had a "marvelous capacity for projecting himself" into other people's lives. He recalled once being together in a New York restaurant where a drunken man began loudly berating Kennedy for his political views. When Walton suggested they leave, Kennedy demurred, saying, "Would you look at that guy's wife and what she's going through?"

* * *

IN THE JOHN F. KENNEDY Presidential Library in Boston, the pre-presidential file on civil rights is a slender folder, sandwiched between "Birth Control" and "Conduct of Government" amid the plethora of subjects that crossed a politician's desk in the first decade and a half after World War II. And yet, with a few notable exceptions, Kennedy had handled questions of race and civil rights deftly and effectively throughout his political career, starting with his first race for Congress, when he called for abolition of the poll tax and measures to combat employment discrimination. In part, that was because he was among the generation of returning servicemen and women whose expectations for themselves and their country had been changed dramatically by a conflict against fascism and dictatorship.

On perhaps no group did the war have a more profound effect than young black servicemen, many of whom—stationed in the cities of Europe and elsewhere—for the first time experienced everyday life without the yoke of Jim Crow. They could not return to Chicago or Boston, much less to Chattanooga or Birmingham, and feel the same way about the status quo. Kennedy realized this, and quickly set about making special outreach efforts to black voters in his first campaign for Congress in 1946. With the help of his college valet, George Taylor, he organized a meeting for five hundred people at a black social organization, the Dunbar Club—and even thought of embellishing the saga of his wartime exploits aboard PT 109 to put himself in command of a diverse crew. "My story about the collision is getting better all the time," he told a friend. "Now I've got a Jew and a Nigger in the story and with me being a Catholic, that's great."

Such language is itself proof enough that Kennedy's attitudes remained unenlightened. There is other evidence, too. Taylor recruited several black college women to join the campaign, but they were not invited to share a luncheon with the candidate's sisters as other volunteers had been. This elicited an unusually frank complaint from the gentleman's gentleman. "Jack, I think that's bullshit," Taylor said. "They're all giving their time. They're all human beings."

Kennedy's reply was dismissive: "George, you're thin-skinned. That's one of the things of the time."

As a freshman in the House, Kennedy supported the Truman administration's surprisingly robust civil rights initiatives, including a ban on segregation in the armed forces, a proposed federal antilynching law, abolition of the poll tax, a permanent Fair Employment Practices Commission, and a strengthening of the Civil Rights Section of the Justice Department. As a member of the House District of Columbia Affairs Committee, he also pressed for broader desegregation of a city that remained locked in the clutches of Jim Crow (except for the airport, the railroad station, and federal cafeterias), partly because the southern barons who ruled Congress believed that if segregation could be maintained in the nation's capital, it could survive in their home states. Kennedy favored home rule for the District (a dream that would not come true for another three decades, and even then in a limited way) and went so far as to try to force a home rule bill out of committee by a parliamentary maneuver. The effort fell short by twelve votes, but Kennedy believed the spectacle of a segregated capital undermined America's prestige in the world, especially in its global competition with an increasingly belligerent Soviet bloc.

Yet Kennedy also kept his distance from organized civil rights groups. He was not a joiner, and just as he did not take membership in Americans for Democratic Action, the anticommunist liberal group formed at the dawn of the Cold War to support liberties at home while opposing Stalinism abroad, so he resisted entreaties from the most venerable civil rights organization, the National Association for the Advancement of Colored People. His aide Ted Sorensen would later say that Kennedy found "the approach of many single-minded civil rights advocates uncomfortable and unreasonable also."

Still, civil rights would play a prominent role in Kennedy's campaign when he sought to move up to the United States Senate in 1952. His Republican opponent that year was Henry Cabot Lodge Jr., a descendant of one of Boston's leading families, who had first been elected in 1936 and whose grandfather and namesake had defeated Kennedy's maternal grandfather, John F. "Honey Fitz" Fitzgerald, for the Senate in 1916. Kennedy brought a strong civil rights platform to the contest, including advocacy of reforming Senate Rule XXII, which allowed a single member to prolong debate indefinitely, unless a two-thirds vote could be mustered to shut off debate. For decades, southern opponents of civil rights had used the provision to block bill after bill, and no civil rights filibuster had ever been broken.

Kennedy took the issue seriously enough that he was moved to write a speech that he drafted by hand and titled "Kennedy Fights for Civil Rights." The first sentence read, "There is nothing worse in life than racial bigotry," but he revised that to end with the word "prejudice," while following up with a second sentence: "There is nothing lower than bigotry." He couched his arguments, as he often would in years to come, in terms of American prestige and the stakes in the Cold War. "Those who view fellow Americans—regardless of race, color or national origin—as anything other than fellow Americans are fostering the very climate in which the seeds of Communism flourish," he wrote. His words were stirring. His prescriptions were less bold. He did not call for the desegregation of public accommodations or schools, for example, and thus in no way really acknowledged the extent of the daily injustices and indignities endured by blacks throughout the South. (It is also not clear that he ever delivered the speech.)

More immediately, at least for Kennedy's prospects in 1952, the head of the Boston branch of the NAACP, Silas Taylor, was hostile to him because of Taylor's long-standing alliance with two older Democrats, Representative John McCormack and former mayor James Michael Curley of Boston, both of whom held Kennedy in minimum high regard. So Kennedy cultivated other black figures, and his campaign subtly adapted its overall slogan—"Kennedy has done and will do more for us"—to conclude, "will do more for *more of* us." And that year, Kennedy did organize two teas for black women. On Election Day, his large margins in the black wards helped him beat Lodge by seventy thousand votes, despite the fact that Dwight D. Eisenhower carried Massachusetts in the presidential race.

No sooner did he arrive in the Senate, however, than Kennedy began treading gingerly on civil rights. The Senate of that day was "the only place in the country where the South did not lose" the Civil War, as the *New York Times* correspondent William S. White put it, and Kennedy took due note. Kennedy's first known speech on *Brown v. Board of Education* came in February 1956, nearly two years after the decision was handed down, when he endorsed it in principle in an address to the Young Democratic Club of New York, but made no mention of how the Supreme Court's ruling should be enforced. For Kennedy was already nursing an ambition that would require support far beyond the Yankee precincts of his home state: a shot at the 1956 vice presidential nomination.

That July, in an appearance on NBC's *Meet the Press*, Kennedy declared that Congress had no role whatever to play in the implementation of the *Brown* ruling. But his usual verbal fluidity failed him when he was asked if the Supreme Court was moving too fast. "No, I don't think—they came to a decision in 1954, it was unanimous and it is the law," he said. Then, equivocating, if not floundering, he added, "I don't think—I am not a lawyer—and I don't think any critique—if you are for the decision, you might say it is high time they did it, and if you are against it, you say they are intervening in political matters." The following month, at the Democratic

National Convention in Chicago, the presidential nominee, Adlai Stevenson, surprised the delegates by leaving the vice presidential selection up to them, and Kennedy and his forces quickly mounted a vigorous bid. Senators Estes Kefauver and Albert Gore of Tennessee sought the prize as well, but neither man had much support in the South. Both of them had refused to sign the so-called Southern Manifesto, a document of commitment to segregation in the wake of *Brown*. So Kennedy, with his equivocal approach, was able to win surprising support in the South, endearing himself to powerful politicians in the region who could help a young man on the move. In the end, Kefauver won the vice presidential nomination, but Kennedy was delighted at the inroads he had made. He was also aware of the price he had paid. He confided to his old family friend Arthur Krock, "I'll be singing Dixie for the rest of my life."

* * *

IN FACT, WHEN IT came to civil rights, Kennedy struggled to square his short-term objectives with his presidential aspirations. In his 1956 book *Profiles in Courage*, a collection of essays about eight United States senators who did the right thing even when doing so was not politically convenient, Kennedy himself had called Reconstruction "a black nightmare the South could never forget." One of the men he lionized in the book was Congressman (later Senator) Lucius Quintus Cincinnatus Lamar of Mississippi, who had promoted the resumption of normal federal-state relations and the withdrawal of Union troops from the South after the war. By contrast, Kennedy painted Charles Sumner, the abolitionist and radical Republican senator from Massachusetts whose own seat he held, as a brittle, unreasonable advocate of harsh Reconstruction policies.

But when the Eisenhower administration's omnibus civil rights bill came before the Senate in 1957, Kennedy knew he had no choice but to support it, given his past stands on the issue.

The two most controversial sections of the 1957 bill were a provision (known as Part III) allowing the attorney general to file suit to enforce constitutional rights, including school desegregation, and a proposed additional provision requiring that local voting registrars accused of barring blacks from the polls be entitled to a trial by jury. On both measures,

Jack Kennedy—acutely mindful of his own presidential prospects—once again sought to avoid controversy.

Part III was the enforcement mechanism at the heart of the bill, and it was considered crucial by all the leading civil rights groups whose support Kennedy had enjoyed. Meanwhile, the southerners fulminated against it as Reconstruction redux, with a northern-dominated federal government dictating to southern states how to run their affairs. In the end, Kennedy voted for Part III, but only after Eisenhower himself had withdrawn his support for it, thus dooming the provision and making Kennedy's vote a completely safe symbolic statement. The jury trial amendment was more complicated. Civil rights groups saw it as a poison pill—a way to assure that all-white southern juries would continue to acquit any local official accused of discrimination. But practical-minded backers of the bill—including Lyndon Johnson, the Senate majority leader—saw it as the best way of placating the southerners and avoiding a filibuster. Kennedy had been inclined to oppose the amendment, but after making a point of consulting with three prominent Harvard Law School professors—who told him that while the amendment would unquestionably weaken the bill, half a loaf was better than none—he voted for it. Once more, he paid a price for his equivocation, as the *New York Times*'s James Reston took him to task for his "11th hour change of heart." Vice President Richard Nixon offered a scathing assessment when the amendment passed: "This is one of the saddest days in the history of the Senate. It was a vote against the right to vote."

Nevertheless, Kennedy understood that even the defanged bill was "a turning point in American social and political thought," as he said in a speech before the vote on the jury trial amendment. "It represents an almost universal acknowledgment that we cannot continue to command the respect of peoples everywhere, not to mention our own self-respect, while we ignore the fact that many of our citizens do not possess basic constitutional rights." And Kennedy sought to keep good relations with such civil rights leaders as Roy Wilkins, the NAACP president, whom he had run into in the Senate restaurant a few days after the vote. In an exchange of notes he initiated, Kennedy later told Wilkins that he could not understand why he was being singled out from among the nearly three dozen non-southern senators who had also voted for the jury trial amendment. Wilkins's answer was direct: he was the only one running for president.

Barely two weeks after final passage of the bill, on September 24, President Eisenhower was forced to send federal troops to Little Rock, Arkansas, after violent demonstrations erupted over the integration of Central High School there. Kennedy's support for this action was tepid, and scarcely a month later, he undertook a mission of his own in Dixie, arranging a meeting with Governor James P. Coleman of Mississippi, whose support he was courting. After a speech in Jackson, Kennedy stayed up late into the night, drinking and talking politics with Coleman and the state's two senators, James Eastland and John Stennis. Kennedy hoped such contacts would help him in 1960, but the meeting with Coleman caused him a more immediate political problem as 1958 rolled around: He faced reelection in Massachusetts, where his pollster Lou Harris's private surveys showed his black support slipping, and his Republican opponent, Vincent Celeste, was running on a strong civil rights platform, accusing Kennedy of selling out to the southern barons. Just as the campaign was heating up, Roy Wilkins of the NAACP began a period of prolonged public criticism of Kennedy in a speech in which he summoned the image of the senator embracing Governor Marvin Griffin of Georgia, one of the country's most rabid segregationists. When Kennedy protested that no such meeting had ever occurred, Wilkins replied that he had simply meant to suggest the possibility of one, given the meeting in Mississippi.

Kennedy now worked with his advisers to fashion a series of civil rights proposals that could be presented as a campaign program, including support for the abandoned Part III of the 1957 bill, revision of the Senate's filibuster rule, and support for antibombing legislation that would impose new federal penalties on whites engaging in antiblack vigilantism. Kennedy had taken another important symbolic step of his own in December 1957: he became the first member of Congress from any New England state to hire a black staff member, Virginia Battle, who became a secretary in his Boston office. The campaign printed thousands of pamphlets with Battle's face on the cover, detailing Kennedy's civil rights record.

Such efforts paid off, and Kennedy won reelection with an increased share of the black vote. Roy Wilkins wrote to congratulate Kennedy, calling his civil rights record "one of the best in the Senate with only our disagreement on the jury trial thing as a debit."

But by the summer of 1959, Kennedy's courtship of southern support for his presidential bid got him in hot water again when he invited Alabama's segregationist governor, John Patterson, to breakfast at his Georgetown home. Jackie Robinson, a staunch Republican, was so incensed that he refused to pose for a picture with Kennedy at a New York dinner. And in November, when Kennedy wrote to Martin Luther King for the first time, introducing himself and asking for a meeting, King didn't even bother to reply.

* * *

IN THE END, KENNEDY would win the Democratic presidential nomination not with the southern delegations, whose support ultimately went to Lyndon Johnson, but by defeating the liberal Hubert Humphrey. Humphrey was one of the Senate's most avid supporters of civil rights, but Kennedy dispatched him in primaries in West Virginia and Wisconsin, and then won the support of big northern states like Pennsylvania at the Democratic Convention in Los Angeles in July 1960, where he chose Johnson as his running mate. His campaign that autumn would depend on both the southern support he hoped Johnson could bring *and* the strong backing of black voters. In his quest for the latter, he enlisted the help of a new adviser, Harris Wofford, a bright young law professor at Notre Dame who had begun writing occasional speeches for Kennedy while still a staff lawyer at the Civil Rights Commission.

One day that August, Kennedy spotted Wofford on the street in Georgetown and gave him a lift to his Senate office on Capitol Hill. "Now, in five minutes, tick off ten things a president ought to do to clean up this goddamn civil rights mess," Kennedy demanded. Wofford had plenty of suggestions, first among them that a president could, with one stroke of a pen, sign an executive order barring discrimination in federally assisted housing. That idea quickly became a staple of Kennedy's speeches, repeated in just those words in a way that would come back to haunt him.

Meantime, Wofford became the head of a special "Civil Rights Section" at Kennedy headquarters, courting black voters in a range of concrete and symbolic ways. Among the section's priorities was a voter registration campaign, which it organized through churches and not the Democratic National Committee, so it would be nonpartisan and could be financed by tax-exempt funds. Kennedy spoke out in favor of the lunch counter sit-ins that had begun in Greensboro, North Carolina, declaring, "It is in the American tradition to stand up for one's rights—even if the new way to stand up for one's rights is to sit down." To help deal with reporters, Kennedy hired Andrew Hatcher, a former journalist then serving in state government in California and an old friend of the campaign press secretary, Pierre Salinger. When a hotel at a campaign stop in Paducah, Kentucky, refused a room to Simeon Booker, the black correspondent for *Jet* magazine, Kennedy moved his entire entourage to other lodging. Finally, on October 11, the campaign convened a daylong conference in New York City on "Constitutional Rights"—a name chosen to avoid offending southern sensibilities—where Kennedy pledged not only legislative but executive action "on a bold and large scale," and added: "This is a moral question, it is upon the president the central responsibility will bear."

But none of these carefully plotted actions could compare to the impact of a single, spur-of-the-moment decision Kennedy would make with regard to an event he could not have planned: the arrest of Martin Luther King on October 19, as he sought to be served in the restaurant of Rich's department store in Atlanta. It was Wofford who set the chain of events in motion, by calling (on his own initiative) his friend Morris Abram, a leading liberal lawyer in Atlanta, who got in touch with the city's progressive mayor, William Hartsfield. Hartsfield promptly announced—to the shock of the Kennedy campaign—that in response to personal intervention from Kennedy, he had worked out a deal for King's release, in exchange for a thirty-day moratorium on further demonstrations while a desegregation plan was formulated.

For public consumption, the Kennedy forces insisted they had merely made a general inquiry into the facts of the case. But when a Georgia judge ruled that King's arrest at Rich's had violated his probation on an earlier charge of driving with an out-of-state license and sentenced him to four months' hard labor in a state prison, the candidate himself reached out to Georgia's governor, Ernest Vandiver, and made a secret deal: if Kennedy would refrain from publicly criticizing the judge's ruling, Vandiver would lean privately on the judge to reverse it. Robert Kennedy, who was his brother's campaign manager, also later spoke with Vandiver, and then with the judge himself.

What happened next was Harris Wofford's brainstorm: a simple, sympathetic telephone call from Kennedy to Coretta King, who was distraught when her husband was manacled and taken to a rural prison farm in the middle of the night. Wofford persuaded Kennedy's brother-in-law Sargent Shriver, who had been active in civil rights work in Chicago, to broach the idea with the candidate. Because Shriver knew the campaign high command was certain to oppose any such move, he waited until he could speak to Kennedy alone. In a hotel room near O'Hare Airport, Shriver made the pitch. The candidate immediately embraced the idea and placed the call, telling Mrs. King simply that he knew she must be worried, and that he was thinking of her. When Bob Kennedy learned what had happened, he was livid. "Do you know that this election may be razor close and you have probably lost it for us?" he exploded at Wofford.

Precisely the opposite proved true. The call got little attention in mainstream newspapers, but the black press played it big. Kennedy's Republican opponent, Richard Nixon, had considered making a similar call himself but concluded it would be "grandstanding," and he refused an entreaty from his most prominent black supporter, Jackie Robinson, to reconsider. Meantime, Wofford and Louis Martin, the black former newspaper publisher who was working as a Kennedy campaign adviser, produced a pamphlet for distribution in black neighborhoods—known as the "blue bomb" for the color of paper it was printed on. It described the case with the headline "'No Comment' Nixon vs. a Candidate With a Heart."

The pièce de résistance came when King's father, the Reverend Martin Luther King Sr., who had previously announced that he could never vote for Kennedy because he was a Catholic, now warmly endorsed him. Kennedy's own comment to Wofford was typically wry. "Did you see what Martin's father said?" the candidate asked. "He was going to vote against me because I was a Catholic but since I called his daughter-in-law, he will vote for me. That was a hell of a bigoted statement, wasn't it? Imagine Martin Luther King having a bigot for a father!"

Then he added, "Well, we all have fathers, don't we?"

* * *

EVEN BEFORE HE TOOK the oath of office, Kennedy offered vivid symbolic proof that the New Frontier would include a new place for black Americans. Harry Belafonte, Nat King Cole, Ella Fitzgerald, and Mahalia Jackson all performed at a glittering preinaugural gala organized by Frank Sinatra (though Sammy Davis Jr. had, of course, been barred because of his interracial marriage), and the great contralto Marian Anderson sang at the swearing-in. As Kennedy reviewed the inaugural parade, he noticed not a single black face in the Coast Guard contingent and immediately called one of his speechwriters, Richard Goodwin, who alerted the new Treasury secretary, Douglas Dillon, whose department was in charge of the fleet. That summer, the Coast Guard Academy hired a black instructor, and the next entering class had four black cadets. Soon enough, Kennedy would appoint more than forty black citizens to significant federal posts. He included Andrew Hatcher's son Avery in Caroline Kennedy's private White House nursery school, and he created, by executive order, a presidential Committee on Equal Employment Opportunity, aimed at combating discrimination in the workforce and chaired by Vice President Johnson himself.

Kennedy also accepted a recommendation from Harris Wofford and Louis Martin to add six significant words to his ringing inaugural address. He declared that the United States was "unwilling to witness or permit the slow undoing of those human rights to which this nation has always been committed, and to which we are committed today, *at home and around the world.*" Those few words had the effect—however little noticed by most commentators—of making civil rights the sole domestic issue singled out in a speech otherwise largely devoted to foreign policy.

But Kennedy did *not* adopt most of the lengthy list of recommendations Wofford had sent him on December 30, 1960, in a memo arguing that when it came to civil rights, "Our jet age ship of state has been flying on only one of its three engines—the Judiciary—while the Congress and the executive have been stalling." Wofford warned that the black vote was "perhaps the most volatile of all the elements making up this year's tight victory," and added, "No one can predict when the Negro cup of bitterness and skepticism is going to overflow." Wofford said that, while the decision would not be popular with civil rights groups and should not be advertised in advance, the president could probably get away without proposing civil rights legislation in 1961, but only if he went "ahead with a substantial executive action program." Such a program, Wofford said, should involve a series of executive orders. These could include Kennedy's campaign proposal to ban segregation in federally supported housing, together with moves to condition federal aid to education on nondiscrimination and an effort by the Justice Department to initiate lawsuits of the sort envisioned by the abandoned Part III of the 1957 Civil Rights Act, to force school desegregation in places where it was lagging.

In the end, Kennedy did not move swiftly on the executive or legislative front. Asked at a news conference on February 1 what executive action he might take on civil rights, the president said only that he had been reviewing the matter "and I'm hopeful that we will shortly conclude that analysis and have some statement to make on it." As for legislation, Lee White, another of Kennedy's civil rights advisers, would recall: "I think his decision was that there was going to be plenty of time to fight the battle of civil rights legislation, that there were many other things that could and should be done in the way of domestic legislation that would benefit all people at the lower end of the economic ladder."

Kennedy did not even appoint a civil rights adviser in the White House until a week later, and then only in the most backhanded way. The Reverend Theodore Hesburgh, president of the University of Notre Dame and a member of the United States Commission on Civil Rights, had come to the White House to lobby the new president for action, complaining, for example, that there were no blacks in the Alabama National Guard. "Look, father, I may have to send the Alabama National Guard to Berlin tomorrow and I don't want to have to do it in the middle of a revolution at home," Kennedy said. He assured Hesburgh, though, that he had a special adviser for civil rights, and that was Harris Wofford. This was news to Hesburgh, who was a friend of Wofford's from their time together on the commission and who had just seen him.

It was also news to Wofford, who had been waiting for a formal offer to join the administration and worrying about his mortgage in the meantime. A few minutes later, he got a call telling him to report to the White House, where he was quickly sworn in as a presidential assistant, without so much as a meeting with the president. The job Wofford really wanted—assistant attorney general for civil rights—went instead to Burke Marshall, a respected antitrust lawyer, whose principal appeal for the president was that, unlike the passionate Wofford, he had no particular background in civil rights.

*　*　*

So IN THE CROWDED two years since 1961, Kennedy had traveled a long, hard road on civil rights. The searing crises of the Freedom Rides, Ole Miss, and Birmingham had left their mark. As he surveyed the morning newspapers on Tuesday, June 11, 1963, the president found yet another horrifying picture—this time not from Birmingham, but from Saigon, half a world away, where a seventy-three-year-old Buddhist monk named Thich Quang Duc had burned himself alive at a busy intersection to protest the policies of President Ngo Dinh Diem of South Vietnam. "Jesus Christ!" Kennedy exclaimed when the attorney general telephoned him first thing that day to talk about the situation at the University of Alabama, which was also very much on the president's mind.

Later that same morning, Deputy Attorney General Nick Katzenbach was prepared to escort two black students, Vivian Malone and James Hood, into the University of Alabama at Tuscaloosa, where Governor Wallace had vowed to resist their admission by standing in the door of Foster Auditorium. The administration had known that such a confrontation was coming, even as it dealt with the violence in Birmingham. Weeks earlier, a federal court had ordered the students' enrollment, and now the White House—still stung by the experience of Ole Miss—was determined to avoid more violence, or a dangerous confrontation with Wallace, who had pledged in his January 1963 inaugural address to maintain "segregation now, segregation tomorrow, segregation forever!"

This time, the Kennedy administration had a carefully choreographed plan: to allow the ritual confrontation that Wallace wanted, then promptly assert federal control of the Alabama National Guard and register the students right away.

The president began his working day at breakfast with the leaders of both parties in Congress, where the Senate majority leader Mike Mansfield told him there simply had to be a civil rights bill. "We're still talking about that," Kennedy said lightly, insisting that he wanted a bill that would not derail the rest of his agenda: "The minimum we can ask for and the maximum we can stand behind." Following Lyndon Johnson's advice, Kennedy had already met privately with the Republican leaders, Everett Dirksen and Charles Halleck, to sound them out about what they might find acceptable in a bill. "No commitments were requested, and none were given," Dirksen would recall, but the Senate Republican caucus had announced, in tepid tones, that it would "support legislation that may be required to meet the problem."

Meantime, in Alabama, the most immediate aspect of the problem was evaporating in the blistering one-hundred-degree heat. Nick Katzenbach—perspiring and towering almost comically over the bantam Wallace—ordered the governor to "cease and desist from unlawful obstructions." Wallace went through the show of denouncing what he called an "unwelcomed, unwarranted and force-induced intrusion" and "a frightful example of the suppression of the rights, privileges and sovereignty of this state." But in short order, after Robert Kennedy asked the president to sign the executive order federalizing the Alabama guard, Wallace stepped aside. The president had missed the initial live broadcast of the confrontation, but he watched a replay in the office of his secretary Evelyn Lincoln and decided he wanted to use the television time he had already tentatively reserved for that night.

Ted Sorensen would have only a few short hours to prepare what he suddenly realized would be one of the most important speeches of Kennedy's presidency. He had no shortage of material. The president had effectively been preparing for years for this moment. Sorensen dug out some sobering statistics that Harris Wofford had gathered for Kennedy to use in his first campaign debate against Richard Nixon in 1960, and that the president had invoked from time to time ever since:

> The Negro baby born in America today, regardless of the section or the state in which he is born, has about one-half as much chance of completing a high school as a white baby born in the same place on the same day, one third as much chance of completing college, one-third as much chance of becoming a professional man, twice as much chance of becoming unemployed, about one-seventh as much chance of earning $10,000 a year; a life expectancy which is seven years shorter and the prospects of earning only half as much.

While Sorensen worked away, the president kept a series of late afternoon meetings—with Averell Harriman, a foreign policy adviser, to discuss coming negotiations on the Nuclear Test Ban Treaty; with Edward R. Murrow, the former journalist who now headed the United States Information Agency, to discuss coverage of the civil rights issue around the world; and with NASA administrator James Webb to discuss the space program.

Finally—after his frantic last round of drafting with the attorney general in the Cabinet Room—the president took his place at his desk and leaned in as the hour struck eight. He began with a recap of the scene in Tuscaloosa, immediately casting the matter as a concern for the whole nation, saying he hoped "every American, regardless of where he lives, will stop and examine his conscience about this and other related incidents." He added, "This is not a sectional issue . . . This is not even a legal or legislative issue alone. It is better to settle these matters in the courts than on the streets, and new laws are needed at every level, but law alone cannot make men see right. We are confronted primarily with a moral issue. It is as old as the Scriptures and is as clear as the American Constitution. The heart of the question is whether all Americans are to be afforded equal rights and equal opportunities, whether we are going to treat our fellow Americans as we want to be treated."

In those few words—among the most eloquent and perhaps the bravest of his life—John F. Kennedy had done what no other American president, not even Abraham Lincoln, had ever done: he had committed his country to assuring full equality for black Americans in the eyes of the law, and had declared that doing so was a moral imperative. Even from the distance of half a century, the words echo magnificently. On the night Kennedy first uttered them, they were lightning bolts in the summer sky.

But if Kennedy's words were ringing, they were also careful—even as he veered from the text with conversational ad-libs from time to time. He had edited Sorensen's final draft with a skilled eye toward bleeding it of needless provocation. Where Sorensen had written that "cesspools of segregation and discrimination exist in every state," Kennedy toned that down to "difficulties over." Where Sorensen had proclaimed, "a social revolution is at hand," Kennedy warned of "a great change." Where Sorensen had lamented that the "pace is still shamefully slow," Kennedy contented himself with "very."

Kennedy did not, however, minimize the scale of the legislation he was seeking. He said he would ask for a bill "giving all Americans the right to be served in facilities which are open to the public," a right that, he added spontaneously, "seems to me to be an elementary right." He said he would also ask for new authority to allow the federal government "to participate more fully in lawsuits designed to end segregation in public education" (the old Part III from 1957), along with greater protections for the right to vote. But legislation alone could not solve the problem, he added. It must be solved, he said, "in the homes of every American in every community across our country" (omitting Sorensen's suggestion that it must also be solved in the "hearts" of people). He paid tribute "to those citizens North and South" who had been working "to make life better for all," adding, "Like our soldiers and sailors in all parts of the world, they are meeting freedom's challenge on the firing line, and I salute them for their honor and their courage."

And then, eleven minutes and seventeen seconds into his speech, the president "ran out of runway," as Lee White would recall. He looked up from his reading copy, stared straight into the camera, clasped his hands on the little reading stand on his desk as the camera pulled back, and went on, extemporaneously, for another two and a half minutes.

"My fellow Americans, this is a problem which faces us all—in every city of the North as well as the South," he said. "This is one country. It has become one country because all of us and all the people who came here had an equal chance to develop their talents. We cannot say to ten percent of the population that you can't have that right; your children cannot have the chance to develop whatever talents they have; that the only way they are going to get their rights is to go in the streets and demonstrate. I think we owe them and we owe ourselves a better country than that."

Then he concluded, "As I've said before, not every child has an equal talent or an equal ability or equal motivation, but they should have the equal right to develop their talent and their ability and their motivation, to make something of themselves. We have a right to expect that the Negro community will be responsible, will uphold the law, but they have a right to expect that the law will be fair, that the Constitution will be color-blind . . . This is what we're talking about, and this is a matter which concerns this country and what it stands for, and in meeting it, I ask the support of all of our citizens. Thank you very much."

Barely a minute after Kennedy went off the air, Martin Luther King dispatched a telegram to the White House, calling the speech "one of the most eloquent, profound and unequivocal pleas for justice and the freedom of all men ever made by any president."

Four hours later, in Jackson, Mississippi, a rifleman hidden in a honeysuckle bush made a decidedly different statement: He shot the NAACP's fearless crusader Medgar Evers dead, in the back, as he walked toward his house from the driveway.

3

The Heart of the Problem

ROBERT FRANCIS KENNEDY WAS not only his brother's attorney general but also his most trusted confidant, so it was no surprise that the longest day of the year should find him working overtime to sell the civil rights bill the administration had sent to Congress just two days before. Together with the president, Bob Kennedy attended a two-hour White House meeting with two hundred forty-four of the nation's most prominent lawyers (sixty-six of them from southern states), along with three of his own predecessors as attorney general, aimed at explaining and promoting the bill.

The meeting was just one in an elaborately planned series of gatherings—of business and labor leaders, women's groups, religious organizations—arranged by the White House staff in the days before and after the bill's introduction as a way of building public support. The meetings were off the record and little mentioned by the White House press office. They were aimed not so much at attracting national publicity as at building grassroots backing—and biracial cooperation—in cities around the country. The Kennedy brothers well understood that they now had a big selling job ahead of them—with Congress and with the nation as a whole—if their bill was to have any chance of passing.

It was no accident that in the president's address to the nation on June 11, he had spoken only in general terms of the measures he would seek. No actual bill yet existed. In the eight days between the president's speech and the administration's formal submission of the measure to the House of Representatives on June 19, the lawyers in Bob Kennedy's Justice Department had worked to finish piecing together a proposal that would achieve two goals: first, that it could pass constitutional muster; and second, that it could win the support of Republicans, who would be crucial in passing any bill, because of the implacable opposition of the southern Democrats. Already, the attorney general had met personally with key legislators, the first step in what would become some eighty hours of official testimony by year's end.

The Justice Department staff lawyers, an all-white crew led by Harold Greene and Norbert Schlei, had debated whether to base the heart of the bill—its prohibition on discrimination in public accommodations—on the Constitution's commerce clause, which granted Congress the power to regulate interstate commerce, or whether to base it on the Fourteenth Amendment's guarantee of "equal protection of the laws." The commerce clause had been used to justify various federal regulatory measures dating back to the New Deal and the Progressive era, but extending its reach into race relations was deeply controversial. The Fourteenth Amendment argument had the strategic advantage of being supported by many Republicans, but also a drawback, because of the lingering 1883 Supreme Court ruling—which had never been overturned—that the amendment did not apply to the actions of private businesses.

In the end, the administration chose to rely on both rationales. Its bill—formally christened H.R. 7152 because it originated in the House of Representatives—was broad, if not quite as ambitious as the most ardent civil rights supporters had hoped it would be. It had seven main provisions:

The **first** would enforce the right to vote in federal elections (but not state contests) through the appointment of government referees. It would not bar state literacy tests, but would require that they be the same for all individuals.

The **second** would outlaw discrimination in hotels, motels, restaurants, and other public accommodations (while exempting, without defining them, private clubs).

The **third** would allow the attorney general to initiate suits to desegregate public schools when asked to do so by someone unable to sue (a less sweeping version of the old, failed Part III from the 1957 bill).

The **fourth** would establish a federal "Community Relations Service" to assist individuals and communities in resolving racial disputes, and relieve the growing pressure on the Justice Department.

The **fifth** would extend the life of the Civil Rights Commission (originally created by the 1957 bill) for another four years.

The **sixth** would prohibit discrimination in federally assisted programs in states and localities.

And the **seventh** would enshrine in law a federal "Equal Employment Opportunity Commission"—a permanent version of the special presidential committee that Kennedy had named Lyndon Johnson to lead—to address discrimination by government contractors.

But—to the chagrin of civil rights groups—this seventh provision pointedly did not include a strong Fair Employment Practices Commission, with power to investigate job discrimination by private companies. Together with the provision to end segregation in public places, such a measure had long been the holy grail of civil rights organizations, and its absence again left them deeply wary about President Kennedy's commitment to a strong bill, after their first flush of enthusiasm over the June 11 speech. For its part, the White House believed that inclusion of an FEPC provision could alienate pro-business Republicans and thus jeopardize the whole bill.

The House Republican leader, Charles Halleck, was keeping his counsel on the bill. In a speech in Atlanta on the same day as the lawyers' meeting at the White House, he declined to state his own views. "I'm not going to admit I'm straddling the fence," he said. "As a leader, it does not do me any good to go one way if the troops go another. I have been asked scores of times about my personal position. I haven't said. I'm being perfectly fair and honest about it. I just don't know."

As it was, Senator Dirksen had already announced his firm opposition to the provision for desegregating public accommodations. So, in a spirit of bipartisanship, majority leader Mike Mansfield introduced the administration's bill verbatim in the Senate—a carbon copy of H.R. 7152—but then joined with Dirksen to offer an alternative, identical in every way, except that the public accommodations section was omitted. Mansfield and another Democrat, Warren Magnuson of Washington, then offered a third bill, covering only public accommodations, which would be referred to the Senate Commerce Committee.

The White House took pains to portray its bill—unveiled the same day as Medgar Evers's burial at Arlington National Cemetery—as a noncontroversial approach to a knotty problem. "The legal remedies I have proposed are the embodiment of this nation's basic posture of common sense and common justice," the president said in his official message accompanying the bill's submission to Congress.

But on Capitol Hill, the southern bulls bellowed in predictable protest. Senator Strom Thurmond of South Carolina railed against the bill as "unconstitutional, unnecessary, unwise and beyond the realm of reason," while James Eastland of Mississippi, the all-powerful chairman of the Senate Judiciary Committee, called it a "complete blueprint for the totalitarian state." Richard Russell of Georgia denounced the measure as "a threatened crime against the whole philosophy of liberty."

By contrast, civil rights groups offered praise for Kennedy's effort, but denounced the president's request for "self-restraint" on further demonstrations and his warning that "unruly tactics or pressures will not help and may hinder the effective consideration of these measures" as unreasonable. Most insisted that the bill did not "fully meet the needs of the times," as Roy Wilkins of the NAACP put it.

It was now Bob Kennedy's thankless job to reconcile those irreconcilable views.

* * *

THE ATTORNEY GENERAL WAS well aware of the task before him. Earlier on the same day as the White House meeting with the lawyers, he had traveled to Philadelphia for a speech at Independence Hall marking the 175th anniversary of the ratification of the Constitution. Quoting Woodrow Wilson's maxim that the Constitution was no "mere lawyer's document" but a "vehicle of life," whose "spirit is always the spirit of the age," Kennedy said such sentiment had special meaning "at a time when the inadequate phrase 'Civil Rights' has come to reflect an urgent nationwide struggle for equality by the ten and a half percent of our people whose skin is not white."

"The time is long past when any sensible American could tolerate the denial of free voting rights to all races, or the existence of 'White Only' signs on public facilities," he added. "Even by the narrowest interpretation, these things are unconstitutional." Then he asked, "Must we now wait, as intelligent modern Americans in a changing society, must we now wait for the Supreme Court to spell out each new particularity of civil rights for us? Whatever color we are, let us hope not."

But there were scores of politically powerful people in Washington and around the country—and millions of ordinary Americans—who would beg to differ on that point. Indeed, on June 12, the very day after President Kennedy's televised speech, southern Democrats in the House of Representatives had helped to defeat what should have been a routine funding bill for the Area Redevelopment Administration, a Kennedy-sponsored program that promoted public works in underprivileged areas.

"That was a tough one . . . wasn't it?" the president asked the House majority leader, Carl Albert, in an exasperated phone call after the vote.

"Oh, it was awful," Albert replied. "This is going to affect mass transit, it's going to kill the farm bill."

"Well," the president replied, his voice grim, "we just have to take 'em as they come."

Even some of the administration's most liberal supporters were unnerved by the sweep of his bill. Arthur M. Schlesinger Jr., President

Kennedy's historian in residence, would record in his diary that soundings by a liberal friend in the Chicago suburbs in the wake of Kennedy's proposals had found "considerable anxiety" over the president's speech, and that people "seemed alarmed over the pace of the integration movement." Still other liberals insisted that the Kennedy administration was moving much too slowly. In a letter to Senator Hubert Humphrey just before the bill was introduced, Andrew Biemiller, the AFL-CIO's chief lobbyist in Washington and himself a former Democratic congressman from Wisconsin, complained that the measure contained no FEPC provision, inadequate provisions on public accommodations, and not enough authority for the government to sue to enforce desegregation. "A patent compromise in a no-compromise situation," Biemiller wrote. "All-out fights are made on all-out measures. How is the public to understand that the administration is going to make an all-out fight when it starts with a halfway measure?" He predicted that the administration's bill would "become a ceiling on what can be done, rather than a floor."

On June 14, several thousand demonstrators marched through downtown Washington, winding up outside the Justice Department building on Pennsylvania Avenue. Bob Kennedy addressed them through a bullhorn from a makeshift platform, taking umbrage at flyers being distributed that suggested there was discrimination in his own department. "There is no discrimination here at Justice," he insisted, noting that he had increased the number of black lawyers in the department from ten to sixty (out of nine hundred). "Any individual can come here and get a job if he is qualified." But he added with some asperity, "I'm not going out and hire a Negro just because he's not white."

It was Bob Kennedy's job to take the heat for the administration. He would recall that he had resisted becoming attorney general in part because he worried that the Justice Department would be so consumed with the controversies of civil rights that having a Kennedy as attorney general would needlessly complicate life for the Kennedy who was president. Now that fear was coming true.

"The fact that I was Attorney General caused him many more problems than if I hadn't been his brother," he would remember. "Instead of talking about Robert Kennedy, they started talking about the 'Kennedy brothers,' which he used to point out to me frequently. It was no longer Robert, the Attorney General, but now they were talking about the Kennedy brothers." The very name Bobby had become a curse, a blood oath, as it was for a policeman in Winona, Mississippi, who had hollered the attorney general's name over and over as he smashed the head of a civil rights protester against the floor in early June. Indeed, *Time* magazine's cover for June 21—under the tagline "Civil Rights: The Moral Crisis"—featured not only a large full-face portrait of Bob Kennedy in the foreground, but a smaller background painting of the two brothers, their heads bowed toward each other in concentration and consultation.

The two men, eight years apart in age, could hardly have been more different. If Jack Kennedy was detached, free-spirited, instinctively ironic, Bob Kennedy was reliable, judgmental, easily angered—"ruthless," in the prevailing thumbnail assessment. "Black Robert," his big brother called him, while Jack's friend Ben Bradlee summed up Bob's self-righteous streak with a play on his middle name: "Saint Francis."

Gore Vidal, writing in *Esquire* that spring, sketched a withering view of the attorney general. "His obvious characteristics are energy, vindictiveness and a simple-mindedness about human motives which may yet bring him down," Vidal wrote. "He has none of his brother's human ease, or charity." Vidal, who shared a stepfather with Jacqueline Kennedy, held a grudge against Bob Kennedy, who had tangled with him at a White House party after Vidal put his arm around the First Lady's bare shoulders, and his assessment was harsh to the point of unfairness. But it nevertheless captured something of the younger Kennedy's edgy essence.

The two brothers had only grown close in adulthood a decade earlier— after Bob managed Jack's successful 1952 Senate campaign and then went on to run his 1960 presidential campaign. But by this point in Kennedy's presidency, they had long since become able to finish each other's sentences, and in almost every crisis—from missiles in Cuba to bombs in Birmingham—theirs were the views that mattered most. "I scheduled a lot of meetings with black leaders and sat in on some of them, but it didn't matter what went on in the meeting," Louis Martin would recall.

"What you had to do when the meeting was over was go into the Oval Office, where J.F.K. and Bobby were, to find out what was really important."

And on this summer solstice, what was really important, to both Kennedys, was whether the civil rights bill was worth all the political trouble it was already causing. "He would ask me every four days, 'Do you think we did the right thing by sending the legislation up? Look at the trouble it's got us in,'" Bob Kennedy would recall of his conversations with his brother. "But always in a semi-jocular way."

The attorney general knew better than most the difficulty of finding a proposal that could pass Congress, while also addressing a problem that he acknowledged was "different from one community to another."

"For the last two and a half years, we have attempted always to work at the local level to see if we could get local individuals, local leaders, political leaders and business leaders, financial leaders, to take action themselves," he had told a meeting of religious leaders at the White House on June 17, as he displayed a map of five hundred communities in the Old Confederacy plus Oklahoma, Kentucky, Maryland, and West Virginia, showing the steps the administration had taken to encourage voluntary desegregation in each. When one of the attorney general's listeners asked whether the administration would now discourage further demonstrations, Kennedy said he would rather have matters settled by negotiation or voluntary action.

"But," he added, "I can understand if I have been abused or misused and treated as a second-class citizen for a long time, where I can't eat in downtown restaurants, where I can't use a restroom or hotel, and I can't get anybody to talk to me as a civilized human being and I can't get any place, there is only one thing for me to do and that is the old American practice of going around with a sign and start picketing."

* * *

ROBERT KENNEDY'S JOURNEY TO the front lines of civil rights—and to the bill he now set out to sell—had been long and slow. He once told the journalist Anthony Lewis that he "didn't lie awake nights worrying" about the issue while he was growing up, and when Lewis asked if he had ever realized "the rather special horror of life for the Negro in the South," he was forced to reply with a flat "No." To his aide LaVerne Duffy, he was blunter: "Honestly, before I became attorney general, I didn't give a shit about civil rights. It never touched my life." In fact, Kennedy spent much of his early life veering between pretending not to give a shit about anything, and struggling—as the third son in his glamorous family and the decided runt among his siblings—simply to keep up and be noticed, especially by his father, who gave him perpetual short shrift in favor of his older brothers, Joe Jr. and Jack—and, later, his younger brother, Ted. Throughout his life, he would be the brooding Kennedy, darker, deeper, more complicated than the other men of the family, except perhaps the patriarch himself. "Who really knew Bob Kennedy?" his friend and aide John Douglas once asked.

As a boy, he briefly had a paper route, but he soon tired of it and began making his appointed rounds in his family's chauffeured Rolls-Royce. As a student at Portsmouth Priory, a solemn Benedictine boarding school in Rhode Island, he was so determined to make the grade that he was caught up in a cheating scandal involving a stolen examination and asked to leave. He transferred to Milton Academy in Massachusetts and in his senior year, in 1943, enlisted in the Navy's V-12 officer training program, which sent him to Harvard while his older brothers were both in combat overseas, taunting him with teasing letters about his stateside status. He flunked the aptitude test for flight training, resigned from Officer Candidate School, and wound up missing the war altogether, serving out his Navy hitch in 1946 as a common seaman aboard the USS *Joseph P. Kennedy Jr.*, the destroyer named for his eldest brother, whose explosives-laden plane had blown up over England on a secret mission in 1944.

After the war, he earned C's and D's at Harvard, not good enough to get him into Harvard Law School, so he enrolled at the University of Virginia, where he became known for his rudeness, scarring the floor of his apartment with football cleats, and allowing an unleashed, ill-tempered German police dog to menace his neighbors. He was hot-tempered and pugnacious. When his father came to make an isolationist speech in Charlottesville and the student paper editorialized, "Mr. Kennedy, the

Dinosaur Is Dead," Bob showed up in its offices, ready to punch someone in the nose.

But the pugnacity masked—and may well even have grown out of—a more admirable quality that Bob had also developed along the way: a strong, unyielding moral sense, perhaps influenced by his exceedingly devout Catholic mother, Rose, whose undisputed pet he had always been. "I enjoyed what you said about the officers not understanding the point of view of the men unless they had done the work themselves," she wrote him while he was scraping paint on his ship at sea. "After your rubbing and scrubbing these months, you will never again be in that position." He was the only one of the Kennedy boys to win his father's promised thousand-dollar bounty for refraining from smoking or drinking until he was twenty-one, and he was physically unable to sit through the compulsory Navy training film showing the graphic consequences of venereal disease. In contrast to his older brother's self-confessed ignorance of the Depression, he once explained, "What we did grow up with was the idea that there were a lot of people who were less fortunate and a lot of people who were hungry—this was during the 1930s—people who had a difficult time."

In 1951, Kennedy invited Ralph Bunche, the distinguished black United Nations negotiator who had won the Nobel Peace Prize, to speak at the University of Virginia. It was Bunche's firm policy never to address segregated audiences, but segregation was the rule in Charlottesville. When other student leaders balked at Bunche's demand, Kennedy became so incensed he was almost incoherent, and he sought the approval of the university's president, Colgate Darden. Suffice it to say that Bunche became the first speaker ever to appear before an integrated audience at the University of Virginia.

By all accounts, Bob first made a strong impression within his family when his Harvard friend Kenneth O'Donnell drafted him into service to manage Jack's flailing 1952 Senate campaign. He had not wanted the job. He was working as a staff lawyer at the Justice Department in Washington, married to his sister Jean's old college roommate, Ethel Skakel, with a child at home and another on the way. But he was prevailed upon to take the assignment, and, as Joseph P. Kennedy's biographer David

Nasaw writes, "Every adjective ever applied to his father was now visited upon the son: abrasive, driven, aggressive and a screamer. But, like his father, he got things done—brilliantly."

Bob built a statewide political organization that owed its allegiance to Jack Kennedy, not to the Democratic Party or the old-line Massachusetts ward heelers whose support their father had been clumsily courting. He brought order, discipline, a strong organization, and fierce loyalty to the effort, and by Election Day old Joe Kennedy was talking up Bob's own political prospects in letters to friends, suggesting he might move to Connecticut to run for elective office. "In that event, we will want to have him make a good legal connection and, if possible, buy some business that would keep him interested—a paper or television station or something like that," Ambassador Kennedy wrote.

In the short term, though, it seemed that there was not enough adjacent airspace for two Kennedys in New England politics. So Bob wound up following Jack to Washington, as a staff lawyer for the new Republican majority on the Senate's Permanent Subcommittee on Investigations—headed by his father's friend, Senator Joseph R. McCarthy of Wisconsin. Kennedy left the committee after just five months—at loggerheads with its snarling chief counsel, Roy Cohn—but he later joined the staff of the Democratic minority and eventually became its chief counsel when the Democrats regained power in 1954. For the rest of his life, Kennedy's work for the McCarthy committee would dog him among liberals who could not understand his sympathy for a Red-baiting demagogue who, fueled by equal parts alcohol and vitriol, ruined lives and careers with reckless charges of subversion, before making the fatal mistake of taking on Dwight D. Eisenhower's beloved Army and finally being censured by his Senate colleagues.

For Bob Kennedy, McCarthy's appeal was twofold: Kennedy, too, was a strident anticommunist, and he believed McCarthy was doing the Lord's work; and he believed that much of the criticism of McCarthy amounted to thinly veiled anti-Catholicism. The same sense of outrage would fuel Kennedy's subsequent and even more celebrated investigation of labor racketeering as counsel of a new Senate Select Committee on Improper Activities in the Labor or Management Field, chaired by John McClellan of Arkansas and including his brother Jack among its members. In that job, Bob pursued Dave Beck and Jimmy Hoffa of the International Brotherhood of Teamsters with the same zeal that McCarthy had reserved for suspected Communists.

But if Kennedy was a typical Cold Warrior in many respects, like his brother, he was also attuned to the emerging issues of human rights around the world. In 1955, he undertook a fact-finding tour of the Soviet Union with another old friend of his father, Supreme Court Justice William O. Douglas, and was so dour and suspicious that he would barely try the local food and resisted being treated by a Russian doctor even when he fell seriously ill. Yet upon his return, he wrote articles for *U.S. News and World Report* and the *New York Times Magazine* in which he argued, "If we are going to win the present conflict with the Soviet Union, we can no longer support the exploitation of native people by Western nations. We supported the French in Indochina for too long."

And like his brother, Bob was becoming more and more aware of the enduring racial injustices suffered by American blacks. He may have chewed out Sargent Shriver and Harris Wofford for engineering John Kennedy's sympathetic phone call to Coretta King in the 1960 presidential campaign, but it was he himself—as campaign manager—who called the Georgia state judge to argue for King's release, in part because of his moral outrage at the severity of the sentence. "The more I thought about the injustice of it, the more I thought what a son of a bitch the judge was," he would later recall, telling Wofford, "It made me so damn angry to think of that bastard sentencing a citizen to hard labor for a minor traffic offense." After the election, when the calls to Mrs. King and the judge had come to be seen as contributing to John Kennedy's close victory, the liberal newspaper columnist Murray Kempton asked Bobby if he was glad they'd been made. "Sure I'm glad," he replied, "but I would hope I'm not glad for the reason you think I'm glad."

Indeed, there was nothing simple or easy about Bob Kennedy or his motives, yet his seriousness—his heaviness—could be leavened with a sly, self-effacing humor. On the morning of his brother's inauguration, when the NBC television correspondent Sander Vanocur encountered

Bob in the Capitol Rotunda and asked on the air how to address him, since he had not yet been confirmed as attorney general, Kennedy just smiled his toothy grin and suggested, "How about Bob?"

* * *

ROBERT F. KENNEDY BECAME ATTORNEY general for one overwhelming reason: his father insisted on it, arguing that Jack needed a senior official in his government whose loyalty and discretion would be absolutely unquestioned, and who could advise the president with unshrinking candor. Bob himself was ambivalent. He would later recall that he was actually eager to get away from Jack for a while. But he knew he could not work on the White House staff or in a sub-Cabinet job; his status as the president's brother would make it impossible for him to function as anyone's subordinate. So, in the face of his father's and brother's insistence, he relented in mid-December 1960 and accepted the appointment. But he chafed when President Kennedy told the 1961 Gridiron Club dinner that he thought it only appropriate that Bobby "get a little experience first," by working in the Justice Department before practicing law (which he had never done). When the president advised him that it was good to make fun of oneself, Bob retorted, "You weren't making fun of yourself. You were making fun of me!"

"Clearly, Bobby was not qualified by any traditional standards," Nicholas Katzenbach recalled. "He was too young, too inexperienced, too political, too brash, too immature in every way. All of these shortcomings were obvious to everyone, including Bobby. What was not obvious was Bobby's determination to do the job well, and his capacity to lead, which had been overshadowed by his devotion to his brother."

With the guidance of his first deputy attorney general, Byron "Whizzer" White, Kennedy recruited a standout team of aides and assistants. His new press secretary, Edwin Guthman, a Pulitzer Prize–winning former reporter for the *Seattle Times*, would later call them—borrowing from Shakespeare's *Henry V*—a "band of brothers." Besides White, an All-American football halfback and Rhodes scholar from the University of Colorado, who as a young naval intelligence officer in the South Pacific had debriefed Lieutenant John F. Kennedy after the sinking of PT 109, they included Katzenbach, another Rhodes scholar by way of Princeton and Yale Law School who had spent more than two years in prisoner of war camps during World War II after the bomber he was navigating was shot down over the Mediterranean. Katzenbach was a professor at the University of Chicago Law School when he was recruited to head the Justice Department's Office of Legal Counsel; he would later succeed White as deputy attorney general.

As his administrative assistant, Kennedy tapped John Seigenthaler, a courtly, lanky reporter for the *Nashville Tennessean*, whose investigations of the local branch of the Teamsters union he had admired. And for the all-important role of assistant attorney general for civil rights he chose Burke Marshall, a lawyer from Yale who had worked in Army intelligence as a Japanese translator and code breaker. When asked at his Senate confirmation hearing what experience he had in the field of civil rights, Marshall answered, "Virtually none," adding that he had "no specific plans" for his division, which had about forty lawyers, compared to about three hundred in the antitrust division. Marshall's own deputy was another unlikely choice: John Doar, a six-foot-two-inch former Princeton basketball player who had trained as an Army Air Forces bomber pilot. Doar, a Republican, had joined the Eisenhower Justice Department from his family's law firm in northwest Wisconsin and was now recruited, he would recall, for a job that "no one else wanted."

Bob Kennedy's new team may have lacked expertise in civil rights, but it had priceless experience of another kind: it had been "tempered by war," as John Kennedy had summed up the passage of power to a new generation in his inaugural address. "Our training as soldiers or sailors made a difference when we confronted civil rights crises," Guthman would later recall. "We could react under pressure to what the situation required."

The editorials on Bob Kennedy's appointment as attorney general may have been scathing, but at his confirmation hearings before the Senate Judiciary Committee, he received surprisingly broad support. The *New York Times*'s James Reston wrote that Kennedy had come "expecting to do battle with Jack Dempsey and instead found himself confronted, most agreeably, by Shirley Temple." Senator Sam Ervin, a country lawyer and former judge from North Carolina by way of the Harvard Law School, praised Kennedy as a man of "profound personal and political courage." Indeed, Kennedy would later recall with some wonder, "The strongest support ever I received as Attorney General came from Southerners," including the powerful Judiciary Committee chairman, James O. Eastland of Mississippi.

Nick Katzenbach would remember Kennedy's "ability to engage the loyalty of each of us, both to him and to each other," and added, "We all participated in the making of policy, and he treated each of us as a valued colleague, not as the head of a division or someone with turf to protect." Lawyers from the antitrust division were asked to weigh in on tax policy, and those from the civil division were asked their opinions on civil rights. "One of the hallmarks of the Kennedys was that they expected you to do everything," recalled William Orrick, who headed the civil division. Remembering his own brief time as a junior lawyer in the department, when higher-ups had ignored him, the new attorney general resolved to get to know as many of the career lawyers as he could, and he walked the hallways, connecting names and faces.

"Don't tell me what I can't do," he would say to his subordinates. "Tell me what I can do." After one early tour of the office with Seigenthaler, Kennedy demanded, "Did you see any Negroes? Get me a study of how many Negroes are working here." Seigenthaler would soon report that of the department's 955 lawyers in Washington, only ten were black. At his first staff meeting in February, Kennedy emphasized the need to integrate the department's offices—north and south—and he wrote to the deans of leading law schools, asking for recommendations about the brightest black students.

To his formal, walnut-paneled office—a converted conference room that he chose because it was bigger than J. Edgar Hoover's office—Kennedy brought a bubbling sense of life, with a varnished mounted sailfish over the mantel, a model of a Chinese junk on a table, a stuffed tiger, and an ever-changing gallery of his children's drawings and artwork hung on the walls with Scotch tape. In violation of government regulations, and to Hoover's extreme annoyance, he often brought Brumus, his large, black, obstreperous Newfoundland retriever, to work, and one or more of his children could be found running in and out of his office even in the midst of the hottest crises. Fifty years later, Kennedy's successor Eric Holder could point to pockmarks in the paneling from the children's stray BB gunfire.

From the start of Kennedy's tenure, the administration's working assumption was that there would be no immediate legislation on civil rights. Instead, the White House and Justice pursued administrative actions. That did not mean Kennedy could ignore the problem. At a meeting in the attorney general's office with top aides on March 6, 1961, Ed Guthman's handwritten notes show that Kennedy and his advisers covered some seventeen points on the matter of civil rights, from "Have U.S. Attorneys study integration laws" to "Leadership by president. Climate of opinion filters down to judges and juries." They considered the idea of a "roving D.A. in the South," and on the question of Alabama, Guthman wrote presciently, "Don't rock the boat on school seg until a Negro student gets into U of A." Guthman also noted that the "Government can't overestimate effect of cleaning up its own operations in South" by hiring more blacks for federal jobs, and added: "Top priority to voting."

That same month, Bob Kennedy told *Look* magazine that civil rights was the "most difficult problem" he faced, "because of the emotional factors involved." Asked about the sit-in movement that had been building in the South since the previous year, he said, "My sympathy is with them morally," but he acknowledged, "Rightly or wrongly, other people have grown up with totally different backgrounds and mores, which we can't change overnight." Asked whether he could envision sending troops to enforce a court order as Eisenhower had been required to do in Little Rock in 1957, he was firm: "I don't think we would ever come to the point of sending troops to any part of the country on a matter like that."

* * *

BY 1963, BITTER EXPERIENCE—with the Freedom Rides, Ole Miss, the Birmingham Spring, and the desegregation of the University of Alabama itself—had shown Bob Kennedy just how naïve he had been about the federal government's required role in civil rights enforcement. He thought he understood the problem of civil rights—and black discontent with the status quo—as well as anyone in Washington. But nothing had prepared him for a devastating encounter that spring, an encounter that would show him how little he really understood—and how much he had yet to learn.

It started with some advice from Dick Gregory, the comedian and activist, to whom Kennedy sometimes turned to take the pulse of black opinion. Gregory was part of a new generation of black comics who were breaking old minstrel stereotypes with more topical humor ("Segregation is not all bad," he would say. "Have you ever heard of a collision where the people in the back of the bus got hurt?") and he now suggested that the attorney general could profit from a meeting with James Baldwin, the black writer and intellectual. Kennedy had met Baldwin the previous year at a White House dinner for Nobel Prize winners, and Baldwin had just published his searing indictment of race in America, "The Fire Next Time," in the *New Yorker.*

Following Gregory's recommendation, Baldwin was invited to the attorney general's home at Hickory Hill for a meeting on Thursday, May 23. Intrigued by their discussion about the problems of urban blacks, Kennedy proposed that Baldwin convene a group of other prominent black figures for a private discussion the very next night, when Kennedy was scheduled to be in New York to meet with chain store owners about desegregating their lunch counters. Baldwin quickly summoned an eclectic group of friends and acquaintances for a meeting that Friday evening in a Kennedy family apartment on Central Park South. The invitees included the playwright Lorraine Hansberry; the singers Lena Horne and Harry Belafonte; the white actor Rip Torn; Clarence Jones, a lawyer and speechwriter for Martin Luther King; Kenneth B. Clark, the psychologist whose studies of black children and their differing reactions to black and white dolls had been used by the NAACP in its arguments to the Supreme Court in the *Brown* case; and Jerome Smith, a young civil rights worker who had joined the Freedom Rides in 1961 and had been repeatedly beaten and jailed and was now in New York for medical treatment.

As if reflecting the emotional divide, blacks and whites sat on opposite sides of the room, and the atmosphere was tense. Torn, who had been born in a small Texas town, tried to break the ice by talking about the evolution of his own attitudes on race, but no one seemed much interested. Clark and others had come ready with statistics and policy ideas, while Kennedy had a list of the administration's accomplishments and a warning about the dangers of extremism preached by Malcolm X and the Black Muslims.

But it was Smith, stammering in frustration and agitation, who set the tone by suggesting that simply having to be in the same room to make his case to the attorney general made him want to throw up. Kennedy, offended, turned away. "You've got a great many very, very accomplished people in this room, Mr. Attorney General," Hansberry bore in, pointing toward Smith. "But the only man who should be listened to is that man over there."

Then Smith went on, recounting his brutal experiences in the South, and saying he did not know how much longer he could remain committed to nonviolence. "You don't have no idea what trouble is," he said. "When I pull the trigger, kiss it goodbye." Baldwin, trying to calm the waters, asked Smith if he would fight for his country. "Never!" he shouted. "Never! Never!"

"How can you say that?" Kennedy demanded, growing redder by the minute, deeply shocked by an attitude so at odds with his own brothers' sacrifices in World War II. But Smith had touched something deep and implacable, and the rest of the room was suddenly with him. "This boy," Horne would recall, "just put it like it was. He communicated the plain, basic suffering of being a Negro. The primeval memory of everyone in that room went to work after that . . . He took us back to the common dirt of our experiences and rubbed our noses in it . . . You could not encompass his anger, his fury, in a set of statistics, nor could Mr. Belafonte and Dr. Clark and Miss Horne, the fortunate Negroes, keep up the pretense of being the mature, responsible spokesmen for the race."

Hansberry turned again to Kennedy. "Look," she said, "if you can't understand what this young man is saying, then we are without any hope at all because you and your brother are representatives of the best that a white America can offer; and if *you* are insensitive to this, then there's no alternative except our going in the streets . . . and chaos."

On and on it went for two hours, perhaps three, "the most intense, traumatic meeting in which I've ever taken part, the most unrestrained interchange among adults, head-to-head, no holds barred . . . *the* most dramatic experience I have ever had," Clark would recall. All of Kennedy's recitation of the administration's record meant nothing—his pleas for understanding, his appeals to reason, carried no weight at all. He was furious, and his anger only increased as the meeting broke up when Clarence Jones approached and thanked him for his help—the secret bail money, Burke Marshall's behind-the-scenes peacemaking—in handling the Birmingham crisis. "You watched these people attack me over Birmingham for forty minutes, and you didn't say a word," Kennedy replied icily. "There is no point in your saying this to me now." To Belafonte, Kennedy simply said, "You know us better than that. Why don't you tell these people who we are?"

"Why do you assume I don't?" Belafonte replied. "Maybe if we were not there telling them who you are, things would not be as calm as they are."

The next morning's *New York Times* carried a front-page account of the session. Baldwin was quoted in it, and Belafonte and others assumed he'd been the source. Kennedy called the Democratic Party's civil rights expert Louis Martin to complain. "I gave him hell," Martin would recall. "I said, 'You go out and make your own appointments without telling me. I could have told you what would happen.'"

"I think that Bobby also sensed that most of the blacks were on the make themselves," Martin added. "They were looking for a place in the sun. He was thinking of them like the Boston Irish in the old days—like Honey Fitz—they were always scrambling."

To Arthur Schlesinger the attorney general complained, "They don't know what the laws are—they don't know what the facts are—they don't know what we've been doing or what we're trying to do." But just days later, Kennedy told Ed Guthman that if he had grown up black, he would feel as strongly about the matter. "He resented the experience, but it pierced him all the same," Schlesinger would recall. "His tormentors made no sense, but in a way, they made all sense. It was another stage in education."

For Bob Kennedy, the crux of the issue was always what could be done. He and his brother both prided themselves on their cold-eyed realism and their contempt for the bleeding hearts, who struck a pose instead of making progress and were "in love with death," as he once put it. "What my father said about businessmen applies to liberals," Bob would say—meaning that they were sons of bitches. Now he was more convinced than ever that action was not only possible, but urgently necessary to address the causes of black unrest.

"I think that what we wanted to do was deal with the problem," he would recall. There had always been only two ways of doing so: either to protect civil rights demonstrators, or to face up to the injustices that were causing the demonstrations. "We didn't feel that the protection of the people was feasible or acceptable under our constitutional system," Kennedy said. "So therefore, what was acceptable was to try to get to the heart of the problem. For the first time, people were concerned enough about it—and there was enough demand about it—that we could get to the heart of the problem and have some chance of success."

* * *

THE ADMINISTRATION'S EFFORTS TO get to the heart of the problem were embodied in H.R. 7152, but its chances for success were by no means clear when a subcommittee of the House Judiciary Committee held the first hearing on the president's civil rights bill on the morning of Wednesday, June 26. Bob Kennedy's appearance did not much help the cause. He was the leadoff witness in the packed hearing room, Room 346 in the northeast corner of the Old House Office Building. (The president himself was half a world away in Germany, defending freedom in his own way by proclaiming, *"Ich bin ein Berliner."*)

Presiding from the curving horseshoe mahogany hearing table was the Judiciary Committee's long-serving chairman, Representative Emanuel Celler of Brooklyn. His official portrait, unveiled earlier that year, stared out over the vaulted chamber, lit by frosted crystal chandeliers.

The attorney general began his opening statement by repeating the president's assertion that a law alone would not solve the problems of injustice and prejudice for black Americans. But, he insisted, "We must launch as broad an attack as possible." He added, "If we fail to act promptly and wisely at this crucial point in our history, grave doubts will be thrown on the very premise of American democracy." (In a bit of editing that his brother would doubtless have approved, he omitted from the middle of that sentence a ringing phrase from his prepared draft, in which he warned that if Congress failed to act, "the ugly forces of disorder and violence will surely rise and multiply throughout the land.")

Kennedy spoke eloquently and at length of the humiliating and arbitrary burdens that segregation placed on blacks throughout the South—with no hint of his own "they can pee before" they go shopping attitude of barely a month before—explaining that a black traveler "cannot rely on the neon signs proclaiming 'Vacancy,' because too often such signs are meant only for white men's eyes." And he couched his argument in the broadest possible economic terms. "The effects of discrimination in public establishments are not limited to the embarrassment and frustration suffered by the individuals who are its most immediate victims," he said. "Our whole economy suffers. When large retail stores or places of amusement, whose goods have been obtained through interstate commerce, artificially restrict the market to which those goods are offered, the nation's business is impaired."

Kennedy explained that the administration had chosen to base the bill on both the commerce clause and the Fourteenth Amendment, in part because of the "vast change" that had occurred since the nineteenth century in the nature of business organization and in part because of a new understanding of what constituted state action. "Today, business enterprises are regulated and licensed by the states to a much greater degree than in 1883," when the Supreme Court held that the Fourteenth Amendment did not apply to private businesses.

Kennedy had a largely sympathetic audience on a subcommittee dominated by liberals, starting with Celler himself. But as the morning dragged into afternoon, and members began to ask questions he considered redundant, the attorney general grew testy. When Representative George Meader, a conservative Republican from Michigan, asked Kennedy if he had read a Republican public accommodations measure that had been introduced in the House earlier that month, he replied, "I have not." That was too much for the measure's sponsor, Representative John V. Lindsay, a liberal Republican from New York's "silk stocking" district with broader political ambitions, who spoke up sharply.

"I am quite deeply disturbed, Mr. Attorney General, that you have never bothered to read this very important legislation," Lindsay said. "In view of the fact that you apparently did not consider these bills at all, I can't help but ask the question as to whether or not you really want public accommodations legislation or not." Lindsay went on to say that the House cloakroom was rife with rumors that the administration was already prepared to water down its own bill.

Kennedy reacted with equal asperity. "I want this legislation to pass," he told Lindsay, chiding him for repeating mere rumors. "I don't think, Congressman, that I have to defend myself to you about the matter." But Lindsay had made an important point, and the Kennedy administration still had a lot to learn about the prickly politics of civil rights legislation. As Celler would point out the very next day, "Frankly, it would be extremely difficult to get a civil rights bill without the support of those on the other side of the aisle."

* * *

ON THE SENATE SIDE of Capitol Hill, the challenge was even tougher. The day after the attorney general's testimony before Celler's committee, Bobby Baker, the secretary to the Senate's Democratic majority, told Mike Mansfield that his nose count had showed it was "virtually impossible" to find even fifty-one solid votes for the bill, much less the sixty-seven needed for cloture. Bob Kennedy would now do his best to improve those odds, in nine agonizing appearances before the Senate Judiciary Committee, to which the Senate version of the administration's bill—known there as S. 1731—had been referred.

The Judiciary Committee's chairman, James Eastland of Mississippi, and its chief constitutional expert, Sam Ervin of North Carolina, had said nice things about Kennedy during his confirmation hearings two years earlier. But that did not change the fact that the Judiciary Committee was the notorious graveyard of civil rights legislation and the first line of defense in the southern Democrats' determination to block this new bill as well.

The first time Kennedy appeared before the committee, at 10:45 a.m. on Tuesday, July 16, he was not even allowed to testify, as Ervin held forth at length on the evils of the bill—with Everett Dirksen, the committee's ranking Republican, looking on. Ervin charged that the public accommodations section could be made to apply "to any shoeshine boy whose sole stock in trade consisted of one can of polish and a rag which had moved in interstate commerce," and he vowed to oppose any bill that would undertake to "deprive private individuals of the right to say how they will use their property, or who they will select to be their customers." As Ervin continued his harangue the next day, railing against the bill's grant of wide discretion to the attorney general in bringing desegregation lawsuits, Chairman Eastland interrupted to ask, "Isn't it true, if we pass this bill, we confer the power of a dictatorship?" Right on cue, Ervin replied, "There is no doubt that this bill, if passed, would confer the power of a dictator upon the president."

When Senators Kenneth Keating, a liberal Republican from New York, and Thomas Dodd, a liberal Democrat from Connecticut, undertook to point out that state laws in the South requiring separate eating and washing places for blacks and whites were already controlling the operations of private business "to a minute degree," Ervin exploded with a circular, Orwellian argument that he would make repeatedly in coming days: such laws, he contended, had no force because the Supreme Court had effectively nullified them in the *Brown* decision in 1954. Leaving aside the cold reality that legal segregation was still the order of the day in hotels and restaurants across the South, Ervin insisted, "At noon on the 17th day of May, 1954, the Constitution suddenly changed its meaning, not as a result of any actions taken by the only bodies that are empowered to change the Constitution: namely the states and the Congress, but by the action of the Supreme Court."

Finally, on the morning of Thursday, July 18, Kennedy himself was allowed to begin his testimony. In a statement that could well have summed up his own feelings before the explosive meeting with James Baldwin and the black intellectuals, he said, "Many millions of white people, especially in the North—people who until recently assumed that the Negro was satisfied with the great social progress of the past twenty years—are now faced with the startling discovery that it's not true; that whatever progress Negroes have made is inadequate to their need for equality. And none of us can deny that their need is real; that their frustration is genuine. We have been unreasonable about it, or ignorant of it, far too long." He noted that even as he spoke, National Guardsmen were patrolling in Cambridge, Maryland, in the face of demonstrations there, and that unrest was brewing in Savannah, Georgia, and Danville, Virginia. "The responsibility of Negro leaders who set these demonstrations in motion is very great, as is the responsibility of the white leadership in every community," he said. "But our responsibilities as a nation are most plain. We must remove the injustices. The alternatives before us are narrow. We can either act or fail to act."

He recited the Justice Department's success in urging voluntary desegregation, but added, "I scarcely need remind this committee that for an American man, woman or child to be turned away from a public place for no reason other than the color of his skin is an intolerable insult—an insult that is in no way eased by the bland explanation that it has been allowed to go on for a hundred years or more." He said that federal laws, from the National Labor Relations Act to the Taft-Hartley labor law and the Fair Labor Standards Act, had all "regulated private business enterprises to remove burdens from the national commerce."

He rattled off some of the grim realities of segregation: Nearly 70 percent of young white people nationwide were high school graduates, but only 40 percent of blacks. In Alabama, only 9 percent of white adults had failed to finish fifth grade, while that description fit more than a third of blacks. In 193 counties across the country, fewer than 15 percent of eligible blacks were registered to vote. (In Mississippi alone, that was true in seventy-four of the state's eighty-two counties.) And he cited an Alabama voting case in which applicants to register were asked to "name the duties and obligations of citizenship." A white salesman had answered, in writing, "Support the law vote," and was registered. A black soldier who wrote, in neat penmanship, "To vote, to obey the laws of Alabama, to bear arms against any enemy, to support the Constitution of the United States and Alabama," was rejected.

When Kennedy had finished, Ervin bore in with the first in a long round of querulous questions, an interrogation that would stretch to more than a dozen hours in all. He first asked the attorney general why the United States had a written constitution, eliciting the concession that it was intended to protect individuals against the power of the state. Then he tried to get Kennedy to admit that the bill was a response to "troublous times" in the streets of Birmingham. "The proposed legislation, other than the voting part and the proposal to extend the life of the Civil Rights Commission, was not offered before the demonstration occurred, was it?" Ervin demanded.

"I don't think," Kennedy replied evenly, "there was a general feeling in the country, or in Congress, Senator, to do much about it."

Next, Ervin wanted to know how many criminal prosecutions the Justice Department had brought in Mississippi or Alabama for denial of voting rights, and Kennedy responded, "To be quite frank about it, I would think it would be virtually impossible to successfully prosecute a criminal case in either one of those states on this matter."

And so it went, on issue after issue: the adequacy of existing statutes; the nature of literacy tests; provisions for special voting referees in localities where fewer than 15 percent of eligible blacks were registered. Ervin, the sole questioner, was relentless, but not without good humor. Kennedy gave as good as he got, but also in an unfailingly respectful tone. As one long hearing concluded, Kennedy said, "Senator, I enjoyed being with you for three years and I enjoy seeing you again." Kenneth Keating interrupted to say, "I did not hear that." Kennedy explained, "I worked for Senator Ervin for three years," only to have Keating respond, "I hope it won't be three more years this time!"

The grilling was so exhausting that, smack in the middle of it, when Ethel Kennedy ran into Ervin at a White House party, she asked, with typical insouciance: "What have you been doing to Bobby? He came home and went straight to bed!"

At another point, when Ervin argued that the civil rights bill would "regulate the use of privately owned property and personal activities within the border of a State after interstate commerce has ceased, merely because the person using such privately owned property or rendering such personal services may use some goods which at some time in the past have moved in interstate commerce or may serve some travelers who have journeyed in time past from one state to another," Kennedy countered that the discrimination itself interfered with interstate commerce. He added, for good measure, that civil rights demonstrations that disrupted business had done so, too.

"If that is so," Ervin snapped, "why don't you ask Congress to pass a law to prohibit those demonstrations?" before apologizing, "Pardon me, I shouldn't interrupt you."

But Kennedy was ready with an answer on this question, too, noting that since May 20 there had been 639 demonstrations around the country, in 174 cities, and 302 of these were exclusively about public accommodations. His message was clear: the only law that would end the demonstrations was a law to end the discrimination.

Ervin wanted to know about beauty parlors, barbershops, and swimming pools. (They would be largely exempted from the bill's provisions, unless they were in hotels, Kennedy replied.) He wanted to know the justification for paying attorneys' fees to successful plaintiffs in civil rights actions, but not for winning defendants. It was, day after day, a dialogue of the deaf, a stalemate neatly summed up on August 8, when Ervin probed the administration's rationale for including a provision to provide assistance to school districts attempting to redress "racial imbalance" in their schools.

"Is it the policy of the administration to encourage transporting children away from their neighborhood schools to schools in other communities for the purpose of getting what some educators may conceive to be racially balanced schools in the other communities?" Ervin demanded.

"No, we have no policy on that, Senator," Kennedy replied.

Then why provide any funds for such assistance?

"There are other solutions to the problems," Kennedy insisted, before turning the tables on the senator: "May I just ask you a question? Do you feel that there is a problem in a number of our major metropolitan areas, at the present time, dealing with racially imbalanced schools?"

"I do not," Ervin said.

"You see," Kennedy went on, "we are not talking the same language, Senator."

"We are both talking English," Ervin replied.

"But that," Bob Kennedy concluded, "is as far as we get."

4

Tell 'Em About the Dream!

Having consulted with lawyers and legislators, with businessmen and clergymen, John Kennedy could no longer postpone a council with the people who had pressed hardest for his new civil rights bill and were most excited about its introduction: the black leaders of the major civil rights groups themselves. And so on this summer morning, he welcomed a cross section of the sometimes feuding coalition of campaigners for equal rights to the Cabinet Room of the White House.

They were known as the Big Six, and they came in solemn array, a group diverse in age, attitude, and experience. There was the silver-haired dean of the movement, A. Philip Randolph of the International Brotherhood of Sleeping Car Porters. The proud and prickly Roy Wilkins, president of the NAACP. The cool, cautious Whitney Young of the Urban League. The mellifluous James Farmer of CORE, whose Freedom Rides had so distressed the Kennedys two years earlier. John Lewis, the brave young chairman of the Student Nonviolent Coordinating Committee, who had been brutally beaten on one of the rides and had already been arrested twenty-four times. And the man who had long since become the most famous—and controversial—face of the cause, Martin Luther King Jr. of the Southern Christian Leadership Conference.

They had been met at the North Portico of the White House by Preston Bruce, a black doorman, and Randolph, Mitchell, and Young wanted to know if Bruce believed Kennedy was fair and sincere about civil rights, or "just another false politician saying things he didn't really mean." Bruce told them that he believed both Kennedy brothers "cared heart and soul about justice for black people," and the president arrived to escort the group to the West Wing.

The president's visitors brought with them some unwelcome news. The previous day, some of them—but not all of them—had announced plans for a massive march on Washington for later that summer, a public demonstration of support for civil rights that Randolph had first contemplated more than twenty years earlier. Despite—or perhaps because of—the tension in the air, there now began what Kennedy's adviser Arthur Schlesinger would later recall as "the best meeting I attended in my years in the White House."

The president and the top aides with him in the room, including the vice president and the attorney general, were not happy at the idea of a giant protest aimed at the Capitol. President Kennedy quickly noted the vital necessity of obtaining support for his civil rights bill from sources other than liberals and the usual civil rights groups—that is, from Republicans and moderates. He warned that many senators, especially those from the sparsely populated states in the Plains and the Mountain West, were reluctant to break a filibuster and cut off debate—for reasons having nothing to do with their stance on civil rights. "They see what has happened to small states in the House of Representatives, and they believe that unlimited speech is the only protection for small states in the Congress," Kennedy said.

When someone asked why no Negroes had been involved in the drafting of the bill, Kennedy replied that the mere perception that the bill was the work of black leaders—especially of King—would mean it could never get out of committee. "We want success in Congress," the president said, "not just a big show at the Capitol. Some of these people are looking for an excuse to be against us. I don't want to give any of them a chance to say, 'Yes, I'm for the bill, but I'm damned if I will vote for it at the point of a gun.'"

In fact, King's aide Andrew Young would later say that the black movement leaders had been helping to draft the bill with their public protests, as surely as if they had been in the room with the Justice Department lawyers. Philip Randolph quietly made a corollary point to the president, noting that "the Negroes are already in the streets," and adding, "It is very likely impossible to get them off. If they are bound to be in the streets in any case, is it not better that they be led by organizations dedicated to civil rights and disciplined by struggle rather than to leave them to other leaders who care neither about civil rights nor about non-violence? If the civil rights leaders were to call Negroes off the streets, it is problematic whether they would come."

The president acknowledged this point, but he nevertheless insisted, "Now we are in a new phase, the legislative phase, and results are essential. The wrong kind of demonstration at the wrong time will give those fellows a chance to prove their courage by voting against us." Vice President Johnson, reflecting his long experience in Congress, offered a lesson in the ways of the Hill and the limits of lobbying. "Not many votes are converted in the corridors," he explained. "Most fellows vote for what they think is right and for what their states want. We have about fifty votes for us in the Senate and about twenty-two against us. What counts is the twenty-six or so votes which remain. To get those votes we have to be careful not to do anything which would give those who are privately opposed a public excuse to appear as martyrs."

James Farmer now echoed Randolph's concern that trying to suppress demonstrations would be counterproductive. Finally, King himself spoke up, saying that the march could serve as a means of dramatizing the issue and mobilizing support in sections of the country that hadn't experienced the problem firsthand. "It may seem ill-timed," he acknowledged. "Frankly, I have never engaged in any direct action movement which did not seem ill-timed. Some people thought Birmingham seemed ill-timed."

"*Including* the Attorney General," the president said drily.

John Kennedy's sardonic streak surfaced again moments later when he told the group, "I don't think you should all be totally harsh on Bull Connor." Schlesinger would recall that there was "an audible intake of breath" around the Cabinet table before the president went on, "After all, he has done more for civil rights than anyone else."

President Kennedy was all too aware that it was the violence on the streets of Birmingham—the violence perpetrated by Connor, yes, but set off by King's determined protests—that had at last forced him to offer the bill. And thanks to King, the president was now in a fight he knew he might not win. He claimed to have just seen a new poll (if it ever existed, it has been lost to history) showing that his national approval rating had fallen thirteen points, to 47 percent, in the aftermath of his June 11 speech. He warned that "a good many programs I care about may go down the drain as a result of this." In sum, he said, "We're in this up to the neck."

Kennedy's summary of the political situation was accurate enough. But the person in the Cabinet Room that morning who was really in it up to the neck—in ways he would never fully understand—was Martin Luther King himself.

* * *

BEFORE THE GROUP MEETING, Kennedy had taken King aside for a private word. The president led the preacher into the Rose Garden where King, unaware of the secret White House taping system, found himself silently wondering whether the president was afraid the Oval Office was bugged. Putting a hand on King's shoulder, the president delivered a serious warning—one that Robert Kennedy and Burke Marshall had already given to a disbelieving King: that two of his close advisers, Stanley David Levison, a New York lawyer and entrepreneur who was King's counselor and closest white friend, and Jack O'Dell, one of his black executive assistants, had ties to the Communist Party.

"I assume you know you're under very close surveillance," Kennedy told King. "They're Communists, you've got to get rid of them."

King's relationship to Stanley Levison weighed heavily on John and Robert Kennedy, because of their paralyzing fear that King—and, by extension, the broader civil rights movement—might be under Communist influence. This concern colored every aspect of their dealings with him. Neither the Kennedys nor King knew the full story. The man who knew the most damaging secrets about both the president and the protester—FBI director J. Edgar Hoover—selectively leaked and withheld information about each man's activities in ways that bred mistrust between them and left both of them vulnerable to Hoover's malevolence.

The president's unease was understandable. At the height of the Cold War—barely eight months after the Cuban Missile Crisis, in the midst of public debate over Kennedy's proposed Nuclear Test Ban Treaty—the mere suggestion that Martin Luther King might have Communist affiliations was so explosive that the Kennedy administration accepted at face value that it had to keep the civil rights leader at arm's length. "If they shoot you down, they'll shoot us down, too," is how Kennedy put it to King in the Rose Garden that day. "So we're asking you to be careful."

For the Kennedys, the reality of leftist support for the civil rights movement was not far-fetched. Nor, for King, would it have been disqualifying. Ever since the 1930s, in years when the civil rights movement had few friends in the centers of established political and economic power, American leftist movements had been in the forefront of support for equal rights, and prominent black activists and entertainers like Paul Robeson and others had been frank in their praise of the Soviet Union while condemning American injustice.

Moreover, the FBI had known since the early 1950s that Levison, who had made a small fortune in a range of overlapping business ventures, had been a major financial backer of the American Communist Party. Levison had met King in 1956, just as the preacher was gaining nationwide fame in the wake of the Montgomery bus boycott, and King quickly came to rely on him as a kind of soul mate and amanuensis who consistently refused payment for his help. "My skills were acquired not only in a cloistered academic environment, but also in the commercial jungle," Levison once wrote to King. "Although our culture approves, and even honors these practices, to me they were always abhorrent. Hence, I looked forward to the time when I could use these skills not for myself but for socially constructive ends. The liberation struggle is the most positive and rewarding area of work anyone could experience."

But it was not until early 1962, via reports from one of the same FBI informants who had prompted the bureau's original interest in Levison, that Hoover learned of Levison's close association with King. The FBI director was delighted to have what he considered damaging information about King, whom he so despised. He promptly informed Bob Kennedy, and within weeks the attorney general had authorized the wiretapping of Levison's office. Hoover's tip also prompted repeated warnings from Justice Department aides to King, who (the wiretaps showed) had just as repeatedly ignored their advice to sever his connections with Levison. The president's own talk with King was meant to be a final, emphatic plea to change his behavior.

What Hoover never told the president or the attorney general—and what emerged only decades later with the release of sealed documents— was that one of the informers who had tracked Levison's actions for the FBI had reported in March 1963 that Levison had definitively severed all of his ties with the Communist Party of the United States, telling associates that he found it "irrelevant" and "ineffective." In fact, it would turn out, Levison had steadily reduced his involvement with the party from almost the moment he met King, his support for the utopian ideal of Marxist ideology now apparently transferred to King's crusade.

Of course, Kennedy knew nothing of the complexities of the Levison matter, even if Hoover did. And the president kept his warning to King so deliberately vague that King could not be sure of the nature of the government's sources. So Hoover held the high card, as usual, and he kept up his sub rosa dirty work. Just days after the Rose Garden conversation with Kennedy, after yet another newspaper leak about Jack O'Dell's continued work for the SCLC, King announced O'Dell's resignation. Stan Levison was another matter. King trusted and needed him too much to cut all ties, whatever the president's advice. After Levison himself warned King that it was too dangerous for the fate of the pending civil rights bill for them to maintain direct contact, they arranged to stay in touch through their mutual friend, Clarence Jones, the young black attorney in New York who had attended the meeting with Bob Kennedy and the black intellectuals in May.

Because of the existing tap on Levison's phone, the attorney general learned of this subterfuge immediately and was predictably outraged. Within days, he ordered the wiretapping of Jones's home and office phones. He also considered acceding to Hoover's request to tap King's own phone, but held off for the time being.

There was one last wrinkle that John Kennedy emphatically did *not* share with King—but that the president knew all too well: J. Edgar Hoover had voluminous evidence of Kennedy's sexual indiscretions, dating back to his wartime romance with Inga Arvad, a Danish journalist whom Hoover had suspected of being a Nazi spy, and continuing into 1962 with Judith Campbell, the sometime girlfriend of both Frank Sinatra and Chicago mob boss Sam Giancana. Barely two weeks after Kennedy's Rose Garden encounter with King, Hoover would warn Robert Kennedy that the FBI had received reports that the president had been involved with Ellen Rometsch, the twenty-seven-year-old wife of a West German army officer stationed at his country's embassy in Washington, who worked by night as a call girl and was suspected of being an East German spy. (The FBI could never confirm the president's involvement, or Rometsch's suspected spying, but the attorney general was concerned enough that he arranged to have Rometsch secretly deported that summer.)

Letting Hoover build his file on King was the price the Kennedys paid for protecting the president's political future and the civil rights bill's prospects. But if their complicity in the surveillance had been known at the time, the revelation would have destroyed their credibility with the leading civil rights groups. A march on Washington, however disruptive it might be, was the least of the Kennedy brothers' worries when it came to Martin Luther King that summer.

* * *

IF BY 1963, MARTIN Luther King was not only the most prominent spokesman for the black cause in America (and in the eyes of his critics and skeptics one of the most dangerous), he had traveled a long road to reach such exalted status. He was the opposite of a plaster saint—and a most unlikely prophet. In fact, for the first four or five years of his life, he wasn't Martin Luther King Jr. at all, but simply *Michael*—"little Mike"—the eldest son and namesake of a onetime Georgia sharecropper who had risen to become the highly respectable, thoroughly bourgeois assistant pastor of the Ebenezer Baptist Church in Atlanta, a church that had been founded by the elder King's father-in-law, A. D. Williams. Only in 1934, when the younger King was five years old, would "Daddy King" formally change both their names to Martin, for reasons that remain unclear but nevertheless stamped the mark of a towering religious reformer on the small, round-faced, almond-eyed boy.

Raised in a secure and loving home in Sweet Auburn, a stable, middle-class black neighborhood in Atlanta, King experienced the delights and travails of a typical childhood. He showed a gift for music (as an adult he would occasionally play bits of the Moonlight Sonata for close friends), and at age ten he sang with the Ebenezer Baptist Church choir at a gala Junior League benefit for the world premiere of Gone with the Wind—an appearance for which his father was censured by his fellow Baptist pastors, both because the ball was segregated and because it involved dancing and drinking.

Despite his clerical heritage, young Martin was a precocious enough thirteen-year-old to startle his Sunday school class by declaring that he did not believe in the bodily resurrection of Jesus Christ. He entered the tenth grade at Booker T. Washington High School at age thirteen in 1942, and two years later he went on to Morehouse, Atlanta's distinguished all-male black college, his way eased by a wartime enrollment shortage, despite what he would later estimate was an eighth-grade reading level. Fastidious in dress and bearing, he was known to his friends as Tweedie. As a teenager, he developed the orotund flourishes of speech and diction for which he would become celebrated. When a teacher asked how he was, he might reply, "Cogitating with the cosmic universe, I surmise that my physical equilibrium is organically quiescent."

King also experienced the sting of racial prejudice from an early age. As a youngster, one of his closest playmates had been a white boy whose father owned a small grocery store near the King house. But after they began attending separate, segregated elementary schools, the child's father forbade them to socialize. Martin watched his father be forced to correct white policemen who presumed to call him "boy," and had himself been made to stand for several hours on a bus returning from a high school oratorical contest in southern Georgia so that newly boarded white passengers might have a seat. As a result, he would recall years later, "I was determined to hate every white person," despite his parents' injunction that, as a Christian, it was his duty to love.

King's spiritual awakening was gradual. Benjamin Mays, the president of Morehouse, was a nationally known theologian who often chided his students for not getting excited about "anything bigger than a hamburger," but King spent most of his college years rebelling at the idea of following his father into the ministry, embarrassed by the emotional effusions of the Baptist worship style. He considered medicine, and then the law. But in the summer before his last year at Morehouse, he decided, seemingly to his own surprise, to become a preacher after all. His father was overjoyed and quickly arranged for Martin to join him in the pulpit at Ebenezer, only to be knocked back by his son's determination to pursue formal religious training.

King's choice of a school was Crozer Theological Seminary in Chester, Pennsylvania, outside Philadelphia, an unusually integrated institution for its day and one where free and critical thinking prevailed. For the first time, King became a diligent student, exposed to the classic works of Plato, Aristotle, and Saint Augustine, together with those of such modern figures as Reinhold Niebuhr and Mohandas Gandhi. He became captivated by the "social gospel" of the theologian Walter Rauschenbusch, which held that humankind could be bettered by a "moral reconstruction of society" that replaced cold capitalism with a "Christian commonwealth." He grew into such a superb preacher that his fellow students would come listen to his sermons just to pick up pointers.

He also fell deeply and painfully in love, in a way that friends would later say left a lifetime emotional scar, because the object of his affection turned out to be the white daughter of a German-born cook at the school. They dated seriously for several months, but King ultimately concluded that interracial marriage was impossible in his chosen line of work in the black church, and he despaired of the hurt such a relationship would cause his mother. He broke off the romance.

After graduation as valedictorian, King again tested his father's patience by heading off to graduate school at Boston University, and a whirlwind courtship and marriage to Coretta Scott, an Alabama farm girl who was studying voice at the New England Conservatory of Music. Despite Daddy King's initial vociferous objections (he had always expected his son to return to Atlanta and marry into black society there), the couple took their vows in front of the elder King in the Scott family's front yard, then spent their wedding night in the only sort of public accommodation that Alabama law would allow them: a spare bedroom in a nearby black-owned funeral home.

Earning his PhD in theology in 1954, King passed up the possibility of a teaching post, or an assignment in some northern city that would have been his bride's preference, for the pastorate of the Dexter Avenue Baptist Church in Montgomery, Alabama. His salary was a princely $4,200 a year, which made him the highest-paid black preacher in town at age twenty-five. In barely eighteen months, he would be famous.

* * *

IF A WEARY BLACK seamstress and NAACP activist named Rosa Parks had not been ordered to stand up and surrender her seat on a crowded Montgomery bus to a white passenger on the afternoon of December 1, 1955, and then been promptly arrested for her refusal to do so, who can say whether there would have been lunch counter sit-ins or Freedom Rides? And if a reluctant but gifted preacher named Martin King had not been willing to assume the leadership of a mass movement to integrate Montgomery's buses in the wake of Parks's protest, who can say when, if ever, there would have been marches and hoses and bombs in Birmingham?

The very night of Rosa Parks's arrest, Montgomery's leading civil rights activist, E. D. Nixon, telephoned King, already locally celebrated for his preaching, and asked him to join in supporting a boycott of the city's bus lines to begin the following week. In his brief pastoral career, King had come to the realization that "the right word, emotionally charged, could reach the whole person and change the relationships of men," as a friend would later recall. Still, he hesitated at first to accept Nixon's invitation. He finally agreed, on the condition that he not be required to do any organizing. But within days, as the boycott got under way with resounding success, King found himself the only person nominated to lead the crusade, as head of the newly created Montgomery Improvement Association. At a mass meeting that night, man and moment converged. "You know, my friends, there comes a *time*, when people get tired of being trampled over by the iron feet of oppression," King intoned, the spirit upon him, and the congregation carrying him along. "There comes a time, my friends, when people get tired of being thrown across the abyss of humiliation, where they experience the bleakness of nagging despair. There comes a time when people get *tired* of being pushed out of the glittering sunlight of life's July and left standing amidst the piercing chill of an Alpine November."

And so it went, night after night and month after month, as King preached and prodded and the boycott dragged on, supported by an elaborate carpool system in which two hundred volunteer drivers supplied some twenty thousand rides a day. "The fight here is between light and darkness," King would say, as he honed what would become a familiar refrain: "The arc of the moral universe is long but it bends toward justice." Soon enough, though, the darkness threatened to overwhelm King. There was a bomb threat, then an actual bomb at his house, then a shotgun blast that blew open his front door. One night he found himself praying aloud at his kitchen table, "Lord, I'm down here trying to do what's right . . . But I've come to the point where I can't face it alone." At that moment, he would recall, he seemed to hear "an inner voice . . . the voice of Jesus," ordering him: "Martin Luther, stand up for righteousness, stand up for justice, stand up for truth. And, lo, I will be with you, even until the end of the world."

King may have found an inner peace, but the Montgomery establishment remained stubbornly impervious in negotiations to end the boycott, until finally, with the help of the NAACP, the boycott's leaders filed suit in federal court. The powers that be in Montgomery retaliated with mass local indictments of the Montgomery Improvement Association's leadership and a request that a state court grant an injunction against the carpool system as an unlicensed transportation network. Just when things looked bleakest, after nearly a year, the United States Supreme Court upheld a lower court ruling that segregation of the buses was illegal. Weeks later, the city government enacted an ordinance allowing blacks to sit virtually anywhere they wanted.

The boycott's impact reached far beyond Montgomery. It made civil rights a national moral cause, and King an international figure. In the ensuing years, he would be summoned with other black notables to the White House by President Eisenhower, would visit Ghana and India and make the cover of *Time* magazine. But he also developed an abiding sense of unworthiness to lead the cause, a fear that his career had peaked too soon, and a gnawing presentiment about his own fate. When a Hollywood producer once discussed how a movie about his life might end, King replied, "It ends with me getting killed."

In the years after Montgomery, King often struggled to find his footing, or at least to top his first act. In 1959, he moved to Atlanta, where he at last assumed copastorship of Ebenezer with his father. Two years earlier he had founded what came to be called the Southern Christian Leadership Conference, an umbrella organization of black clergy dedicated to fighting for civil rights across the South. This caused considerable consternation for Roy Wilkins and the NAACP, which had been founded in 1909 and was the nation's largest and oldest civil rights organization, one that had always believed the route to justice lay through carefully calibrated legal challenges to segregation. King's tactics of direct action marked him as a dangerous upstart.

Indeed, King's very prominence made him a figure of controversy for other movement leaders and white politicians alike. He may have led the mass meeting at the height of the Freedom Rides in Montgomery in the spring of 1961, but his refusal to get on the bus himself angered the young riders. So did his reason for declining: "I think I should choose the time and place of my Golgotha." It was at this point that the activists of CORE and the Student Nonviolent Coordinating Committee began referring to King derisively as "De Lawd," for the God character in the 1930s play *The Green Pastures*.

Among those Americans skeptical of King was John F. Kennedy. Despite his sympathetic phone call to Coretta King during the 1960 campaign, Kennedy would not meet with King himself until nine months into his presidency, on October 16, 1961, and only then after repeated importuning from Harris Wofford. At their meeting in the White House family quarters, King spotted a copy of the Emancipation Proclamation and urged Kennedy to issue a proclamation of his own, a "Second Emancipation," declaring all segregation illegal under the Fourteenth Amendment. The president responded with politesse, asking King to propose a draft, but the idea went nowhere.

"Unlike the president's relations with Whitney Young and Roy Wilkins, which were easy and sophisticated, there was always a strain in his dealing with King, who came on with a moral tone that was not Kennedy's style and made him uncomfortable," Harris Wofford would recall.

In fact, King's whole Birmingham campaign in 1963 grew out of his determination to prick Kennedy's conscience, to make him uncomfortable. In his famous "Letter from Birmingham Jail," King couched his manifesto in ringing tones that surely struck the perpetually detached Kennedy as self-referential and overwrought. "I am in Birmingham because injustice is here," King wrote. "Just as the prophets of the eighth century B.C. left their villages and carried their 'thus saith the Lord' far beyond the boundaries of their own home towns, and just as the Apostle Paul left his village of Tarsus and carried the gospel of Jesus Christ to the far corners of the Greco-Roman world, so I am compelled to carry the gospel of freedom beyond my own home town."

For his part, King found Kennedy all too cool. On a walk after dinner at Wofford's house the night of that first meeting with the president in 1961, he confided of Kennedy, "I'm convinced that he has the understanding and the political skill but so far I'm afraid that the moral passion is missing."

* * *

BY THE TIME OF the June 22 White House meeting with King and the other leaders, Kennedy had at last demonstrated moral passion on civil rights. But his political caution in counseling against a march on Washington still prompted divergent reactions from his visitors, as they demonstrated immediately upon leaving the White House.

Speaking to reporters, Roy Wilkins of the NAACP was noncommittal about participating in any march. "That little baby does not belong to me," he said. Just that spring, Wilkins had bearded King: "In fact, Martin, if you have desegregated *anything* by your efforts, kindly enlighten me."

"Well," King had replied, "I guess about the only thing I've desegregated so far is a few human hearts."

Wilkins still favored "quiet, patient lobbying tactics" over street action. But he could hardly deny that John Kennedy's own heart had apparently been one of those moved by King's Birmingham campaign.

Indeed, black opinion on civil rights was no more monolithic than its white counterpart. There had been tensions between King and Wilkins dating all the way back to the Montgomery bus boycott, when King argued that the NAACP should provide even more financial support to the effort than it already was by paying the costs of the suit challenging Alabama's transportation segregation law, and defraying the legal costs of the boycott leaders who had been indicted. Those tensions grew when King created the SCLC. Wilkins, the grandson of a Mississippi slave and nearly thirty years older than King, regarded the NAACP's pursuit of strategic litigation, which had produced such landmark rulings as *Brown v. Board of Education*, as the key to success. The two men's dueling approaches had met at last in Medgar Evers's protests in Jackson, Mississippi, earlier that spring. Wilkins reluctantly joined that campaign and was arrested for the first time in more than thirty years of civil rights work. "We've baptized Brother Wilkins," King told Stan Levison.

Despite their prominence, King and Wilkins by no means constituted the whole of the civil rights coalition's leadership. For their part, James Farmer of CORE and John Lewis of SNCC, who had been instrumental in the Freedom Rides, looked askance at King and Wilkins as too tepid. King had tried to redeem himself with the Young Turks in the aftermath of the Freedom Rides by lending his support to a desegregation movement in Albany, Georgia, in late 1961 and 1962, but it had largely fizzled. Meantime, John Lewis regarded Urban League president Whitney Young as not really a movement figure at all but as the leader of a social service organization for northern urban blacks.

The one figure the whole group revered was the stately Philip Randolph, who had been meeting with presidents since Martin Luther King was in knee pants. He had first dreamed of a march on Washington in 1941, when he had threatened to bring a hundred thousand demonstrators to the capital to protest the lack of black hiring in the burgeoning defense economy on the eve of World War II. Only when Franklin D. Roosevelt agreed to sign an executive order calling upon employers and labor unions to "provide for the full and equitable participation of all workers in defense industries, without discrimination because of race, creed, color or national origin," and setting up a Fair Employment Practices Commission empowered to investigate grievances and track compliance, did Randolph relent.

So when the march's organizers next met at the Roosevelt Hotel in New York City on July 2 to refine their plans, there was universal agreement that Randolph should chair the effort, with the power to select his own deputy. Randolph's prestige was such that even Wilkins could not succeed in blocking his controversial choice: Bayard Rustin, a fifty-one-year-old black Quaker with a long record of support for leftist causes and a flamboyant quasi-British accent. Rustin's opponents argued that his youthful flirtation with the Communist Party, his refusal to serve in the military, and his 1953 arrest in California on a morals charge for performing oral sex on two men in a parked car should disqualify him. (Robert Kennedy himself would call Rustin "an old black fairy.")

But Rustin was an organizational genius, and Randolph trusted him totally. He had helped King organize the Montgomery boycott, and he later helped get the SCLC off the ground. Now Rustin turned his attention to the Washington march, which he estimated would cost $65,000 and draw a hundred thousand people. The date was fixed for August 28, a Wednesday, and the plan was for the bulk of marchers to arrive early that morning and leave the same night, so as not to overwhelm the city. Any idea of a protest at the Capitol was scrapped in favor of a solemn procession in memory of Medgar Evers from the Washington Monument to the Lincoln Memorial, where there would be a program of music and speeches. Lobbying visits to members of Congress would be closely supervised; all banners and placards would be created by the organizers, not individuals; and a large contingent of black New York City police officers would help serve as marshals. The sound system had to be top-notch, so that marchers could hear the speeches and heed instructions. No detail was too mundane, down to the need for chemical toilets. Years later, John Lewis would delight in the memory of Rustin's declaring, "Now we cawn't have any disorganized pissing in Washington."

* * *

RUSTIN AND HIS COLLEAGUES were not the only ones busily organizing on behalf of the bill that summer. A broad coalition of the nation's mainstream religious denominations was undertaking a strategic lobbying campaign of its own, aimed at moving the hearts and minds of white Americans—and their legislators—with pinpoint precision. Leading Protestant, Catholic, and Jewish groups—often coordinated by the umbrella organization of the National Council of Churches—plotted a crusade aimed at having maximum impact on Congress. Victor Reuther, a prominent Methodist layman and the brother of Walter Reuther of the United Automobile Workers, headed a planning group that suggested concentrating the legislative efforts on a limited number of states, especially in rural areas of the Midwest. Traditional civil rights groups were weak in such places—except in a handful of big cities—and the black vote nearly nonexistent, but churches were strong and well organized. As President Kennedy himself had noted, the support of senators from such states— many of them Republicans—would be vital in the fight for cloture.

So the church groups mounted a series of conferences and organizing workshops in states from Ohio to the Dakotas. Theologians and pastors joined forces with such movement figures as Clarence Mitchell, the chief lobbyist for the NAACP, to instruct local groups on how best to contact their congressional delegations by telephone, telegram, and letters, emphasizing the moral and religious dimension of the civil rights fight. The Leadership Conference on Civil Rights, an umbrella group that had been founded in New York in 1950 to lobby for a federal Fair Employment Practices Commission, moved its headquarters to Washington in July 1963 and began working closely with James Hamilton, the Washington representative of the National Council of Churches. Hamilton had joined the Council in 1958, and much of his early work involved such bread-and-butter issues as obtaining favorable tax treatment for churches and clergy. But as the 1960s dawned, the Council had become more involved in social justice issues, lobbying to improve wages and working conditions for migrant farm workers, for example. As religious activism on civil rights grew, Hamilton developed a mailing list of some five thousand state and local religious groups to whom he could now send periodic updates or urgent "action memos" on the status of H.R. 7152.

"The Middle West and on a bit into the Mountain States—that was the churches' assignment," Hamilton would recall, "because labor was in the East. So we had our work cut out for us there." Perhaps the churches' most powerful educational tool was the flood of horrifying news pictures from Birmingham and elsewhere. "I think people in the Midwest and in other areas began to see what the problems were, what's happening," Hamilton said. "The attitudes began to change." But the churches themselves were also "working with a little more sophistication in terms of how the political process actually works than perhaps we had heretofore," Hamilton added.

* * *

IF THE RELIGIOUS GROUPS found themselves waging an unlikely battle in the public square, Bayard Rustin and his fellow march organizers soon had an unlikely ally: John Kennedy himself. Unable to stop the march, the president determined instead to make sure it succeeded. When he asked aides who was really running it, and the answer was unclear, he replied, "Well, I'll run it then."

So as desultory hearings on his civil rights bill groaned on in the House and Senate Judiciary Committees, the president endorsed the march at his news conference on July 17, calling it a "peaceful assembly calling for a redress of grievances," and adding, "I think that's in the great tradition." But he also issued a warning that the paramount goal now was the passage of his bill. "So I would suggest that we exercise great care in protesting so it doesn't become riots," he said. "And, number two, that those people who have responsible positions in Government and in business and in labor do something about the problem which leads to the demonstration."

That same day, the District of Columbia coordinating committee for the march issued a memo soliciting help from churches to be used as assembly points and seeking some overnight lodging for marchers who would be coming from too far away to follow the preferred plan of arriving that morning and leaving the same night. There would be fifty-one assembly points around the city (one for each state, plus the District of Columbia). "Only those citizens who are committed to non-violence as a creative means of protest are urged to participate," the memo warned.

On Capitol Hill, the politicians who were wrestling with H.R. 7152 girded for the invasion. Burke Marshall would later recall the congressional leadership as "scared to death of the march, just totally irrational." If that was so, they did not let on publicly, instead insisting that the march would not influence their views. "I do not intend to be disturbed or dismayed by demonstrations and denunciations," declared Everett Dirksen, who was still smarting that he had not received more black support in his 1962 reelection campaign in Illinois despite a long record of pro-civil-rights votes. His counterpart in the House, Representative Charles Halleck of Indiana, noted that there were strict rules and regulations governing activities at the Capitol and allowed that the drill team from Purdue University in his home district had recently been denied permission to perform there. And Representative William McCulloch of Ohio, the ranking Republican on the House Judiciary Committee, whose support for the bill was crucial, insisted, "They're not going to bluff me. Doctors, lawyers, everybody could start marching and there would be no end to it."

At the Justice Department, Bob Kennedy assigned John Douglas, now the head of the civil division and the son of Paul Douglas, the liberal senator from Illinois who was one of the civil rights bill's biggest supporters, to coordinate the government's share of the planning. In twice-daily meetings over the next five weeks, Douglas worked with John Reilly, who headed the Justice Department's office of United States attorneys, to sketch a battle plan.

As with Bayard Rustin, no detail was too small. Douglas worked with the UAW and the National Council of Churches to assure a respectable white turnout. King had led a peaceful march of 125,000 people in downtown Detroit on June 23, and Reilly went to school on the lessons learned there. "No cop under two years and no left-handers," he scribbled in his working notes. (The ban on left-handers may have been intended to ensure proper coordination should nightsticks be needed, but it may also have been Reilly's Irish slang for anyone not up to snuff.)

"Troops and cops should be talked to—smile—help," Reilly continued. Among the endless questions to be resolved: "Time program starts. Who ends the program? Route to be taken to White House. Which gate do leaders enter?" The president had agreed to meet the leaders at the White House *after* the march, one more inducement to keep it peaceful. Yet another crucial matter: "Security of sound system. (Can we cut it off)." Liquor stores would be closed, and marchers urged to pack food that would not spoil in the August heat. And finally, a special demand from Douglas to the Washington police, who reluctantly agreed: *no dogs.*

"All this arranging and orchestrating was alarming to many of us at SNCC," John Lewis would recall. "The sense of militancy, which was so central to most of our efforts, which was so much a part of our definition of ourselves, was being deflated. Civility had become the emphasis of this event. It was becoming a march *in*, not *on*, Washington. The whole thing seemed to have been co-opted by the government—co-opted very deftly."

In a bizarre example of just how far the administration was willing to go to stage-manage the event, Reilly's notes urged administration officials to meet with an executive at the local Metromedia television affiliate in Washington, which was to broadcast a postmarch roundtable with King and other leaders. The panel was to be moderated by J. Richard Kennedy, an old friend of James Farmer and Philip Randolph. Kennedy was not only a novelist and the screenwriter of *I'll Cry Tomorrow*, a weepy biopic about the alcoholic singer Lillian Roth, but also Harry Belafonte's former business manager. And he was as well—totally unbeknown to Belafonte or the other civil rights figures—the Central Intelligence Agency's principal source of domestic intelligence on the civil rights movement, and an old enemy of Stan Levison's.

Reilly even suggested that J. Richard Kennedy "should be briefed on how J.F.K. and Pierre"—the White House press secretary, Pierre Salinger—"would like show to go—line questioning should take." At the time, however, the press and public knew next to nothing about the nature or extent of the government's involvement in planning for the march, and that suited Douglas, Reilly, and their Justice Department colleagues just fine.

In the midst of all this elaborate orchestration, a sour note sounded. In early August, Martin King took ten days' vacation with his family at Clarence Jones's house in the Riverdale section of the Bronx, and there the FBI wiretap soon picked up conversations that set J. Edgar Hoover's blood boiling: salacious sex talk, intimations of infidelity, a loose, unplugged aspect of King's personality that reinforced Hoover's deepest doubts and suspicions. On August 13, the director sent a confidential two-page summary of the findings to Nick Katzenbach at the Justice Department, who passed it along to Bob Kennedy, who bucked it straight up to the president with the driest of cover notes: "I thought you would be interested in the attached memorandum."

* * *

WEDNESDAY, AUGUST 28, DAWNED GLORIOUSLY in Washington, with sunrise at 5:33 a.m. The FBI's crowd forecast, duly passed along to John Douglas and apparently hoping for the worst, suggested a small turnout, while a Gallup poll about a week before the march had shown that close to two-thirds of the public disapproved of the event. George Meany, the president of the powerful AFL-CIO, declined to participate, and ordered the union's headquarters building closed and barricaded for the day.

Indeed, in the early morning hours, the streets of the city were eerily empty. But soon the chartered buses began rolling into town like clockwork, more than fifteen hundred in all. One group of marchers had walked 237 miles from Brooklyn; another man had roller-skated all the way from Chicago. Two thousand D.C. police officers, and like numbers of national guardsmen and volunteer marshals, were on patrol—with thousands more troops on standby alert at Bolling Air Force Base and at Fort Myer across the Potomac River in Virginia.

Eleanor Holmes Norton, a native Washingtonian and Yale law student who had been helping organize the march from Rustin's headquarters in Harlem, volunteered to keep the New York office open overnight to deal with any last-minute questions, in part because she knew that meant she would get to fly down to Washington, rather than take a bus. As her plane approached her hometown, she could see the gathering throngs below. "When I saw the number of people at various sites, it was clear to me that this was going to be an absolutely big success," she would recall.

Robert Kennedy's intrepid commandos were at their assigned posts: John Douglas at police headquarters from 6:00 a.m. to midnight and John Reilly at Union Station in the early morning and then at the Lincoln Memorial for the day's program. Bayard Rustin's elaborate sound system had been sabotaged the day before, but was rebuilt overnight by the Army Signal Corps. (Reilly had solved the problem of what to do if the speeches got too incendiary: he himself would man the loudspeaker switch, and substitute a 78 rpm record of the great gospel diva Mahalia Jackson singing "He's Got the Whole World in His Hands.")

The Big Six civil rights leaders—with the exception of James Farmer, who was in jail in Louisiana as the result of a protest there—spent the morning in meetings with the bipartisan congressional leadership, first Mike Mansfield and Everett Dirksen in the Senate, then Speaker John McCormack and Minority Leader Charles Halleck in the House, while a biracial contingent of Hollywood and Broadway celebrities recruited at King's request by Harry Belafonte prepared to muster out. (Belafonte had persuaded Charlton Heston, a Republican who had played Moses in *The Ten Commandments*, to attend, lending the artists' delegation a pious, bipartisan air.) The Senate Democratic whip, Hubert Humphrey, joined his legislative assistant John Stewart and his wife, Nancy, in the basement of the First Congregational Church downtown to make a breakfast of pancakes and sausage for the delegation from Minnesota.

George Stevens Jr., the head of the motion picture division of the United States Information Agency, the government's Cold War propaganda arm, dispatched the independent filmmaker James Blue and a dozen newsreel cameras around town to make a documentary about the day to be shown in embassies, libraries, and mobile trucks around the world. (Representative John Rooney of Brooklyn, the crusty chairman of the House appropriations subcommittee that controlled the agency's budget, would later ask Stevens, "Have you thought about getting a security clearance for your leading man?" while Bob Kennedy worried that a shot of a young white woman laughing and smiling in conversation with a black seatmate would not go over well in some quarters.)

News organizations feared the worst. The *Washington Post*'s city editor, Ben Gilbert, had leased two huge walkie-talkies and a base unit at great expense and sent a young general assignment reporter named Philip Kopper out "looking for 'trouble,'" as Kopper would recall. George Lincoln Rockwell and some members of his American Nazi Party showed up at the Mall only to get chased away by whites about 7:00 a.m.; after that, there was "no trouble at all," Kopper said. "We were reduced to calling in color stuff, all of it rather rosy." The *New York Times* went even further, sending its star Washington columnist and resident prose poet Russell Baker aloft in a chartered helicopter. "We had low-altitude clearance," Baker would recall, "so as the morning passed without so much as a fist fight in progress anywhere I directed the pilot on low-level sightseeing swoops on the houses of friends and colleagues, then took a close look at the roof shingles on my own house and, finding them sturdy and storm-proof, had the pilot drop me at National Airport and moseyed up to the Lincoln Memorial."

Shortly before 11:00 a.m. a disembodied voice from a loudspeaker near the Washington Monument rang out. "We are trying to locate Miss Lena Horne," it said. The performers on the Mall included Joan Baez; Peter, Paul and Mary; and Bob Dylan, who sang a mournful hymn about "the day Medgar Evers was buried from a bullet that he caught."

Suddenly, the vast throng—in the end, it would be more than two hundred thousand people, more than twice the hoped-for size—began quietly walking westward toward the Lincoln Memorial, as King and the other leaders scrambled to reach the head of the line. Diahann Carroll, who had just ended her run in *No Strings*, a groundbreaking Broadway musical about an interracial romance, marched hand-in-hand with James Garner, the popular star of the television western series *Maverick*. A bearded Paul Newman marched with his wife, Joanne Woodward, while Marlon Brando twirled an authentic cattle prod from Gadsden, Alabama, the kind used to subdue civil rights demonstrators.

About seventy-five members of Congress attended the rally, and as they took their reserved seats on the steps of the Memorial, the crowd began chanting *Pass the bill! Pass the bill!* "I remember seeing Ted Kennedy waving and smiling and I thought, 'Well, he doesn't get what we're yelling at him,'" recalled Greg Craig, a young Exeter graduate on his way to Harvard (who would later work on Kennedy's Senate staff and serve as White House counsel for Barack Obama). The president had advised his youngest brother not to appear, in case of any trouble, and he had debated up to the last minute before deciding to go.

At the White House, the president himself could not resist trying to get a glimpse of the march. He went to the mansion's third-floor solarium with Preston Bruce, the doorman, and though they could not see the marchers on the Mall, they could hear the singing and could sense its power.

* * *

MARIAN ANDERSON WAS TO have begun the formal program with the national anthem. But she was stuck in traffic and did not make it in time, so the lyric soprano Camilla Williams stepped in at the last moment with a soaring version of "The Star-Spangled Banner." Backstage at the Memorial, however, in a small room behind Daniel Chester French's massive statue of Lincoln, disharmony reigned.

The night before, an advance copy of John Lewis's proposed speech had been circulated, and some passages raised alarm bells all over town. Lewis had used words like "revolution" and "masses" and "radical." He attacked the administration's civil rights bill as "too little, too late" and said that SNCC would not support it. He vowed to "march through the south, through the heart of Dixie, the way Sherman did." That was too much for Patrick Cardinal O'Boyle, the Catholic prelate of Washington, who was to deliver the invocation but who now told Bob Kennedy and Burke Marshall that he could not possibly do so unless the speech was changed. When Rustin assured the cardinal that a satisfactory outcome could be reached, he agreed to proceed, but he vowed to get up and leave his seat unless he received a revised text at least ten minutes before Lewis delivered it.

Lewis and his fellow activists had ample reason to question the Kennedys' motives and commitment. On August 9, the Justice Department had won federal perjury indictments against nine civil rights activists in Albany, Georgia, charging that they had lied about whether they had picketed a white-owned store there in retaliation for its owner's vote in a civil suit against the county sheriff, L. W. "Gator" Johnson. A local black man, Charlie Ware, had sued Johnson for shooting him in the head and neck while arresting him on a charge of public drunkenness, and an all-white jury ruled in favor of the sheriff. The Justice Department contended that the picketers' actions could be construed as a form of juror intimidation. But its intervention in the case stood in sharp contrast to Bob Kennedy's repeated insistence that the federal government had no power to protect the Freedom Riders or other demonstrators, and the indictments were now seen as an effort to appease southern sentiment in the wake of H.R. 7152's introduction.

But the march's leaders did not want Lewis's strong words to cause the Washington establishment to revoke its approval of the event. So they surrounded him and asked for compromise—which he resisted. Roy Wilkins accused Lewis of "double-crossing" the people who had come to support the bill. Finally Philip Randolph himself made a deep, personal appeal. "I have waited twenty-two years for this," he told Lewis and his SNCC colleagues Courtland Cox and Jim Forman. "I've waited all my *life* for this opportunity. Please don't ruin it." Then he turned to Lewis, ready to cry, and implored, "John, we've come this far together. Let us stay together."

Lewis relented, and soon, even his watered-down version had the crowd roaring its assent. "We will not stop," he cried. "If we do not get meaningful legislation out of this Congress, the time will come when we will not confine our marching to Washington. We will march through the south . . . but we will march with the spirit of love and with the spirit of dignity that we have shown here today. By the force of our demands, our determination and our numbers, we shall splinter the segregated south into a thousand pieces and put them back together in the image of God and democracy. We must say, 'Wake up, America. Wake up!' For we cannot stop, and we will not be patient."

Then it was Mahalia Jackson's turn to sing—live, not on John Reilly's trusty record—and she stirred deep feeling in the crowd with a wrenching gospel standard, "I've Been 'Buked and I've Been Scorned."

By prearrangement, King spoke last. Philip Randolph introduced him in grandiloquent tones as "the moral leader of our nation . . . Dr. Martin Luther King, J-R!!" King's prepared text, too, had already been issued, and as he began delivering it, he spoke of the pledges of the Constitution and the Declaration of Independence as a "promissory note" that had been returned to black Americans marked "insufficient funds." It was a metaphor worked out with the help of Clarence Jones, who had recalled his feeling of awe as he had stood in the bowels of the Chase Manhattan Bank the previous spring, signing a promissory note for $100,000 in bail money for the Birmingham protesters from Nelson Rockefeller.

"We have come to this hallowed spot to remind America of the fierce urgency of now," King went on, insisting that "this sweltering summer of the Negro's legitimate discontent will not pass until there is an invigorating autumn of freedom and equality." He invoked the same words from the Old Testament prophet Amos that he had used in Montgomery nearly eight years earlier: "No, no, we are not satisfied, and we will not be satisfied until justice rolls down like waters and righteousness like a mighty stream."

Then a voice in the crowd—legend holds that it was Mahalia Jackson herself—cried out insistently, "Tell 'em about the dream, Martin, tell 'em about the dream!" And suddenly King pushed his text aside and began ad-libbing—as John Kennedy had in his speech promising the civil rights bill on June 11—launching into a passage he had used before in Detroit and Chicago, a refrain that began, "I still have a dream . . ."

"It is a dream deeply rooted in the American dream," he continued, steadily gathering steam. "I have a dream that one day this nation will rise up and live out the true meaning of its creed: We hold these truths to be self-evident, that all men are created equal . . . I have a dream that my four little children will one day live in a nation where they will not be judged by the color of their skin but by the content of their character. I have a dream today!"

He went on, summoning the words of the Prophet Isaiah, dreaming of a day when "every valley shall be exalted and every hill and mountain shall be made low," as the crowd roared its assent. And finally, in a shattering crescendo, he invoked the stirring words of Samuel Francis Smith's "America," "Let freedom ring!"

"Let freedom ring from every hill and molehill of Mississippi, from every mountainside, let freedom ring. And when this happens, when we allow freedom to ring, when we let it ring from every village and every hamlet, from every state and every city, we will be able to speed up that day when all of God's children—black men and white men, Jews and Gentiles, Protestants and Catholics—will be able to join hands and sing in the words of the old Negro spiritual, 'Free at last, free at last, thank God Almighty, we are free at last!'"

It was a full five minutes before Clarence Jones could make his way through the cheering crush to grab King's arm. "Martin!" he said. "Today you were smokin'! Just smokin'! Coltrane and Parker rolled into one!"

At the White House, John Kennedy, who had never heard a complete speech by King, was watching on television, and had a similar view. "He's damned good," he told aides, one thoroughbred assessing another. "Damned good!"

* * *

IN FACT, IT WAS hard to tell who was happier about the day's outcome, the marchers or the president himself. When Kennedy greeted the march leaders in the Cabinet Room at five o'clock, he reached out to King, a glint in his eye, saying, "I have a dream." When King, already self-conscious about the praise being heaped upon him, asked if Kennedy had heard Walter Reuther's fiery speech, in which the union leader declared, "We cannot *defend* freedom in Berlin so long as we *deny* freedom in Birmingham," the president brushed him off with, "Oh, I've heard him plenty of times."

When it became clear that none of the marchers had eaten since breakfast, Kennedy ordered coffee and sandwiches from the White House mess, and Wilkins embarked on a sober argument that the march had shown massive grassroots support for civil rights, exemplified by the marchers' willingness to lose two or three days' pay. He enumerated the shortcomings of Kennedy's bill—no Fair Employment Practices Commission, inadequate power for the attorney general to bring suits to rectify discrimination—and pressed for a stronger one. Reuther seconded that thought, while Randolph raised the importance of keeping blacks in school. Kennedy picked up that theme, saying blacks would do well to follow the example of Jews, who had overcome discrimination through emphasis on education.

But, as usual, the president was pessimistic about the bill's legislative prospects, and he resisted any provisions that might make it even harder to pass. He rattled off a state-by-state review of Democratic votes in the House: "Alabama, of course, none. Alaska, one. Arizona, you've got one sure and one doubtful." At best, the president reckoned, he could count on 160 Democratic votes, meaning that he would need 60 Republicans, and they "are hard to get."

At this, Randolph spoke up, saying that if the situation were as grim as Kennedy suggested, "It's obvious that it's going to take nothing less than a crusade to win approval for these civil rights measures. Nobody can lead this crusade but you."

The meeting broke up just after six, and the leaders scattered to their hotel rooms. At 10:30 that night, in Huntington, West Virginia, a letter was postmarked from H. L. Pemberton, who signed as "Ex-Democrat." Addressed to "John Kennedy, c/o Luther King White (?) House, Washington, D.C.," it read, in its unpunctuated entirety, "Grab the nigger vote you just lost mine."

And the next day, the deputy FBI director, William Sullivan, composed a memo, endorsed by J. Edgar Hoover, that swiftly circulated throughout official Washington. "In the light of King's powerful demagogic speech," it read, "we must mark him now, if we have not done so before, as the most dangerous Negro of the future in this country from the standpoint of communism, the Negro and national security."

* * *

FOR THE NEARLY QUARTER million people who came to Washington that day, the march was an indelible experience. "It was clearly, of all the places to be on the face of the planet, that was the place to be at that particular moment in time," Greg Craig would recall. But John Lewis found himself disappointed that the news coverage emphasized the Sunday school picnic aspect of the day. "Too many commentators and reporters softened and trivialized the hard edges of pain and suffering that brought about this day in the first place," he would remember, "virtually ignoring the hard issues that needed to be addressed, the issues that had stirred up so much trouble in my own speech."

The march's practical, political impact was harder to judge, at the time, and even a half century later, its influence on events remains a matter of debate. Kenneth Teasdale, legislative counsel to Mike Mansfield, was watching the march from a balcony at the Capitol with "a couple of Southern Senators," who took note of a spectacle in which "not one single bad thing happened."

"And they said, 'Well, that means there's going to be a civil rights bill,'" Teasdale would remember.

A Gallup poll that July showed that public support for a federal law requiring desegregation of public accommodations was clearly divided, with 49 percent of the nation in favor and 42 percent opposed. By September, a narrow majority—54 percent—was in favor of the idea, while opposition had dropped to 38 percent.

Nick Katzenbach was not so sure about the march's impact on Capitol Hill. "I would like to think the march was instrumental in the passage of the civil rights bill," he would write years later, "but as far as I could see, it had no effect on members of Congress who were undecided. But it did, then and later, in the memory, have an important impact on the average American television viewer. It was, I think, the beginning of an American commitment, with respect to which Congress was, as it so often is, just a little bit behind."

As the summer of 1963 wound down, hope was in the air that Congress was at last beginning to catch up.

PART TWO

THE HOUSE

5

A Compromise Between Polar Positions

ON THE SAME DAY that the civil rights leaders met in New York to plan the March on Washington, Burke Marshall flew to Dayton, Ohio, for a crucial meeting on the long march to passage of H.R. 7152. Marshall was reserved to the point of shyness (he had sat in virtual silence through much of his job interview with Bob Kennedy) but that very diffidence, combined with a piercing intelligence, made him a superb negotiator, as his experience with the feuding camps in Birmingham two months earlier had proved.

This morning, Marshall's quarry was Representative Bill McCulloch, the ranking Republican on the House Judiciary Committee. McCulloch was an important member of Congress, but in the custom of the day, he still kept his hometown law office in Piqua, twenty-eight miles north of Dayton, and had agreed to a meeting with the assistant attorney general to review the bill. McCulloch's son-in-law David Carver met Marshall at the Dayton airport and then escorted him to a long lunch at the local country club while McCulloch addressed a meeting of Piqua's Rotarians. "Bill had an engagement, but he also wanted it clear that he was not at

Marshall's beck and call," Carver would recall. Marshall could play the same game; at one point on their meandering tour of the Miami Valley, Marshall spotted a hardware store and told Carver to stop the car. "I need some nails," he said, went in, and returned with a sack to tuck in his briefcase.

When it was at last time for the meeting, Marshall trudged to the second floor of the Piqua National Bank Building, where McCulloch's comfortable office was advertised with Sam Spade–style letters painted on the window, proclaiming the name of his firm: McCulloch, Felger, Fite and Gutmann. The sole decoration was a framed copy of an excerpt from Edmund Burke's letter to the electors of Bristol, in which he had declared: "Your representative owes you, not his industry only, but his judgment; and he betrays, instead of serving you, if he sacrifices it to your opinion."

Judgment was precisely what Bill McCulloch had been delivering to the voters of Ohio's Fourth Congressional District since 1947. In many ways, he was a conventionally conservative Republican, an avatar of fiscal probity with consistently low ratings from the liberal group Americans for Democratic Action and equally high ones from its conservative counterpart, Americans for Constitutional Action. He supported school prayer and gun rights, opposed foreign aid and federal involvement in education. "There is no such thing as easy money from Washington," he declared during his 1948 campaign, adding, "If you expect to measure your Congressman's ability by what money he can get from Congress, I would rather not be returned." He was among the few members of Congress who never spent his entire office allowance, but instead returned the excess funds to the government.

But despite the fact that the population of his district was less than 3 percent black, McCulloch had also long been an avid supporter of civil rights, though he preferred the term "equal rights," his daughter Ann Carver would recall, paraphrasing the Constitution's guarantee of "equal protection" of the law. He liked to observe, "The Constitution doesn't say that whites alone shall have our most basic rights, but that we all shall have them." On January 31, 1963—four and a half months before John Kennedy's speech to the nation—McCulloch had introduced his own civil rights measure in the House. He described it as "a comprehensive bill, which seeks to advance the cause of civil rights in the United States," adding, "At the same time, however, it is a bill keyed to moderation. And the reason for moderation is obvious: We members of the Republican Party are honestly desirous of proposing legislation which stands a chance of enactment. Anyone, of course, can introduce grandiose legislative schemes. But reaching for the sky, rather than aiming for the possible, is a form of showmanship we don't wish to engage in. Reality is what we live by and accomplishment is what we seek. For only in compromise, moderation and understanding are we able to fashion our society into a cohesive and durable structure."

As the spring wore on, however, the House Judiciary Committee chairman, Emanuel Celler, had yet to schedule a single hearing on McCulloch's measure—or on any of nearly ninety similar Republican-backed bills, including the one from New York's John Lindsay that would become such a contentious topic during Robert Kennedy's testimony in June. So McCulloch was more than ripe for Burke Marshall's appeal on this July day. But he had two strict conditions.

First, McCulloch told Marshall that he expected the administration to support a strong but practical bill, one that could pass the full House, and then to fight for that very same bill in the Senate, without accepting amendments that would weaken its impact or effectiveness. McCulloch had supported the 1957 and 1960 civil rights bills, only to be dismayed when their toughest provisions—including Part III of the 1957 bill—were bargained away in the Senate. If Kennedy's new bill suffered a similar fate, he warned, House Republicans would oppose it when it came back to the House for approval—and no civil rights bill could pass either house without substantial Republican support. Second, McCulloch wanted the White House not to exploit the bill for partisan advantage, but to give full and public credit to the bill's Republican supporters as well.

Marshall accepted McCulloch's terms, and an improbable alliance was born. But the terms were tough, and it is hard to overstate the impact that McCulloch's demand for an uncompromising bill would have on all the subsequent legislative strategy and debate. His insistence on no softening of the measure in the Senate—and his undoubted ability to deliver Republican votes for or against the bill—all but assured that the administration would have to attempt something that had never before succeeded in American politics: to break a civil rights filibuster in the Senate, rather than avoid one by watering down the bill. The administration had by no means settled on such a strategy by the time of Marshall's meeting with McCulloch. It would be lucky for John Kennedy—and for his bill—that this single strong-willed, small-town lawyer also happened to be the most fair-minded of men.

* * *

WILLIAM MOORE MCCULLOCH WAS born in 1901, to a Scots American family that had been abolitionists before the Civil War. He was raised on the family homestead in Holmes County, attended one-room schools, and then rode off on his bicycle to seek his college education at the nearby College of Wooster before earning a law degree from Ohio State University. After graduation, he taught school for a year before moving to Jacksonville, Florida, where he began the practice of law—and first witnessed the day-to-day realities of Jim Crow segregation. He returned to establish a thriving law practice in Piqua and steadily rose in local politics, first winning election to the Ohio House of Representatives, then serving as its minority leader before becoming speaker in 1939 when the Republicans took control. His ability to win the trust and respect of colleagues from both sides of the aisle earned him the nickname "the red-headed lion," and he lived modestly, commuting almost daily the ninety miles from Piqua to the state capitol in Columbus. In 1943, he enlisted in the Army at age forty-two—well beyond the potential reach of the draft— and served almost two years in the European theater as a captain.

At the war's end, when leaders of Piqua's local NAACP chapter determined to integrate the local bus station's lunch counter in the Favorite Hotel, across the street from McCulloch's office, it was McCulloch to whom they turned in case legal help should be needed. But the owner promptly desegregated the establishment in response to the NAACP's demands, and McCulloch's aid was not required. Nevertheless, he maintained regular contact over the years with the local NAACP activists, Emerson and Viola Clemens, sending them copies of the *Congressional Record*, consulting them on race-related questions, and inviting their daughter, Colleen, to socialize with his own two daughters, Nancy and Ann.

A frugal man of simple tastes, he favored red suspenders and loved pumpkin pie (served with cold turkey gravy at the local Elks Club). After his election to Congress, he was apt to be seen stuffing his own campaign literature into envelopes for mailing, or sending literature on the care and feeding of infants to new mothers in his district. He worked seven days a week, employed an office staff of one or two, and returned home to Ohio every June to make the rounds of the seven counties in his district, borrowing a room in each local courthouse where he kept office hours and open house for his constituents, a pencil always ready in his shirt pocket for taking notes. He drove fast but eschewed official congressional license plates, pulling them out of the glove box only if he was stopped for speeding as he made his rounds. "He was very frugal," his daughter Ann recalled. "He was really a Scotsman." McCulloch once wrote a constituent, "I have never spent nearly as much in an election campaign as my salary as a Congressman has been, and I do not propose to do it now or in the future."

One of his favorite phrases, with family or friends, was "Are you sure?"—as if by testing their assumptions, he might test his own. He liked a martini, but his limit was one. "If I ordered a second drink, I would get a look or an 'Are you sure?'" his son-in-law David Carver, Ann's husband, would recall. McCulloch was a director of a local bank in Piqua, and as such reviewed the list of overdrawn depositors at each monthly meeting. Carver's name once turned up on the list, and McCulloch put $200 into his account but warned him, "I will call it but you won't know when, so don't spend it."

On most matters, McCulloch was right in sync with his district. But on civil rights, especially, he was leading the way. "His constituents were very conservative," one of his young administrative assistants, Joe Metz, would recall. "He was teaching them, too." His reasoning was simple: "How can one oppose these clear mandates of the Constitution?"

McCulloch had an unusually nuanced and thoroughly considered view of his job. "The function of Congress is not to convert the will of the majority of people into law; rather its function is to hammer out on the anvil of public debate a compromise between polar positions acceptable to a majority," he would tell his House colleagues on the eve of his retirement in 1972, contrasting their work with the direct democracy of a town meeting, in which one position always prevails and the other loses. "In a republic, representatives vote *for* the people. There is discussion and debate. There are amendments. There is opportunity for compromise. It is less clear that there is a losing side."

* * *

MCCULLOCH'S DEMOCRATIC COUNTERPART ON the Judiciary Committee, chairman Emanuel Celler, could hardly have been more different—though the two had by this point served on the committee together for sixteen years and, with their wives, were good friends. Celler, a scrappy, balding, bespectacled lawyer from Brooklyn, had first been elected to Congress during the Harding administration, and by 1963 he was the second-longest-serving member in the House. (A half century later, he would still rank as the fourth-longest-serving member in history.) The grandson of German Jewish immigrants, he had been a tireless crusader for civil rights and liberalized immigration policies—in an era when Congress had imposed strict nation-of-origin quotas intended to reduce immigration from Southern and Eastern Europe, thus excluding many Jews and Catholics. In Brooklyn, his law practice prospered through his sponsorship of private bills—special legal exceptions tailored to individual needs—for immigrants. But on the national scene, he was a fierce liberal who had vigorously battled Senator Joseph R. McCarthy, accusing him at the 1952 Democratic Convention of "undermining the faith of the people in their government" and of seeking to "sow suspicion everywhere, to set friend against friend and brother against brother."

Yet the very differences between Manny Celler and Bill McCulloch now allowed for a most unusual division of labor—one that would produce serious short-term strains and stresses for their friendship, and for H.R. 7152.

Throughout that summer and into the fall, the conservative McCulloch would become the Kennedy administration's strongest friend on the civil rights bill. In a series of secret back-channel meetings with Nick

Katzenbach, Burke Marshall, and the lawyers at the Justice Department, he would work to make sure that H.R. 7152 could draw enough Republican support to pass the House and survive the Senate. Among the kinds of changes McCulloch sought were provisions to make the bill more palatable to northerners. So, for example, he proposed to alter the section of the bill dealing with public school desegregation, to permit the federal government to give technical and financial assistance to help local school boards address problems of desegregation, but not to address problems of racial imbalance in schools in neighborhoods that happened to be heavily segregated. Such a move meant the bill would bar legal segregation in the South while accepting de facto segregation in the North.

Given Congress's instinctual resistance to anything that might smack of interference in its prerogatives by the executive branch, and the Kennedy administration's understandable wariness about Republican motives, the alliance with McCulloch was unorthodox, to say the least. It was born of necessity, but it bore fruit.

"The negotiations were essentially between Nick and Burke and McCulloch," recalled David Filvaroff, who arrived in the Justice Department as a young aide to Katzenbach in the fall of 1963. "He was very reasonable. He cared about one thing: When others would stand up and talk about a Kennedy power grab leading toward dictatorship, he would stand up and say, 'This is a reasonable, moderate bill,' and you could just see all the air go out of the other side."

"Bill McCulloch became the conscience of the bill," recalled Robert Kimball, the legislative aide to Representative John Lindsay. "He was so respected because he wasn't an ideologue. If he took a position on something, he brought along a lot of colleagues."

If McCulloch was now the administration's improbable insider, it fell to Manny Celler to placate the outsiders—the Leadership Conference on Civil Rights and other activist groups—and his own liberal colleagues, many of whom remained skeptical of the Kennedy administration's commitment to the cause and wanted to strengthen the bill. Their strategy was to present the Senate with a maximalist piece of legislation, so that even if parts of it had to be bargained away (as they assumed would happen), what remained would be as far-reaching as possible. They were not privy to the deal that Marshall and McCulloch had struck, forswearing any watering down of the bill in the Senate.

Instead, liberal House members and the civil rights groups had begun to get wind of McCulloch's quiet cooperation with the administration and were determined to counter what they assumed would be his weakening influence.

So all through July, as Sam Ervin continued his courtly torture of Robert Kennedy before the Senate Judiciary Committee, and as the Senate Commerce Committee heard from such hostile witnesses as Ross Barnett and George Wallace (who predicted that the civil rights bill would "destroy free enterprise"), Celler welcomed a parade of liberal stalwarts to his own hearings of the House Judiciary subcommittee he chaired and ran personally, known as Subcommittee No. 5. These included George Meany, the leader of the AFL-CIO; Joseph Rauh, the veteran civil rights lawyer who had drafted Franklin Roosevelt's original executive order on fair employment practices; Norman Thomas, the perennial Socialist Party presidential candidate; and Walter Fauntroy, the Southern Christian Leadership Conference's Washington representative. They all testified as to the ways in which H.R. 7152 could and should be made stronger. By Friday, August 2, the subcommittee had held twenty-two days of hearings and compiled some seventeen hundred pages of testimony.

At times, even Celler had his limits. When James Farmer of CORE testified before the committee in late July, he advocated strengthening the bill's first section, on voting rights, to make it apply to state elections as well as federal ones. Celler lectured him, "That was left out deliberately, not on principle but on expediency. It would be very difficult to get the bill through, the whole package through, if we had such a provision."

"When we ask for one half of a loaf," Farmer rejoined, "we get one quarter of a loaf. We ought to ask for what we want and then fight for it."

For the civil rights groups, this was the crux of the matter. And ultimately, Celler could not resist his fellow liberals' entreaties or their increasingly sharp attacks. When the detailed "markup," or subcommittee drafting, on H.R. 7152 began in earnest in closed hearings on Tuesday, September 10, Celler presided over a process in which the Kennedy administration's bill would be steadily strengthened. He himself offered an amendment to broaden the bill's voting rights provisions, by accepting proof of a sixth-grade education as de facto qualification for voting in any state with a literacy test. Representative Robert Kastenmeier of Wisconsin proposed to have the bill cover state and local elections—the very measure that Celler had scoffed at James Farmer for suggesting just weeks before. And though a Gallup poll, released around this same time, found that 50 percent of the country believed that the president was moving too fast on civil rights, outside events would soon strengthen the liberals' hand further.

* * *

ON SUNDAY, SEPTEMBER 15, A bomb planted at the Sixteenth Street Baptist Church in Birmingham took the lives of four little girls in their Sunday school best. Police gunfire in response to rock throwing by an angry crowd of black youths left a teenage boy dead, and yet another black teenager was killed when a white Eagle Scout who had just attended a segregationist rally fired on him without provocation. Birmingham was already in turmoil that fall, because of George Wallace's defiant resistance to a court order that blacks be admitted to three public schools there, and in the wake of the bombing another round of full-scale rioting erupted, leading Martin Luther King to plead with the White House once again for federal intervention.

Four days after the bombing, King and several black leaders from Birmingham met at the White House with the president. During the meeting, King declared, "The real problem that we face is this. The Negro community is about to reach a breaking point." But the president once again insisted that the administration had no legal grounds for sending troops. Four days later, Kennedy would tell a group of white civic leaders from Birmingham that he was equally powerless to curtail black demonstrations. "It may be the feeling in Birmingham that this administration can move these people in and out," Kennedy said. "I'm just telling you flatly we can't do it."

Kennedy's response to the latest violence was to send two presidential emissaries to Birmingham on a fact-finding mission: Kenneth Royall, a North Carolinian who had served as secretary of the Army in the Truman administration, and Earl "Red" Blaik, the legendary West Point football coach. That move left civil rights leaders badly disappointed, because Blaik had fielded all-white teams at the military academy and Royall had resisted integration of the Army. Some thoughtful southern whites were no more impressed with Blaik and Royall's efforts, and in the end, they never even produced a formal report to the White House.

E. L. Holland, the sympathetic editorial page editor of the *Birmingham News*, wrote to Ed Guthman at the Justice Department on October 3 expressing his concern that Blaik and Royall had "been 'snowed,' sold a bill of goods," by the white business community in Birmingham. "Nobody in any established position of leadership has yet dared say publicly the first word of reality as to what has to be done. They still dread the term 'concession,' and not only that, they still dread any soothing synonym for 'concession.'" He concluded, "This is wholly confidential, of course, and I trust you will protect me, for I am wholly vulnerable."

Kennedy's handling of the new Birmingham crisis left the leaders of the civil rights groups more skeptical than ever of his administration's commitment, and of its intentions about the bill. And so, just as the White House and Bill McCulloch feared, the liberals on Subcommittee No. 5 kept the pressure up from their end, steadily reshaping H.R. 7152 in ways that made it more in line with what the civil rights groups wanted, but that also jeopardized its prospects in the full House. In mid-September, Representative Byron Rogers of Colorado offered an amendment to the bill's education section allowing the attorney general to intervene in cases in which a person was denied access to virtually any public facility operated by any state or local government, including parks and libraries. Bob Kastenmeier proposed to amend the public accommodations section to include almost every form of business, including private schools and law firms (while maintaining the administration's exclusion for small boardinghouses). Celler himself offered a new section that would allow federal appellate courts to review civil rights cases that had been sent to unsympathetic state courts by federal district court judges.

By the end of the month, still more liberal amendments had been added, all with Celler's support. Rogers offered a new section granting the attorney general broad authority to initiate or intervene in pending civil suits charging discrimination, while Peter Rodino of New Jersey proposed to give the bill's equal employment section real teeth by giving the proposed Equal Employment Opportunity Commission the authority to investigate discrimination by any business with more than twenty-five employees and, after an administrative hearing, to order such practices stopped. (This would replace the weak employment discrimination provision in the administration's bill, which covered only government contractors and lacked any enforcement mechanism.)

Up to this point, Celler had let the subcommittee proceed in a casual way, with tacit understandings of agreement but no binding votes on the bill or the various amendments. In part he followed this course because the president's all-important tax bill was pending in the full House, and the administration did not want to give southern opponents of civil rights any reason to vote against that measure in retribution. But once the House passed the tax bill on September 25, Celler's demeanor changed. On October 1, he began to ram through the amended civil rights bill—summarily accepting amendments from liberal Democrats and squelching Republican alternatives. Celler was content to load the bill with liberal provisions, confident that they could yet be traded away for passage by the full House. The next day, the amended H.R. 7152 passed Subcommittee No. 5 on a series of voice votes and was favorably reported to the full Judiciary Committee. Civil rights leaders were jubilant.

But Bill McCulloch was livid.

For weeks, he had been working, at considerable risk to his own reputation and standing in his party, to avoid just this outcome. He and the Justice Department lawyers had worked out a middle-ground approach to the desegregation of public accommodations—one that Celler had said in the past that he could support. So he was shocked to learn that Celler now supported a bill that would extend the law's reach to almost every form of private enterprise, including private schools and law firms. "It's a pail of garbage," McCulloch told the *Wall Street Journal*.

President Kennedy was almost as distraught. He had been receiving upbeat reports from Katzenbach and from his legislative liaison, Lawrence O'Brien, that a more moderate bill was on track, only to have Celler accede to the liberals' demands at the last minute. To the White House, it did not matter that Celler himself believed he was pursuing the time-honored civil rights strategy of passing a strong subcommittee bill that could later be watered down in the full Judiciary Committee, again on the House floor, and finally in the Senate. That was the playbook that had worked—albeit to produce flawed final products—in 1957 and 1960. But this time around, Bill McCulloch had already rejected such a strategy, and the Republican votes that would be needed for passage in the full House rested in his hands. Manny Celler had now done nothing but raise the hopes of the civil rights groups and liberals, who, by themselves, could provide scant vote-getting help in the uphill legislative battles to come.

The president's frustration with the purists boiled over on September 30, in a meeting with the Reverend Eugene Carson Blake of the National Council of Churches. "The fact of the matter is, as you know, that a lot of these people would rather have an issue than a bill," the president complained. "But, as I said from the beginning, to get a bill, we got to have bipartisanship." And the key to that—the key to getting the needed Republican votes—was Bill McCulloch. "McCulloch can deliver sixty Republicans," Kennedy said. "Without him, it can't be done."

In the Washington of 1963, McCulloch's power was neither mystic nor wholly personal, though he was deeply respected on both sides of the aisle. His power flowed from his status as the senior Republican on one of the House's most powerful committees. The House was so big and unruly that, by tradition, the leaders of both parties deferred to their committee chairmen and ranking members, as even the president—who in his years in Congress had never been much of a legislator—well understood.

"To get the Republicans," Kennedy repeated, "we've got to get McCulloch and we've got to get as strong a bill as McCulloch can take. And that's the best way to get action." As for the liberals and civil rights groups, he said, "They have to be dissatisfied. I don't mind what they say, or you know, they're going to do a lot of complaining.

"I'll go as far as I can go, but I think McCulloch has got to come with us, or otherwise it is an exercise in futility."

* * *

As if the Kennedy brothers did not already have enough trouble with Manny Celler, at this very moment they faced yet a new round of complications involving Martin Luther King and J. Edgar Hoover—complications that might also make it harder to pass H.R. 7152. To make matters even worse, the catalyst for these complications was a longtime Senate protégé of Lyndon Johnson's, Robert G. Baker.

Bobby Baker had come to the Senate as a fourteen-year-old page in 1943, and though he was twenty years younger than Johnson, he had become one of his important early teachers and guides in the folkways of the institution. By the late 1950s, with Johnson's steady backing, Baker had risen to the post of secretary to the Senate's Democratic majority, the man who made the trains run on time, and the best-known wheeler-dealer and fixer on Capitol Hill. By October 1963, he had become something else: the subject of an investigation into that very wheeling and dealing, and thus a source of potential embarrassment to both Lyndon Johnson and John Kennedy.

The Baker inquiry—begun by a handful of sharp-eyed journalists but soon picked up by Senator John Williams of Delaware, the ranking Republican on the Finance Committee and a self-appointed ethics watchdog—was broad, stretching from Baker's investment in a vending machine company that sought lucrative business from federal aerospace contractors, to his backing of a splashy resort motel on Maryland's Eastern Shore. But the aspects of his activity that involved Johnson and Kennedy were all too specific—even if still unknown to the public.

First, Baker had arranged for a Maryland insurance broker, Don B. Reynolds, to write a $100,000 life insurance policy for Johnson after he had trouble getting coverage in the wake of his 1955 heart attack. Johnson paid the $2,500 commission, Baker would later explain, but wanted something else in return: Reynolds would have to advertise on the television station that the Johnsons owned in Austin, Texas. And if a Maryland insurance broker's being forced to advertise on Texas TV was not payback enough, the Johnsons also wanted a new Magnavox stereo set, which Reynolds bought wholesale for $542.25 and shipped to their home. The gift of a mere vicuña coat had forced Dwight Eisenhower's White House chief of staff, Sherman Adams, to resign in 1958, and Johnson was wary of anyone poking around in his personal finances, an area in which he knew he was vulnerable, having accumulated great wealth while on the public payroll.

Second, it was Bobby Baker who owned the smoky Capitol Hill retreat—known as the Quorum Club—where Ellen Rometsch, the German beauty whom the FBI suspected of being a spy, was a regular entertainer of senators of both parties. And it was Baker who would claim to have sent Rometsch to the White House to share her favors with the president.

So when Baker abruptly drank four martinis at lunch and resigned his Senate post on Monday, October 7, just before a scheduled meeting with Mike Mansfield and Everett Dirksen to defend himself from John Williams's inquiries, Robert Kennedy was understandably alarmed. The attorney general well understood that J. Edgar Hoover knew all about the rumors swirling around Baker and Rometsch, and it cannot have been a coincidence that just three days later, on Thursday, October 10, he at last authorized Hoover's request for wiretaps on Martin Luther King's home and office. "There would have been no living with the Bureau" if he had refused, Kennedy would later tell a friend. Days later, the attorney general humbled himself even further with Hoover by asking the director to persuade Mansfield and Dirksen that no good could come—for either party—from an inquiry into Rometsch's sexual exploits. In one more telling way, Hoover once again held the upper hand—over King, over the Kennedys, and, as his adversaries knew, over H.R. 7152 itself.

* * *

J. EDGAR HOOVER WAS NOT the only one in Washington exacting a price from the Kennedy brothers that October. Bill McCulloch and his fellow Republicans insisted that the White House would have to help clean up the mess that Celler and the House liberals had made of H.R. 7152. The man chosen to deliver that message to the administration was a character every bit as singular as McCulloch or Celler—the House minority leader, Charles Abraham Halleck of Indiana.

Halleck, a scrapper from Hoosier farm country, had been gleefully battling Democrats since the days of the New Deal. The historian Eric Goldman once described his political views as "just left of King George

III." He was a lawyer and onetime state prosecutor, and the highlight of his political career may well have been his nomination of his fellow Indianan, Wendell Willkie, for the Republican presidential nomination in 1940. (Halleck nursed abiding resentment that he had been narrowly passed over for the vice presidential nomination in 1948 by Thomas E. Dewey, who chose Earl Warren instead.) He had become the House Republican leader in 1959 by challenging and toppling his predecessor, Joseph Martin of Massachusetts. Now, with his W. C. Fields nose and gravelly midwestern twang, he was one half of the Republican congressional leadership, teamed with his Senate counterpart, Everett Dirksen of Illinois, in a weekly news conference of loyal opposition that the *New York Times*'s Tom Wicker had dubbed "The Ev and Charlie Show" and that President Kennedy compared to the popular television drama about Prohibition-era gangsters, *The Untouchables*. Halleck was the bull terrier to Dirksen's baleful basset hound, the drum to his flute, the sandpaper to his velvet, as the liberal columnist Mary McGrory put it.

Halleck held court in a hideaway office off a basement corridor of the Capitol, presiding over what he called "the Clinic," his bibulous answer to former Speaker Sam Rayburn's famous "Board of Education," the private group of pals and protégés with whom Rayburn shared his opinions and wisdom regarding pending legislative business over Virginia Gentleman bourbon and branch water. In Halleck's salon, the tipple of choice was Grant's Stand Fast Scotch. He was, a friend would recall, a man who "never succumbed to the modernist theory that booze interferes with brain function." (When Larry O'Brien once told Lyndon Johnson that Halleck worried that he might have been a little rough in a telephone call with Johnson because "he had a couple of pops," Johnson demurred, "No, every time I talk to him, he's drinking." "Yeah, well, you catch him after noontime, that's the way it has to be," O'Brien replied.)

Now, on Tuesday, October 8, the very day that the amended bill arrived at the full Judiciary Committee, it was Halleck who met with Nick Katzenbach and John McCormack, the elderly Speaker of the House. Halleck told them that the Republicans would go halfway toward fixing the flawed subcommittee bill, but only halfway. They would also need backing from the liberal Northern Democrats on the full Judiciary

Committee. Otherwise, he threatened, the Republicans would oppose any softening amendments, condemning the bill to certain death at the hands of the southern segregationists on the House floor.

Like Bill McCulloch, Halleck had hardly any black constituents in his western Indiana district. If his support for civil rights was less emphatic than McCulloch's, he had nevertheless consistently opposed poll taxes and had supported the 1957 Civil Rights Act, though such stands won him little support from the folks at home, whose letters filled his in-box. Among the hostile communiqués he received circa 1963 was a bogus application for membership in the NAACP that asked the respondent to list "Number of children claimed for relief check," "number of legitimate children (if any)," and "Total children fathered (if known)," and to describe his marital status as "shacked up," "making out," or "worn out."

In fact, almost certainly because of his bona fides as a scrappy conservative, Halleck was under assault that summer from constituents and other correspondents demanding to know what he intended to do about the Kennedys' civil rights program. On June 16, W. E. Black of Indianapolis sent the minority leader a letter that began, "I am writing to you to find out what Kennedy and his little brother, that he put in as Attorney General, are trying to do to the white people of America. We all know it is for votes." The same day, Frank Farr of San Diego demanded, "Would you care to have niggers in your home, marrying into your family, of course you would not. They have only been out of Africa and the trees for a short period of time."

Halleck's delicate situation as Republican leader had been summed up earlier that summer in a private note he had received from Gettysburg, Pennsylvania, on the cream-colored, gold-embossed stationery of Dwight D. Eisenhower himself. Noting that President Kennedy had been lobbying for his support on the civil rights bill (and insisting, with his usual diffidence on the subject, that "I, as a layman, was not able to suggest the details that might be useful"), Ike suggested it might be a good idea for the Republicans to let the Democrats stew in their own juices a bit.

Because strong Republican support would be required for the passage of any bill, Eisenhower continued, "The picture presented, then, is a curious one. The Democratic Party, while normally completely unified at election time, always becomes immersed in a hopeless civil war when anything remotely touching the race question is brought up in Congress . . . It puts you and your Republican colleagues in a rather awkward position. The electorate has declined to give the Republicans responsibility for leading the nation, yet the implication is that Republican Congressmen have a responsibility of overcoming the errors committed by the elected majority." The former president concluded that he would support legislation "that seemed to me applicable, proper and constitutional," but he added, "The situation is one that certainly poses tough decisions upon us all, first as good citizens, second as Republicans."

Eisenhower's letter is revealing, showing as it does how the Republican Party's most revered elder statesman could view the civil rights bill through the cold-eyed prism of partisan politics. By contrast, Charlie Halleck, the dogged Republican "gut-fighter," was finding himself thrust into the role of statesman by default. The same partisan loyalty that made Halleck a political scrapper meant that he was loyal to his party's ranking campaigner for civil rights. That was Bill McCulloch, and McCulloch had already given his word to the administration. For better or worse, he and Halleck would now help the Kennedys salvage their bill.

* * *

THE FIRST STEP IN the Kennedy administration's elaborate dance of reclamation was Robert Kennedy's summons of Manny Celler to the woodshed—or at least to the Justice Department, where he gave the chairman a stern talking-to for not following the administration's earlier wishes on the bill. "It was unpleasant," Kennedy would recall. "But you see, we'd lost him. The problem was, it wasn't just a gratuitous lecture. We'd lost him, and he wasn't giving any leadership. He'd indicated that he'd come along with us—and then hadn't . . . The reason that I was as strong as I was, was that he was no good to us with his present posture at the time. He liked me, and I liked him, but we'd lost the bill. So I just put the facts on the table: that the bill was going to go down the drain and we needed some leadership from him."

Celler was not happy, as Burke Marshall would recall. "He thought he was being scolded and he *was* being scolded," Marshall said. "He did resent it at the time. But then, I think, he finally came around and accepted it." He also agreed to sit down with McCulloch and the Justice Department lawyers to forge a bill that would meet everyone's requirements.

The attorney general was willing to play his painful part, too, by making a return pilgrimage to the Judiciary Committee. There, on Tuesday, October 15, he testified (in executive session, whose gist quickly became public) in favor of a scaled-back bill. "Differences as to approach and emphasis must not be permitted to be escalated into the arena of politics—or else the country will be the loser," he said. He ticked through a point-by-point analysis of his objections to the amended bill—twenty-six pages of prepared testimony in all—suggesting the adoption of revisions that had already been quietly agreed to by McCulloch, Celler, and the lawyers at the Justice Department.

Together with Marshall and Katzenbach, Celler and McCulloch had done their best to remove the most objectionable provisions in the subcommittee bill—effectively rewriting H.R. 7152 behind the scenes. The negotiators agreed to apply the voting rights provisions of Title I only to federal elections, as originally envisioned, and not to state and local contests, as the liberals wanted. They scaled back the public accommodations section to accede to McCulloch's wishes that personal service firms such as law firms and medical practices not be covered. And they deleted completely the broad powers that would have allowed the attorney general's intervention in almost any civil rights matter.

In his testimony to the Judiciary Committee, Bob Kennedy now summed up his views on these changes, focusing on the provision that would give the attorney general sweeping powers of intervention. The civil rights groups had intended this provision as a means of protecting demonstrators like the Freedom Riders. Kennedy countered that giving the federal government such power might encourage state and local authorities to abdicate their own responsibilities, "thereby creating a vacuum in authority which could be filled *only* by Federal force." As he left the hearing room, Kennedy told waiting reporters, "What I want is a bill, not an issue"—just the opposite of the dismissive formulation that his brother had used in deriding the high-minded purism of the liberal groups.

The next morning, continuing the agreed-upon ritual, Celler announced that he, too, had changed his mind and would support a scaled-back bill. Predictably, the civil rights groups hit the ceiling. Clarence Mitchell of the NAACP called it a "sellout," and he was especially irked that Robert Kennedy had testified in closed session. "Everybody in there is a white man and what they are doing affects ten percent of the population that is black," he said. James Farmer allowed that such "political expediency brought me to the point of nausea." The Leadership Conference on Civil Rights said that the attorney general's action was "almost as if Birmingham hadn't happened."

What the liberals saw was compromise and surrender. What they could not appreciate—in part because of the mutual mistrust that had built up—was the Kennedys' hard-headed determination to produce a bill that could pass the House, by any means necessary. And even as Bob Kennedy ate his plate of crow, still more trouble was brewing behind the scenes to pose a threat to the bill.

On Friday, October 18, three days after Kennedy's testimony, J. Edgar Hoover—perhaps emboldened by the attorney general's authorization of the wiretap on Martin Luther King—issued a top-secret memo detailing King's contacts with Stanley Levison and other alleged Communist-influenced figures, real or imagined, and added a scathing, vituperative attack on King's character. The FBI director sent copies not only to the president and attorney general, but also to the secretary of defense, the CIA, and the military intelligence services. "It was a very explosive document, in the sense that it was at the time the bill was before Congress," Burke Marshall would recall. Bob Kennedy promptly ordered Hoover to recall all existing copies, including the attorney general's own. But the damage had been done. The memo had gone "all around the damn place," Katzenbach would remember, and had shocked generals and senators alike. On October 21, the attorney general approved additional electronic surveillance of the Southern Christian Leadership Conference's headquarters in Atlanta.

* * *

EVEN BEFORE BOB KENNEDY's pilgrimage to the Judiciary Committee, Manny Celler had agreed to get the process of revising the bill rolling with an amendment to restrict the bill's voting rights provisions to federal elections. To offer this measure he had handpicked Representative Roland "Libby" Libonati, a stalwart member of Mayor Richard J. Daley's Chicago Democratic machine—and a onetime lawyer for Al Capone—who could usually be counted on to follow the party line. When the full Judiciary Committee met on the morning of October 10, Libonati made his motion, as arranged. But for procedural reasons, the committee was forced to adjourn before a vote could be taken. That gave Bob Kastenmeier—the liberal author of the proposal to extend coverage to state elections in the first place—a chance to block Libonati's move.

Kastenmeier enlisted the help of Representative William Dawson, the dean of Chicago's Democratic delegation and one of only five black members of Congress. Dawson promptly lobbied Libonati to change his position. Libonati had his pride and did not want to look like anybody's stooge, especially if he was one. His resolve was further softened when he happened to catch a television appearance in which Manny Celler, his own pride on the line, continued to insist for public consumption that he would resist efforts to weaken the bill. That was enough to push Libonati over the edge.

"I'm watching television and who do I see on the television but my chairman," Libonati complained. "And he's telling 'em up there in his district that he's for a strong bill, and he doesn't have anything to do with any motion to cut the bill down. So when I hear that, I says to myself, 'Lib, where are we at here, anyway?'"

So when the Judiciary Committee reconvened nearly two weeks later on the morning of Tuesday, October 22, with Libonati's pending motion as the first order of business, he promptly withdrew it. Complete chaos ensued in the hearing room, as liberals and conservatives on the committee jockeyed over what to do next. Some southerners wanted to send the whole bill back to the subcommittee. That so angered liberals that they threatened to simply report the sweeping bill passed by Subcommittee No. 5 to the full House.

At last, Representative Arch Moore, a pro-civil-rights Republican from West Virginia, grew so disgusted by all the maneuvering, and by Celler's failed Kabuki dance, that he moved to send the strong subcommittee bill to the full House with a favorable recommendation—the course the administration and Bill McCulloch most feared, because they believed that this version of the bill could never pass. "The shame of our times," Moore said, "is that the subject of civil rights" had been "made the butt of political opportunism" in Congress. "The committee chairman was forced to label the subcommittee bill 'drastic,' irrespective of the fact that it was his bill. Amendments were offered and withdrawn. Signals were called and then missed."

Manny Celler was trapped. He knew that Moore had enough votes to prevail, simply because the liberal Democrats on the committee would be happy to join in supporting the measure the civil rights groups most wanted, while the southern Democrats would be glad to conspire in reporting out a bill they believed was doomed to failure on the House floor. Only the sound of the noon bell—which meant that the full House was in session and, following the custom of the day, committee meetings had to be concluded—spared Celler immediate defeat. The chairman set the committee vote for one week hence, on October 29. The Kennedy administration would live to fight another day—and it was President Kennedy himself who would have to do much of the fighting.

* * *

THE PRESIDENT'S FIRST STEP was to summon the bipartisan House leadership to a meeting in the Cabinet Room just after 6:00 p.m. on Wednesday, October 23. Speaker John McCormack and Majority Leader Carl Albert; Charles Halleck and his minority whip, Les Arends of Illinois; and Celler and McCulloch joined the president, the vice president, the attorney general, Katzenbach, and Marshall for a freewheeling two-hour meeting that veered between angry griping by the Republicans and recurrent attempts at strategizing by a charged-up president.

Halleck had met earlier that day with the Republicans on the Judiciary Committee and had gotten an earful of their discontent. "I think it's only fair to say that this damned thing has gotten all fizzled up and fouled up, into where some of the guys on our side who are normally pretty steady-going . . . they've got themselves all boiled up," he told the president.

Kennedy was sympathetic but noted that he, too, had taken heat—from the liberals and civil rights groups—and volunteered to lobby Judiciary Committee members himself. "I'll say we get the Democrats together and say that I think you're crazy, and that you're going to bear the responsibility for no bill if you follow this course," the president said to Halleck. "If we do that, it seems to me, you can get your people." A few moments later, McCulloch acknowledged, "Well, I don't think we're too far apart." That excited the president, who exclaimed, "My God! I could sit . . . we could do this thing," but Halleck and his Republican colleagues quickly insisted the matter was not so simple.

"Hell, you see, Mr. President," Halleck explained, "there's been a feeling among a lot of our guys, Manny's subcommittee—and I don't know whether he is responsible or not—but they loaded this thing up, way beyond anything you asked and way beyond anything we ought to do. And then the feeling got abroad that we were supposed to be the goats. We are supposed to go ahead and emasculate the damned thing."

At this, Kennedy interrupted to say, "No, we've done that, we're the goats." The president went on, offering to make Halleck's job easier by first persuading a majority of Democrats on the committee to accept a bill more like the original one, so that Halleck could assure his fellow Republicans that the Democrats would share the blame. He pressed for action as soon as possible.

But Halleck and McCulloch had to vent a bit more. At one point, McCulloch interjected that he and his angry colleagues believed he had been "taken for a ride" by Celler's actions in the subcommittee, while Halleck insisted that the president had more power over the wayward Democrats than he did over his Republicans. "You're in a damn sight better position to work yours over than I am to work mine over," Halleck said, prompting laughter all around.

In the end, Kennedy proposed a compromise: if he could get a majority of Democrats on the Judiciary Committee "who are willing to take the heat, and a majority of you fellows do, that's a reasonable position."

Halleck countered that he would try to produce seven Republican votes—half the party's membership on the committee—to block Arch Moore's motion.

As the meeting broke up, Katzenbach, Celler, and McCulloch agreed to meet the next morning in Katzenbach's office to go over the outlines of a compromise agreement, and Halleck promised to poll his members and get back to Kennedy with a tally by noon the next day. Joining his friend Ben Bradlee for dinner in the upstairs residence a few minutes later, Kennedy complained that "trying to touch Charlie is like trying to pick up a greased pig." But he acknowledged in the next breath, "It's a lousy bill as it now stands."

At the urging of Lyndon Johnson, Kennedy agreed to meet with the northern Democrats on the Judiciary Committee the next morning (the southerners being a lost cause) to try to sell them on a compromise. He did so despite the misgivings of Larry O'Brien and others, who worried that "the president's personal prestige would be so much on the line if it didn't work," as Burke Marshall would recall. So on that Thursday, October 24, the Democrats, escorted by Celler, arrived in secret at the Diplomatic Entrance of the White House for their meeting with Kennedy. "We want to pass something," the president told them. "We sympathize with what you've done, but we can't pass the bill in its current form."

One member, Representative George Senner of Arizona, spoke up to say, "We're with you, Mr. President," but there was no stampede to second him because, without an agreement from Halleck and McCulloch, Kennedy still had no clear alternative to give to the liberals. The meeting broke up without any definitive result.

Meantime, the noon deadline for the report from Charlie Halleck came and went with no call, until finally a nervous Kennedy himself telephoned the minority leader at 12:45 p.m. "Mr. President, I'm terribly sorry," Halleck explained. "I had a hard time catching a couple of my fellows but I just talked to the last one . . . I was just about to call you with good news—I've got you the votes to get your bill out of the committee."

* * *

KENNEDY WAS DELIGHTED, BUT the challenge remained to fashion a substitute measure that would eliminate the most objectionable parts of the subcommittee bill while retaining enough teeth to attract the wavering liberals. In that effort, the work of Bill McCulloch and Nick Katzenbach would be crucial.

McCulloch knew that before he could reach any accommodation with Celler and the Democrats, he first had to resolve his own differences with the liberal Republicans on the Judiciary Committee, especially John Lindsay, the ambitious, charismatic New Yorker who was already in search of bigger things. Lindsay was not a member of Subcommittee No. 5, but McCulloch liked him and had arranged for him to join in the subcommittee's deliberations, so he was conversant with all the discussions on the bill. If Lindsay and the other Republican liberals on the full Judiciary Committee did not have an acceptable alternative, they were now all but certain to vote to send the strong bill to the floor.

So on Friday, October 25, McCulloch asked his staff counsel, William Copenhaver, to seek out Lindsay's aide, Robert Kimball, to ascertain what Lindsay might be willing to accept in terms of a compromise. The answer was that Lindsay so distrusted the administration that he was unlikely to accept any deal. But the two aides promised to keep talking, and by Sunday, Lindsay himself agreed to come to McCulloch's office in the New House Office Building where the Ohioan had been working through the weekend, as usual. Together with Copenhaver and Kimball, they went through the bill section by section and, each by turns giving the other concessions on language and substance, managed to resolve their differences. Lindsay was especially gratified that McCulloch had agreed to accept a strong public accommodations measure.

Now it remained to reach agreement with the administration, and in the meantime, Nick Katzenbach had an inspiration of his own. Knowing how important a strong Equal Employment Opportunity Commission—the so-called FEPC provision that the White House had omitted from its own original bill—was to liberals who wanted teeth in the bill to fight employment discrimination in the private sector, Katzenbach turned to an old friend from New Jersey, Representative Frank Thompson, a Democratic member of the House Education and Labor Committee, to ask he if had any ideas. Thompson wondered whether Katzenbach had considered a Republican-sponsored measure that the labor committee had earlier approved, which would require any fair employment practices commission, if it wanted to force action, to do so in federal court, where both labor and management would be entitled to a trial, and not by administrative action. Such a measure would split the difference between having a commission that could merely oversee government contractors (as the administration had proposed) and one that could unilaterally force action on private industry (as the liberals on Subcommittee No. 5 had wanted).

Katzenbach floated the idea with McCulloch, who liked it. It was, after all, a Republican-sponsored idea, and so it should not cost any Republican votes, while it might yet sway a wavering liberal or two to support the scaled-back bill. (McCulloch did warn Katzenbach, though, that Charlie Halleck, who had long been notoriously wary of fair employment laws, might not accept the proposal.)

On Monday morning, October 28, just a day before the scheduled vote, Katzenbach met with McCulloch, Copenhaver, and Kimball in a secret rendezvous in Room 410 of the frayed Congressional Hotel on Capitol Hill, where Kimball kept an apartment, to go over the proposed compromise, including the new FEPC provision. The revised bill was weaker than the Subcommittee No. 5 version but a good deal stronger than the administration's original bill. The result: the voting rights section was limited to federal elections only; the public accommodations section would cover hotels, sports stadiums, theaters, and restaurants, but not barbershops and beauty parlors; the public facilities section dropped the provision that would allow the attorney general sweeping powers to file suit to desegregate parks, libraries, and the like, allowing him only to intervene in suits already filed by others or when he received written notice that an aggrieved person could not sue for lack of funds or fear of personal harm; and the section on discrimination in federally assisted programs restricted the government's ability to cut off funds for noncompliance.

* * *

WITH THE COMMITTEE VOTE looming the next day, it now remained for the president himself to put the screws to the Judiciary Committee's northern Democrats one last time. He did so at four o'clock on Monday afternoon in yet another meeting at the White House, where he polled them one by one. Kennedy knew he needed ten Democratic votes and could so far count on only three: Celler; George Senner, the Arizonan who had expressed his support in the meeting the previous week; and Harold Donohue, an old comrade from Massachusetts. Two more were likely: William St. Onge of Connecticut, who was hospitalized and had given his proxy to Celler; and Jack Brooks of Texas, a close ally of Lyndon Johnson's. That meant the president needed at least five more votes, and as he went around the Cabinet room, the results were mixed.

Once more, Roland Libonati—who had caused so much trouble in the first place by withdrawing his initial motion to weaken the bill—proved a pain in the president's neck, announcing that he would refuse to accept the new compromise. Kennedy was so irked that he briefly ducked out of the meeting to telephone Libonati's patron, Mayor Daley in Chicago. "Roland Libonati is sticking it right up us," Kennedy complained. "He's standing with the extreme liberals who are gonna end up with no bill at all."

"He'll vote for it," Daley exclaimed. "He'll vote for any goddamned thing you want!"

At that Kennedy laughed and said, "Well, can you get him?" and Daley suggested that Ken O'Donnell tell Libonati to call him in Chicago. But the president suggested it might be better for Daley himself to call Libonati later, "Otherwise, 'cause he might think—"

"That's better," Daley promptly agreed. "But he'll do it."

"That'd be good," Kennedy said. (Indeed, later that night, Libonati sent word to the White House that he would support the president.)

Yet again, the meeting ended inconclusively, with Kennedy still uncertain of just how many votes he could count on.

But by 9:30 on Tuesday morning, October 29, when the president convened one last meeting at the White House with McCulloch, Halleck, and the usual suspects, Kennedy reported that he believed he now had nine votes to oppose Arch Moore's pending motion to send the liberal bill to the floor. "And we hope maybe Libonati will support us," he added.

"We've got at least seven and maybe another on our side," Halleck reported.

That meant sixteen votes—just one short of the seventeen needed to block Moore's motion. In fact, Halleck, canny as ever, was understating his tally on purpose; he already had a certain eighth vote in hand. But he had only pledged to Kennedy the support of half the committee's Republicans—and seven fulfilled that promise. Now he was waiting to see whether the president could produce his promised half of the Democrats— that is, ten.

"I think we got a pretty good bill here," Kennedy said. "We've got the FEPC that the Republicans—"

At this reference to Nick Katzenbach's handiwork—the new Equal Employment Opportunity Commission proposal—Halleck interrupted, "Let's understand one thing, Mr. President. You know my concern about FEPC. And so I wouldn't want it understood here that when this gets out on the House floor that I support FEPC."

Kennedy rejoined in disbelief, "That's the Republican FEPC!" Indeed it was, and Katzenbach's inclusion of it was doubly clever, because it was not only a Republican measure, but one that had been sponsored by three young Republican Turks—Robert Griffin of Michigan, Charles Goodell of New York, and Albert Quie of Minnesota—who had recently challenged Halleck's leadership. The trio had engineered a successful effort to knock off Halleck's conservative deputy minority whip, Charles Hoeven, in favor of an up-and-comer from Michigan named Gerald R. Ford. Whatever Halleck's protestations, Kennedy knew he would be hard-pressed to oppose the FEPC provision now.

At 10:45 that morning, Chairman Celler called the Judiciary Committee to order. Leaving nothing to chance, the Justice Department had prepared a six-point script for him to conduct the meeting. The first step was a roll call vote on Arch Moore's pending motion to send the liberal bill to the House floor. The number needed to defeat the motion was seventeen, exactly half the thirty-four votes available that morning. (One of the committee's thirty-five members was absent, and a motion fails on a tie vote.) Because tradition dictated that the roll of the majority party be called first, the results of the president's lobbying efforts were soon clear.

He got his ten votes—but Roland Libonati's was not among them. The feckless ward heeler had changed his mind yet again, and the tenth vote came from a most unlikely candidate, Ed Willis of Louisiana, a staunch segregationist who was nevertheless a close friend of both Celler and McCulloch and who returned their friendship by voting with them. A total of nine Republicans—two more than Halleck had promised—also voted against the motion, which was defeated 19–15.

The next task was for Celler to read the first sentence of the pending liberal bill and then move to strike everything following it, in favor of the new fifty-six-page compromise measure. The text of the new bill had been hand-delivered to all the committee members overnight, so none could claim they had not seen it before voting on it. The next requirement was the reading of the new bill and the committee's aged clerk, William Foley, whose constitution was frail, barely managed to finish it by 11:52 a.m., just eight minutes before the full House would convene and force the committee to adjourn. Celler raced through the remaining steps, giving himself sixty seconds to explain the bill, and McCulloch equal time, before Peter Rodino of New Jersey called for a vote and an end to all discussion. Celler then ordered a vote on the new bill, which passed 20 to 14 just as the noon bell sounded, announcing the start of the House floor session. The administration had won ugly, but it had won.

Reactions ran to form. The president called the bill "comprehensive and fair" and said it would "provide the basis for men of good will in every city in our land to work together to resolve their racial problems within a framework of law and justice." But the Leadership Conference on Civil Rights, quoting Roy Wilkins, said the bill was "inadequate to meet the needs of 1963." The biggest loser was probably Roland Libonati, who confided to a colleague in the aftermath of the vote that he had received word from the Daley machine that his political career was over.

After the vote, President Kennedy called Charlie Halleck with his thanks. "Well, you did a great job," the president said.

"Oh, well, thanks," Halleck replied, adding, "I got a lot of mad people up here."

Kennedy laughed and assured him, "Oh, but that's all right," and Halleck acknowledged, "I know, you've got a few."

"You really did what you said," Kennedy told the minority leader, one smooth operator admiring another.

"I hated to overpromise," Halleck replied.

Then Kennedy turned his scorn on Libonati, but with a twinkle that referenced his own close election in 1960, which many had credited to Mayor Daley's delivery of Illinois. "Evidently that Cook County machine isn't as strong as we hear," the president said.

"I got a little trouble on my side," Halleck concluded, "a lot of guys bitching . . . and so I ain't sure they'll make me leader again but . . . I don't give a damn."

Halleck's break with his usual conservative-southern coalition was remarkable. The columnist Murray Kempton wrote that he had "violated the compact with the southerners which is the heart of his tactics" and had "stifled lust at the smell of a bleeding Democrat, which is the inner-most response of his natural being." The *Washington Post* editorialized that Halleck's "action would have brought down a government in many parliamentary legislatures."

In fact, that same afternoon, someone placed a furled umbrella on the Republican leadership's desk on the House floor, a gesture meant to compare Halleck's actions to Neville Chamberlain's appeasement of Hitler in 1938. The next day, sixty-eight House Republicans—40 percent of the caucus—held a secret meeting to protest Halleck's decision to support the bill without consulting the Republican Policy Committee. "They aren't organizing a revolt," said Representative Melvin Laird, an influential young Republican from Wisconsin. "But Halleck has been warned." Another angry Republican member, quoted anonymously in the newspapers, was blunter. "We had Kennedy locked in a box on civil rights and Charlie Halleck gave him the key," he said. "Now Kennedy will get credit for the bill among the Negroes, and the white voters will blame the Republicans for helping to pass it. So we are damned either way."

Days later, a postcard signed with an illegible scrawl arrived in Halleck's office from Xenia, Ohio. "You used to be the fair haired lad from Indiana," it read. "NOW YOU ARE THE HAIRY APE OF THE PARTY—HOPE THE PARTY BOUNCES YOU."

For the rest of their days, the Kennedy brothers professed some puzzlement about just why Halleck had agreed to support their bill when he could have chosen to embarrass them with an election year coming up. Nick Katzenbach thought Halleck did so out of loyalty to McCulloch. "If the senior Republican on a committee was for something, then the party leader was for it," he would recall. Near the end of his life, Halleck offered his own answer. "They couldn't understand that once in a while a guy does something because it's right," he told Charles Whalen, a fellow Republican congressman who, with his wife, Barbara, wrote a sympathetic history of the bill, and of the Republicans' crucial role in its passage. "I had a few experiences. I had a black driver. We used to go down to Warm Springs, Virginia, to see friends. We'd stop at a little bit of a restaurant. I'd go in and ask if he could go in with the Hallecks. They said no but they would be glad to serve him in the car. The goddamned thing just didn't look right to me. Hell, I didn't do it for political advantage. The colored votes in my district didn't amount to a bottle of cold pee."

Bill McCulloch had the same point of view. Ten days after the bill cleared the Judiciary Committee, he told the *Dayton Journal Herald*, "My purpose is to remove this bill from the political arena. I just want the people to know it has the imprint of both parties."

* * *

IN THE AFTERMATH OF the committee vote, however, some liberals worried that the makeshift coalition that had brought the bill this far could not hold. H.R. 7152's next stop before the House floor would be the all-powerful Rules Committee, which would set the terms for its debate by the full House. And the committee's all-powerful chairman was Representative Howard Smith of Virginia, a staunch segregationist whose usual method for burying bills he disliked was to retreat to Cedar Hill, his farm in Fauquier County, to check up on the livestock.

Kennedy himself was frustrated and fretful. On a political trip to Pennsylvania on the day after the Judiciary Committee passed the bill, his motorcade passed through sparse crowds in the racially tense wards of South Philadelphia, "one of the poorest receptions Mr. Kennedy has had in a major city since he became president," the *New York Times*'s Tom Wicker wrote. Not only the civil rights bill, but also the president's long-pending tax bill, was now stalled on Capitol Hill. "I think it is unfortunate," he said at his news conference on November 14. Five days later, in his regular weekly meeting with the Democratic congressional leadership, he professed astonishment that Congress had so far passed only four of the twelve standard appropriations bills, with the end of the session in sight. "What are you doing up there?" he demanded.

Two days later, on Thursday, November 21, Charlie Halleck refused to shoulder any blame for the president's languishing legislative program. "With the Democrats in control of the White House and every government agency and with a two-to-one majority in the Senate and a three-to-two majority in the House of Representatives of the Congress, Mr. Kennedy can have no alibi," he said at his regular weekly news conference with Everett Dirksen. "Any censure of Congress is a censure of the Democrat Party and of the lack of presidential leadership."

The very same day, Halleck made it clear that he was not above calling in a chit or two for his support of Kennedy on civil rights. He wrote Frederick Hovde, the president of Purdue University, the biggest educational institution in his district, that he was lobbying the administration hard to put a new electronic research center for NASA on the university's campus in West Lafayette, Indiana. "My inclination is to talk to the president personally, but he left Washington this morning for a trip to Texas," Halleck wrote. "Possibly I can get in touch with him early next week. In any event, that is my intention."

6

A Good Man in a Tight Spot

NOT THREE HOURS AFTER the fateful shots rang out in Dallas, the thirty-sixth president of the United States was aloft in Air Force One winging his way back to Washington with the body of the thirty-fifth president in a heavy bronze casket in the aft of the plane. Lyndon Johnson had suffered a great shock. No one yet knew whether he himself might have been the target of an assassination plot. Half the president's Cabinet was airborne over the Pacific, diverted from a planned trip to Japan and now also returning to Washington. John F. Kennedy's widow and aides, huddled together by his coffin, were numb with grief or blind with rage—or both—and drowning their sorrows in Scotch. Confusion and uncertainty reigned.

But as he sat in the high-backed chair in the presidential stateroom that only hours before had been another man's, Johnson knew just what he wanted to do. He drew a small notepad from the desk and wrote:

1. Staff
2. Cabinet
3. Leadership.

Moments later, Malcolm Kilduff, an assistant White House press secretary and the ranking spokesman on the Texas trip, was on the plane's radio with his colleague Andrew Hatcher back at the White House.

"On arrival, on arrival," Kilduff said of the new president, "he will meet with at the White House . . . he will meet with the leadership . . . He will meet with the leadership . . ."

"Now is that bipartisan leadership or Democratic leadership?" Hatcher inquired.

"That is *wholly* bipartisan, *wholly* bipartisan," Kilduff answered. "Over."

Kilduff meant the bipartisan congressional leadership, of course. But the leadership in question that November afternoon was—*wholly, wholly*—Lyndon Johnson's own. And with John Kennedy's agenda— from the tax bill to civil rights—squarely stalled on Capitol Hill, he was wasting no time.

"I was a man in trouble, in a world that is never more than minutes away from catastrophe," he would recall. "I knew it was imperative that I grasp the reins of power and do so without delay. Any hesitation or wavering, any false step, any sign of self-doubt, could have been disastrous. The nation was in a state of shock and grief. The times cried out for leadership."

Johnson once told his biographer Doris Kearns Goodwin that he had "detested every minute" of his vice presidency, but the summer and fall of 1963 had been the absolute nadir of that famously thankless job—and perhaps the worst time of his whole life. He was mocked by sneering Kennedy aides as "Rufus Cornpone," repeatedly needled and cruelly humiliated by the attorney general, and shut out of important policy deliberations by the president himself. (John Kennedy's private name for his No. 2 was "Riverboat.") In 1961, according to the diaries of the president's secretary, Evelyn Lincoln, Johnson had spent just ten hours and nineteen minutes alone with the president. By 1963, that figure was down to one hour and fifty-three minutes. The popular CBS television show *Candid Camera* had asked a random sample of the public, "Who is Lyndon Johnson?" and the answers ranged from, "No, I don't know him . . . I'm from New Jersey," to "He's not president. Am I getting close?" *Time* magazine had declared that "power has slipped from his grasp," while *The Reporter* had published a headline that summed up his has-been's fate: "Whatever Happened to Lyndon Johnson?"

He looked, his once and future aide Harry McPherson would recall, "absolutely gross. His belly was enormous and his face looked bad, flushed, maybe he had been drinking a good deal . . . His life was not causing him to come together physically, morally, intellectually, any way. On the contrary, it must have been a tremendous frustration."

"I really don't have anything going for me," Johnson had told John Kennedy's legislative liaison, Larry O'Brien. "They don't listen to me as they used to."

Now, in a flash, in an instant—in the crack of fire from a mail-order rifle—all that had changed, and Lyndon Johnson was in charge, while the New Frontiersmen with him aboard the big blue and white Boeing 707 despaired. "I thought they were just wineheads," he would recall years later. "They were just drinkers, just one drink after another coming to them to try to drown out their sorrow, and we weren't drinking, of course."

Instead, the new president fortified himself with hot vegetable soup and crackers, and when Air Force One touched down at Andrews Air Force Base outside Washington just after 6:00 p.m., Johnson made a statement whose eloquent brevity might have pleased Jack Kennedy: "I will do my best. That is all I can do. I ask for your help—and God's."

Barely two hours later, in the vice president's suite in Room 274 of the Old Executive Office Building adjacent to the White House, Johnson asked for help from the congressional leaders who had been his colleagues for so long. (He had briefly kept them waiting while he finished writing condolence notes to Caroline Kennedy and John Kennedy Jr.) The new president had already had his press aide George Reedy draft a joint statement reassuring the world that American policy would not be changed because of "a very abrupt and sudden transition." The journalist Hugh Sidey would later recall that in this meeting, "perhaps more than in anything else, lay the real clue to his flawless assumption of power." It had no real purpose, except as a ritual display in a world where such meetings were a way of life, in which some men summoned and others came. For years as Senate majority leader, Johnson had convened hundreds of such meetings. As vice president, he had not. Now he was again the one doing the summoning and, Sidey believed, "those men understood."

As the meeting broke up, one senator held back a moment for a private word—Hubert Humphrey, Johnson's old comrade in arms. "He put his arm around me and said that he needed me desperately," Humphrey would recall. That was true enough, but it was also a phrase that Johnson, a proud man alert to the pride of other men, would use countless times in the hours and days after the assassination. Less than an hour later, the president gave a subtler indication of his thinking—and of the political implications for the task ahead, including passage of the stalled civil rights bill. In a telephone call to Supreme Court Justice Arthur Goldberg, he praised the Senate minority leader, Everett Dirksen, summing up his meeting with the leadership by saying, "Needless to say, the Republicans were really better than the Democrats."

As the endless day at last wound down, Johnson summoned his aides Cliff Carter, Bill Moyers, and Horace Busby—together with a Houston advertising man named Jack Valenti, whom he had dragooned into service that afternoon in Dallas without so much as a suitcase of clothes—to the Elms, his sprawling French-style house in the Spring Valley section of Washington. After greeting several dozen close friends and colleagues who had been waiting for him, the president ordered a glass of orange juice and, finally, as midnight neared, gathered the aides in his bedroom for a restless monologue. He vowed to pass not only the stalled civil rights bill, but also the still barely dreamed-of social welfare measures—health insurance, aid to education—that would soon be known as the "Great Society." None of the aides felt compelled to offer much in the way of commentary. "If LBJ had said he was going to ride Pegasus to the nearest star, I would have bet on it," Valenti would recall.

Johnson's wife, Lady Bird, recorded a simpler, clearer-eyed sentiment in her diary entry for that night. Lyndon had always been, she recalled, "a good man in a tight spot."

* * *

WHEN HE FINALLY LET them go to their own bedrooms sometime between 3:30 and 4:00 a.m. on the morning of Saturday, November 23, Johnson had told his aides, "Get a lot of sleep fast. It's going to be a long day tomorrow." True to his word, the new president was back in the White House before nine the next morning. Like the grieving Kennedy team, who had to observe all the solemn rituals of national mourning, Johnson would be occupied with ceremonial duties. Unlike them, he also had to run the country—and he set about doing so with his trademark energy, zest, and zeal.

The night before, Johnson had reached out to the three living former presidents—Herbert Hoover, Harry Truman, and Dwight Eisenhower—and now Eisenhower was in the White House complex, down from his farm at Gettysburg. In Johnson's outer office, the old general picked up a yellow pad and began making notes of advice to the new president, suggesting that he address a joint session of Congress in a speech of "not over ten or twelve minutes," making the point that "it will be your purpose to implement effectively the noble objectives so often and so eloquently stated by your great predecessor." Johnson was grateful enough for the gesture that he would reproduce Ike's memo verbatim in his memoirs. But on this sad Saturday he had already thought of just such moves. In early afternoon, he telephoned Ev Dirksen to ask his opinion of a joint session address. "I believe it'd be *reassuring* to the country," the senator from Illinois replied.

In this moment, Johnson faced innumerable challenges: reassuring allies around the world of the steadiness of Washington's course; undertaking a detailed investigation of an assassination that still remained a mystery; persuading the grieving Kennedy aides that he—and their country—needed all the help they could give him; consolidating his support with old allies; and reaching out to skeptical would-be adversaries. But perhaps no challenge loomed larger or more immediately in his mind than moving Kennedy's stymied legislative agenda in Congress. So just after 2:00 p.m., he called Senator George Smathers of Florida, who had not only been Kennedy's closest friend in the Senate but was also a longtime ally of Johnson and a skilled vote counter. Smathers was a member of the powerful Finance Committee, and Johnson wanted his take on the status of Kennedy's tax cut bill, which had been subject to weeks of desultory hearings by the committee's fiscally conservative chairman, Harry F. Byrd of Virginia, who opposed the measure as too costly.

Smathers informed Johnson that he had cut a deal with Byrd, who had agreed at last to move the hearings along in exchange for a pledge that the handful of Democratic liberals on the committee would oppose any effort to take the bill out of his hands and send it directly to the Senate floor. Still, Smathers warned, "I'd hate to see you make [the tax bill] a big issue because I'm afraid we're not going to be able to do it." This was bad news indeed, because if the tax bill were still pending once the infinitely more controversial civil rights bill wound up in the Senate, the southern caucus would hold it and everything else hostage to civil rights. Johnson had worried about just this outcome when Kennedy had first talked of proposing the bill in June.

Then Smathers, a political moderate and a shrewd judge of people, reported on a conversation he had had with Hubert Humphrey after the congressional leadership's meeting with Johnson the night before, a "*most* interesting visit," he called it. Smathers said he had told Humphrey, a fierce advocate of civil rights and a darling of the Senate's liberal caucus, that he would be a logical vice presidential candidate for 1964, but only if he could "keep these damn liberals in line, and keep things going," in the Senate. Humphrey, Smathers continued, "was not at all averse to that idea," and agreed that the Democrats should work together to keep the new president from looking like "an old Texas oilman" who would not be committed to the Kennedy agenda.

Over the next three days, as he joined Jacqueline Kennedy and a raft of foreign leaders in the carefully choreographed pomp of public mourning, Lyndon Johnson would spare no effort to reassure anyone and everyone that his first priority was the passage of his fallen predecessor's program, especially the civil rights bill. "I knew that if I didn't get out in front on this issue," the liberals "would get me," he would recall. "They'd throw up my background against me, they'd use it to prove that I was incapable of bringing unity to the land I loved so much . . . I couldn't let that happen. I had to produce a civil rights bill that was even stronger than the one they'd have gotten if Kennedy had lived. Without this, I'd be dead before I could even begin."

So on Monday evening, November 25, after Kennedy's state funeral and meetings with such visiting dignitaries as Charles de Gaulle, Johnson addressed a gathering of some thirty-five of the nation's governors—all that the White House had been able to catch before they headed home—in Room 274 of the Old Executive Office Building. In a riveting talk, Johnson described the horror of the scene in Dallas. "Here is our president shot in the head and his wife holds his skull in her lap." He went on, "We have to do something to stop that hate, and the way we have to do it is to meet the problem of injustice that exists in this land, meet the problem of inequality that exists in this land, meet the problem of poverty that exists in this land, and the unemployment that exists in this land."

And the best way to do *that*, Johnson said, was to pass the tax bill *and* the civil rights bill, "so that we can say to the Mexican in California or the Negro in Mississippi or the Oriental on the West Coast or the Johnsons in Johnson City that we are going to treat you all equally and fairly. And you are going to be judged on merit and not ancestry, not on how you spell your name."

Less than an hour later, Johnson was on the phone to Martin Luther King with a similar message. King had not been invited to Kennedy's funeral but came on his own anyway, and Johnson now called to thank him for having made supportive remarks about the new president in a television interview. "We know what a difficult period this is," King said.

"It's a—it's just an *impossible* period," Johnson replied, the weight of the world on his shoulders. "We got a civil rights bill that hasn't even passed the House, and it's November, and Hubert Humphrey told me yesterday that everybody wanted to go home. We got a tax bill that they haven't touched. We just got to let up—not let up on any of them and keep going."

Two days later, at 12:30 p.m. on Wednesday, November 27, Johnson went before the joint session in the House chamber, where he had first sat as a young congressman twenty-six years earlier. In his audience were eighty-seven House members and seventy-eight senators who had served with him. And in the front row of the First Lady's box in the gallery, one seat away from Lady Bird herself, was Zephyr Wright, a college graduate and a black woman, who for twenty-one faithful years had been the

Johnson family's cook and was even then planning their Thanksgiving dinner of turkey and cornbread dressing for the next day.

"Let us put an end to the teaching and the preaching of hate and evil and violence," Johnson declared. "Let us turn away from the fanatics of the far left and the far right, from the apostles of bitterness and bigotry, from those defiant of law, and those who pour venom into our nation's bloodstream. I profoundly hope that the tragedy and the torment of these terrible days will bind us together in new fellowship, making us one people in our hour of sorrow."

Then, borrowing from Lincoln, he concluded in words both high-flown and homey, "So let us here highly resolve that John Fitzgerald Kennedy did not live—or die—in vain. And on this Thanksgiving Eve, as we gather together to ask the Lord's blessing and give him our thanks, let us unite in those familiar and cherished words:

> America, America
> God shed his grace on thee,
> And crown thy good
> With brotherhood,
> From sea to shining sea."

* * *

THE SPEECH TO CONGRESS was the American public's first wide window into the character, personality, and style of Lyndon Johnson, and the reaction to it was effusively positive. But he was not a simple man.

"He was thirteen of the most interesting and difficult men I ever met," his onetime aide Bill Moyers would recall, while his longtime adviser George Reedy, who understood him as well as anyone, believed, "He was a man of too many paradoxes."

"Almost everything you find out about him you can find a directly contrary quality immediately, and your problem is always which quality was real and which quality was assumed," Reedy would recall. "Or maybe neither quality was real. Or maybe both were real, who knows?"

Hubert Humphrey once called him a "tidal wave . . . he went through the walls." He could be tender and thoughtful, crude and cruel. He could be gentle and solicitous, heedless and egomaniacal. He could be brave and forthright, cowardly and devious. "He had an animal sense of weakness in other men," Moyers judged. "He could inflict on them a thousand cuts before flying in at his own expense the best doctor to heal them or, if that failed, a notable for the last rites." The least—or most—that can be said of him is that he came by his contradictions honestly.

Later in life, Johnson liked to brag, "My ancestors were teachers and lawyers and college presidents and governors when the Kennedys in this country were still tending bar." But, in fact, he had a childhood of sometimes wrenching privation and emotional complexity—an upbringing that left lasting and painful scars. Yes, his mother, Rebekah Baines, came from an upright line of Baptist worthies and had graduated from Baylor University, a rare accomplishment for a woman in her time and place. And yes, his father, Sam Houston Johnson, was finishing his second term in the Texas state legislature when Lyndon was born on August 27, 1908. But the Baines family had lost its money in bad business dealings, and Sam Houston Johnson had a checkered financial career as a small farmer and dealer in real estate and cattle. Lyndon grew up first in a cabin on the family homestead on the Pedernales River, and then in a frame house in nearby Johnson City in the Texas Hill Country. Austin was two days away on dirt roads that turned to mud at the first rain. "To know fully the disabling conditions of Johnson's youth can only increase admiration for the inexplicable power of his will," Johnson's biographer Doris Kearns Goodwin has written.

From his earliest days, he would be torn between his mother's pretensions to culture and gentility and his rough-hewn father's determination that she not make a sissy out of him. One of his first memories, from about the age of five, was of his father cutting off his long curls one Sunday morning when Rebekah was away at church. She refused to speak to her husband for a week, just as, three years later, she would refuse to speak to Lyndon when he declined to continue the violin and dancing lessons she had arranged for him. Years later, as senator and president, he would replicate this "Johnson freeze-out" on aides or friends he considered disloyal.

In 1924, after his father lost his legislative seat and the family was living at the poverty level, Johnson took off with some friends in a Model T for California and a series of jobs picking grapes, washing dishes, and fixing cars—and finally as a clerk to a lawyer who was a cousin of his mother. Two years later, he returned to Texas and the only college available to him, Southwest Texas State Teachers College at San Marcos. There, despite his academic deficiencies and lack of money, he ultimately mastered campus politics, defeating the ruling student fraternal organization in which athletes were king by creating a rival group that supported debate, drama, and the glee club. By sheer relentlessness and force of personality ("He could look busy doing nothing," one contemporary would recall), he became the editor of the college paper, a star debater, and an honors student. "His greatest forte," his classmate Bill Deason would remember, "is to look a man in the eye and do a convincing job of selling him his viewpoint."

To pay for his senior year at San Marcos, Johnson took a job that would mark him for life, as a teacher in the Mexican school in the small Texas town of Cotulla, where his twenty-eight fifth, sixth, seventh, and eighth graders lived in shanties and were barely literate. He quickly organized clubs and games, spelling bees and a band. "His being there," one student said, "was like a blessing from the clear sky." He himself would later say, "You never forget what poverty and hatred can do, when you see the scars on a hopeful face of a young child. They never seem to know why people dislike them. But they knew it was so, because I saw it in their eyes."

After graduation, he briefly held another job teaching public speaking and business arithmetic at Sam Houston High School in Houston. But soon enough he would embark upon the vocation that had always been his calling: politics, first as secretary to a newly elected Texas congressman, Richard Kleberg, the owner of the giant King Ranch (from whose office he led a caucus of the other congressional aides), and then, barely more than five years later, as a congressman himself. Along the way, he had conducted a whirlwind courtship of Claudia Alta Taylor, a genteel East Texan whose family nickname was Lady Bird and who became the flywheel that lent a measure of balance to his overpowering drive.

Following a pattern he would establish time and again, he attached himself to older, more powerful men—in this case, Speaker Sam Rayburn and President Franklin D. Roosevelt himself—and he rose rapidly. In brief, essentially ceremonial Navy service in World War II he rode as an observer on a single bombing run against a Japanese base in New Guinea, winning the Silver Star, the military's third-highest decoration for valor, from General Douglas MacArthur himself while the rest of the crew went unrewarded. (Johnson himself apparently drafted a letter saying that he did not deserve the award, but there is no evidence he ever sent it, and he was wearing the Silver Star lapel bar in Dallas on November 22.)

In 1948, by a dubious margin of eighty-seven votes, he won election to the Senate, and before the end of his first term, he had become the Democrats' minority leader, ascending to the majority leader's office when his party took control in 1955.

Johnson's extraordinary rise in the Senate had been aided by the affections and affinity of the men who ruled the chamber, the southern Democrats, led by Richard B. Russell of Georgia. But he was more than smart enough to know that the very quality that had fueled his rise—his southernness—would now limit his prospects for the biggest job of all, the presidency.

"There were no 'darkies' or plantations in the hill country where I grew up," he would recall. "I never sat on my parents' or grandparents' knees listening to nostalgic tales of the antebellum South. In Stonewall and Johnson City I was never a part of the Old Confederacy. But I was part of Texas . . . And Texas is a part of the South."

In fact, in his very first speech on the Senate floor, an hour-and-twenty-five-minute broadside against the Truman administration's civil rights proposals in 1949, Johnson had declared, "We of the South who speak here are accused of prejudice. We are labeled in the folklore of American tradition as a prejudiced minority." But, he insisted, "We are not speaking against the Negro race. We are not attempting to keep alive the old flames of hate and bigotry. We are, instead, trying to prevent those flames from being rekindled. We are trying to tell the rest of the nation that this is not the way to accomplish what so many want to do for the Negro."

So it came as a shock that after years of voting against civil rights measures—against elimination of the poll tax or literacy tests, against federal antilynching laws—Johnson would shepherd the first civil rights law since Reconstruction through the Senate. To many liberals and civil rights groups, Johnson was the villain who had watered down the 1957 Civil Rights Act's most sweeping provisions. But the plain truth was that he was also the reason that any bill passed at all. George Reedy would recall that Johnson's motives for supporting the bill were "highly mixed"— and presumably included his own presidential ambitions—but were in no way driven by personal prejudice.

By Johnson's own account, his epiphany on civil rights was gradual, but it was real. In his Senate days, besides Zephyr Wright as cook, he and Lady Bird employed two other black servants: Helen Williams as a housemaid and her husband, Gene, as driver, gardener, butler, and breaker-in of new shoes. (His feet were the same size as Johnson's, so he could soften up each fresh pair the boss bought.) At the end of one Senate session, Johnson asked Gene Williams if he would not only drive the extra Johnson family car back to Texas for the summer, but take the family dog—Little Beagle Johnson, like everyone else in the clan, LBJ—along for the ride.

"Senator, do I have to take Beagle?" an obviously reluctant Williams asked.

When Johnson probed, as doubtless only he could, for the source of Williams's hesitation, his driver confessed:

> Well, Senator, it's tough enough to get all the way from Washington to Texas. We drive for hours and hours. We get hungry. But there's no place on the road we can stop and go in and eat. We drive some more. It gets pretty hot. We want to wash up. But the only bathroom we're allowed in is usually miles off the main highway. We keep going till night comes, till we get so tired we can't stay awake anymore. We're ready to pull in. But it takes us another hour or so to find a place to sleep. You see, what I'm saying is that a colored man's got enough trouble getting across the South on his own, without having a dog along.

At the time, Johnson would recall, "there was nothing I could say to Gene." But Johnson himself had done menial jobs that the idiom of the day had derided as "nigger work." He himself, poor and struggling, had "always ordered the egg sandwich, and I always wanted the ham and egg."

* * *

THE PARADOX OF JOHNSON's role as John Kennedy's running mate in 1960 is that he was chosen to help Kennedy win Texas and the South, but his own growing support for civil rights, and his alliance with Kennedy, made that job all the harder—even in his own home state. Four days before the election, Johnson and Lady Bird were accosted in Dallas by an angry crowd of demonstrators, including many women, as they attempted to enter a Democratic rally at the Adolphus Hotel. The crowd waved placards declaring, LBJ SOLD OUT TO YANKEE SOCIALISTS, and pulled off Lady Bird's gloves, as spit flew her way. Johnson waved away the Texas National Guard officers who tried to intercede and endured the crowd's abuse, later telling the rally, "I wanted to find out if the time had come when I couldn't walk my lady through the corridors of the hotels of Dallas."

If civil rights leaders viewed Johnson with suspicion and distrust because of his Texas roots and his past legislative compromises, they, too, were beginning to change their views. Roy Wilkins of the NAACP would recall an audience with Johnson after the vice president had returned from a goodwill trip to Senegal in 1961. Wilkins had come to deliver an NAACP complaint about discrimination at a Lockheed Aircraft Corporation Plant in Marietta, Georgia—where the workers' time cards were in separate colors for blacks and whites—that had just won a $1 billion federal contract. "We're working on that," said Johnson, who had been assigned by Kennedy to be the administration's point man on employment discrimination. By the end of the year, the plant had hired two hundred black workers and had made fifty-nine promotions, including, for the first time, some to professional jobs. What impressed Wilkins just as much, though, was Johnson's account of his experiences in Senegal. "When I looked into the eyes of the mothers there, they had the same look as the people in Texas," the vice president said. Wilkins concluded that Johnson was "sentimental, old-fashioned, manipulating, but at bottom somehow sincere. He didn't have to talk that way. You could tell by his tone that behind all the soft soap, there was genuine feeling."

In February 1963, when Johnson learned that a political banquet he had been invited to address in St. Augustine, Florida, the following month would be segregated, he at first refused to attend. Ultimately, he arranged for two tables of blacks to be seated in a prominent place in the dining room and accepted the invitation. On the plane back to Washington, he was "happier than he had been for months," George Reedy would recall. As that spring wore on, and the crisis in Birmingham exploded, Johnson became more and more outspoken on civil rights. When he learned that Marian Anderson would be performing at the University of Texas in Austin, he invited her to spend the weekend at his ranch. He addressed the annual banquet of the black press club in Washington, warning that action on civil rights was urgently needed and saying, "The hours are short and we have no moral justification in asking for an extension." And in a Memorial Day address at Gettysburg, he was the most eloquent and emphatic of all, going well beyond anything the president himself had yet said on the topic by declaring: "One hundred years ago, the slave was freed. One hundred years later, the Negro remains in bondage to the color of his skin. The Negro today asks justice. We do not answer him—we do not answer those who lie beneath this soil—when we reply to the Negro by asking, 'Patience.' It is empty to plead that the solution to the dilemmas of the present rests on the hands of the clock. The solution is in our hands."

"Until justice is blind to color," he added, "until education is unaware of race, until opportunity is unconcerned with the color of men's skins, emancipation will be a proclamation but not a fact."

In the group meetings with civic leaders that the White House arranged that early summer to build support for the civil rights bill, Arthur Schlesinger and other witnesses would recall that the vice president was invariably more articulate, and more passionate, on the subject than the president himself—and more knowledgeable, too.

Yet even as Johnson spoke out on the issue in public (and, indeed, because he did speak out), he continued to suffer in his dealings with the

Kennedy White House—and with the Kennedy brothers. Because he believed his candid counsel was not wanted, Johnson did not often give it, especially in group staff meetings where he feared that any critical comment to sound a note of caution on legislative strategy would be seen as disloyal or leaked to the press to paint him in an unfavorable light. His old comrade Bobby Baker would recall that Johnson had always "felt that if he said something, they'd leak it to the *New York Times* or somebody, and try to make him look like he didn't know what he was talking about, to be disdainful." When he finally unburdened himself, in his impassioned telephone conversation with Ted Sorensen on June 3, 1963—a week before the president announced the bill—Johnson had plenty to say.

"I think he's got to have his bill," Johnson told Sorensen, but added, "I think he ought to make them pass some of this stuff"—like the tax bill—"before he throws this thing out." Johnson warned that every other item on the president's agenda would be held hostage to civil rights once the bill was on the floor of the House or Senate. "They're going to cut his outfit off and put it in their pocket and never mention civil rights," he said. "So I'd move my children through the line and get them down in the storm cellar and get it locked and key, and then I'd make my attack."

When Johnson uttered those words in June, he had no power to carry them out. "Don't try to kill the snake until you have the hoe in your hands," he liked to say. Now, in November, he had the hoe in his hands, he was in charge, and his was precisely the strategy that he intended to follow.

* * *

As he took power and plotted his course, little escaped Lyndon Johnson's notice, and civil rights was always on his mind. He had asked his personal pilot, Air Force Major James Cross, who had been flying the vice president's small Lockheed Jetstar, to become qualified as quickly as possible to command the larger Boeing 707 that usually served as Air Force One, and on Thursday, November 28, Thanksgiving Day, Cross dictated a memo for the president saying, "It is my thought that you might wish me to make a careful selection of other crew members from a wide cross-section of American culture."

The next day, the president met with Roy Wilkins about how to force action on the civil rights bill in the Rules Committee. "Johnson talked quickly, earnestly," Wilkins would recall. "It was the first time I had really felt those mesmerizing eyes of Texas on me . . . He put all his being into the task. Leaning forward, almost touching me, he poked his finger at me and said quietly, 'I want that bill *passed*.'" Johnson added, "I'm going to help wherever the Constitution will let me," but noted, "I can't do the lobbying myself. I don't think you would expect me to do that."

But the only way to pass the civil rights bill was to get it out of the House Rules Committee, where Chairman Howard Smith, universally known as "Judge" for his prior judicial service in Virginia, so far showed no sign of even being willing to hold the first hearing on the bill that had passed the Judiciary Committee on October 29.

The Rules Committee is the turnstile at the entry to the House of Representatives, the body that sets the terms and conditions—and exacts the price—for debating most every bill that reaches the House floor. Unlike the Senate, with its tradition of unlimited debate, the House is so large that legislative action would grind to a halt without limits on speaking time and procedures that its 435 voting members must follow. It is the Rules Committee that spells out those limits and procedures—those rules—and these can have major effects on a bill's ultimate fate.

Howard Smith well knew that the surest way to doom a bill he disliked—and he disliked many—was to refuse to grant it a rule at all. And there were only three conceivable ways to force his hand, none of them easy.

The first way was so far-fetched as to be impossible: a procedural move known as "Calendar Wednesday," under which, on any Wednesday, the Speaker of the House is allowed to call the roll of committees in alphabetical order and any chairman can order a bill already reported out of his committee directly to the floor. In theory, this meant that Manny Celler could demand consideration of the Judiciary Committee's compromise bill. But the catch was that the bill would have to be disposed of by day's end, and eleven other committees would be called on before the roll reached the letter *J*—half of them with southern chairmen who would be more than willing to run out the clock.

The second option, under House Rule 11, would allow any three members of the Rules Committee to request that the chairman hold a meeting. If, after three days, he had not scheduled one, a simple majority of the committee could compel a meeting at a specified date and time, to consider a specified topic. But because of the southern conservatives' dominance of the Rules Committee, any such move would require Republican support, and Charlie Halleck and his House leadership, respectful of the seniority system, had always resisted questioning a chairman's prerogatives or interfering in committee affairs.

The third option would be a "discharge petition," which, if signed by a majority of the whole House, or 218 members, could send the bill out of the Rules Committee directly to the floor. It was this last option that Lyndon Johnson now began to pursue—secretly, but emphatically.

* * *

THE SAME DAY THE president met with Wilkins, he telephoned Dave McDonald, the president of the United Steelworkers of America, and confided, "We're going to have to get a discharge petition."

"I can't say that myself," Johnson added, "but it's already filed . . . And I think if there's ever a time when you really talk to every human being you could . . ." The president said the Democrats might provide 150 signatures to start but would still need at least sixty to seventy Republicans to join them. "They'll be saying they don't want to violate procedure," Johnson predicted, adding that the Democrats' answer would have to be that "a man's entitled to a hearing." If such a move succeeded, the president said, "that would almost insure passage in the Senate, because they could see it—we had the power to discharge them and therefore we'd have the power to apply cloture." But, he warned, "don't be quoting the fact that I'm calling you, because—that'll just *create* problems." And, the president added, "If we fail on this, then we'll fail on everything."

Three days later, on Monday, December 2, Johnson telephoned Representative Richard Bolling of Missouri, one of the most stalwart liberals in the House, who agreed that a discharge petition was "the only lever we've really got in our arsenal." But when the president held his first weekly meeting with the Democratic congressional leadership at the

White House the next morning, he was not impressed with the reliability of their head count, so after breakfast he telephoned Majority Leader Carl Albert and asked for a more complete poll. By day's end, the Hill was abuzz with reports of the president's interest, and Anthony Lewis of the *New York Times* was able to report that there was "some evidence of a dramatic impact on the situation."

Johnson did not confine his efforts to counting noses. He actively lobbied the Republican leadership of both houses, inviting Ev Dirksen to breakfast at the White House on Wednesday, December 4. "Now he is the president—my president—and words can never be put in his mouth," Dirksen told the *Chicago Tribune*. "So now I can tell you only that he contacted me, not what he said." It was Charlie Halleck's turn to break bread the next day, and since Johnson was still living at the Elms, just a few blocks from Halleck's own house in Spring Valley, he stopped to pick up the minority leader for the morning ride downtown together in the presidential limousine, with motorcycle escort, flashing lights, and sirens—"quite a little trip," Halleck would recall. The ride was followed by a hearty meal, with "thick bacon—the kind he knew a fellow from Indiana would like," Halleck told reporters.

The president also met with the leadership of both the AFL-CIO and the Business Advisory Council on December 4, telling the latter that he knew there were many Republicans among them, and that if the civil rights bill did not get out of the Rules Committee, "it's going to be right in the Republicans' lap." And he warned them: "I am the only president you have; if you would have me fail, then you fail, for the country fails."

Halleck and Bill McCulloch had made it plain that they opposed the discharge petition, again out of fealty to seniority and a reluctance to second-guess a chairman's wishes, even one of the opposite party. A discharge petition was, indeed, a drastic step. Since 1932, when the prevailing discharge rule was adopted, 333 motions to discharge bills from committee had been filed. Of those, only thirty-two had received enough votes to be placed on the House calendar, fourteen had passed the House, and just two became law. "This move for a petition is irritating some people who materially helped rescue the civil rights legislation from the sticky morass in which partisan political considerations had apparently placed it," McCulloch complained.

But one of McCulloch's fellow Ohio Republicans was providing Johnson—and H.R. 7152—with some quiet help of his own.

Representative Clarence Brown, a gruff former newspaper publisher and a stalwart conservative, was the ranking Republican on the Rules Committee. He was also a close friend of McCulloch, whose district adjoined his own. Like McCulloch, Brown had long supported civil rights, and he had two historic black colleges—Wilberforce and Central State—in his district. On the evening of December 4, Brown stopped by Judge Smith's office to serve notice that he had enough Republican votes on the committee to trigger the option Smith had always feared most: to force him to hold a hearing. "I don't want to run over you, Judge, but . . . ," Brown said. That is all he said, but Smith knew what he meant. The next day, the chairman announced that the Rules Committee would begin hearings "reasonably soon."

That same day, December 5, Johnson turned his attention to the chairman of the Senate Finance Committee, Harry Byrd of Virginia, who was being just as stubborn about the tax bill pending in his committee as Smith was about the civil rights bill in his. Byrd, elfin and rosy-cheeked, was invariably courtly and so perpetually soft-spoken that listeners often had to strain to hear him. But he was also an implacable racist who, once spying Joseph Rauh and Clarence Mitchell in the Senate gallery, had shaken his fist at them and exclaimed of the longtime civil rights lobbyists, "There they are—the Gold Dust twins!" That was a reference to the crude, caricatured tutu-wearing black twins who had once adorned the label of a popular scouring powder. Byrd was wealthy—he owned the nation's largest private apple orchards—and a fierce fiscal conservative. He was adamantly opposed to John Kennedy's proposed tax cut, and appalled at the prospect of a federal budget that was set to exceed $100 billion for the coming year.

But Harry Byrd was something else as well: he was one of those powerful older men whom Lyndon Johnson had worked so hard to cultivate in his Senate days, and whom he would now court as never before. Whereas Jack Kennedy had complained that negotiating with the immovable Byrd was "a pillow fight in the dark," Johnson was able to get Byrd to do what no one else had been able to do: let the tax bill move along through his committee, despite his personal opposition. Byrd's price: a solemn promise from the president to bring in the federal budget at under $100 billion.

In all these fevered early days of consultation and conversation, of strategizing and nose counting about the civil rights bill, there was one person intimately involved in the effort to pass it to whom Lyndon Johnson did not talk—indeed, to whom he would not talk even once, for the whole month of December, and well beyond: the attorney general, *his* attorney general, Robert Francis Kennedy.

* * *

As REGARDED CIVIL RIGHTS, there was a bitter twist in Johnson's rift with Bob Kennedy. Both men had come slowly to the cause and both were now passionately committed to it. But by late November 1963, there was so much accumulated mutual distrust, enmity, and—in Johnson's case—fear between them that neither could fully appreciate the other's concern. Their division became one of the defining political realities of the decade, and the comedian David Frye, a demon mimic of both, would imitate Kennedy by saying, "Despite what you've heard, Lyndon Johnson and myself are becoming like brothers: Cain and Abel."

They were as unlike as two people could be, and their mutual ill will went back to at least 1955, when Ambassador Joseph P. Kennedy had offered to finance a 1956 presidential campaign for Johnson, if he would take Jack Kennedy as his running mate. Johnson politely declined, assuming that the elder Kennedy's real calculus was that any Democrat would lose to Dwight Eisenhower and thus a Johnson defeat would pave the way for his son's own candidacy in 1960. But Bob Kennedy never forgave what he regarded as a slight, and matters were not improved four years later, when Bob was sent to the LBJ ranch to sound out Johnson on his intentions for 1960. Embarking on a deer hunt, Johnson handed Bobby a powerful shotgun, whose kick knocked Kennedy to the ground. "Son, you've got to learn to handle a gun like a man," Johnson drawled.

Black Robert would seek his revenge at the Democratic National

Convention in Los Angeles on July 14, 1960, when he spent the better part of a day trying to get Johnson to give up the No. 2 spot on the ticket that his older brother had just held out. To the end of his life, Bob would maintain that Jack had merely offered the vice presidential nomination as a courtesy, never expecting Johnson to take it. In fact, John Kennedy's own actions made evident that he wanted Johnson—who could help carry Texas—and was worried about making a firm offer that Johnson could then embarrass him by rejecting. The precise sequence of events has been in dispute for more than half a century, but the outcome was clear: Lyndon Johnson became John Kennedy's running mate but never forgot that Bob Kennedy had tried to humiliate him by taking the prize away. For his part, Bob Kennedy would always remember that a prominent Johnson supporter—referencing his brother's serious but undisclosed health problems (he suffered from the life-threatening adrenal insufficiency known as Addison's disease)—had called John Kennedy a "spavined hunchback," or that Johnson himself had referred to Joseph P. Kennedy as a "Chamberlain umbrella man."

The distrust would only grow after John Kennedy won the presidency. Mindful of the enormous power Lyndon Johnson had wielded as Senate majority leader—for the last half of the 1950s, second only to that of President Eisenhower himself—President Kennedy went out of his way to treat Johnson with public respect, making sure that he and Lady Bird were invited to official state functions. But real chemistry was elusive—their Boston-Austin styles were so different—and the Johnsons were sometimes left off the list when the Kennedys held glamorous private dinner dances for friends. On February 20, 1962, as the president and vice president watched television coverage of John Glenn's historic orbital space flight, Johnson was heard to mutter, "If only John Glenn were a Negro!" It became one of the president's favorite stories, an example of how Johnson was always counting votes and playing angles.

As for substance, Kennedy denied Johnson's request to become the first vice president in history to have an office next to his in the West Wing (though he did give him one in the adjoining Executive Office Building, which gave Johnson a leg up on Richard Nixon, whose only vice presidential office had been in the Capitol). The president simply ignored Johnson's even bolder proposal for an executive order that would put the vice president in general charge of defense and space programs. The two assignments the president did give Johnson, the chairmanships of the National Space Council and the President's Committee on Equal Employment Opportunity, were not as impressive as they sounded on paper, since the first panel was purely advisory and the second mostly toothless.

During the Cuban Missile Crisis, in October 1962, Johnson had, at almost every turn, advocated the opposite course from the one that Kennedy ultimately took. He had opposed the idea of a naval blockade, favoring surprise airstrikes instead. He also opposed the secret deal that ended the crisis, in which Soviet missiles were withdrawn from Cuba in exchange for the withdrawal of outmoded American missiles from Turkey, and he was pointedly excluded from the crucial meeting of the president's advisers at which the final strategy was set.

By the spring and early summer of 1963, with pressure building on the administration for action on civil rights, the attorney general twice burst into meetings of Johnson's Committee on Equal Employment Opportunity, rattling off skeptical questions about why it had not succeeded in producing more jobs for blacks across the South and, at the second meeting on July 18, walking out while Johnson was trying to answer his questions and explain the committee's record.

None of these encounters, grim as they were for Johnson, could compare with the bitter tensions that now erupted in the wake of the assassination. Bob Kennedy was incensed that Johnson had thoughtlessly telephoned him—and not some legal functionary—about the requirements for being sworn in as president aboard Air Force One before leaving Dallas, and resentful that Johnson had later insisted that the swearing-in had been performed at the attorney general's insistence. Johnson, in turn, was insulted and confused that when the presidential plane landed at Andrews Air Force Base, the attorney general rushed aboard in shock and ran past him to Jacqueline Kennedy without so much as a greeting. There was a contretemps over precisely when Johnson should occupy the Oval Office for his official business. (He ultimately waited three days.) When the new president held his first Cabinet meeting the day after the assassination, Kennedy at first resisted attending, then insisted there be no photographs during the meeting.

Finally, on the afternoon of November 27, just after Johnson had finished his address to Congress, he invited the attorney general to the Oval Office in an attempt to air their differences. "You can't let your people talk about me and I won't talk about you," Johnson said. The encounter was awkward and tense and resolved nothing, and the two men would not meet again for nearly two months. In the interim, Johnson reached out to intermediaries. On December 11, the president telephoned Ken O'Donnell to ask "what we can do about Bobby."

"Tell me, and it won't ever come from you," Johnson implored. "But we don't know. And ignorance is a terrible thing. If you were down in Texas trying to shoot a deer, you might need a little knowledge from us. So we *need* some of these things."

"During all of that period, I think [Bobby] seriously considered whether he would let me be president, whether he should really take the position [that] the vice president didn't automatically move in," Johnson would recall, with obvious hyperbole. For his part, Bob Kennedy would recall, "Our president was a gentleman and a human being . . . This man is not . . . He's mean, bitter, vicious—an animal in many ways. You know, as I say, I think his reaction on a lot of things is correct, but I think he's got this other side of him in his relationships with human beings which makes it very difficult, unless you want to kiss his behind all the time."

* * *

JOHNSON LIKED HAVING HIS behind kissed as much as anyone—and probably more than most—but it was his own kissing up to others that was paying off as his presidency took root. On December 13, he assured Harry Byrd that he was "working on my budget every night," and promised to "get you a budget I think you'll be proud of," so the Finance Committee could move the tax bill to the floor. "You bother me any time," Johnson told Byrd. "You help me, though, get that bill out. I know you're against it, but you're a good chairman and you help them vote. You're tired of this talking yourself."

Byrd responded with a single word: "Right!"

And five days later, on December 18, Howard Smith announced that he had scheduled hearings on the civil rights bill in the House Rules Committee, to begin January 9 and to be finished by the end of the month.

But before Congress could wrap up business for the year, a new crisis arose. Both houses had passed separate versions of a long-pending $3 billion foreign aid appropriations bill, and the final conference report reconciling them was pending in the House on Saturday, December 21, with many Democratic members having already begun drifting out of town in anticipation of the Christmas recess. As if to make peace with his conservative critics in light of his civil rights compromise, Charlie Halleck took advantage of the moment to vote down a provision that would have given the president discretion to allow the Export-Import Bank to provide credit guarantees for private grain sales to Communist countries. An unnamed White House source told the columnist Mary McGrory that Halleck's move was an attempt by the "Midwest isolationist wing" of the Republican Party to "impose its will upon the foreign policy of the United States."

The president canceled plans to fly to his Texas ranch and spent that Saturday afternoon on the phone rounding up absent members for a second vote—to be taken two days later, on Monday, December 23, in what turned out to be the midst of a snowstorm that delayed trains and planes throughout the mid-Atlantic region. But when the Monday vote came, another procedural hurdle loomed. Because the measure had not "rested on the speaker's desk" for the required twenty-four hours, it would need a two-thirds majority to pass on this day, and it failed.

"Well, I'll be damned," Johnson exclaimed when Larry O'Brien called him with the news. Johnson had already resolved to take the extraordinary step of holding the House over for a revote the next day, Christmas Eve, when only a simple majority would be required. And he had also decided to invite every member of the House and Senate who was still in town over to the White House for a bourbon and eggnog reception early that evening. "Bird, let's have Congress over tonight!" he had called out to the First Lady.

O'Brien and other aides were skeptical of such a last-minute charm offensive, but the president pressed ahead. "I don't care if only twenty come," he told Carl Albert, and he warned O'Brien, "You be damn sure you're there to introduce them."

In the end, more than two hundred members showed up for the five o'clock party in the East Room, just as the black crepe of mourning for John Kennedy was coming down after thirty days and Christmas greenery was going up. Johnson himself lit a Yule log in the fireplace, then climbed up on a gilt chair.

"Your attention, please," the president said, as he proceeded to apologize to Charlie Halleck, "if anyone down here said anything ugly about you." He praised the legislators who had "labored through the vineyard and plowed through the snow" to vote. "We're Americans first," the president said. "I hope we can disagree without being too disagreeable."

The House passed the foreign aid bill the next morning, in a special 7:00 a.m. meeting, ending the longest peacetime session of Congress in American history to that point. "At that moment," Johnson would later recall, "the power of the Federal government began flowing back to the White House." A year-end *Newsweek* poll found that the public blamed Congress by a margin of two to one for the partisan gridlock, while support for the civil rights bill stood at 62 percent.

* * *

ON THE AFTERNOON OF the congressional reception, Johnson was feeling expansive. He had summoned the celebrity hairdresser and makeup artist Eddie Senz from New York to work on his wife and daughters—and his secretaries to boot—all the while pleading for a reduced price, saying, "I'm a poor man; I don't make much money." (His estimated net worth was $14 million, or roughly $100 million in today's currency.) "Now, bring whoever you need and we'll pay their transportation," the president told the stylist, "but we can't pay you much else." After Senz arrived, Johnson called Lady Bird in the White House residence to check up on his progress, asking especially about one of his secretaries, Yolanda Boozer. "She's got to have about a bale cut off if I'm going to look at her through Christmas," Johnson declared.

Meantime, the president had it in mind to strike another visible blow for civil rights. For some time, he had had his eye on Geraldine Whit-

tington, an attractive young black secretary in the office of Ralph Dungan, who had handled political appointments and Latin American policy
for John Kennedy. Now, just before ten o'clock on this snowy Monday
night, he telephoned Whittington at her home in distant Northeast
Washington, across the Anacostia River, with a proposal.

"Gerri, where are you?" the president called out into the receiver.
"Gerri?"

"Hello?" Whittington replied.

"Where are you?" the president repeated.

"I'm at home. Who's this?"

"This is the president."

"Oh!"

"What are you doing?"

"Oh, I think someone's playing with me," Whittington replied in a
soft, cultured voice.

"No, no, they're not," Johnson insisted. "I want to talk to you about
our work, honey. Where are you—at home?"

"Oh, yes, I am."

"Are you busy?"

"No, I'm not."

"Can you come down here immediately?"

"Oh, I'd be glad to."

"Come on down. I've got Jack Valenti and we want to talk to you
about a little reassignment."

"Oh, yes, sir."

"If you need a car sent out for you, I'll get one, but you can get a cab
quicker, can't you?"

"Well, as a rule I can, Mr. President, but inasmuch as the weather
is so . . ."

Whittington gave her address and phone number and the president
continued, "All right . . . He ought to be there in fifteen minutes. How far
are you away from the White House?"

"Oh, I guess about twenty-five minutes."

"Twenty-five minutes!"

"Yes."

"That's a hell of a long way. Do you walk to work?"

"No, sir, I don't," Whittington giggled.

"Okay, get ready now and get your walking clothes on."

Unable to contain his enthusiasm until Whittington arrived, Johnson called his assistant press secretary Andy Hatcher at 10:15 to announce his intention to hire Whittington and ask about her references.

"She's got good character? Good ability? . . . Respected by all her employees?" the president asked. Assured that the answers were all yes, Johnson then telephoned Roy Wilkins and Whitney Young to share the news. (A month later, Johnson would arrange to announce Whittington's hiring to the nation at large by having her appear—along with an "all-girl" orchestra leader, a bird seed salesman, and the actor Van Heflin—on the popular Sunday night CBS game show *What's My Line?* in which panelists tried to guess a contestant's occupation.)

At 11:00 p.m., Whittington finally arrived outside the Oval Office to find the president, Jack Valenti, Walter Jenkins, and Cliff Carter in a discussion that suggested the president might need some fresh administrative help, as Johnson complained bitterly about misspelled names in official correspondence. "These dumbbells! Who in the hell?" he spat.

Valenti interrupted. "That girl is here—Gerri Wilkerson, or whatever her name is."

"I want to talk to her, and keep everybody else out of here," Johnson replied, adding, "Now listen, it's Gerri *Whittington* . . ."

"Come in, honey," the president said. "Pull up a chair."

Shortly afterward, Johnson telephoned two of his other secretaries, Juanita Roberts and Marie Fehmer, presumably to arrange for Whittington's hiring. The following morning he upended his newest secretary's plans for a quiet holiday with her mother, whisking her off instead to Philadelphia for the funeral of Congressman William Green and then on to the LBJ ranch for the holidays.

A week later, on New Year's Eve, with Lady Bird resting at the ranch with her relatives, the president took Fehmer, Whittington, and a third secretary, Vicki McCammon, off to Austin by helicopter for a round of parties, including a cocktail reception for his aide Horace Busby at the Forty Acres Club, the faculty club at the University of Texas. A group of professors had been boycotting the club because of its rigid segregationist policy, so just before his entourage entered, the president slipped Gerri Whittington's arm through his.

"Does the president know what he's doing?" E. Ernest Goldstein, a Texas law professor, asked Bill Moyers.

"He always knows what he's doing," Moyers answered.

Whittington herself asked the president the same question. "I sure do," he replied.

On January 2, 1964, when a still stunned Goldstein called the club to make sure it would be all right if *he* brought black guests, the answer was clear: "Yes, sir. The President of the United States integrated us on New Year's Eve."

7

A Great Big Vote

LYNDON JOHNSON RANKED AMONG the most stubborn and prideful of men, but in pressing for the civil rights bill, he humbled himself in striking ways. Just days after John Kennedy's funeral, he had reached out to one of his most vocal critics, Joseph Rauh, one of the founders of Americans for Democratic Action and the general counsel of the Leadership Conference on Civil Rights. As a delegate to the 1960 Democratic Convention, Rauh had jumped to his feet in anger at the news that Kennedy had chosen Johnson as his running mate, shouting in full view of television cameras, "Jack! Don't do it, Jack!" But in early December 1963, a stunned Rauh got a call from the White House, inviting him to accompany the president to the funeral of former governor and senator Herbert Lehman of New York—a rapprochement so striking that it prompted a front-page story in the *Washington Post*.

"If I've done anything wrong in the past," Johnson told Rauh in a subsequent White House meeting, "I want you to know that's nothing now—we're going to work together."

Now, on this January morning, Rauh was in the Oval Office, and with Johnson's permission, he had brought with him an equally skeptical colleague: Clarence Mitchell of the NAACP. "Johnson had been dealing with me on the legislation, and I knew that wasn't right," Rauh would recall. "Clarence Mitchell was the leading civil rights lobbyist and it would only work if Johnson treated him so."

Two more different personalities could hardly be imagined than Clarence Mitchell and Joe Rauh. Rauh was a fiery, fast-talking Harvard-trained lawyer who had first come to Washington during the New Deal, had drafted the executive order that created the Fair Employment Practices Commission, had battled McCarthyism, and had stood perpetually on the ramparts for nearly all of the post–World War II liberal causes. Mitchell was a courtly former newspaper reporter for the *Baltimore Afro-American* who had recently earned a night school law degree from the University of Maryland after years of working for the NAACP. He still commuted daily to Washington from Baltimore and was such a tireless and ubiquitous advocate in the corridors of Capitol Hill that he would come to be known as "the 101st senator," at a time when there were no black men in that body. In his personal attitude, and on issues other than civil rights, Mitchell was essentially a conservative, and Rauh liked to tease him by saying, "Clarence, if you were white, you would be a reactionary."

Mitchell and Rauh had tangled with Johnson over his watering-down of the 1957 and 1960 laws. Now, however, the president offered a pleasant surprise. While he acknowledged that he would oppose any efforts to strengthen H.R. 7152 in the House—honoring the Kennedy administration's compromise with Bill McCulloch the previous fall—the new president also assured his visitors that he would not brook weakening the bill in the Senate, either.

"I don't care how long it takes," Johnson said. "I don't care if the Senate doesn't do one other piece of business this year, you've got to keep this bill on the floor . . . You can tell anybody, the President of the United States doesn't care if this bill is there forever. We are not going to have anything else hit the Senate floor until this bill is passed."

For the moment, the challenge remained to get the bill out of the House Rules Committee, which was currently holding its fifth hearing on H.R. 7152 under Judge Smith's stubborn, slow-walking command. The chairman had begun his promised review on January 9, around a big table in the committee's compact hearing room, H-313, on the House side of the Capitol. He pronounced the bill "as full of booby traps as a dog is full of fleas."

Manny Celler, testifying that same day in support of the bill, was more accurate in summing up the prevailing feeling about the civil rights movement, and by implication the bill, when he told Smith, "You can no more stop it than you can stop the tide . . . The die is cast, the movement cannot be stayed."

Indeed, the day before Johnson's meeting with Mitchell and Rauh, the president's chief congressional nose counter, Larry O'Brien, had told him that there appeared to be 220 House members in support of the bill's passage, two more than needed for a discharge petition to succeed, and for the bill to pass. So pressure was building on the eighty-year-old Judge Smith, who had begun to renege on his pledge to hold expeditious hearings and was instead dragging them out in a last stand.

"He was a fox," Representative John Dingell of Michigan would recall. "His great skill was to make you think he was agreeing with you and that you had a commitment, which you never did. And so everybody would think they had a deal with him, and they didn't."

John Lindsay's aide Robert Kimball, who had been assigned to shadow Smith's hearings, got another perspective when he ran into the judge in a hallway one day as the hearings approached. "He thought he was too old to be doing it and others should step up," Kimball would recall. "The judge knew that they were going to be beaten and he had to go down fighting. He said to me, 'You're going to run over us.'"

Smith's reaction to his anticipated defeat was to torture his witnesses all the more. When Bill McCulloch testified on January 15 that the bill was "comprehensive in scope but moderate in application," Smith demanded to know who had written the compromise version. "I assisted in writing this bill," McCulloch replied, adding that "staff people on the Judiciary Committee participated in redrafting this bill, duly constituted and appointed and confirmed people in the Department of Justice helped write the bill—the same general people who often help in writing difficult and technical bills which are considered by the Judiciary Committee." With this careful phrasing, McCulloch glossed lightly over the crucial roles played by Burke Marshall and Nick Katzenbach, which was what Smith was driving at in the first place. When Smith asked how it was that the Judiciary Committee had allowed McCulloch a "whole minute" to explain the bill before the lightning-fast vote in October, McCulloch just smiled and said, "Because of my receding red hair."

Smith bearded McCulloch about the seeming unfairness of hotel barbershops being covered by the law while independent ones would not be. McCulloch replied by citing the case of a black Ohioan who had recently successfully sued a barber under a seventy-five-year-old state antidiscrimination law, only to have Smith rejoin, "They do strange things in Ohio." McCulloch then simply quoted from "The Present Crisis," James Russell Lowell's nineteenth-century antislavery poem:

> New occasions teach new duties
> Time makes ancient good uncouth
> They must upward still and onward
> Who would keep abreast of truth.

If Howard Smith was on the ropes, Lyndon Johnson was leaving nothing to chance with the House Republican leadership. Having already worked over Charlie Halleck at their bacon breakfast in December, he quickly turned to the subject of the NASA research center that Halleck wanted to secure for his district at Purdue University—the very subject that Halleck had hoped to broach with Jack Kennedy after his return from Texas. "I'm sitting here with Charlie Halleck and he's breathing down my neck," Johnson told NASA administrator James Webb over the telephone on Saturday, January 18, with Halleck by his side. "He wants to know what he can tell his people when he's running for reelection that he's done for them lately, and he wants to know what we *can* do for Purdue."

"Let me talk with him and see if he and I can work out something that he'll come back to you and tell you he's pleased with," Webb replied.

"If he's not satisfied when he comes back to me, why, then, I'm going to be talking to you again," the president warned.

Now, three days later and just hours after his meeting with Mitchell and Rauh, Johnson was on the phone again with Webb, who told the president he had met that very morning with Halleck and suggested that, with Halleck's help in the House, NASA might be able to finance a building to the tune of some $750,000—along with a series of research grants (for which he noted Purdue was well suited)—that might amount to an additional $300,000 or $400,000, spread over three years. "The net effect, Mr. President," Webb added, "is that if you tell him that you're willing to follow this policy as long as he cooperates, I can implement it on an installment basis. In other words, the minute he kicks over the traces, we stop the installment."

"All right," Johnson replied.

And it just so happened that two days later, the Republicans on the House Rules Committee, led by the ranking member, Clarence Brown of Ohio, let it be known that they were consulting with their party's leaders and with their Democratic counterparts about lighting a fire under Judge Smith. Before the day was out, the chairman had capitulated. "I am opposed to the speedup just as I am opposed to the bill," Smith announced. But he nevertheless added that the hearings would end with an up-or-down vote a week hence, on Thursday, January 30.

For Clarence Mitchell, the assistance rendered by otherwise conservative pro-civil-rights Republicans like Clarence Brown and Bill McCulloch was heartening proof of a lesson he had learned the hard way—that it was wrong to "cram people into tight molds." Brown's decency had helped Mitchell to "see many members of Congress in a new light," he would recall. As the most prominent black lobbyist before a Congress that still had just five black members, Mitchell was forced to be resourceful and resilient in seeking support, and in taking it where he could find it. His own life's challenging path had helped him sharpen just such skills.

* * *

CLARENCE MITCHELL JR. WAS born into genteel poverty in Baltimore in 1911, in a family that would total ten children. His father, Clarence Maurice Mitchell, was a talented musician (he played guitar, violin, and piano) and in a bigger town or less racist era might have made a career of those skills. But he had to settle for work as a waiter at the elegant Rennert Hotel. Mitchell's mother, Elsie, took in laundry and table boarders to help make ends meet, and for the rest of his life Clarence despised fish and cabbage, because he associated their smell with the big pots his mother had on the stove next to her laundry water. Young Clarence himself worked virtually full time from his earliest days. He delivered ice and coal, worked in a confectionery store, and served as an overnight elevator operator at the Rennert, finishing his shift at 8:00 a.m., just in time to get to high school.

In 1928, though he could barely afford it, Mitchell arrived at Lincoln University in Oxford, Pennsylvania. Founded in 1854 as a refuge for runaway slaves, Lincoln had produced legions of black doctors, lawyers, legislators, and other professionals, and by the time Mitchell enrolled it was known as "the black Princeton." Mitchell earned tuition money by working one summer season as a busboy at the all-white Gibson Island Club on Chesapeake Bay—alongside a fellow Baltimorean named Thurgood Marshall, whose father was the club's headwaiter.

Graduating in the depths of the Depression, Mitchell decided there was little immediate promise in trying to pursue a profession that might otherwise have interested him—such as the law—since even most lawyers seemed to be struggling. So instead he accepted a $15-a-week job as a reporter for the *Baltimore Afro-American*. His first big assignment was to cover the aftermath of a notorious lynching in Princess Anne, Maryland, on the Eastern Shore. The case involved a twenty-two-year-old "feeble-minded" black man named George Armwood, who had been accused of attempted assault on an elderly white woman and was seized from jail by a mob of a thousand and beaten and hanged.

Mitchell missed the actual murder, but he arrived the next morning in time to see Armwood's scorched and blackened corpse with one ear missing "and his tongue between his clenched teeth," in a sign of "his great agony before death," as Mitchell would write in the *Afro-American*. He would never forget the sight. "When you see a fellow human being with a rope around his neck, and skin coming off his body," he said, "you don't need to add any touches of horror." Mitchell would later travel to Alabama to cover one of the trials of the Scottsboro Boys, nine black youths accused of raping two white women in 1931. The Jim Crow justice system's infamous mistreatment of the young defendants helped build support for the modern civil rights movement.

But Mitchell wanted a job more stable than newspaper reporting, and he applied for an Urban League fellowship for graduate study at the Atlanta School for Social Work. He ultimately became executive director of the League's office in St. Paul, Minnesota, and in 1941 he returned east, to work in various federal agencies during World War II, including the Fair Employment Practices Commission. In 1946 he joined the Washington bureau of the NAACP and became its director and chief lobbyist in 1950—a job he would hold for the next twenty-eight years.

Lobbying on behalf of civil rights legislation required sacrifice, persistence, and infinite patience with mundane details and the smallest signs of progress. Mitchell was well suited to the task. "When I began working for the NAACP, we had periods of great financial difficulties," he would recall. "It was usually after some awful crime that our finances would improve. Someone observed that the persons who believed in civil rights were not moved to fight or work except in times of emotional distress. I think this is true of many humans."

Mitchell had been a driving force in the Eisenhower administration's advocacy of the 1957 and 1960 civil rights bills. With his carefully trimmed mustache, dignified bearing, and scratchy border-state twang, he virtually lived on Capitol Hill, and he had made it a point to cultivate civil relationships with even some of the most implacable southern segregationists.

Andrew Biemiller, the AFL-CIO's longtime chief lobbyist, would recall that he hardly ever went to Capitol Hill without running into Mitchell, so constant was his presence there. "He was a very busy guy. I don't know where he got all that energy," Biemiller said. Trim and athletic in his youth, by 1964 Mitchell was a bit overweight. "In the summer, I've got this picture of Clarence bursting into your office, tie a bit loose, shirt out, mopping his brow, cursing the Southern Democrats," Hubert Humphrey's legislative director John Stewart would recall. "He sure kept you honest. You weren't going to get away with anything with Clarence."

Mitchell endured regular indignities in his daily work. Nearly every time he testified before the Senate Judiciary Committee, its chairman, James Eastland, would arrange to be absent. On one occasion when Eastland was present and Mitchell had been waiting through testimony by other witnesses, the chairman simply called out, "Anybody else wants to testify?" to avoid having to utter the words "Mr. Mitchell."

Mitchell's method for dealing with such treatment was to make sure his own conduct was above reproach. Joe Rauh would remember one occasion when he and Mitchell were about to cross a street in Washington, and as Rauh began to step into the intersection before the light had turned green, he felt Mitchell's hand making him wait. "Being Clarence's fellow traveler down the halls of Congress forty years hasn't been so damn easy," Rauh would recall. "First this guy walks so fast and so far I can't keep up with him. Around noon, I get hungry and he doesn't eat; at about late afternoon, I want a drink and he doesn't drink." But Mitchell could also "get very emotional," John Stewart would recall. Rauh thought he was "the ideal lobbyist, in the sense that he never boiled over, but he was able to boil over when the situation called for boiling over. He had the patience of Job, but knew when the right moment had come to substitute eloquent anger for patience."

When Mitchell encountered Manny Celler in the corridor of a House office building after the Judiciary Committee passed the compromise civil rights bill in October, the chairman asked, "Well, Clarence, is your tail between your legs?"

"No, Mr. Celler," Mitchell snapped back. "I wish my teeth were in somebody's pants. I'm not the kind of dog that keeps its tail between its legs."

In a taxi on the way back to the NAACP's offices that day, Mitchell slumped back in his seat, a colleague would recall, and "with a wry smile" said, "I resent being treated like a fool."

* * *

ON JANUARY 30, AT the Rules Committee's tenth hearing on H.R. 7152, Howard Smith at last gave up the ghost. He was well aware that the Republicans were eager to get the bill onto the House floor and disposed of in time for them to fan out for the party's traditional Lincoln's Birthday round of speeches and fundraisers on February 12. (Lyndon Johnson knew that, too, and had warned Charlie Halleck, "If I were you, Charlie, I wouldn't dare [go out] and try to make a Lincoln Birthday speech that'll laugh you out of the goddamned park when Howard Smith's got his foot on Lincoln's neck.")

As he had promised the week before, on this day, Smith reluctantly called for a vote on Resolution 616, the measure setting the ground rules for House debate of H.R. 7152. "The question is," he said in his hard-to-hear Virginia drawl, "shall the resolution pass?" The vote was 11 to 4, with only the committee's diehard southern Democrats in opposition. Now it was the whole House's turn.

At noon on Friday, January 31—with the galleries packed with the bill's supporters, including Katzenbach, Marshall, Rauh, and Mitchell— the House of Representatives convened in its marble-trimmed, wood-paneled chamber, its upper reaches papered in a blue-green shade of silk brocade, with bas-reliefs of famous lawgivers from Moses to Thomas Jefferson staring down from on high. The session began with a prayer from the House chaplain, the Reverend Bernard Braskamp, who quoted from Saint Paul's letter to the Galatians: "As we have therefore opportunity, let us do good to all men." The majority leader, Carl Albert of Oklahoma, promptly noted the absence of a quorum (or 218 members, half the body), and the three bells of a quorum call rang out throughout the Capitol and the two adjacent House office buildings as members began streaming into the chamber.

Ray Madden, Democrat of Indiana, presented Resolution 616, the Rules Committee's road map for consideration of H.R. 7152, which called for ten hours of floor debate, evenly divided between the two parties, with members eligible to speak for five minutes on any proposed amendment. Madden noted a fact that Clarence Mitchell must have found gratifying, if long overdue: the bill was the first legislation to come before the

Congress with provisions "almost identical with the platforms of the two major parties" in the 1960 presidential election.

Clarence Brown of Ohio appealed to his colleagues to "conduct this debate on so high a plane that we can at least say to our children and grandchildren, we participated in one of the great debates of modern American history, and we did it as statesmen and not as quarreling individuals." He pledged that the bipartisan leadership had agreed that every member of the House who might wish to do so would be allowed to offer any amendment he or she wished. But William Colmer of Mississippi was having none of that. "What is the rush?" he demanded. "I ask, Mr. Speaker, is all this done out of fear? Is the Congress of the United States to yield to threats of further demonstrations by minority group leaders— blackmail, if you please? . . . To what end will this bring us? Is the Congress to comply by legislation with the demands and even riots of every organized minority group in the country?"

Resolution 616, authorizing the terms for debate, passed overwhelmingly on a voice vote.

Now it was time for the debate itself. Manny Celler, as the bill's floor leader, moved that the House resolve itself in a "Committee of the Whole," to permit general discussion and the offering of amendments. This practice dated back to the early days of the British Parliament, when members wanted to get the speaker of the House of Commons out of the chamber during consideration of bills, as political power shifted from the monarchy to the elected assembly, and the speaker's role evolved from being the monarch's spokesman into becoming the spokesman for the House. The House of Representatives had conducted debate on major legislation in the same way since the time of the Founders. Celler's motion was approved, and the debate began.

Armed with voluminous notebooks of background material prepared by his Judiciary Committee staff and the Justice Department lawyers, Celler said that H.R. 7152 "bestows no preferences on any one group."

"What it does," he added, "is to place into balance the scales of justice so that the living force of our Constitution shall apply to all people, not only to those who by accident of birth were born with white skins."

Bill McCulloch spoke next, answering a charge from Colmer that the bill was being rushed, by insisting, "Not force or fear . . . but the belief in the inherent quality of man induces me to support this legislation . . . No one would suggest that the Negro receives equality of treatment and opportunity in many fields of activity today . . . Hundreds of thousands of citizens are denied the basic right to vote. Thousands of school districts remain segregated. Decent hotel and eating accommodations frequently lie hundreds of miles apart for the Negro traveler . . . These and many more such conditions point the way toward the need for additional legislation . . . This bill is comprehensive in scope yet moderate in application. It is hedged about with effective administrative and legal safeguards."

But Representative Ed Willis of Louisiana countered that the bill was "the most drastic and far-reaching proposal and grab for power ever to be reported out of a committee of the Congress."

The battle was under way.

* * *

IF THE CHALLENGE IN the Judiciary Committee had been to keep the bill from being loaded up with strengthening amendments that would make it too hard to pass, the challenge on the House floor was to prevent it from being weakened by amendments from the segregationists. That would be no easy job, because the practical effect of the House's sitting as a Committee of the Whole was to permit members to vote on proposed amendments without having their votes recorded by name. And because just one hundred members constituted a quorum in the Committee of the Whole, a hostile amendment could easily be passed with a comparative handful of votes, unless enough pro-civil-rights members were present to block it. That required the pro-civil-rights forces to make sure there were sufficient numbers of pro-civil-rights members on the floor whenever a vote was near, to head off any attempted mischief. And *that* meant that Clarence Mitchell, Joe Rauh, and their allies would have to stake out the House galleries at all times, able to recognize members by face as they appeared. Moreover, because House rules prohibited note taking in the visitors' galleries, Mitchell and his team would have to remember the running tallies in their heads.

To carry out the effort, the Leadership Conference set up temporary headquarters in the dowdy Congressional Hotel across the street from the House office buildings on Capitol Hill, where the spotters convened each morning to review the lay of the land before the House went into session. To supplement his own work, Mitchell drafted about a dozen diligent young people to patrol the hallways of the Capitol and the two adjacent House office buildings, corralling friendly members who might be absent from the floor. They worked under the watchful eye of Jane O'Grady, an energetic twenty-four-year-old graduate student fresh from the University of California at Berkeley, with a master's degree in political sociology, who had come to Washington as a lobbyist for the Amalgamated Clothing and Textile Workers Union. Mitchell "was as patient and as kindly as could be," O'Grady would recall, "and he came up with things for us to do, even if we were not the most knowledgeable."

Each morning, O'Grady and her troops—who would quickly be dubbed "O'Grady's Raiders"—stationed themselves in the offices of sympathetic House members like Frank Thompson, the New Jersey Democrat who was leading the Democrats' efforts to corral votes. Thompson had been recruited for this task because the majority whip, Hale Boggs of Louisiana, was a southerner and could not afford to be seen as publicly supporting the bill, even though he was a close ally of Lyndon Johnson.

Thompson and his colleagues devised a buddy system in which seventeen pro-civil-rights members would each be responsible for knowing the whereabouts of about half a dozen others. Every time a vote seemed near, Thompson would initiate a telephone tree to spread the word. (In the recollection of Nick Katzenbach, Thompson also supplied "a great deal of liquor" to any members whose support might ever be wavering.)

Meantime, O'Grady and her raiders, waiting beside whatever telephone they could cadge from a friendly office receptionist, would be alerted by a pay phone call from the spotters in the gallery. They would then race from office to office, rounding up members from lunch breaks or visits to the gym—an army of human paging devices. "It was nuts, but I didn't know that then," O'Grady would recall years later. "I don't think it's ever even been replicated, because it was such a nutty idea." Like many another nutty idea, it would prove effective. "By the third or fourth day," she recalled, "you'd poke your head in and smile and say, 'Just checking.' And the secretaries would yell, 'He's all right! You don't have to come in here!'"

Tallying the floor votes on amendments was just as daunting. "Even if you sat and watched them from the gallery, it wasn't easy to tell how members were voting on amendments," Marvin Caplan, the executive director of the Leadership Conference, would later recall. That was because votes occurred in three possible ways. The chair would first ask for a simple voice vote on any amendment. If this proved inconclusive, members would then be asked to stand by turns, for or against the proposal. If fewer than one hundred members were present, any member could initiate a quorum call, bells would ring, and members would come pouring into the chamber from all over the Hill for a still more formal vote.

"The chair would designate 'tellers,' one for the amendment and one against," Caplan remembered. "All the members would then troop up the center aisle ('looks like a sheep's run,' one of our gallery watchers once remarked) while the tellers, standing opposite each other, would clap and count each shoulder as it passed under their hands and, in the end, call out the totals to the chair," with the ayes recorded first. From high above in the galleries, the spotters would have to keep track of these subtle movements and hope that the running tallies they were keeping in their heads were correct. Even journalists—the only spectators allowed to take notes—had a hard time being sure who was voting how, because, after voting, the members would walk up the center aisle toward the exit, with their backs to the press gallery behind them.

"This really aroused a lot of concern in Congress," Clarence Mitchell would recall. "So much so that we were asked to stop the notification process, and people promised if we stopped, they would be sure to stay on the floor. And then, of course, there were a few who said, 'How do you know how I voted? You're not supposed to make notes or write in the gallery.'"

Mitchell and his allies made this jerry-built system work in their favor, as even the segregationists acknowledged. James A. Haley, a Florida Democrat, contended that without the "vultures in the spectators galleries, who were controlling votes in the House, or at least calling the turn on them . . . I do not think you would have twenty-five votes for this monstrous bill."

* * *

DELIBERATIONS ON THE BILL resumed on Saturday morning, February 1, and stretched into the evening, with supporters and opponents offering general lines of defense and attack. Howard Smith condemned H.R. 7152's swift passage by the Judiciary Committee, and insisted, "The only hearings that were ever held on this bill were held over the protest of a great many people, before the Committee on Rules. Apparently, nobody who favored this bill wanted the people to know what was in it," or what "it proposes to do for 90 percent of the people of this country whose liberties are being infringed upon." He added, "What we are considering now is a . . . monstrosity of unknown origin and unknown parentage."

Manny Celler and Bill McCulloch both denied southern claims that they had agreed to oppose all amendments. In fact, they had resolved to allow any modifications that seemed constructive—even if offered by southerners—to preserve as much comity as possible. But it was true that they had privately vowed to stand in lockstep against any effort to water down the bill. At his news conference that same day, Lyndon Johnson offered a somewhat less ringing assurance when asked if he believed the bill would have to be weakened to pass the Senate. "No, I do not think it will have to be substantially trimmed," he said, "and, yes, I do expect a filibuster."

On Monday, February 3, discussion turned at last to the bill's first section. Each of H.R. 7152's major provisions had by now acquired the formal numerical "title" by which it would be known for the rest of its journey through the House and Senate, and Title I covered voting rights in federal elections. Dick Poff, a Virginia Democrat, proposed an amendment to give defendants in cases of alleged voting rights violations the same rights as the attorney general to request a hearing before a panel of three federal judges. In keeping with their strategy of accepting amendments that did not seriously weaken the bill, Celler and McCulloch backed the measure and it passed by a 100-to-68 standing vote. Another amendment, by Bill Cramer of Florida, to include Puerto Rico under the terms of the bill was also accepted.

But over the next two days, a half dozen hostile amendments were rejected by substantial margins, including one from Howard Smith that would have applied Title I's voting rights guarantees only to elections that were exclusively for federal offices. The bill's supporters noted that any state could then exempt itself from coverage merely by including a single nonfederal office on the ballot. The amendment was defeated by a 55-to-155 standing vote.

On Tuesday, February 4, debate moved on to Title II, the public accommodations section, long considered the most controversial part of the bill. For the pro-civil-rights forces, Title II's provisions would bring a long-overdue end to the humiliations and indignities of Jim Crow, the cruel apartheid that condemned blacks and whites to separate spheres in virtually all public places in the South. Indeed, as Bill McCulloch liked to note, for hundreds of years Anglo-Saxon common law had required innkeepers to serve anyone who could pay and whose person and decorum were seemly. But for the segregationists, Title II would usurp centuries of private property rights and commingle the races in intimate settings, in defiance of generations of accepted southern custom. It was—for both sides—the visceral, emotional heart of the bill.

As reported out of the Judiciary Committee, Title II barred discrimination in restaurants, soda fountains, hotels, theaters, and concert halls, while exempting the so-called Mrs. Murphy boardinghouses with five or fewer rooms for rent. Barbershops, retail stores, bowling alleys, and the like were not specifically covered unless they were inside or contained a covered business. So, for example, a hotel barbershop would be covered, as would a retail store that operated a lunch counter or restaurant.

The bill's critics contended that Title II would go so far as to equate private discrimination with state action. In response, Charles Goodell, a pro-civil-rights Republican from New York, offered an amendment intended to make the public accommodations section more palatable by changing the definition of discrimination that would be "supported" by state action and thus covered by the Fourteenth Amendment. The Judiciary Committee bill had barred discrimination that was "carried on under color of any law, statute, ordinance, regulation, custom or usage; or is required, fostered or encouraged by action of a state or a political subdivision thereof." Goodell proposed to add three crucial words, requiring that state or local discriminatory action be *"enforced by officials."* Goodell said his aim was to make it clear that there would have to be "some kind of action, some kind of *activity*," in support of discrimination, as was the case in many southern states where Jim Crow laws were still on the books. Ed Willis, Democrat of Louisiana, then offered an amendment to Goodell's amendment, striking the use of the broad word "fostered," leaving only the narrower terms "required" and "enforced." That had the effect of further restricting Title II's sweep—if only in a rhetorical way. Both amendments passed by voice vote after Justice Department officials let it be known that they did not believe these changes would substantively weaken the bill.

Such displays of bipartisan spirit did nothing to assuage the cantankerous Judge Smith. At one point, he erupted in fury that a podiatrist who happened to have an office in a hotel building would be covered by the act. "If I were cutting corns," Smith spat, "I would want to know whose feet I would have to be monkeying around with. I would want to know whether they smelled good or bad." (But this outburst never appeared in the *Congressional Record*; availing himself of every member's privilege to revise or extend his remarks for publication, Smith later had the comments stricken.)

Then Smith proposed a devious kind of "double-dog-dare-you" amendment, one motivated by deep cynicism but not without logical appeal: a provision that no one could be compelled to render labor or service without his consent—absolving a restaurant owner from serving blacks if he chose not to, for example. "This amendment merely implements the Thirteenth Amendment," which had barred slavery and involuntary servitude, Smith said. "See if you can vote against it. I defy you to do it." But defy him members did, and the measure failed, 107 to 149.

* * *

BY THE NEXT DAY, Wednesday, February 5, the segregationists knew they were losing the fight. Dick Poff of Virginia offered an amendment to exclude from the bill's provisions those establishments that were included only because they were in a covered facility (hotel barbershops, for example). It failed 70 to 123. A proposal by Bill Colmer to exempt *all* barbers and beauticians was defeated 69–114. But it was an amendment by George Meader, a Republican from Michigan, that had Bill McCulloch most worried. Meader proposed to limit Title II's coverage only to those businesses situated or advertised immediately adjacent to interstates or major roadways. Opponents argued that such a measure would cover only 7 percent of roads in the United States.

McCulloch gently upbraided his colleague. "He comes from Ann Arbor," McCulloch said. "If that great Michigan football team was on its way to Miami to play that great school down there in Florida, and a Negro family were traveling with them and could not get service in Ft. Lauderdale, Florida, what could be done? There is just no teeth in this amendment and it should be defeated." It was, 68 to 153.

Indeed, the pro-civil-rights forces were doing so well that many southerners had simply stopped showing up for the debate. F. Edward Hebert, a segregationist Democrat from Louisiana, went so far as to praise his worthy opponents. "You are here on the job," he said. "I disagree with you, but I respect you and I admire your courage and your determination to be here and be counted."

In fact, it was hard not to marvel at the bipartisan coalition that had now made it through three full days without any damaging amendments. Clarence Mitchell would recall especially the dogged persistence of his Ohio Republican namesake, Clarence Brown, who was enduring agonizing arthritis but "was always present on the floor to vote against crippling amendments." With a reassuring nod or wink, Brown would let Mitchell know the bill was on track. "He was waging a terrific battle just to stand erect, but his voice always rang out strong and clear," Mitchell remembered.

On Thursday, February 6, the bill's managers worked through Titles III (public facilities) and IV (public education), accepting a few non-threatening amendments but rejecting most. Then came Title V, the

Civil Rights Commission. The commission's mere existence had been a thorn in the segregationists' side since 1957. Now the persistent Ed Willis of Louisiana proposed that the commission not be required to investigate the membership practices of any "bona fide fraternal, religious or civic organization." Though neither Manny Celler nor Bill McCulloch entirely approved, to keep harmony with Willis, a Judiciary Committee colleague, they acceded. "I am interested in getting this bill passed," Celler said simply. The amendment passed on a voice vote.

McCulloch was more concerned when Byron Rogers, a Colorado Democrat, proposed to restore language from the Kennedy administration's original bill, extending the commission's life only for four years instead of making it permanent, as McCulloch and John Lindsay had insisted in their October compromise. This was a "particularly acute" issue, Robert Kimball would recall, and prompted concern that the Johnson administration might be waffling. But the issue did not seem central enough for McCulloch to dig in his heels, and he let the amendment pass on a voice vote.

* * *

A MUCH MORE SERIOUS drama—the tensest moment in the debate so far—erupted the next day, Friday, February 7, as the House moved to consider the bill's next section, Title VI, which allowed for the cutoff of federal funds to states and localities found to be practicing discrimination. This section, too, was loathed in the South, where segregationists feared it would be used broadly to punish local school districts. Representative D. R. Matthews of Florida called Title VI the "Let the Little Children Suffer Title," and demanded to know whether a class in an agricultural vocational school that put on a performance of *Othello* in blackface would lose federal aid, or whether a primary school class that sang Stephen Foster's words, "Darkies, how my heart grows weary," would risk losing its school milk subsidy.

Finally, just before 5:00 p.m., with debate growing hotter and the southerners clearly on the ropes, Democrat Oren Harris of Arkansas, the powerful chairman of the House Committee on Interstate and Foreign Commerce, offered a dramatic amendment that would have drastically changed Title VI and threatened the bill. He proposed to restore language from the Kennedy administration's original bill, which would merely have repealed provisions in existing federal law that permitted segregation in federally supported programs, and given the president discretionary authority to withhold funds from discriminatory programs. The administration's original language had also given the president the sole power to prescribe the conditions needed to assure nondiscrimination, and did not provide that the withholding of aid should be subject to review by the courts.

Bill McCulloch had insisted that any cutoff of funds be subject to judicial review as part of his compromise with the White House in October. Now Harris proposed to jettison that procedural safeguard, making the bill unpalatable to McCulloch and his like-minded colleagues, who wanted to be sure that such thorny questions could be aired in court and not decided by executive fiat.

The Harris amendment left the pro-civil-rights Republicans blindsided. Most astonishing of all, the Democratic majority whip, Hale Boggs, one of President Johnson's closest friends in Congress, who had not even appeared on the House floor during the debate so far, now rose to support Harris's proposal. The Republicans, led by John Lindsay, immediately cried foul. Lindsay leapt to his feet, calling the Harris amendment "the biggest mousetrap in a beautiful ribbon" that had been offered since debate on the bill began and insisting it would "gut" the bill.

"I am appalled that this is being supported in the well of the House by the Majority Whip," Lindsay exclaimed. "Does this mean there is a cave-in in this important title?" Lindsay and his allies worried that Boggs "was doing something at the behest of the leadership," and perhaps even of the president himself, Robert Kimball would recall.

Bill McCulloch had been off the floor in the men's room when Boggs first spoke up in support of Harris. But now he was back in the chamber and was fed up at what seemed the latest betrayal of his good faith. He had already salvaged H.R. 7152 from Manny Celler's runaway Subcommittee No. 5. He had worked with the Kennedy White House to forge a workable compromise. Only the previous day, he had watched as the Democrats had allowed the life of the Civil Rights Commission to be limited to another four years, instead of being made permanent, as he had wanted, and as the White House had agreed in October. Now Hale Boggs's move looked like the latest effort—perhaps an effort backed by Lyndon Johnson himself—to do just what everyone had promised Bill McCulloch would not be done: pare down the bill.

The *New York Times*'s account of the moment described McCulloch's face as white. But his wife, Mabel, watching from the gallery with Roy Wilkins beside her, knew him better. "Look," she told Wilkins. "Bill's face is red. He's mad."

McCulloch took the microphone to say he had been "absent from the floor on important official business" when the amendment came up, then added: "If we pick up this old provision from the bill which did not get consideration and which does not provide for judicial review, I regret to say that my personal support for the legislation will come to an end."

In hindsight, Robert Kimball judged, McCulloch and Lindsay might have overreacted, and it was soon clear that the Harris proposal did not have support from the White House. But in the wake of McCulloch's emphatic declaration, there was stunned silence—and for the civil rights supporters, cold fear—before the amendment was voted down 80 to 206 on a standing vote. Every single Republican voted with Bill McCulloch, who had saved the day yet again.

* * *

NOTHING IN THE SEVEN days of debate so far could compare with the circus that erupted on Saturday morning, February 8, as the members considered Title VII, the section of the bill barring discrimination in employment on the grounds of race, creed, religion, or color. Once again, Judge Smith was the culprit.

"Mr. Chairman, I offer an amendment," he drawled, before handing the clerk a piece of paper, from which he then read, "After the word 'religion' insert 'sex' on pages 68, 69, 70 and 71 of the bill." Howard Smith, that courtly, chivalrous, devious country squire, had just proposed to include women as a protected class in the bill. Barely able to suppress a smile, he urged his colleagues to rectify "this grave injustice . . . particularly in an election year." Two hours of panicked pandemonium ensued.

In fact, Smith's move could not have come as a surprise. At the moment he spoke, just two states in the Union—Hawaii and Wisconsin—had laws prohibiting sex discrimination in employment. On the contrary, many states had laws offering special exemptions and protections for female employees, limiting the hours they could work, or the weight they could lift, or the dangerous jobs they could perform. Such measures had been sought during the earlier decades of the twentieth century in a spirit of progressivism. But since at least World War II, women's rights groups had been strongly pressing for laws barring sex discrimination, as Judge Smith himself well knew.

In 1956, during the initial debate over the creation of the Federal Civil Rights Commission, Smith had supported an amendment to include gender discrimination in the commission's jurisdiction, arguing, "If this iniquitous piece of legislation is to be adopted, we certainly ought to try to do whatever good with it we can." Clarence Mitchell, fearing that the inclusion of gender would amount to a poison pill that could kill the whole bill, organized opposition to it, and Manny Celler joined in, but the provision was accepted over their opposition. While the bill creating the commission passed the House, it ultimately failed to pass the Senate. The commission idea was then successfully revived as part of the 1957 Civil Rights Act—but without the sex provision.

From the moment John Kennedy proposed H.R. 7152 in 1963, some rights groups, led by the National Women's Party, pressed to have sex discrimination covered by the bill, and the cause was backed by Representatives Martha Griffiths, a Michigan Democrat, and Katherine St. George, a Republican from New York. Griffiths, for one, believed that Smith's support could insure a least a hundred votes on the House floor. On January 9, the very day the Rules Committee had begun its hearings on the bill, Smith told Manny Celler that the National Women's Party wanted to know "why you did not include sex in this bill."

Celler, who for all his other virtues was a notorious male chauvinist and a bitter foe of long-running efforts to pass an equal rights amendment to the Constitution, countered: "Do you want to put it in, Mr. Chairman?"

"I think I will offer an amendment," Smith replied.

Twelve days later, Bill Colmer brought up the issue again in the Rules Committee, and on January 26, May Craig, one of the most prominent female Washington correspondents of the day, asked Smith on *Meet the Press* if he would offer an amendment from the floor.

"I might do that," the judge replied.

Now, at the eleventh hour, Smith had done just that, and Manny Celler was livid. He warned that such language would be an "entering wedge" for the ERA, and fretted that it could lead (as it, indeed, eventually did) to the overturning of state laws aimed at protecting women, to the drafting of women into the military, and to revisions in alimony and rape laws. (As it happens, Judge Smith would have probably been all too glad to see state laws limiting working hours and conditions for women overturned, since Virginia's many textile mills depended on cheap female labor.)

The Democrats had suspected that Judge Smith might make mischief, so they were armed with rebuttal arguments gathered in advance. Representative Edith Green, an Oregon Democrat, now rose to quote a letter from the American Association of University Women opposing the amendment. "I do not believe this is the time or the place," Green said.

Clarence Mitchell, Joe Rauh, and Marvin Caplan of the Leadership Conference all shared the fear that Smith's amendment "could doom the bill, but we had no choice," Caplan would recall. And so Mitchell rushed down from his perch in the gallery to call Congressman James Roosevelt of California, the son of Franklin Roosevelt, off the floor and urge him to inform the bill's managers that the sex provision would, in the end, strengthen the bill.

Whatever Smith's deepest motives, it was now a bipartisan coalition of five women members who took up the fight: Frances P. Bolton, Republican of Ohio; Catherine May, Republican of Washington; Edna F. Kelly, Democrat of New York; and Martha Griffiths and Katherine St. George. Countering Celler, St. George declared: "I can think of nothing more logical than this amendment at this point. We outlast you. We outlive you, we nag you to death . . . We are entitled to this little crumb of equality. The addition of the little, terrifying word 's-e-x' will not hurt this legislation in any way."

In the largest counted vote on any measure considered that day, Smith's amendment passed 168 to 133 on a teller vote (with mostly southern and Republican support, Martha Griffiths, who was one of the tellers, would recall). As the tally was announced, one woman in the gallery shouted out, "We've won! We've won!" while another cried, "We made it! God bless America!" before male doorkeepers escorted them out of the chamber.

Perhaps emboldened by the success of Smith's gambit, Representative John Ashbrook, a conservative Republican from Ohio, now offered an amendment proposing that "it shall not be unlawful employment practice for an employer to refuse to hire and employ any person because of said person's atheistic beliefs." McCulloch held his tongue, while Celler simply said, "There is no need for your amendment." It passed anyway, 137 to 98 on a standing vote.

* * *

THE NINTH AND FINAL day of debate began on Monday morning, February 10, with Celler and McCulloch again staving off the vast proportion of proposed amendments to Title VII, the bill's employment discrimination section. They accepted a handful, including one from the reactionary William Colmer of Mississippi that would allow employers to refuse to hire Communist Party members.

As the afternoon ground on, Celler and McCulloch plowed through the bill's remaining sections, defeating still more amendments—including an attempt by the South Dakota Republican E. Y. Berry to finance economic development efforts on Indian reservations. It was now apparent that the bill would pass that evening. About four o'clock, Clarence Mitchell and Joe Rauh were sitting in the House gallery, taking a breather and savoring their anticipated success, when a message came that the White House was trying to reach them, and Rauh ducked out to a pay phone.

"What have you done to get the bill on the floor of the Senate?" Lyndon Johnson demanded, heedless, for the moment, of the reality that no bill had yet actually passed the House. "You've got to go see Mansfield right away and talk about all of this." Minutes later, Johnson called Roy Wilkins with the same message. "No lobbyist could ever outdo Lyndon

Johnson," Wilkins would recall. "He even knew how to raise you on the pay phones."

Titles VIII and IX—providing for the collection of voting statistics by race, and for the review by the highest federal appeals courts of civil rights cases bounced back by district courts to state courts—passed with little fuss.

The last substantive amendment to be considered was a proposal by Robert T. Ashmore, a South Carolina Democrat, to create a new Community Relations Service to help localities peaceably resolve race-based disputes. Such a measure had first been proposed by Lyndon Johnson as part of the 1957 bill, and then was revived in the Kennedy administration's original bill, before being dropped in the Judiciary Committee negotiations in October. Celler and McCulloch happily accepted the idea now, in part because they knew that if the service worked as intended, it might minimize federal intervention in local affairs, an issue of concern to conservatives in both parties. It passed on a voice vote, as a newly numbered Title X.

There was one more round of procedural wrangling as members at last ended their deliberations as the Committee of the Whole—where recorded votes on amendments had not been permitted—and resumed sitting as the House, where one-fifth of the members could force an on-the-record vote on any amendment adopted in the Committee of the Whole. John Bell Williams, a Mississippi Democrat, tried to force such a vote on Judge Smith's "sex" amendment and John Ashbrook's protection for atheists, but his attempt failed, as did an effort by Bill Cramer of Florida to recommit the entire bill to the Judiciary Committee. Finally, Speaker John McCormack asked the members, "Shall the bill pass?"

One by one, the members answered the roll call, until the final tally was 290 to 130 in favor of passage. One hundred fifty-two Democrats and one hundred thirty-eight Republicans voted aye, with ninety-six Democrats (eighty-six of them from the states of the Confederacy) and thirty-four Republicans (including ten from the South) voting nay.

The lopsided margin was deeply satisfying for the bill's supporters. "It was sort of a source of great pride, feeling of success that we'd done

something we should have, earned our keep," Representative John Dingell of Michigan would recall. *Congressional Quarterly* estimated that
"well over a thousand persons from every state in the union" had come
to town to lobby for the bill, representing organizations as diverse as the
AFL-CIO, the National Council of Churches, and the Japanese-American
Citizens League. (By contrast, the Chamber of Commerce and the National
Association of Manufacturers—business lobbies that might have been
expected to weigh in, especially on the public accommodations section—
were largely neutral and noninvolved.)

The pro-civil-rights forces' diligent gallery-watching efforts paid off.
Of the 124 amendments offered to the bill (including amendments to
amendments), only thirty-four were adopted, and most of those were
technical. And the strategic lobbying by the church groups in the Midwest bore fruit, too: there was only a single "no" vote among the fifty-five
representatives from Illinois, Indiana, and Ohio, while eight of the twelve
representatives from Iowa, Nebraska, and South Dakota—all of them
Republicans—also voted in favor of the bill.

In gratitude to the members and aides who had tolerated her raiders'
days of bird-dogging, Jane O'Grady stayed up most of the night with
Peggy Roach of the National Catholic Conference baking vanilla sugar
cookies frosted with chocolate equal signs to take around to the offices
the next day.

At the White House, President Johnson worked with Larry O'Brien
and Pierre Salinger to draft a statement thanking the key players, taking
particular care to mention McCulloch and Halleck by name. "I think
naming Halleck is an advantage, in that it puts the arm a little bit on our
friend Ev Dirksen," Salinger advised. "I think so, too," Johnson agreed.
(At the same time, ever sensitive to local sensibilities, Johnson wondered
whether it would help or hurt to thank Majority Leader Carl Albert, who
was taking heat from his Oklahoma constituents for his support of the
bill. Five minutes later, after consulting with Speaker McCormack, Johnson called Salinger back to say, "Just go ahead and include" Albert, but
after all the fuss, it appears that no statement was ever issued.)

Then Johnson launched a round of congratulatory thank-you calls.
He just missed Bill McCulloch, who was already on his way to Bermuda

for an intergovernmental conference on European migration (or, in other words, a brief vacation). When he reached Charlie Halleck just after 8:30 p.m., Johnson said, "I was mighty proud of you," and Halleck replied, "By golly, we got this thing back of us—and with a great big vote, Mr. President . . . It's been a good debate and wound up in pretty good feeling . . . and I think maybe is going to be all right." In fact, the voluble Halleck had been oddly silent throughout the entire debate, perhaps still atoning for his perceived perfidy of October. He made no statement of either support or opposition on the bill, and the Republican Policy Committee never once met to discuss it, because to have done so would have been to expose the party's lingering internal divisions over whether to support first Kennedy, and now Johnson, on civil rights. When Halleck went home to make a Lincoln Day speech in Indiana and another in Nebraska, he made no mention whatever of the civil rights bill.

Outside the Capitol, in the cold and falling snow, Clarence Mitchell waited on the steps with Roy Wilkins, who was preparing to film a television interview. As Wilkins talked, Mitchell suddenly found himself sensing the full meaning of the vote. "I knew that we had just won an important part of the fight, but hearing it as a news comment helped to give it perspective and historical depth," he would recall. "I have always loved the Capitol and now there was a reason for a faster pulse-beat when I looked at it." Mitchell headed over to the Congressional Hotel, where the Leadership Conference team was celebrating. "Someone put a champagne glass in my hand, but remembering I did not drink, quickly exchanged it for a glass of tomato juice," he would remember. "We were all happy. I doubt very much that any group of persons lobbying for a bill really liked each other as much as we."

* * *

LESS THAN AN HOUR after the final vote, at 9:07 p.m., Lyndon Johnson asked the White House telephone operators to find Robert Kennedy. The attorney general came on the line as the president was talking with Larry O'Brien in the Oval Office.

"Bobby?" Johnson asked.

"Hi, Mr. President," Kennedy replied.

"Congratulations."

"Yeah, it was very nice, wasn't it," Kennedy continued.

"I thought it was wonderful—290 to 130," Johnson answered. "You can't do better than that."

"No, I would think that would put a lot of pressure on them in the Senate, wouldn't you?" Kennedy asked.

"Yeah," Johnson said, adding that Kennedy should now work with O'Brien and the Senate Majority Leader, Mike Mansfield, about how to put the bill directly on the Senate calendar, without a stop in the Judiciary Committee, where James Eastland of Mississippi would be just as determined to bury it as Howard Smith had been in the House.

"Now, will we be able to talk with you tomorrow?" Kennedy asked.

"Yes, sir," Johnson replied.

That was significant, because Johnson and Kennedy had barely seen each other since the assassination—much less plotted civil rights strategy. After the still grieving Kennedy took his family on a Colorado skiing vacation for Christmas, Johnson had hoped to divert him in mid-January by sending him on a diplomatic mission to try to persuade President Sukarno of Indonesia from delivering on his threat to "crush" the newly independent Federation of Malaysia, which shared a common border.

Kennedy was able to work out a tentative agreement for a cease-fire and negotiations on the border dispute, but when he returned to Washington, expecting to brief the president in private, he was instead asked to put on a dog and pony show for Johnson and the ranking members of the Senate Foreign Relations and Armed Services Committees. Johnson never followed up on the report, leading Kennedy to conclude that the president's intentions had not been sincere to begin with.

This was the context in which the two met privately on the afternoon of Tuesday, February 11, after a group strategy session with O'Brien, Katzenbach, and Marshall about how to handle the bill in the Senate. It was the sharpest, bitterest encounter the two men had ever had, and while their accounts of it would differ slightly in language and emphasis, the weight of the evidence suggests that Johnson's tone was, as the columnist Charles Bartlett would remember, "so . . . *savage*."

The casus belli was a Democratic operative named Paul Corbin, who had been a loyal Kennedy infighter since the 1960 campaign and now held a minor job at the Democratic National Committee. Sometime in early February, Corbin had shown up in New Hampshire, which would hold its presidential primary on March 10, to help organize a write-in campaign for Robert Kennedy, aimed at boosting his prospects as Johnson's vice presidential running mate. Corbin, always a bit of a loose cannon, was operating independently, but he was known for his unswerving loyalty to Bob Kennedy, who returned the favor, defending him to his many critics even in the Kennedy circle. Johnson himself was only a write-in candidate in New Hampshire—having expected no opposition, he had not bothered to file for the ballot—but he suspected the worst, and he now ordered the attorney general to have Corbin fired.

Kennedy balked, saying he hadn't even known Corbin was in New Hampshire and insisting that Corbin had always been loyal to John Kennedy, "who thought he was good."

Johnson replied in no uncertain terms that *he*, not Jack Kennedy, was now the president.

"Do it," he ordered.

"I know you're president," Kennedy replied—Johnson would later say that "tears got in his eyes"—"and don't you ever talk to me like that again."

That evening, after consulting with top officials of the Democratic National Committee, Johnson telephoned Kennedy at the Justice Department to tell him that Corbin was being fired. Kennedy insisted Corbin was "harmless," but the president maintained he had become "quite a problem," because he did not want anyone at Democratic headquarters taking sides on prospective running mates. He added that he had sent Kennedy to Indonesia because he wanted to "keep things equal" among potential nominees.

"Don't ever do a favor for me again!" Kennedy exploded. The attorney general spent the next four or five minutes staring out the window into the snowy night before gathering some papers into his briefcase and murmuring to a watching Ed Guthman: "I'll tell you one thing: this relationship can't last much longer."

That same night, a couple of dozen blocks from the Justice Department, four young men from Liverpool played their first American concert for more than eight thousand ecstatic fans at the sold-out Washington Coliseum, less than forty-eight hours after their stateside debut on *The Ed Sullivan Show*. Their opening number: "Roll Over, Beethoven."

"What do you think of President Johnson?" a reporter asked the Beatles at a press conference from the stage just before the show. John Lennon and Ringo Starr replied in unison, "Never met him."

PART THREE

THE SENATE

8

You Listen to Dirksen!

After lyndon johnson's weekly White House breakfast meeting with the Democratic congressional leadership, his old friend Hubert Humphrey, the voluble Senate majority whip, stayed behind for a private word. The day before, when H.R. 7152 arrived in the Senate, the majority leader, Mike Mansfield, had named Humphrey as the bill's floor manager for the coming fight, and now Johnson, that past master of legislative tactics and peerless student of the Senate's realities, had a few words of strategic advice.

In most ways, Humphrey was an ideal choice to shepherd the civil rights bill through the southern Democrats' guaranteed filibuster. He was buoyant, resilient, relentless—respected by colleagues on both sides of the aisle and both sides of the civil rights question—and perhaps no issue had meant more to him throughout his political career. As the idealistic young mayor of Minneapolis and Democratic candidate for the Senate from Minnesota in 1948, he had electrified the Democratic National Convention in Philadelphia by proposing a bold civil rights plank from the convention floor, after the party's platform committee had declined to adopt it.

"There are those who say to you—we are rushing this issue of civil rights," Humphrey told the astonished delegates, ad-libbing what would become the most famous passage in one of the twentieth century's most celebrated political speeches. "I say we are one hundred and seventy-two years late. There are those who say—this issue of civil rights is an infringement on states' rights. The time has arrived for the Democratic Party to walk out of the shadow of states' rights and into the bright sunshine of human rights!"

With the help of key big city bosses eager to appeal to black voters, Humphrey's motion carried the day, and he won his Senate race as well. When Humphrey arrived in Washington in January 1949, his brashness at first rubbed the Senate's old bulls the wrong way; it was a fellow freshman, Lyndon Johnson, already a Capitol Hill veteran from his years in the House, who helped their colleagues understand that the big-hearted liberal from Minnesota was worthy of acceptance by the club. Now, fifteen years later, Humphrey was a loyal lieutenant by the new president's side, and Johnson took the opportunity to point out what he saw as the Minnesotan's greatest vulnerability.

"You bomb throwers make good speeches," the president said. "You have big hearts, you believe in what you say you stand for, but you're never on the job when you need to be there. You spread yourself too thin making speeches to the faithful." By contrast, Johnson warned, Richard Russell knew all the rules of the Senate and how to use them, while the liberals and civil rights supports could never seem to get organized.

"He was relentless, goading me, challenging me, belittling liberals in general as inept in dealing with parliamentary situations," recalled Humphrey, who understood that his handling of the bill would amount to one long audition for the vice presidential nomination on Johnson's ticket that fall. "He shook his head in apparent despair, predicting that we would fall apart in dissension, be absent when quorum calls were made and when critical votes were being taken."

"I would have been outraged if he hadn't been basically right and historically accurate," Humphrey would remember. "As it was, I suffered his attack mostly in silence, with an occasional protest that things had changed. Having made his point, he shifted the conversation and more quietly and equally firmly he promised he would back me to the hilt. As I left, he stood and moved toward me with his towering intensity: 'Call me whenever there's trouble or anything you want me to do.'"

Nicholas Katzenbach, recalling this same period, retained a vivid impression of Johnson's management style, especially as it compared to Robert Kennedy's. "President Johnson, in contrast with Bobby, almost always told you not only what he wanted accomplished but, in excruciating detail, how he thought you should do it." Even before his session with Humphrey, Johnson had given Katzenbach his own talking-to, cornering him at a White House reception on February 11—the same day as the president's blowup with Bob Kennedy over Paul Corbin—demanding to know how Katzenbach and the Justice Department intended to get the bill through the Senate.

"I think we have to try for cloture," Katzenbach replied.

That was a tall order. Under the rules then in place, achieving cloture required two-thirds of the Senate, or sixty-seven votes, to cut off debate—in a body that prided itself on its willingness to allow unlimited debate on any issue—and one in which a single senator's objection could cause business to grind to a halt. Indeed, Senate Rule XXII, the rule that provided for cloture, had not even been adopted until 1917, and in the twenty-eight cloture votes taken since then, only five had succeeded. In the eleven times cloture had been proposed for a civil rights measure, it had been defeated every time. The representatives of small and western states whose support would most be needed to overcome the southern Democrats' opposition to civil rights had always been especially reluctant to vote for cloture, since unlimited debate was the principal means by which they could ensure that the Senate paid obeisance to their states' interests. The Senate's senior member, Carl Hayden of Arizona, in the Senate since 1927 and first elected to the House of Representatives in 1911, a year before Woodrow Wilson won the White House, had never voted for cloture.

So Johnson was deeply skeptical that cloture could succeed this time. He made it clear to Katzenbach (and everyone else) that he favored wearing down the aging southern caucus with round-the-clock sessions, as he had done with the 1960 civil rights bill. The problem with this approach was twofold. First, Mike Mansfield refused to accept it, fearing that marathon sessions might literally kill some of the Senate's older members. And second, Bill McCulloch was steadfastly insisting—as he had since his first meeting with Burke Marshall in July 1963—on no compromise, no weakening of H.R. 7152 in the Senate. That meant that cloture was the most logical strategy for forcing a vote on the bill that had passed the House, however difficult it might be to achieve.

"Talking voting details with the man who knew the Senate better than anyone was a little daunting," Katzenbach would recall. But the deputy attorney general had solid grounds for his argument. For one thing, only the year before, the Senate had voted for cloture on the 1963 Satellite Communications bill, suggesting that members' long-standing reluctance to invoke it was softening. Katzenbach also believed that members would be embarrassed to confess that they had voted to cut off debate on a technical measure like a communications bill while refusing to allow an up-or-down vote on a major constitutional question like civil rights. Katzenbach estimated the administration could get fifty-seven to sixty votes with reasonable ease—by combining about fifty pro-civil-rights Democrats with a handful of liberal Republicans. But the president would need a total of at least half the Senate's thirty-three Republicans to prevail.

And whatever his private doubts about such a strategy, Lyndon Johnson knew there was only one man who could deliver those Republican votes: his old comrade, the Senate minority leader, Everett Dirksen of Illinois, who from the start had expressed strong opposition to the public accommodations section at the heart of the bill.

"The bill can't pass unless you get Ev Dirksen," Johnson now told Humphrey. "You and I are going to get Ev. It's going to take time. We're going to get him. You make up your mind now that you've got to spend time with Ev Dirksen. You've got to let him have a piece of the action. He's got to look good all the time. Don't let those bomb throwers, now, talk you out of seeing Dirksen. You get in there to see Dirksen. You drink with Dirksen! You talk with Dirksen! You listen to Dirksen!"

On February 12, 1963, President John F. Kennedy held a reception at the White House to mark Lincoln's Birthday and the one hundredth anniversary of the Emancipation Proclamation. Seated left to right are Ethel Kennedy, Lyndon and Lady Bird Johnson, and John and Jacqueline Kennedy. Behind them are some of the eight hundred black guests, who included many civil rights leaders and entertainment figures.

Fred Shuttlesworth, Ralph D. Abernathy, and Martin Luther King Jr. march in work clothes on Good Friday, April 12, 1963, in Birmingham, Alabama, eschewing Easter finery to protest the segregation of downtown department stores. King would be arrested and placed in solitary confinement, where he would write "Letter from Birmingham Jail."

In Birmingham in May 1963, public safety commissioner Eugene "Bull" Connor's police dogs lunge at seventeen-year-old Walter Gadsden, an image that outraged President Kennedy—and the world.

Deputy Attorney General Nicholas deB. Katzenbach wipes his face as he confronts Governor George C. Wallace at the "schoolhouse door" on June 11, 1963, over the integration of the University of Alabama.

That same evening, President Kennedy delivers a nationally televised speech proposing comprehensive civil rights legislation.

Attorney General Robert F. Kennedy makes impromptu remarks to civil rights protestors gathered outside the Justice Department on June 14, 1963.

The civil rights advocate Joseph L. Rauh (below left) confers with Clarence Mitchell and Roy Wilkins of the NAACP about lobbying strategy in August 1963.

NAACP LEGISLATIVE STRATEGY CONFERENCE ON CIVIL RIGHTS

Part of the interdenominational throng of demonstrators who descended on the National Mall on August 28, 1963, for the March on Washington.

Unlikely allies: Representatives William McCulloch of Ohio (left), the ranking Republican on the House Judiciary Committee, and Emanuel Celler of New York, the committee's chairman, were crucial backers of the civil rights bill, designated as H.R. 7152.

"The Ev and Charlie Show": Senate Minority Leader Everett McKinley Dirksen of Illinois (seated) and House Minority Leader Charles A. Halleck of Indiana, Republicans whose support for H.R. 7152 was indispensable, conferring on the set of NBC's "Meet the Press."

Representative Howard Smith of Virginia (below), the chairman of the House Rules Committee, was one of the most powerful Southern Democrats in the House and an implacable foe of the bill.

"Let Us Continue": President Lyndon B. Johnson addresses a joint session of Congress on November 27, 1963, vowing to pass the late President Kennedy's stalled agenda, including the civil rights bill.

Geraldine Whittington, President Johnson's newly hired secretary, with civil rights leaders in the Cabinet Room. Left to right: James Farmer of the Congress of Racial Equality, Roy Wilkins of the NAACP, Whitney Young Jr. of the National Urban League, and Martin Luther King Jr. of the Southern Christian Leadership Conference.

A copy of H.R. 7152, annotated by the House of Representatives' parliamentarian upon the House's passage of the bill on February 10, 1964.

Senator Hubert H. Humphrey
of Minnesota, the Democratic
majority whip and floor leader
for the civil rights bill.

The Johnson Treatment: Lyndon Johnson
lobbies Everett Dirksen.

Senator Richard B. Russell Jr. of Georgia, the indefatigable leader of
the Senate's Southern bloc through a record-setting filibuster, and
segregation's staunchest defender.

* * *

EVERETT MCKINLEY DIRKSEN WAS the single most flamboyant senator of his day, with a rumbling baritone foghorn of a voice that Bob Hope called a combination of Tallulah Bankhead's and Wallace Beery's, and that the *New York Times*'s drama critic Brooks Atkinson once likened to "the froth on a warm pail of milk just extracted from a fat Jersey cow." He kept his vocal cords lubricated with a daily gargle of Pond's cold cream and water (which he swallowed) and subsisted on a diet of Sanka, cigarettes, Maalox, and bourbon whiskey. He let his graying, curly hair arrange itself in a deliberate tousle—the better to stand out from the crowd, he once confessed—and he was fond of briefing reporters in the Senate press gallery while sitting atop a table in the lotus position. For years, he had waged an unapologetic campaign to make the marigold the national flower. When he took to the floor for one of his signature stemwinders, an excited cry would spread through the corridors: "Ev's up!" Senator Albert Gore Sr. of Tennessee once strained the Senate's rule of civility by accusing Dirksen—not without reason—of "pompous verbosity," then apologized with mock praise, singling out his voluble colleague as "the inimitable and euphonious sockdolager from Illinois, one of the most ariose, mellifluous, dulcifulent orators" in the chamber.

But if Dirksen was the consummate Senate show horse, he was also a master of rules and procedures and a meticulous legislative draftsman, an expert on the fine print of pending bills, with a crackerjack legal staff. The light in the backseat of his official limousine burned bright each night as he pored over memos and reports on the hour-long drive home from Capitol Hill to Heart's Desire, his farm overlooking a branch of the Potomac River in Sterling, Virginia.

He was born in "Beantown," an immigrant enclave on the edge of Pekin, Illinois—so called because its hardscrabble residents grew vegetables to eat, not flowers to admire—at the beginning of 1896, ten months before the election to the White House of William McKinley, the popular Republican politician for whom he was named. His parents, Johann Frederick and Antje Conrady Dirksen, were staunch Republicans of stolid German immigrant stock. Everett was an early and passionate reader, waking on cold winter mornings to rub one barefoot leg against another to warm up while still in his nightshirt as he held a book in one hand. When he was five years old, his father suffered a crippling stroke, and he died four years later, leaving Everett and his brothers to milk cows, slop hogs, and tend 150 chickens and fifteen hives of bees to help stock their mother's butter-and-egg stand.

By the time he reached high school, he was vice president of his class, the 150-pound center on the football team (proudly known then, and until 1981, as the Pekin "Chinks"), the business manager of the year-book, and a good student of German and history. His vocabulary was so large that a classmate once surmised "he must have swallowed a diction-ary," and his senior yearbook declared that he suffered from hopeless "big-worditis." In 1913, he won an oratorical contest sponsored by a Prohibition society that sent him to compete in the finals in Lexington, Kentucky, where he met the reigning orator of his age, the three-time losing Democratic presidential candidate and current secretary of state, William Jennings Bryan. When Dirksen asked the great man's advice about public speaking, the reply was simple: "Always speak to the folks in the back rows, my boy, and the rest will be sure to hear you."

Dirksen went off to the University of Minnesota to study prelaw, but his college days were interrupted by Army service in France in World War I, where he was a balloon surveillance officer floating 3,500 feet above the lines, observing and redirecting artillery fire. He never went back to school, but the war had provided its own kind of education, including a lesson in prejudice that would stick with him into the thick of the civil rights debate. Dirksen's mother had received a commemorative picture of Kaiser Wilhelm II as a premium for subscribing to a local German newspaper, and she kept it on her wall, along with an American flag in the window, commemorating Everett's service abroad. That "did not deter a self-appointed group of local loyalty monitors from coming to our home without legal process of any kind and by sheer intimidation demanding that the photograph be handed over for destruction," Dirk-sen would recall years later. "Such are the little violations of liberty."

On his return to Illinois, Dirksen held an assortment of jobs before going into partnership with his brothers in a wholesale bakery business, whose motto was, "If it's made of dough, we make it." He rolled piecrust and kneaded bread, but mostly he made sales calls, which enabled him to get to know a wide range of small businessmen throughout the region.

At the same time, he was active in amateur theatricals with the Pekin Players and took the lead in a Chinese-themed romance, *A Thousand Years Ago*, in which a fetching local girl named Louella Carver played the Princess of Pekin. She became his wife in real life. During their courtship, in 1924, he wrote her from a business trip outside Memphis, Tennessee, with a midwestern burgher's withering view of the South.

"In a sense, girlie, this is terrible country," he complained. "One would think that the Creator had either run out of fair material for this part of the South or had purposely created it as it is for punishment. Nothing but yellow and red soil from which the energy and fertility has been sapped years ago, and at the same time the energy and ambition of those who till the land must have flowed away and left a residue of indolent white trash and niggers who live in unpainted slatterns and seeming care not what happens from this day to the next."

By this same period, Pekin itself, which had been abolitionist territory before the Civil War, had fallen under the sway of the Ku Klux Klan, which in 1923 took over the *Pekin Daily Times* as its local mouthpiece. In 1920, just thirty-one black residents lived in Pekin; by 1940, not a single one was left, and it became a notorious "sundown town," in which blacks knew they should not be caught after dark. But Dirksen himself felt an almost mystic kinship with his fellow Illinoisan Abraham Lincoln, and he would never pander to racist sentiment, from his earliest days in public life supporting efforts to outlaw the poll tax and ban lynchings.

Dirksen's pathway to political office was his involvement in the American Legion, which brought him a wide circle of acquaintances throughout central Illinois. In 1927, he was elected to the part-time job of city commissioner in Pekin, and just three years later he challenged the incumbent Republican congressman in a primary, losing by 1,100 votes. Two years later, in the depths of the Depression, Dirksen won the nomination, and the seat—in a district that included the nearby city of Peoria, then the state's second largest, and a major railroad and distilling center—with a campaign that carefully avoided explicit embrace of either Herbert

Hoover or Franklin Roosevelt while urging economic reforms. He saw the Capitol dome in Washington for the first time when he arrived to take up his duties as a freshman member of Congress.

In his early years on Capitol Hill, he supported some aspects of the New Deal but was otherwise a conventional conservative isolationist—until September 1941, three months before Pearl Harbor, when the looming American involvement in World War II caused him to take a more internationalist stance. In 1944, he ran his own brief campaign for the White House, which many in the party saw mainly as an effort to deny the nomination to the Republicans' liberal 1940 standard-bearer, Wendell Willkie. After World War II, he voted for the Truman Doctrine, the United Nations, and the Marshall Plan, but he also remained a staunch backer of the party's conservative wing, led by Senator Robert A. Taft of Ohio.

In 1947, he began experiencing severe vision problems, and doctors at Johns Hopkins Hospital in Baltimore advised removal of his left eye. Instead, he temporarily retired, but by 1950 he felt strong enough to challenge an old friend from the American Legion, the Democrat Scott Lucas, for his seat in the United States Senate. With the support of Joseph R. McCarthy, the senator from neighboring Wisconsin who was just then beginning his campaign to "kick the perfumed pinks and punks out of our State Department," Dirksen won. Two years later, backing Taft at the Republican Convention in Chicago, Dirksen unleashed pandemonium on the floor by pointing his finger at the party's moderate 1944 and 1948 presidential nominee, Thomas E. Dewey, and bellowing: "We followed you before and you took us down the path to defeat!"

Taft's loss of the nomination to Dwight D. Eisenhower was a bitter pill, and Dirksen spent most of Ike's first term veering between grudging support for the president and nipping away at his policies, keeping a "foot or finger in every possible camp," as Lyndon Johnson's aide George Reedy would recall. Among Dirksen's policy differences with Eisenhower was civil rights, and the senator was far ahead of the president on the issue, as early as 1953 proposing a federal civil rights commission and grants and aid aimed at encouraging southern states to ease segregation. He pressed for an endorsement of the Supreme Court's *Brown* decision in the 1956 Republican Party platform, eventually retreating to a statement that the party "accepts" the decision in the face of Eisenhower's reluctance to go further.

He vigorously supported the 1957 Civil Rights Act in the Senate, opposing Eisenhower's willingness to drop Part III, with its powers of federal intervention in desegregation cases, and opposing Johnson's proposed jury trial amendment. "Seldom in my long legislative experience have I seen . . . so many ghosts discovered under the same bed," he declared at one point in the debate, "but I am confident that if the civil rights bill is enacted, the heavens will not be rent asunder, the waters will not part, the earth will not rock and roll, and we will go on."

But, as his biographer Byron Hulsey has written, Dirksen knew that he had "hamstrung himself by speaking out so clearly in the early stages of the debate. In the future, he kept his thoughts to himself and thus retained more flexibility as legislation snaked its way through Congress."

* * *

WITH H.R. 7152 NOW before the Senate, Dirksen was in an ideal position to capitalize on just such flexibility, and he had not yet made his full intentions clear. From the first, he had told John Kennedy he would support the bill—with the glaring exception of its symbolic and practical heart: Title II, on public accommodations. Dirksen also had serious concerns about Title VII, the section on fair employment. And while the Republicans in his caucus were not as divided as their Democratic counterparts on civil rights, it would be no simple matter for Dirksen to round up a majority of Republicans in support of the House-passed bill.

Of the Senate's thirty-three Republicans, twenty-one, including Dirksen himself, could be classified as conservatives, with deep concerns about the degree of intrusion into free enterprise and private property that H.R. 7152 would entail. Just five Senate Republicans were regarded as moderates, while seven—including such stalwart supporters of civil rights as Jacob Javits and Kenneth Keating of New York, Clifford Case of New Jersey, and Thomas Kuchel of California—were reliable liberals. So finding the twenty-odd Republican votes needed for cloture was by no means guaranteed, as Dirksen well understood.

Hubert Humphrey knew that, too, and Lyndon Johnson's emphatic lectures notwithstanding, Humphrey was hardly sitting on his hands. He knew that managing the bill would "test me in every way," he would recall, but he had his own considered strategy for getting the job done. "This time I assured myself, it would be different," he added. While the southerners talked, "we would organize." Humphrey decided to appoint seven floor captains, one for each section of the bill, to manage debate, with the help of large green three-ring binders full of background material compiled by the Justice Department and kept handy on the floor at all times. Philip Hart of Michigan would be responsible for the voting rights section, Joseph Clark of Pennsylvania for equal employment, Warren Magnuson of Washington for public accommodations, and so on.

Humphrey had a well-earned reputation as the Democrats' reigning Happy Warrior. He had emerged from a bitter, brutal primary campaign for the presidential nomination against John Kennedy in 1960 with his good humor intact ("I think I did pretty well for a Protestant," he would tell the Gridiron Club in 1963), and as majority whip had become a valued Kennedy loyalist in Congress—and a frequent goad on civil rights. Now he resolved to use all his considerable charms in pressing for a strong bill.

"I had to make up my mind as to my mental attitude and how I would conduct myself," he would remember. "I can recall literally talking to myself, conditioning myself for the long ordeal." He added, "I made up my mind early that I would keep my patience. I would not lose my temper and, if I could do nothing else, I would try to preserve a reasonable degree of good nature and fair play in the Senate . . . I knew that if the southerners could get the pro-civil rights people divided and fighting among themselves, the opponents would win."

From the minute the bill arrived in the Senate on February 17, Mike Mansfield was equally prepared. After the clerk read H.R. 7152 for the first time, the majority leader made sure he would retain as much control as possible over it. Invoking a parliamentary tactic, he objected to a second reading of the bill, which allowed him to short-circuit what would normally have been the next step in the legislative process: immediate referral of H.R. 7152 to James Eastland's Judiciary Committee, a graveyard of civil rights legislation as full of tombstones as Howard Smith's House Rules Committee. Instead, by blocking a second reading, Mansfield preserved his own power over the bill's path, and he announced that he would soon move to place it directly on the Senate calendar. "We hope in vain if we hope that this issue can be put over safely to another tomorrow, to be dealt with by another generation of Senators," he said. "The time is now."

But Mansfield, a courtly, laconic former professor at the University of Montana, also shared Humphrey's view that debate should be civil and dignified. "This is not a circus or a sideshow," he insisted. "We are not operating a pit with spectators coming into the galleries late at night to see Senators of the Republic come out in bedroom slippers without neckties, with their hair uncombed and pajama tops sticking out of their necks." Some Democrats chafed at Mansfield's relaxed hand. One of his own staff lawyers, Charles Ferris, would recall that he learned to be careful in drafting memos on pending legislation for his boss, because Mansfield would immediately share them with Dirksen. "Mansfield always was, you know, from our point of view, too deferential to Dirksen," Humphrey's chief legislative aide, John Stewart, would recall. "But he believed in fairness and he believed that each senator deserved full respect and opportunity to function in the Senate and that's what made the Senate a different and distinctly important institution, and those qualities had to be preserved."

The degree to which Mansfield and Humphrey were in charge of the Senate action was reflected in the degree to which Lyndon Johnson chafed at their pace. On Wednesday, February 19, the day after the president's first meeting with Humphrey as floor manager, Richard Russell and his southern caucus met and vowed to use every tactic at their disposal to delay the bill. That same afternoon, talking by telephone with Agriculture Secretary Orville Freeman, Humphrey's old friend from Minnesota, Johnson expressed frustration that a pending cotton-wheat bill—a bill that Johnson wanted out of the Senate before the civil rights bill hit the floor—was gumming up the Senate calendar, in part because the Senate had not been in session to receive a required report from Freeman's department. "Oh, that god-damned, no-good outfit," the president said. "I never saw a Senate operate like that one in my life. I just don't know *what* to do."

The next day, with his aide Bill Moyers on another extension, Johnson complained to Mansfield that Mary McGrory of the *Washington Star* had called Moyers to say that she had been unable to discern any clear or coordinated strategy for passing the bill, or any active consultations between Democrats and Republicans. "Well she hasn't been around to see me," Mansfield replied. "She hasn't been around to see Hubert." Johnson acknowledged that it was up to Mansfield "to arrange the strategy because if I got into it, they'd say I was bossing the Senate and directing them." He suggested Mansfield himself call McGrory and tell her "that you discussed at the breakfast the other morning what the plans of the leadership were, and that they're satisfactory to the White House, but that you make those decisions yourself." Finally, noting McGrory's close relationship with Robert Kennedy, Johnson said, "Justice, I imagine, Mike, is starting this. She's got awfully close sources over there . . . She's just a troublemaker and they want to start the trouble."

In fact, Humphrey and Mansfield already had a considered strategy, and they had consulted extensively with Bob Kennedy, Nick Katzenbach, and Burke Marshall about it. They were also well prepared to work with pro-civil-rights Republicans. On Friday, February 21, Dirksen named Thomas Kuchel, a strong civil rights supporter from California and one of his party's liberal stalwarts, to serve as the Republican floor manager for H.R. 7152. His top aides had already been closely consulting with Humphrey's, and Humphrey quickly welcomed Kuchel as my "co-partner."

But by early the following week, with the civil rights bill, the cotton-wheat bill, and the long-sought tax bill all stacking up in the Senate, Johnson could once again not resist a word or two of micromanagement. On Tuesday, February 25, the president advised Humphrey that it made sense to delay consideration of civil rights for a few more days, until the agriculture subsidy bill could be passed, in part because its passage might appease the southern senators whose states depended on those crops. But as a southerner himself—and a man about whom the most avid civil rights supporters were still somewhat skeptical—he did not want to be seen as driving the train. "Now, on your civil rights things, Hubert, I think you've got to be *awfully* careful that you don't leave that at the White House, because they'll say it's a plot of the cotton South," the president insisted.

"No," Humphrey dutifully replied, "I'm taking the full responsibility."

The next day, Wednesday, February 26, the tax bill conference report at long last passed the full Senate. Johnson had kept his pledge to bring in a federal budget under $100 billion, and Harry Byrd had kept his promise to allow the tax bill to proceed. With that business out of the way, Mike Mansfield promptly asked that H.R. 7152 be read for the second time. Then, invoking a provision under Senate Rule XIV, the majority leader asked that the bill be placed directly on the Senate calendar—an unusual procedure that nevertheless required only a simple majority vote. Richard Russell immediately objected that this course would violate the Senate's Rule XXV, which had been passed *after* Rule XIV, calling for all bills to be referred to the relevant standing committee. But as Russell himself would have been the first to remember, he had lost this very point of order in 1957, when the Senate voted to let that year's civil rights bill bypass the Judiciary Committee, and now the Senate's presiding officer, Lee Metcalf of Montana, simply cited the 1957 precedent as controlling, and overruled Russell.

Interestingly, in 1957, Mansfield had voted to send the civil rights bill to committee (as had John Kennedy and Lyndon Johnson) while Everett Dirksen, eager to help the Eisenhower administration get its bill through, had voted to place the bill directly on the calendar. Now, however, with his own commitment to H.R. 7152 still equivocal, Dirksen, the senior Republican on the Judiciary Committee, took the opposite tack. He argued that the only witness ever to testify before the committee on the bill had been the attorney general himself (in those long summer colloquies with Sam Ervin), and that Title VII, the fair employment practices measure inserted in the compromise House bill, had never been considered by any Senate committee at all.

Russell's and Dirksen's objections were joined by Wayne Morse, an Oregon Democrat and strong civil rights supporter who was nevertheless a stickler for Senate procedure and traditions. "We would make a great mistake if we put this bill directly on the calendar and proceed to turn the Senate into a Committee of the Whole and debate it," Morse insisted. But, Humphrey rejoined, the civil rights bill *had* been in committee—Eastland's committee. "The problem was that it did not come out of committee," he said. "I have been around here long enough to know that the only way civil rights legislation can really be gotten before this body is through extraordinary, but legal, means." Several hours of heated debate now followed, but in an ominous sign for Russell and the southerners, Mansfield carried the day, 54 to 37, with twenty Republican votes.

And then, in an apparent gesture of goodwill that stunned both civil rights supporters and opponents, Mansfield himself requested unanimous consent that the bill be referred to the Judiciary Committee after all, with instructions that it be reported back "without recommendation or amendment" by Wednesday, March 4. Mansfield apparently did so in hopes of winning eventual support for cloture from Senator Ernest Gruening, a Democrat from Alaska and another stickler for procedure, but the immediate effect of his gesture was to alienate nearly everyone else. Jacob Javits of New York shot to his feet and objected to the unanimous consent request, thus blocking Mansfield's gambit.

Before the Senate could debate whether to actually take up H.R. 7152—to make it the Senate's "pending business"—the pro-civil-rights forces would have to endure a few more days of debate on the cotton-wheat bill. That did not really bother Hubert Humphrey, who was playing a long game.

"He used to say, you can read the Bible all the way through, and you can read the Constitution from beginning to end, and you can memorize the Bill of Rights, and you'll never see the word 'efficiency' mentioned once," recalled Walter Mondale, who would serve alongside Humphrey in the Senate in the 1970s. "And he had time. He would use time, use time, use time. He decided not to do it in a hurry, but do it slowly and well."

* * *

WHEN GOD HANDED OUT glands, Humphrey's longtime press secretary, Norman Sherman, liked to say, Hubert took seconds. Indeed, throughout his life he seemed possessed of some perpetual excess of energy, a drive that could only be released in talk, action, and then more talk. He always had, Richard Russell once complained, "more solutions than we have problems."

Hubert Horatio Humphrey Jr. was born in 1911, in Wallace, South Dakota, and grew up in nearby Doland, population 660, where his father was a struggling druggist. Hubert Humphrey Sr. was a rare Democrat in a Republican town, one who, the locals liked to say, "never sells you a pill without selling you an idea." He was himself a font of loquacious energy, and he told his son, "Stay out of bed as long as you can. Most people die there." Even before he was able to reach the taps of the soda fountain in his father's store, young Hubert went to work. Hard times hit the Dakotas early, and when Hubert was sixteen years old, his family was forced to sell their house to pay the bills; it was the first time he saw his father cry, and he never forgot the sight.

In Doland's small high school, Humphrey played football and basketball, ran the half mile, acted in plays, blew the baritone horn, and graduated as a star debater and the valedictorian. "I sometimes wonder what would have happened if I had gone to a large high school," he would recall. In 1929, he lit out for the University of Minnesota in Minneapolis, some three hundred miles from home, and made ends meet by getting a job washing dishes in the basement of—of course—a drugstore, where he survived by eating the mistakes, the returned food and milkshakes, from the lunch counter upstairs. At the end of his freshman year, his father thought there might not be enough money to send him back, but finally he decided Hubert simply had to return, because "There's only one thing to do here and that's just fade away and go broke."

Soon enough, though, Humphrey's college career was interrupted, and he dutifully went home—like George Bailey in *It's a Wonderful Life*—to help his father, who had now moved to Huron, South Dakota, run one of the Walgreen chain's first drugstores, an emporium, Humphrey would recall, that rarely did twenty-five dollars a day in business in those lean years. Finally, in 1932, realizing that if this was to be his lot, he had better learn the trade, Humphrey went off to a six-month pharmaceutical cram course in Denver, learning in six months what other students absorbed in four years, then returning to Huron to work in the store from 7:00 a.m. to midnight most days. To supplement their income, he and his father mixed their own patent medicines—for humans and hogs alike—including a concoction called "Humphrey's Sniffles," intended to compete with Vicks nose drops but made with vegetable oil and a touch of benzocaine, "so that even if the sniffles didn't get better, you felt it less."

Somehow in the midst of those long workdays, Humphrey met and began courting Muriel Buck, a girl from a prominent local family with whom he was able to share dreams he found it hard to confess to others. "Maybe I seem foolish to have such hopes and plans," he wrote her in August 1935 from Washington, where he had gone to attend his sister's graduation from George Washington University, "but Bucky, I can see how someday, if you and I just apply ourselves and make up our minds to work for bigger things, we can someday live here in Washington and probably be in government politics or service. I intend to set my aim at Congress. Don't laugh at me, Muriel. Maybe it does sound rather egotistical and beyond reason, but Muriel I do know others have succeeded. Why haven't I a chance?"

Hubert and Muriel were married in September 1936—at eight o'clock in the morning, so the drugstore would not have to be closed during the busiest hours. The newlyweds were happy with each other, but Humphrey was miserable in his work, suffering headaches and nausea. Finally, he told his father that he knew it was time to go back to college in Minnesota. "I wanted to learn something, anything, new," he would recall. He signed up for twenty-one credit hours, though the limit was fifteen. Because he had been gone from the campus for six years, he came back as a contemporary of former students who were now assistant professors, and he and Muriel formed an energetic social circle, surviving on hamburger, root beer, and good talk. He graduated in June 1939, having finished three years' work in two, and accepted a $450 fellowship for graduate study in political science at Louisiana State University.

There now began "a most difficult and impecunious time," Humphrey would recall, as Muriel made sandwiches every morning for Hubert to take to campus to sell for a dime. In a Louisiana where Huey Long's son Russell was the LSU student body president, Humphrey discovered the roiling, gothic nature of southern politics, and also the brutality of Jim Crow. Growing up in south Dakota, the only blacks he had ever encountered were workers on road crews building a highway from Doland to Redfield, and he would ride their mule-drawn dump trucks and chat, to the shock of his mother. When he first saw separate White and Colored signs for drinking fountains and toilets, Humphrey would recall, "I found them both ridiculous and offensive. I remember my naïve reaction: 'Why, it's uneconomic.'" (Years later, as Senate majority whip, he would always ride in the front seat with his black chauffeur, Tom Graham, because he thought it looked pompous to sit in the back.)

Returning to Minnesota, Humphrey took a job with the Workers' Education Program, a jobs training effort under the auspices of the Works Progress Administration, in which he came to know labor leaders throughout the state. In 1943, to his considerable surprise, he was recruited by labor groups to run for mayor of Minneapolis at age thirty-two, one of eleven candidates competing in a nonpartisan open primary. He lost by slightly less than six thousand votes, but two years later, he tried again and won by more than thirty thousand votes.

Minneapolis had a "weak mayor" system of government, in which the city council traditionally held the dominant role. But Humphrey had the sole power to appoint the police chief, and he used it to name a tough new commander, who took on gambling and graft in what was then still a wide-open town. Humphrey raised license fees to pay for more and better-trained police officers, all the while fighting Communist influence in the Minnesota Democratic-Farmer-Labor Party, which he had helped create. "By 1948, newspapers in Minnesota had begun to describe me as ambitious, as though it were a sin," he would recall. In fact, he was sinful (or virtuous) enough to win the DFL nomination for Senate that year.

* * *

HUMPHREY'S SUCCESSFUL INTRODUCTION OF the civil rights plank at the Democratic National Convention that summer—and his Senate victory alongside Harry Truman's upset comeback that fall—made him an instant national celebrity. The January 17, 1949, issue of *Time* put his face on the cover, with a stylized tornado whirling in the background, and described him as "a glib, jaunty spellbinder with a 'listen-you-guys' approach." But his new colleagues in the Senate, where the power still rested disproportionately with the southern barons, were not so impressed. While Humphrey watched from the gallery as the last special session of the Eightieth Congress concluded, one senator after another studiously ignored him, until Lister Hill of Alabama finally noticed him and asked him to come down to the floor.

It did not go unnoticed when Humphrey took a black staff member, Cyril King, later governor of the Virgin Islands, to lunch in the Senate dining room, only to be told by an embarrassed black headwaiter that they could not be served. Humphrey made such a fuss that they were seated, but in the Senate cloakroom one day soon thereafter, he was crushed to his core to hear Richard Russell mutter, "Can you imagine the people of Minnesota sending that damn fool down here to represent them?" The *Saturday Evening Post* pronounced Humphrey "the Senate's gabbiest freshman."

But gradually, Humphrey's ebullience, good humor, and essential decency would win over even his most stubborn colleagues, and by 1964 he was as esteemed a member of the club as any man. Milton Young, a North Dakota Republican who suffered from recurrent debilitating migraine headaches, would never forget Humphrey's sensitivity. Humphrey, the former pharmacist, could always tell when Young was suffering an attack, and he would go around the chamber getting members to talk more softly so Young "could stay in the Senate without abusing his headaches," Walter Mondale would recall. "He always believed that if you really put your mind to it . . . and brought a lot of bright people in, that you could solve anything, that there were no intractable problems," Humphrey's longtime aide Bill Connell remembered.

In 1960, Humphrey had every reason to be bitter at John Kennedy after their primary fight. Instead, he campaigned for him vigorously in the general election, reminding an overwhelmingly Scandinavian and Protestant audience in northern Minnesota that the Vikings had occupied Ireland for a hundred years and had intermarried with the local Celts. "Look at Kennedy!" Humphrey exclaimed. "See that rusty reddish hair, those blue eyes, that ruddy complexion? Why, he is one of us!"

* * *

ON THE AFTERNOON OF Friday, February 28, two days after the passage of Mike Mansfield's motion to put the bill on the Senate calendar, H.R. 7152's floor managers, Humphrey and Thomas Kuchel, met in Humphrey's office with their key legislative aides. This bipartisan gathering of senators and aides would become a daily—sometimes twice daily— ritual in the long fight to pass the bill, its precise makeup and meeting place varying from time to time but its mission never changing in the months ahead.

On this occasion, the group was joined—as it often would be—by Clarence Mitchell and Joe Rauh to plot the first steps in strategy. All who were present agreed that they should accept nothing less than the House version of H.R. 7152, and that they should stay in close touch with Bill McCulloch and Manny Celler as the Senate action unfolded. Kuchel proposed that the Senate not allow any committees to meet during the coming civil rights debate. "It doesn't bother me if the committees do not meet," he said. "This should be a show." Humphrey warned that the Senate should prepare to meet from 9:00 a.m. to midnight, including Saturdays, and that the pro-civil-rights forces would need "faith and perseverance." Russell, he warned, would run "a war of nerves. He will yell, 'Benedict Arnold, traitor and lynch law.' He is like that French general who always said, 'Attack, attack, attack!' If he were on a bear hunt, he would let rabbits out of the cage and have the hounds chase them. He doesn't want us to get bear."

Humphrey well understood the paradox of the coming filibuster—a term that derives from the Dutch word for "freebooter," or pirate, and that had come to be used in the Senate after the Civil War to describe those who would hijack debate. A filibuster would place the greatest burden not on the southerners, who would simply have to show up one or two at a time to talk in desultory opposition, but on the pro-civil-rights forces, who would have to be able to produce fifty-one senators on the floor any time the southerners called for a quorum in order to keep Senate business from grinding to a halt. It was this very reality, Mike Mansfield believed, that had resulted in the weakening of the 1960 civil rights bill. Round-the-clock sessions had not so much worn down the southerners, who could hold the floor with only a handful of well-rested troops, but "rather the exhausted, sleep-starved, quorum-confounded" proponents of civil rights, who were only too happy to compromise in the end.

Quorum calls not only gave the filibusterers time to rest their feet and voices, they also posed a keen parliamentary risk for the pro-civil-rights troops. Under the Senate's rules, each member was allowed to deliver just two speeches on the same subject in a single "legislative day." If a quorum could not be mustered, the Senate would have to adjourn—instead of simply recessing, as was its more typical practice—thus starting a new legislative day, allowing the southerners to make even more speeches in opposition. (If each filibusterer simply made two twelve-hour speeches, that alone could use up eight to ten weeks of debate.) Moreover, if the Senate adjourned while a motion to consider the civil rights bill was pending—as Mike Mansfield had announced the motion to consider H.R. 7152 soon would be—the motion would die, and the process of calling the bill up would have to start all over again the next day. So it was of utmost importance, as a demonstration of will if nothing else, that the pro-civil-rights side be able to deliver a quorum on demand and keep the current legislative day alive.

To that end, Humphrey set up two platoons of about twenty-five members each, and each day, one platoon would be expected to answer every quorum call. Together with Humphrey and his title captains, Kuchel and his Republican troops, and the handful of southern Democrats that could always be counted on to be on the floor, that system could be expected to produce the warm bodies needed for a quorum.

Humphrey's aide John Stewart, a twenty-nine-year-old political science graduate student from the University of Chicago, came up with another innovation: a daily mimeographed newsletter, written with style and wit, to be distributed by the pro-civil-rights forces, summing up floor debate and the state of play, listing the quorum duty rosters, and generally helping "to keep Senators and their staffs fully informed."

All this careful planning—and Bill McCulloch's steadfast insistence on no compromise on the House bill—left the civil rights proponents hopeful that they had at last reversed the long-standing dynamic that had prevailed in the Senate. "You had a situation where you really couldn't compromise and expect to have anything other than a huge mess on your hands," Stewart would recall. "And in that set of circumstances, common sense prevailed and told you that, you know, in the past it has always been the advocates who have blinked. And once you blink in a filibuster situation, you're doomed. It may take a while, but you're basically doomed to lose the core of what you're after, so you can't blink. And if you just hold out long enough, there will be countervailing power that will—that you'll flip the whole equation such that it's the filibusterers who are the ones who are going to blink."

Whatever Lyndon Johnson's apprehensions about trying to win cloture, no one understood this reality better than he. At his news conference on Saturday, February 29, the president was asked whether he would be willing to compromise on the public accommodations section or otherwise water down the bill. "I have never discussed this with anyone and I would suspect that those rumors which you talk about, which I have read about, are strictly Republican in origin," the president insisted. "I will say that the civil rights bill which passed the House is the bill that this administration recommends. I am in favor of it passing the Senate exactly in its present form. I realize there will be some Senators who will want to strengthen it, some who will want to weaken it. But so far as this administration is concerned, its position is firm and we stand on the House bill."

But privately, Johnson still had his doubts about the Senate leadership team. On Friday, March 6, the president asked Larry O'Brien to make certain that Bob Kennedy agreed with Humphrey and Mansfield's easy-does-it approach. "Now, you be damned sure the attorney general agrees to the procedures they're following," Johnson instructed O'Brien.

"You know Mike a helluva lot better than I do," O'Brien replied. "But I didn't get any impression, I haven't . . . he's been. Anytime you bring up all night sessions, he really bridles, you know, just gets stiff-backed and by God, he's just not going to do it."

"I just want to be sure the attorney general approves of this," Johnson again insisted. "Because I sure don't. And if they agree with him, all right. But my judgment is they ought to start right out going right around the clock until they get it."

"Well, I have a feeling that he'll—" O'Brien began, before the president again interrupted him.

"You be sure that you explain to him that's my judgment on the matter, but I want them to handle the bill, and I'll work with them any way I can. And if Hubert and them work it out, that's their business. They ain't going to damn sure put it in my lap because I'm for civil rights—period. And that means all night, every night. I'll stay here all night, every night, to do it myself and I've passed two of them myself. And I never passed them on any nine-to-four basis."

Bob Kennedy and Burke Marshall would later say that Johnson wanted the attorney general's approval at every step of the way because the president did not see how the bill could pass and did not want to shoulder the sole blame for its failure. But that very evening, the president showed that he needed no reminder of what the fight for the bill was about. As he worked late in the Oval Office, Lady Bird corralled him and Gerri Whittington and Marianne Means, a Hearst Newspapers reporter who was one of the president's favorite journalists, to head to the White House swimming pool for a predinner dip. They found suits for both women but, as Lady Bird noted in her diary, "Lyndon was astonished that Gerri Whittington couldn't swim, and in his very forthright way, he said, 'What's the matter, couldn't you go in any public pools?' And she, I must say, with very creditable poise, said, 'That is right, so I never learned to swim.'"

* * *

IF HUMPHREY AND HIS allies were cautiously optimistic about the coming battle, Richard Russell was not. He had vowed a fight "to the bitter end," but speaking on the CBS News program *Face the Nation* on Sunday, March 1, he offered a pessimistic political analysis of the southerners' plight. "President Kennedy could have lost this bill completely, or in large part, and not one of those who were affected directly by it would have held it against President Kennedy," he said. "I think President Johnson feels that if he loses any substantial part of it, that it will cast all of his statements of support for it in doubt as to their sincerity. That really makes it a much more difficult position as to any possible compromise than there would have been had President Kennedy not met his tragic fate."

9

We Shall Now Begin to Fight

THREE WEEKS AFTER H.R. 7152 arrived in the Senate, Mike Mansfield at last prepared to offer his motion to consider the bill. The final roadblock had been removed the previous Friday, March 6, when the cotton-wheat bill passed the Senate. At his news conference the next day, President Johnson said, "I believe the Senate is prepared now to diligently apply itself, and I hope it stays on the subject until a bill is passed that is acceptable." He declined to estimate the length of the coming debate. "I don't think anyone really knows how long the matter will be discussed," he said. But he did predict that "the majority of the Senate will have an opportunity to work its will," which was a veiled way of acknowledging that the southern filibuster would have to be broken.

One day later, on Sunday, March 8, Hubert Humphrey appeared on NBC's *Meet the Press* and, blithely ignoring Everett Dirksen's openly voiced doubts about the bill, predicted that the Republican leader would regard the civil rights issue as "a moral, not a partisan, one." "I believe we can win this time," Humphrey said, "because there is a time in the affairs of men and nations when an idea comes to fruition. I really believe the

American public recognizes the need for civil rights legislation." He told the program's moderator, Lawrence Spivak, "There will be no wheels and no deals and no compromise that will in any way fundamentally affect or alter this bill." When one of the program's panelists, May Craig, asked about Howard Smith's sex amendment, which had been incorporated into the House bill, Humphrey smiled and answered, "I think we can accept that provision and it is a workable one."

Now, just hours before the Senate was due to begin consideration of the bill, Humphrey met in his office with the bipartisan floor leaders' group for a pep rally. "The House bill is a good bill," Humphrey assured the gathering. "In fact, there is so much good with it that it is hard to tamper with." Moreover, Humphrey told his colleagues, they would be getting plenty of help from a powerful and newly organized group of allies. "The secret of passing this bill," he confided, "is the church groups."

Organized religion had played a key role in American political debates from abolition to Prohibition. But never before had mainline denominations wielded their clout on the question of civil rights in ways they were now prepared to do. Led by the National Council of Churches and its Washington representative, James Hamilton, and working closely with the Leadership Conference on Civil Rights, the interfaith coalition had kept up a ceaseless stream of lobbying activity since the previous summer. Workshops aimed at organizing grassroots efforts had been held in places like Denver, Indianapolis, and Columbus, Ohio. (Of all the letters received by Charlie Halleck about H.R. 7152 in the weeks when the bill was under active consideration in the House, more than four in ten were from correspondents who identified themselves as associated with church groups.)

For his part, Tom Kuchel's aide Stephen Horn carried an index card in his wallet with careful notation of the religious denominations of seven Republican senators he believed might vote for cloture (Bourke Hickenlooper of Iowa was a Methodist, for example, while his Hawkeye colleague Jack Miller was Catholic.) Newspaper accounts of the debate over the bill had kept equally close track of religious affiliation, with one long article in the *Charlotte Observer* noting the denomination of every key player in the House debate.

Now, with the Senate poised to take up the bill, the National Council of Churches issued a bulletin on March 6. THE CRUCIAL SENATE FIGHT IS ABOUT TO BEGIN, it warned. THE EFFORTS OF THE RELIGIOUS FORCES OF OUR NATION WILL AGAIN BE THE DECIDING FACTOR . . . THE BATTLE AHEAD OF US WILL ONLY BE WON AS WE CONVINCE OUR SENATORS THAT WE ARE DEEPLY COMMITTED TO THIS CIVIL RIGHTS BILL AS AN IMPORTANT STEP ON THE ROAD TO FREEDOM AND JUSTICE FOR ALL AMERICANS.

Hubert Humphrey's aide John Stewart and his wife, Nancy, were active in their local United Church of Christ, and throughout the Senate debate on the bill Stewart regularly contributed articles to *Christianity & Crisis*, the liberal biweekly Christian journal that had been founded in 1941 by the theologian Reinhold Niebuhr to urge American intervention in World War II. Stewart's article in the March 2 issue was titled "The Testing of Lyndon B. Johnson," and it offered an insider's perspective on the coming fight.

Because the Senate did not have the usual option of trading away parts of the House-passed bill, Stewart wrote, "The normal complement of expendable items that provide the currency of the legislative process is simply not available to the president under existing circumstances." At the same time, he noted, "the southern opponents will be dealing with a constellation of forces never before assembled in support of civil rights legislation. Under this combination, the filibuster may reveal itself to be a paper tiger. President Johnson appears ready to find out."

* * *

IT WAS ONE OF the mid-twentieth-century Senate's many quirks that its "morning hour," the period at the beginning of each workday reserved for routine housekeeping tasks—the reading of the previous day's journal, the presentation of memorials and committee reports—actually took place in the afternoon and lasted two hours, or until 2:00 p.m. if the Senate convened as usual at noon. During the morning hour, a motion to consider a bill—that is, to make it the pending business of the Senate— was not debatable. So if Mike Mansfield had wanted to call up just any old bill as the first order of business on an ordinary Monday, he might have done so in a matter of seconds.

But March 9, 1964, was no ordinary Monday, and H.R. 7152 was not just any old bill. So, a few minutes after noon, when Mansfield offered a routine motion to dispense with the reading of the previous day's journal, Richard Russell was first on his feet, asking that the journal be read "slowly and clearly enough for all members of the Senate to understand." With a wink to a watching Hubert Humphrey, Russell made his aim clear: to drag out the proceedings past 2:00 p.m., when the morning hour would end and Mansfield's motion to consider the bill would again be debatable.

"Mr. President," Russell intoned, explaining the reasoning behind his delaying tactic, "this measure not only is the strongest of its kind to be proposed since Reconstruction. It is much more drastic than any bill ever presented even during the days of Reconstruction. And I state unhesitatingly that no member of the Reconstruction Congress, no matter how radical, would have dared to present a proposal that would have given such vast governmental control over free enterprise in this country so as to commence the process of socialism."

Two hours and five tedious minutes later, Mike Mansfield again took the floor, to make his motion to consider H.R. 7152, and his message was solemn. "There is," he said, "an ebb and flow in human affairs which at rare moments brings the complex of human events into a delicate balance. At those moments, the acts of governments may indeed influence, for better or for worse, the course of history. This is such a moment in the life of the nation. This is that moment for the Senate."

The southerners were unmoved by Mansfield's ringing appeal. They simply began talking—hour after hour, then day after drowsy day—in what amounted to a kind of prefilibuster on the question of whether to simply take up the bill. The fear among civil rights supporters was that they might just keep talking, preventing the Senate from even beginning to consider H.R. 7152, until Congress adjourned for the Republican Convention in July.

Humphrey and Kuchel and their troops could only do their best to stay organized. On the afternoon of March 10, the bipartisan floor leaders group agreed to have David Filvaroff, the young Justice Department lawyer who had helped draft the bill in the House the previous fall, or one of his colleagues always on duty to answer any questions that pro-civil-rights senators might have about the bill during the debate. Peter Smith, another young Justice Department lawyer, had started work just the day before, and his first assignment was to "sit in the gallery and take note of anything that the Democratic right-wing nuts would say, and if there wasn't an immediate response, and a correct one, from Humphrey or one of his people, we were to run down" to Senator Warren Magnuson's hideaway office just off the Senate floor, "and write up what the answer should be," and send it onto the floor for use by Humphrey and his troops.

For his part, Russell had organized three teams of six southerners each to take responsibility for action on the floor. Humphrey countered with six teams of his own, each of whose leaders was expected to produce four to six of his colleagues after every quorum call. There now began a pattern on the pro-civil-rights side that would last throughout the debate: Each morning, the floor managers, their staffs, and Justice Department aides would meet to go over plans for the day. At least twice a week, Clarence Mitchell and Joe Rauh would join them. And every evening, the Senate staffers would reconvene to review the day's action and tie up any loose ends. Such diligence impressed even Lyndon Johnson, who asked Larry O'Brien about the possibility of inviting the hardworking aides and their wives to the White House for a little break.

By Wednesday, March 11, as the southerners drawled on, the civil rights supporters were already talking about how to handle the touchy matter of senators who wanted to offer amendments to strengthen the House bill. At their meeting that day, Joe Rauh told the bipartisan floor leaders group that the Justice Department was so concerned about upsetting Bill McCulloch with any amendments that it had asked Clarence Mitchell to take a position against even those that would strengthen the bill—which Mitchell said he could not do. When Rauh wondered if there was any "jelling" in the situation yet, John Stewart replied that things were "still fluid," to which Patricia Connell of Senator Kenneth Keating's office could not resist adding, "It is better fluid than frozen." The harried staffers looked for humor wherever they could find it. On Thursday, March 12, Kuchel's legislative aide Stephen Horn, who kept a detailed diary of the deliberations of the floor leaders' group, noted, "It is a very jocular crowd. Department of Justice representatives are no longer present."

By that same day, Stewart's journalistic brainchild, the daily civil rights newsletter slipped under senators' office doors overnight, was beginning to cause a stir. A typical issue noted that there had already been seventy days of public hearings on the civil rights bill, with 275 witnesses and 175 written statements, running to a record of 5,792 printed pages.

But the southerners were not impressed. "Who writes these mysterious messages," an irritated John Stennis of Mississippi inquired, "which come to Senators before the Congressional Record reaches them, and in them attempt to refute arguments made on the floor of the Senate?"

"There is no doubt about it," Humphrey proudly replied. "The newsletter is a bipartisan civil rights newsletter. For the first time, we are putting up a battle." Then, in a typical gesture of magnanimity, he announced, "If anyone wishes to have equal time, there is space on the back of it for the opposition."

Indeed, Humphrey was proving that it was possible to disagree without being disagreeable. Near the end of this same day, Senator Willis Robertson of Virginia made a speech excoriating every section of the bill, and when he was done, strode over to Humphrey and offered a small Confederate flag pin for the majority whip's lapel. Humphrey accepted the offering and praised Robertson (the father of the future televangelist Pat Robertson) for his "eloquence and his great knowledge of history and law, but also for his wonderful . . . gentlemanly qualities and his consideration to us at all times."

Robertson returned the compliment in the highest terms, noting that "if it had not been for the men from Wisconsin and Minnesota, when Grant finally came down to Virginia, we would have won, but they formerly belonged to Virginia. We could not whip them." The pair then ambled off arm in arm to Humphrey's office to share a drink.

* * *

ON SATURDAY, MARCH 14, Lyndon Johnson taped a television interview with the three major networks, reviewing his first hundred days in office, to be broadcast the following night. "The Negro was freed of his chains a hundred years ago," he said, "but he has not been freed of the problems brought about by his color and the bigotry that exists. I know of nothing more important for this Congress to do than pass the Civil Rights Act as the House passed it."

As the southerners' talkathon continued, the civil rights proponents kept up their own side of the debate, not only on the Senate floor but in the daily newsletter. The March 16 edition cited "The High Cost of Racial Discrimination to Our Economy," quoting a 1962 report by the White House's Council of Economic Advisers saying that the nation's gross national product might rise 2.5 percent if barriers to discrimination in employment were removed, and by 3.2 percent if there were no barriers in education. "This, of course, in no way measures the heaviest cost of all—the loss of human dignity accompanying racial discrimination," the newsletter noted.

That same day, Robert Kimball of John Lindsay's staff reported to Stephen Horn that Bill McCulloch was getting "progressively worried" about the protracted Senate debate, as civil rights disturbances continued around the country. A protest over a segregated barbershop in Yellow Springs, Ohio, not far from Piqua, had turned violent and led to the arrest of one hundred people, many of them students at Antioch College, leaving the Ohio delegation "up in arms," Kimball added. He said McCulloch now estimated that the House Republicans would lose 25 percent of the votes they had obtained for passage of the bill if the vote were retaken today. That was worrisome, because H.R. 7152 would have to go back to the House for final approval if the Senate changed so much as a word.

By this point, the strain on the pro-civil-rights forces was showing in other ways, too. It took them sixty-seven minutes to complete a dinner-hour quorum call, and the newsletter of March 17 chided, "The more promptly that the Senate responds to such quorum calls, the more efficiently we can proceed."

In Humphrey's quest for ways to bolster support for the bill, no idea seemed too far-fetched. In a memo to his staff, the majority whip noted that the actor Marlon Brando had told him that he had sounded out Johnny Carson, Steve Allen, Jack Paar, and Hugh Downs about promoting the bill on their television shows, and Humphrey expressed enthusiasm about the possibility. Humphrey's aide Bill Connell urged him to ask Lyndon Johnson to lobby top network executives to join the cause, and went so far as to draft a memo from Humphrey to the president, urging that they enlist entertainers popular in the Midwest—including Lawrence Welk, Bob Hope, John Wayne, and the cast of *The Beverly Hillbillies*—to stage a television special promoting civil rights as a way of pressuring wavering Republican senators to support cloture. (There is no evidence the memo ever made it to the White House, and nothing came of the idea.)

But the bipartisan floor leaders' group also took some care not to overplay its hand, agreeing in a meeting on March 18 that it was too early to enlist large numbers of union members or average citizens to come lobby the Senate in person. "If fifty Negroes came," Clarence Mitchell suggested, "the newspapers would say they are overrunning the town." By this point, the southerners were dragging out debate by asking unanimous consent to make off-topic speeches that would not count against their allotted total on civil rights, and had so far used only twelve of the thirty-eight speaking slots available to them under the two-speeches-a-day rule. The calendar might read March 19 in the Capitol itself, but in the Senate it was still the legislative day of March 9. Joe Rauh and others argued that the slowdown was not so bad, and actually favored the pro-civil-rights forces, allowing them more time to gain support for the bill while avoiding any votes on cloture when success was still uncertain.

At a meeting with the floor leaders' group in Humphrey's office on Friday, March 20, Kuchel suggested asking Bill McCulloch to come and join one of their daily meetings. Nick Katzenbach, who was present that day, reported that he was not sure McCulloch would do so, noting that while the congressman had always opposed weakening amendments, he had been equally careful not to say what kind of strengthening amendments he might support. After the meeting, Kuchel and Stephen Horn met Robert Kimball for coffee in the Senate dining room, and Kimball informed them that McCulloch was under pressure from other House Republicans to "go slow" in the face of unfavorable mail and mounting public concern over continuing civil rights demonstrations.

Finally, by March 24, word began to circulate on Capitol Hill that the southerners were ready to allow a vote on the Mansfield motion to consider the bill. Jerry Grinstein of Warren Magnuson's staff reported that the southern caucus had voted 7 to 5 to let the bill come up. The precise reason for this about-face has never been clear, but the best guess is that Richard Russell had begun to fear that continued foot-dragging on the mere consideration of the bill might prompt more Republicans to support cloture once H.R. 7152 reached the floor.

Once again, the pro-civil-rights side went out of its way not to be seen as gloating. Stephen Horn drily noted in his diary, "There is a feeling that Martin Luther King should stay out of the gallery when the vote is underway" on the motion to consider.

On March 26, after sixteen days of what *Time* called "drone and drawl talk," Mansfield at last got a vote on his motion to consider H.R. 7152, and it passed overwhelmingly, by a vote of 67 to 17—a blow to the southerners. But then Wayne Morse, a stickler to the end, offered a motion to recommit the bill to the Judiciary Committee, with instructions to report it out by April 8. Everett Dirksen would have accepted this course, but Mansfield moved to table—in effect, reject—the motion. Mansfield carried the day, but only by a much closer vote of 50 to 34, with six northern and western Democrats and nine Republicans (including Dirksen) supporting Morse, in a sign of just how difficult it would be to break the filibuster. (Mansfield was especially worried that if the bill went to committee, it would come back to the floor without any privileged status, and the fight to get it on the calendar and make it the pending business would have to be waged all over again.)

Richard Russell was philosophical. "A skirmish has been lost," he said. "We shall now begin to fight the war." Martin Luther King was just as determined. He threatened "direct action" if the bill was not passed by the first of May.

* * *

MONDAY, MARCH 30, THE day after Easter, was anything but springlike on Capitol Hill. It was cold and snowing, and the early-flowering forsythia and cherry blossom buds were frozen as Roger Mudd of CBS News took up his camera position on the Senate steps in galoshes and a snap-brim felt hat, interviewing Hubert Humphrey, who had been forced to borrow a too-large overcoat from the CBS Washington bureau chief, Bill Small, at the last moment.

But inside the Senate chamber, the bright sunshine of human rights beamed hot from Humphrey's heart as he began his fifty-five-page opening speech in support of H.R. 7152.

"I cannot overemphasize the historic importance of the debate we are beginning," Humphrey told his colleagues, on what just happened to be the ninety-fourth anniversary of the ratification of the Fifteenth Amendment, which had prohibited federal and state governments from denying a citizen the right to vote based on "race, color or previous condition of servitude." "We are participants in one of the most crucial eras in the long and proud history of the United States, and, yes, in mankind's struggle for justice and freedom which has gone forward since the dawn of history." The stakes, the majority whip added, were of the largest possible scale. "If freedom fails here—in America, the land of the free," he demanded, "what hope can we have for it surviving elsewhere?"

Three and a half hours later, after Humphrey had gone through the bill, title by title and point by point, his Republican counterpart, Tom Kuchel, actually managed to out-talk him, making a fifty-six-page address of his own. "This issue should not be a partisan fight," Kuchel said. "It should be, and is, an American fight. The record that is being made in the Senate today will go a long way, not merely to demonstrate that the Senate desires to pass legislation in the civil rights field, but also to provide the people of this country and all branches of government with the clear and unequivocal intention by which the bill will be fashioned in plain English."

From the White House, Lyndon Johnson telephoned Ted Kennedy, to praise him for a television appearance in support of the bill the day before, and to assure him once more of his commitment as "just a trustee that's trying to carry on the best I can" to pass the bill as a memorial to John Kennedy. "We're going to put over his program," Johnson said, "and he's going to be proud of it—if we all survive."

If anyone on that late March morning understood the potential pitfalls ahead for the civil rights bill, it was Lyndon Johnson. But the president and his allies knew something else: that the mood of the country was changing. Just twenty-four hours earlier, on Easter Sunday, the Reverend Billy Graham had held a service for thirty-five thousand intermingled black and white congregants in a football stadium in Birmingham, the largest integrated audience in the history of Alabama. Even as the Senate opened debate on the bill, the Supreme Court was hearing oral arguments on the Prince Edward County, Virginia, school discrimination case, in which the county had simply closed all its schools rather than accept integration, a move that Solicitor General Archibald Cox told the court amounted to an "experiment in ignorance." That same week, Mrs. Malcolm Peabody, the mother of the Republican governor of Massachusetts, and a group of fellow demonstrators were arrested in St. Augustine, Florida, for attempting to integrate the restaurant of the Ponce de Leon Motel, in the same city where Lyndon Johnson's stand for desegregation had lasted for precisely one evening the year before.

The mood of the Senate itself was changing, too, with liberal freshman Democrats like Birch Bayh of Indiana, Daniel Inouye of Hawaii, and George McGovern of South Dakota—all young World War II–era veterans—bringing a fresh perspective and a new concern for social justice to the institution. Bayh had managed black G.I. baseball players in postwar occupied Germany. Inouye had lost an arm fighting in Italy with his segregated, all Japanese-American regiment, but came back to face fresh prejudice. "When I returned home from the war, from the hospital with four ribbons and a captain's bar," he recalled, "I was denied entrance to one of the big restaurants" outside Honolulu.

For all the presumed drama of the opening day of debate, the scene in the Senate was oddly ordinary. Humphrey's and Kuchel's voices floated out toward the pale yellow marble-trimmed walls of a mostly empty chamber, and disappointed tourists trudged into the galleries above at quarter-hour intervals in search of something that might pass for debate. "Let there be extended debate, full debate, debate on every section, subsection and title," Humphrey declared. "But the difference between extended debate and a filibuster is that debate is designed to give life to legislation, and is designed to arrive at a decision—either affirmative or negative—a decision of will, yea or nay. A filibuster is designed to kill legislation, to bury it, to paralyze it."

* * *

HUMPHREY AND KUCHEL HELD the floor so long that Richard Russell did not have a chance to begin the southern rebuttal until the following day, Tuesday, March 31. When he did, he was livid with Humphrey, complaining that the majority whip had spoken for four or five hours. "For some reason," Russell allowed, "he appears to think that he not only calls the tune but does all the dancing." When Humphrey rejoined that he had spoken only for three hours or so, the dour Senator Spessard Holland of Florida interjected, "It merely seemed like a longer time, so little was actually said."

The southerners accused the pro-civil-rights forces themselves of staging a filibuster, with their extended speeches in support of the bill, even as Russell drily acknowledged, "It may take some time for us to discuss the bill adequately." When Kuchel noted that a "clear majority" of senators favored the bill, Russell pounced. "The Senator assumes, of course, that a majority is always right," he said. "That is the most violent and erroneous assumption that has ever been asserted. A minority has the responsibility to undertake to correct the views of any majority."

Soon enough, Russell's bumptious colleague Strom Thurmond of South Carolina—who held the Senate's all-time filibuster record for his twenty-four-hour, eighteen-minute tirade against the 1957 civil rights bill—was on his feet to undertake the task of correction. Thurmond began with Title I, which barred unequal application of voter registration requirements in federal elections. He insisted that such protections were unnecessary because the NAACP was already busy bringing voting rights suits, and added, "Today, the Negro is almost a favored class of citizen in America." Thurmond argued that a recent report of the United States Commission on Civil Rights had found not a single confirmed report of voter discrimination in South Carolina.

Senator Jacob Javits of New York, well prepared by the Justice Department briefing books at hand, was quick to contend that an absence of sworn complaints of discrimination should not be taken as proof of anything. He noted that in McCormick County, South Carolina, only one of forty-nine registered black citizens appeared to have voted in the 1960 presidential primary, and none in the general election.

George Smathers of Florida, a segregationist of a more genteel stripe, couched his arguments on a loftier plane. "The proponents seek to set fire to the barn in order to get rid of a couple of rats," Smathers said. "We are doing a good job. If we are permitted to continue to do it, in time the evil will disappear, and citizens will no longer be deprived of the right to vote because of race, color or creed."

But Thurmond was having none of this. He spoke skeptically of the constitutionality of the entire Fourteenth Amendment, because it was passed during Reconstruction, when the South was under the heel of the northern boot. This was too much even for Hubert Humphrey, who was moved to exclaim, "I never thought I would live to see the day when anybody would doubt that the Fourteenth Amendment was as much a part of the Constitution as the Bill of Rights."

Such a day had now come, and the fight was on in earnest.

* * *

THE MAN LEADING THAT fight for the South—the man who had led it with devastating effectiveness for more than a generation—was perhaps the most respected, and also the most quietly feared, man in the Senate: Richard Brevard Russell Jr., the courtly, learned, lonely bachelor from Winder, Georgia, who had come to Washington at the dawn of the New Deal and in the ensuing three decades had become the acknowledged master of the Senate's rules and procedures and the proud custodian of its unspoken codes and folkways.

"Baseball fan. Roman bearing. Tends toward hypochondria," is how Roger Mudd of CBS summed Russell up in a succinct sketch that spring. "Almost impossible to anger but a devastating debater . . . Modest. His *Congressional Directory* biography totals seven words."

Indeed, by this stage in his long and distinguished career, Russell had no need to impress anyone, friend or foe. The son of a family that had lived in Georgia and North Carolina since colonial times—"descended from the oldest and choicest American stock," an admirer said—Russell was, as his fellow southerner Lady Bird Johnson once put it, "Quality."

Russell's great-great-grandfather, a British sympathizer during the Revolution, had been forced to flee to the Bahamas, but the family eventually returned and Russell's own father became a lawyer, Superior Court judge, and finally chief justice of the Georgia Supreme Court. Like every southern boy, as William Faulkner once wrote, young R. B. Russell grew up always able to imagine that it was not yet two o'clock on the afternoon of Pickett's Charge at Gettysburg, when the tide had not yet turned and defeat was not yet inevitable for his beloved South. He was taught to cherish every fact and legend of regional gallantry and valor, and when Lyndon Johnson's daughter Luci married Patrick Nugent in 1966, "Uncle Dick" Russell's gift to her would be an inscribed copy of *Gone with the Wind*.

By age twenty-five, he was speaker pro tem of the Georgia State Assembly, and at thirty-three he was elected governor, sworn in by his own father, the chief justice. Just two years later, in 1932, he won a special election to the United States Senate, where he became a staunch supporter of Franklin Roosevelt's New Deal farm legislation and rural electrification (and he would be the driving force behind creation of the National School Lunch Act after World War II). But by the late 1930s, he was also a leader of the "Conservative Coalition" of southern Democrats and midwestern and western Republicans that held the balance of power in Washington.

When Lyndon Johnson arrived in the Senate in 1949, he asked Bobby Baker who was the most influential senator. Baker replied that while all senators were equal, Dick Russell was the most equal, "incomparably the truest current Senate type, and incomparably the most influential man on the inner life of the Senate," as the journalist William S. White would write. In fact, when the Senate faced a difficult task—such as the investigation into Harry Truman's firing of General Douglas MacArthur in 1951—it was Russell to whom the Senate turned. Soon enough, Lyndon Johnson made it his business to be assigned a seat on Russell's powerful Armed Services Committee, listening and learning at the hand of a teacher he called "the Old Master."

And Johnson, with his gift for courting and flattering and winning over older men to his side, soon accomplished a feat even more extraordinary. He enticed the solitary Russell to after-work suppers and, later, Sunday brunches at his and Lady Bird's welcoming home on Thirtieth Place, Northwest. Russell had largely shied away from Washington social life, and Lady Bird said it was all but impossible to get him to accept an invitation far in advance. But the Johnsons persisted, and in those friendly, filial, spur-of-the-moment get-togethers, Lyndon Johnson was, indeed, learning from a master.

Russell eschewed the crude populist racism of southern demagogues like Theodore Bilbo of Mississippi and "Cotton Ed" Smith of South Carolina—and for that matter, the showy, seriocomic antics of Strom Thurmond. Instead, he grounded his implacable opposition to desegregation in the Constitution itself. Indeed, he always took care to refer to the southern caucus that he led as the "Constitutional Democrats." As a result, national magazines and newspapers whose correspondents stood in awe of Russell's legislative skills took pains to portray him as being "at opposite poles from the stereotype some Northerners hold of a Deep-Dixie segregationist—the gallus-snapping, Negro-baiting semi-illiterate," as *Newsweek* put it in 1963. *Time* said he "admired and respected" blacks in "that special, paternal, Southern way." Many journalists wanted to believe, as the *Saturday Evening Post* reported as early as 1951, that Russell was "far more liberal in his heart than he is in his votes."

* * *

YET DICK RUSSELL'S VOTES told a stark story. In 1949, he led the fight to change the cloture rule to require two-thirds of the whole Senate to cut off debate, instead of just two-thirds of those senators present. (He once said he would "vote to gag the Senate when the shrimp start whistling 'Dixie.'") After the Supreme Court's *Brown* decision in 1954, he drafted the final version of the southerners' "Declaration of Constitutional Principles," less grandly known as the "Southern Manifesto," calling the decision "a clear abuse of judicial power" and promising to use "all lawful means to bring about a reversal of this decision which is contrary to the Constitution and to prevent the use of force in its implementation." (Lyndon Johnson was one of only three southern senators who refused to sign.) Russell denounced the 1957 Civil Rights Act that Johnson labored so craftily to pass as sure to create "unspeakable confusion, bitterness and bloodshed in a great section of our common country." After it passed, a constituent wrote to him to say he was fighting a losing battle.

Russell responded that he was trying to delay desegregation "ten years if I'm not lucky, two hundred years if I am." In the debate over the 1960 civil rights bill, he organized his three squads of southerners to break the back of the exhausted civil rights supporters, block cloture, and gut the legislation.

And in occasional public flashes, bits of his deepest private views emerged. During World War II, he made no secret of his belief that blacks lacked physical courage even if, as he once told his sister, they were quick to kill in anger. To a constituent who objected to black and white troops using the same hospitals (and even the same maternity wards) on southern Army bases, he wrote, "It is a terrible mistake and I hope we will be able to convince the Army of it before it is widely advertised and becomes a serious issue." In a debate over one of his pet causes—cutting the budget of Franklin Roosevelt's wartime Fair Employment Practices Commission, he told his colleagues, "Any man who wants to take a position that he is no better than the Negro is entitled to his own opinion. I do not think much of him, but he can think it."

"I don't like to say too much about people like Senator Russell," Lyndon Johnson's loyal cook, Zephyr Wright, would tell an oral history interviewer after both men were dead, "because he was at the Johnsons' quite a bit. To me, when he was there, naturally he portrayed a different way of life than he did in Congress, because he was a very nice person. But when I read about him and heard about the things he was doing and saying in Congress, then I got a very different feeling about him."

What Russell was saying and doing in Congress in the spring of 1964 could not have pleased Zephyr Wright. On March 16, during the debate on the motion to consider the bill, he revived an old chestnut, proposing a program of voluntary "racial relocation," which would offer government subsidies aimed at achieving a black population in each state "as near to the national average as practicable and feasible." Under such a plan, the federal government would pay blacks to move north and west, and white northerners to move south, with the goal of producing a black population of 10.5 percent in all regions. The *Atlanta Constitution*, the most influential newspaper in his own state, took him to task for perpetuating "for all the nation to see an image which Southerners are trying to overcome, the callous attitude that Negroes can be moved about like chess pawns." State Senator Lamar Plunkett of Georgia allowed that "the people of Georgia are now going forward with a little different beat of the drum. Those who are not thoroughly conversant with it may lose the beat." But Russell was unapologetic, telling *Business Week*, "I'm not an anthropologist, but I've studied history. And there is no case in history of a mongrel race preserving a civilization, much less creating one." Russell's proposal went nowhere.

In truth, for all his erudition, for all his mastery of the rules, Russell had limited options, as he knew better than anyone. In 1952, spurred on by the sentiment so often repeated in Washington with a sigh—that Dick Russell would make a better president than any man in national life, if only he weren't from the South—Russell himself had decided to test the proposition by actually mounting a campaign for the White House. He failed, miserably, and some of his best friends thought he was never again quite the same psychologically. "It's one thing to know something academically," George Reedy would say. "It's another to have it hit you in the face."

Now even some of Russell's onetime allies were throwing his own words back at him, and the beat was changing. He was sixty-six years old, and his emphysema was bothering him more and more. He was exhausted by the dual demands of the filibuster and his service on the special commission, chaired by Chief Justice Earl Warren, charged with investigating the Kennedy assassination—an assignment that Lyndon Johnson had forced upon him. His best hope for the southerners that spring was to keep talking—with luck, until summer, when he knew the Senate would have to break for the presidential nominating conventions and then be unable to wrestle with anything so contentious in the middle of a fall election campaign. "We knew there was no way in hell we could muster the necessary votes to defeat the civil rights bill," Russell's fellow Georgian Herman Talmadge would recall. "But we thought we could filibuster long enough to get the other side to agree to amendments that would make it less offensive."

*   *   *

As THE FILIBUSTER BEGAN, however, Russell had one other hope besides prolonged talk: Everett Dirksen, who on the very day the southerners began their counterattack on the bill was marshaling his own forces. Like Lyndon Johnson and Hubert Humphrey, Russell knew that Dirksen was the wild card—in fact, the trump card—in the whole civil rights debate. And Dirksen's publicly expressed doubts about the public accommodations and fair employment practices sections of H.R. 7152 entitled Russell to think he might yet win the Illinoisan to his side.

But even as the southerners trumpeted their determination to defeat the bill, Dirksen was making it clear to his fellow Republicans that he was already looking for a way to make H.R. 7152 more passable. All during the prefilibuster over the motion to consider, Dirksen had largely stayed out of the public parliamentary maneuvering. Instead, he worked quietly with his key legal aides on the Judiciary Committee—Cornelius "Neal" Kennedy, Clyde Flynn, and Bernard Waters, known collectively as "Dirksen's Bombers"—to analyze the bill. "Dirksen asked us to take a look at the bill and make it as acceptable as possible to as large a number of people as possible," Flynn would recall. "We met with him literally fourteen hours a day, month after month," Kennedy remembered.

Dirksen and his staff concluded that Title VII, covering employment discrimination, would pose particular problems in northern states like Illinois that already had strong fair employment statutes. "If the powers granted in this Title are exercised," the minority leader wrote to Walter McAdoo, executive vice president of the Keystone Steel & Wire Company, a large employer in Peoria, "it will be one great headache for industry and business all over the country."

Dirksen's concern was also fueled by an intense employment discrimination controversy in his home state involving Motorola, the big electronics company that was a major employer in suburban Chicago. Earlier that year, a black hearing examiner for the Illinois State Fair Employment Practices Commission had ordered Motorola to hire a black applicant who had failed an ability test and had directed the company to stop using the test on the grounds that it discriminated against "culturally deprived and disadvantaged groups." The case, which was still pending before the full commission, had become a cause célèbre among conservative opponents of Title VII, who contended that it presaged the sort of overreaching that a new federal Equal Employment Opportunity Commission would attempt.

On March 31, at a closed-door meeting of the Republican Policy Committee, the party's Senate brain trust, Dirksen outlined some possible amendments to Title VII that might keep the bill from "harassing businessmen," as he put it. These included proposals aimed at easing employment record-keeping requirements, plus other measures intended to avert conflicts between state and federal fair employment rules and to give precedence to states with effective laws already on the books. He also floated the far more controversial idea of revising Title II of the bill, the all-important public accommodations section, to allow for voluntary compliance within one year, before the attorney general could sue for an injunction to block discriminatory practices. It was his first effort to share his evolving ideas beyond his own inner circle, and he took in his colleagues' views. They persuaded him to hold off on any changes in Title II for the moment.

As Dirksen tested the Republican waters, the pro-civil-rights forces were facing a crucial test of their own. At the meeting of the bipartisan floor leaders' group on Wednesday, April 1, Joe Rauh declared: "Let's face it. We have a bill now which is beyond our wildest dreams." But with the first weekend of the filibuster fast approaching, and the probability that many senators would be out of town campaigning in an election year, Humphrey's allies worried that they would be unable to muster a quorum for the projected Saturday session on April 4.

In fact, they failed to produce the needed bodies—to disastrous embarrassment. When the Senate convened at eleven o'clock that morning (still the "legislative day" of March 30, of course), Mike Mansfield, following standard procedure, noted the absence of a quorum, and the clerk began to call the roll. Humphrey was forced to announce the expected absence of more than forty Democrats, for one reason or another, while Kenneth Keating announced that a dozen Republicans were also hors de combat. This led the presiding officer, Mansfield's Montana colleague, Lee Metcalf, to announce that a quorum was not in fact present.

If the Senate lacks a quorum, the rules allow only two options: adjourn or take action to produce a quorum. Since adjournment would allow the southerners to start a new legislative day, Mansfield immediately moved that the Senate sergeant at arms be directed "to request the attendance of absent Senators." And then, knowing full well that even such a move could not produce a quorum with so many senators out of town, Mansfield short-circuited that process by asking Metcalf whether a motion to recess until Monday would be in order, so that the two-speech clock would not have to start all over again on a new legislative day, allowing the southerners to prolong the filibuster even further. Because the roll call had not yet started, Metcalf ruled that the motion was in order. "I am afraid we are face to face with a travesty on the legislative process," Mansfield told his colleagues. "I believe it is a shame and an indignity upon this institution. In order to prevent this situation from turning into a farce, I move . . . that the Senate now stand in recess until Monday morning next at 10 o'clock." Forty-one excruciating minutes after it had convened, the Senate did just that.

For their part, a majority of the southerners had not even bothered to show up that morning, and most of the handful present in the chamber voted in favor of the motion to recess, apparently satisfied that the failure to produce a quorum was humiliation enough for the pro-civil-rights side.

An embarrassed Humphrey explained after the vote that too many senators "just wouldn't stay in town." But ever the optimist, he predicted, "I'll bet there'll be so many Senators here Monday that you will think each state sent four."

When Humphrey and his pro-civil-rights allies convened that Monday morning in his office, the majority whip was unbowed. Having been told by Kuchel and other Republicans of Dirksen's potential amendments to Title VII, Humphrey urged his colleagues not to dismiss Dirksen's ideas out of hand. "My position is no amendments, but I want to praise Dirksen," Humphrey said. "He's not trying to be destructive. He's trying to be constructive. There's no chance of getting cloture unless we have Dirksen."

* * *

ON THAT MONDAY, APRIL 6, the filibuster edged into its second week. There were few new arguments to be made, so the southerners just kept on making the same old ones. George Smathers complained that if the bill passed, "There will have to be an Attorney General's section as big as the Pentagon building in order to hold all the lawyers that will have to be employed." Then, in practically the next breath, he acknowledged, "It would be less than candid of me to say that in the past, in parts of the South, discrimination has not been practiced against Negro citizens. It is true that there has been discrimination; and I'm afraid there will be discrimination, so long as we are human beings and so long as we remain alive." He went on to say that, because of Reconstruction, southerners themselves knew something of discrimination, and added, "I point out that on the floor of the Senate, we who come from the South are but a small group, with a membership of only some 18. No Southerner has been elected President of the United States for more than 100 years. Why? Because of discrimination."

Smathers's Orwellian interpretation of Reconstruction was a sign of the perverse lengths to which the southerners would go to defend the peculiar institution of Jim Crow. Over and over again in the weeks and months of the long debate, they would resort to sophistry and solipsism, sarcasm and spitefulness, that would have been shocking enough in the antebellum era, much less in the second half of the twentieth century.

The segregationists suggested that H.R. 7152 should be called "the Discrimination Act of 1964," as John McClellan of Arkansas put it, or "a bill to regulate the American people," as Herman Talmadge of Georgia suggested.

"The good Lord did as much segregating as anyone I know of when he put one race in one part of the world and another race in another part of the world," Russell Long of Louisiana said early in the debate. "We folks in the South are not hypocrites about this matter. We think it is absolutely desirable that the white people should continue to be white and that their children and grandchildren should be the same; and we let our children know that we think just that. We think it desirable to encourage the colored people to exert themselves in the same direction." To this homily, Paul Douglas of Illinois replied drily, "In spite of the protestations that have been made by our Southern friends that they do not want mixing of the races, race-mixing has occurred in the past in the South, and most of it was not initiated by the Negroes."

On another occasion that April, Long was moved to muse: "Would it not be fair to ask what kind of fix the colored folks would be in if they had not been brought to this country, but had been allowed to roam the jungles, with tigers chasing them, or being subjected to the other elements they would have to contend with, compared with the fine conditions they enjoy in America." And on the same day, Long engaged in a collegial colloquy with Strom Thurmond on the subject of the police methods used to subdue civil rights demonstrators.

"Is the Senator familiar with the fact that the prod sticks have been described as cattle prodders because they have been used on cattle?" Long asked. "Is the Senator further familiar with the fact that the prod sticks are not designed for cattle but are designed for exactly the kind of 'animals' that they are touching: namely, reluctant human beings who insist on getting in the way of a policeman?"

Thurmond gamely replied: "It seems to me that a stick of that kind might be appropriately used. There is not very much electricity in one. I remember once going through a secret organization ceremonial—a fraternal organization. There was a man after me with one of those sticks and I ran for about 100 yards. I had to run fast to keep ahead of that stick because while it mostly tickled, it tickled pretty much. It would force one to move—it does not hurt anyone—but it is a practical means of getting people to move on." (The daily civil rights newsletter cited this exchange under the heading "Quote Without Comment.")

Sometimes, the southerners simply told lies, as the incorrigible James Eastland of Mississippi did when he interrupted a speech by William Proxmire of Wisconsin about race-based economic and employment discrimination. "I have lived in the South my whole life," Eastland sputtered. "I have not seen the first instance of economic discrimination in the South."

Proxmire then read from a United States Department of Agriculture Report on Greenwood, Mississippi, that found that nearly half the daily attendees in the public schools were black, yet Negro students received only one-fifth of the free school lunches distributed in the district. "I live near Greenwood, Mississippi, and I do not believe a word of that," Eastland shot back.

"This is from the Department of Agriculture," Proxmire insisted.

"That does not mean it is true," Eastland replied. "I know the conditions there. I know the conditions in my own area. I live in the county adjoining Greenwood. They get exactly the same treatment and there is no such thing that I know of as economic discrimination there."

The exchanges were not without humor. Willis Robertson of Virginia, complaining about Title VII's requirements for nondiscrimination in employment, told of a Jewish banker who had approached him, saying he would not want to have to employ blacks or gentiles because they would not know his business. Informed that he might well have to, Robertson said, the banker exclaimed, "Then I had better sell out right now!" Hubert Humphrey could not resist asking, "Can the Senator from Virginia inform us whether that would be a good opportunity for a bargain?"

But no amount of levity could mask the fundamental gravity of the debate. One day in mid-April, Olin Johnston of South Carolina undertook to lecture the civil rights supporters, insisting: "There is considerable evidence that segregation in the South has worked far better than integration in the North. Repeated incidents of mob actions in the streets of Southern cities—and cities all over our land—should not make us lose sight of the fact that Southern states, despite their relatively low per capita incomes, do not have the high rates of crime and juvenile delinquency of those states which are hotbeds of agitators against so many American institutions."

Soon thereafter, Sam Ervin of North Carolina joined Johnston in offering Jacob Javits, the liberal Republican civil rights supporter from New York, "our gratitude for his willingness—notwithstanding his failure to cure the racial ills of New York—to try to ram a new law down the throats of the people of our states."

"Does not the Senator from South Carolina," Ervin continued, "think that, as we say in North Carolina, 'That is downright kind and generous of the Senator from New York'?" Javits jumped into the debate to say, "I am delighted to be the object of such affection by these two distinguished Senators from the South. But it strikes me that charm never covered up a running sore. And that is what we are dealing with."

* * *

ONE DEVELOPMENT OUTSIDE THE Senate chamber that Richard Russell hoped his delaying tactics might work in the southerners' favor was a strong showing by George Wallace's white supremacist presidential campaign against Lyndon Johnson for the 1964 Democratic presidential nomination. Wallace's candidacy was symbolic; he never expected to win. But all eyes were on the Wisconsin primary on Tuesday, April 7. In fact, Wallace won a surprising 33.9 percent of the vote that day, racking up big tallies in Milwaukee's white ethnic neighborhoods, and taking 264,000 votes against 511,000 for Governor John W. Reynolds, who was running as Johnson's surrogate. Reynolds had said that even a 100,000-vote showing by Wallace would be a "catastrophe," but Hubert Humphrey was now quick to dismiss Wallace's performance as "a flop, F-L-O-P."

And indeed, the Wisconsin results did little to affect the progress (or lack thereof) in the Senate's debate over H.R. 7152. On the day of the primary, Senator Abraham Ribicoff of Connecticut conducted a vigorous defense of Title VI, the provision covering antidiscrimination in federally financed programs, which would allow (but not compel) Washington to cut off funds to state and local programs that practiced racial discrimination. "Of all the provisions of this civil rights bill," Ribicoff told the Senate, "none rests on so simple and so sound a principle as does Title VI. That principle is taxpayers' money, which is collected without discrimination, shall be spent without discrimination. The principle requires no argument. It is based on simple justice. It is based on decency." But John Stennis of Mississippi countered that the measure would "grant all this power to Federal departments and agencies . . . in a carte blanche bill."

That afternoon, Stephen Horn of Tom Kuchel's staff talked to John Lindsay's aide Robert Kimball, who told him that Bill McCulloch had returned home from a trip to Ohio "shaken up" by the impact that a grassroots advertising campaign by a segregationist group called the "Coordinating Committee for Fundamental American Freedoms" was having on "rational people." The work of John C. Sattefield, a former president of the American Bar Association, and William Loeb, the rabidly conservative publisher of the *Union Leader* in Manchester, New Hampshire, and financed in part by public funds from the State of Mississippi, the committee had run newspaper ads around the country denouncing H.R. 7152 as a "$100 Billion Blackjack."

Meantime, Everett Dirksen kept noodling over his proposed amendments to the fair employment section. On April 7, he briefed the Republican Policy Committee on his latest ideas. These included a provision under which no federal action could be taken to resolve an employment discrimination complaint where a state law or fair employment agency already existed without first giving state authorities ninety days to resolve the matter. Dirksen would also limit the powers of the federal Equal Employment Opportunity Commission to seeking voluntary compliance with its findings. He did not want federal record-keeping requirements to be superimposed on existing state agencies. He would include union hiring halls among the "employment agencies" covered by the bill, to make sure that employers would not be blamed for hiring decisions that were in fact dictated by unions. And he would specify that the results of technical studies by the commission would be made public but that the findings of individual efforts at conciliation would not. He would give all enforcement powers under Title VII to the federal courts, and not to the commission itself. He also proposed to delete Howard Smith's "sex" provision from the House bill. And at a press briefing after the private luncheon, he surprised reporters and other senators alike by declaring that he might just like to strike Title VII altogether.

Dirksen was testing the waters, trying to ascertain what kind of measures his own Republican caucus would accept. But such public rumblings alarmed the pro-civil-rights forces. Humphrey once again urged forbearance, arguing that Dirksen was still sounding out his own troops, not making any final pronouncements. At a meeting of the bipartisan floor leaders' group on Thursday, April 9, Humphrey advised that he and his colleagues should "follow the course of not being openly antagonistic to Dirksen. The Republicans must carry the fight. Let the Republicans argue it out with their own leader. Dirksen told me that if he could not get support, then he would have to retreat."

In the same meeting, in a sign of just how closely H.R. 7152's supporters in both parties were cooperating, Stephen Horn suggested that the pro-civil-rights Republicans believed "that Dirksen will go through his public acting process, take a licking and then be with us." He asked how many Democratic votes would be available to turn back Dirksen's potentially "gutting amendments," and when Humphrey's aide John Stewart replied, "Between thirty-five and forty," Horn exulted, "Then we've got him."

But they didn't have him yet, as no less an expert than Lyndon Johnson knew. That same day, as he waited in the Oval Office to be connected on a telephone call to Richard Russell, the president read aloud to Jack Valenti from a draft statement on civil rights. "We're going to pass the civil rights bill," the president read. "Nothing has happened to deter us from that course. The demands of justice and decency will make that certain." Then he stopped and asked Valenti, "Do you think that's true?"

Even as the president worried, the civil rights cause got a small shot in the arm from a rare moment of emotion on the Senate floor, as Ted Kennedy, seventeen months into his tenure as the junior senator from Massachusetts, made what he would forever after refer to as his "maiden speech," though he had actually earlier made brief remarks on the Nuclear Test Ban Treaty and Northeast Airlines.

"A freshman Senator should be seen, not heard; should learn, not teach," Kennedy said, as his wife, Joan, and sister-in-law Ethel listened intently in the gallery, on a day in which the Senate would sit for thirteen and a half hours, the longest one-day stretch of debate in the filibuster so far. "This is especially true when the Senate is engaged in a truly momentous debate." Then he went on to speak of his state's own long history in absorbing waves of immigrants, and of overcoming discrimination "by persuasion where possible, by law where necessary."

"We have not suffered from this effort," he added. "Indeed, we have been strengthened." Finally, his voice breaking, he said, "My brother was the first president of the United States to state publicly that segregation was morally wrong. His heart and soul are in this bill. If his life and death had a meaning, it was that we should not hate but love one another; we should use our powers not to create conditions of oppression that lead to violence, but conditions of freedom that lead to peace."

No Republicans were present to hear Kennedy's speech. They were caucusing with Dirksen, to hear him outline his proposed amendments. As Stephen Horn had suggested, Dirksen was now undertaking to find out just where the fissures in his caucus lay, and predictably enough, it was the liberals in his flock who balked first at his ideas. Margaret Chase Smith of Maine, one of two women in the Senate and Dirksen's longtime friendly adversary in a campaign to name a national flower (she favored the rose), implored him to retain Judge Smith's "sex" amendment, noting that it had been included in the House bill with strong support from Republican congresswomen. (Humphrey was under equally strong pressure to retain Smith's amendment; John Stewart was lobbied fiercely by Betty Friedan, who only the year before had published *The Feminine Mystique* and who now told Stewart, "If Senator Humphrey and his cronies have any thought about dropping sex from the coverage of this bill, I'm here to tell you they'd better forget about that, because if they do that, you don't know what trouble is.")

The Republican caucus reached no quick consensus on Dirksen's proposals. But there was widespread concern among civil rights supporters that Dirksen's emphasis on state action to correct employment discrimination would allow southern states to create their own sham fair employment agencies or commissions, which could then take precedence over federal efforts and delay effective relief. After the caucus, Kenneth Keating said the proposed amendments "would seriously weaken the effectiveness of the bill," while Clifford Case said that it might be necessary "for those of us who favor a strong civil rights bill to take the position from now until Kingdom Come" of opposing cloture, or anything other "than an effective bill." One unnamed moderate told the *New York Times*, "The Senator from Illinois may not be Mack the Knife but he's certainly Ev the Dirk."

* * *

From the other end of Pennsylvania Avenue, Lyndon Johnson wasted no chance to press the case for H.R. 7152, even with such an implacable foe of the bill as Senator Robert Byrd of West Virginia, a former Ku Klux Klan member who was otherwise a staunch Johnson ally and had supported him in the 1960 presidential race. On April 10, Byrd sought Johnson's support for a candidate for a federal judgeship in West Virginia—a Byrd ally who was thought to be too old for the job and had been deemed not qualified by the American Bar Association's screening panel. Byrd reminded Johnson of his long loyalty, then added, "The only thing I won't go along with, Mr. President, you and I have already discussed, and that's the civil rights bill."

"Well, you don't have to go along on it," the president replied. "But make them vote on it. Don't let them keep me up there on the vote, damn it."

"Oh, no, no," Byrd rejoined. "No, sir. I wouldn't make them vote on it, because I know if they vote on it, they're going to get it." Johnson chuckled as Byrd went on, "And if a man starts to come in my house, if I can't beat him with my fists, I'm going to take a poker to him. So the only way we can win here is not to let them vote."

"I don't pass that bill, they'll beat me," the president complained, adding: "I might send you off on a tour or something, some of these days, before they vote cloture . . . I don't want you to—"

But Byrd interrupted, "I wouldn't leave Dick Russell for all the tours in the world."

10

Alternatives and Substitutes

As THE FILIBUSTER DRAGGED on, the pro-civil-rights forces grew increasingly worried about the prospect of Everett Dirksen's promised amendments. At the bipartisan floor leaders' group meeting this morning, Joe Rauh questioned Stephen Horn about the status of Dirksen's proposals. "Keep smiling," Horn counseled. Humphrey arrived late for the meeting, but announced that he had talked Dirksen down from some seventy amendments to about fifteen. Clarence Mitchell warned that if Dirksen's amendments prevailed, "it will be a disaster. There will be a Negro revolution around the country."

"We don't plan on letting them pass," Humphrey reassured him. "Don't you break out in a sweat, Clarence."

By this point, tensions were rising between Mitchell and Rauh and their colleagues in the Leadership Conference on Civil Rights—who wanted the strongest possible bill—and Humphrey and his fellow legislators, who wanted the strongest possible bill that could *pass*. Their joint Monday and Thursday meetings took on the air of a shadow play, because Mitchell and Rauh well knew that Humphrey and the other senators and their aides were making the real decisions, and sharing their deepest concerns, only in their own private meetings. "The worst thing they can do with me is tell me what to do," Humphrey said of the civil rights groups around this time. "I want a bill. I think I'm smarter than they are. You can't give people blood tests every fifteen minutes" on the purity of their civil rights support.

Humphrey's aide John Stewart was even blunter, confiding to his diary, "It has become increasingly clear that the civil rights groups must be handled with great care and maturity. In short, it is simply impossible to permit the civil rights groups to call the shots on this legislation. It is a good object lesson that you must even be willing to go against your strongest supporters when dealing with legislation of such tremendous scope."

"There are enough groups and interests in this nation so that certain accommodations simply have to be made if there is to be a bill," Stewart added, thinking not only of the business community, whose concerns weighed so heavily on Dirksen, but of all the other manifold constituencies with a stake in the bill. "This is a fact which the civil rights groups, looking at the bill from their very narrow perspective, simply cannot comprehend. And, what is even more distressing is that they immediately interpret any particular change in the legislation as some manner of dastardly sell-out. Clarence Mitchell's bi-weekly eruptions in the leadership meetings only testify to this fact."

On this spring Monday afternoon, the beleaguered civil rights troops sought surcease by trooping off to the *other* Washington Senators' season opening game, assuming that comity might prevail for such a beloved annual ritual. But that hope collapsed at 2:20 p.m. when the spoilsport Spessard Holland of Florida noted the absence of a quorum on the Senate floor, and the announcer at D.C. Stadium alerted the watching crowd. Fifteen pro-civil-rights senators had to hustle back to work while Richard Russell, perhaps the biggest baseball fan of the bunch, just smiled and stayed in his seat.

On the floor of the Senate, shortly before midnight that same day, George Smathers sought to explain that he understood how high the passions about civil rights ran among black Americans. Humphrey interrupted him. "I would like to ask the Senator if he thinks that either the

Senator from Florida or the Senator from Minnesota knows what it feels like to be a Negro and to be told he cannot come into a restaurant?" Humphrey demanded. "What is happening is not so much economics, even though it amounts to economic deprivation. It is not so much education, even though we know people have been denied education. What is happening is humiliation, the lack of a sense of dignity which has been imposed upon people."

"I know something about discrimination," Smathers defensively replied. "I recall that when I was in the Marine Corps, some of us could not enter certain officer areas to eat. We had to eat Spam. Those at the club ate steak, because they happened to be aviators."

"That," Humphrey retorted, "is a dictatorship called the military establishment."

As the southerners droned on and the pro-civil-rights forces waited to see the full import of Dirksen's amendments, they were sometimes at a loss as to what to do next. When in doubt, they simply let the southerners talk. But strains were showing. "We want them to make fools of themselves," Humphrey said in the floor leaders' meeting in his office on Thursday, April 16. "If they run out of speeches on this, then they will have amendments. We will have to plan on cloture. Nobody won a war on starving the enemy. We must shoot them on the battlefield."

Clarence Mitchell interjected, "You are shooting the friends if you trade with Dirksen."

"We don't have sixty-five votes for cloture," a frustrated Humphrey insisted. "Unless we are ready to move in our clothes and our shavers and turn the Senate into a dormitory—which Mansfield won't have—we have to do something else. The president grabbed me by my shoulder and damn near broke my arm. He said, 'I'd run that show around the clock.' That was three weeks ago. I told the president he is grabbing the wrong arm. I have the Senate wives calling me right now asking, 'Why can't the Senator be home now?' They add, 'The place isn't being run intelligently.' Sometimes I'm working for longer hours. The president says, 'What about the pay bill? What about poverty? What about food stamps?' Clarence, we aren't going to sell out. If we do, it will be for a hell of a price."

At this point, the bells indicating a quorum call on the Senate floor rang out and the majority whip got up to go. "I'd better answer the quorum," Humphrey laughed. "It would be a hell of a thing, if I missed it."

* * *

ON THAT SAME THURSDAY, April 16, Dirksen at long last introduced his fair employment amendments to Title VII, which had now been reduced to ten in number. They were, he said, "the fruit of long study and staff work and consultation with the people in business, in industry, in the contracting field, and in nearly every other field of economic activity."

Dirksen's proposals would:

- Allow the new federal Equal Employment Opportunity Commission to take jurisdiction in discrimination cases after six months if a state agency had done nothing. Six months after that, if conditions had still not changed, an aggrieved employee could file a lawsuit and the commission could intervene to compel compliance with a court order. (Dirksen's original idea had been to let state fair employment commissions claim jurisdiction in such cases until their actions were deemed ineffective by a court, but the pro-civil-rights forces said this would allow southern states to set up sham fair employment agencies in a deliberate move to stymie federal action.)

- Include union hiring halls in the definition of an employment agency. This provision was intended to ensure that employers would not be punished for discrimination that had really been inflicted by labor unions.

- Make the EEOC's technical studies on discrimination available to the public.

- Delete a provision from the House-passed version of Title VII that would allow a third party—such as the NAACP—to file an employment discrimination complaint on behalf of an individual. Under Dirksen's proposal, the employee himself would have to file.

- Prohibit the EEOC from making public anything said or done by it or an aggrieved employee during efforts to resolve the complaint.

- Restrict the filing of employment discrimination suits to the jurisdiction where the alleged offense had occurred and delete a provision allowing for suits in the location of a company's home office.

- Strike out the House-passed proposal allowing employers to refuse to hire atheists.

- Require courts to find that any illegal act of discrimination had been willful, not inadvertent.

- Delete a provision allowing courts to appoint a special master to investigate the facts of discrimination cases.

- Stipulate that in states having fair employment laws, employers and unions need keep only the records required by existing state law, not a separate set of records under the federal law, and allow federal courts to require employers to comply with the EEOC's request for evidence when they refused to provide it voluntarily.

Dirksen also announced that he would propose an eleventh amendment—which reporters quickly dubbed a "mystery amendment"—at a later time. But the minority leader did not yet "call up" his proposals—that is, he did not ask to have them made the pending business of the Senate—because he was still testing the waters. His paramount goal was to protect the thirty states that already had their own fair employment laws. As it happened, seventeen of these states were represented by a total of twenty-three Republican senators, whose votes would be needed for cloture.

But would Dirksen's proposals fly with his fellow Republicans, much less the civil rights supporters? That afternoon, Robert Kimball reported to Stephen Horn that Bill McCulloch had accepted some of Dirksen's ideas, but found others objectionable, including the idea of state agencies preempting federal action. Kimball further reported that Charlie Halleck did not "give a damn" about Dirksen's proposals one way or the other. The two Republican staff aides agreed that Dirksen was being "dramatic, and wants to show when he finally lands on our side that the matter has been thoroughly considered."

That evening, Humphrey and Kuchel's staff analysis estimated that the civil rights forces could ultimately get sixty-four of the sixty-seven votes needed for cloture. But they agreed that not all of those votes were yet nailed down, and Dirksen himself was still listed as "doubtful."

When Humphrey and the floor leaders' group met the next day, Friday, April 17, they faced a question that would dog them repeatedly in coming days and weeks: were they willing to deal with the Dirksen amendments? Indeed, should they accept any amendments at all? Should they test the waters by seeking cloture on some amendments that might be acceptable, or hold out until they were certain they could win cloture for the whole bill? Nick Katzenbach warned that, once the civil rights backers accepted any amendments, "we've lost our virginity," and would be vulnerable to more. For his part, Humphrey told reporters that if the Senate had not begun voting on amendments by the following week, he would ask for round-the-clock sessions.

On Saturday, Humphrey and Kuchel met at the Justice Department with Bob Kennedy and his top aides to go over the Dirksen amendments. They agreed that they would need to see the totality of Dirksen's proposals—including his still threatened amendment to Title II, the public accommodations section—before issuing any detailed response, or beginning any horse trading. But a casual comment that the attorney general made to the press after the meeting briefly sent Joe Rauh and Clarence Mitchell and the other members of the Leadership Conference on Civil Rights into a tailspin.

When a reporter asked Kennedy whether he still felt the same about the Equal Employment Opportunity Commission in Title VII as he had the previous fall—when he had said he would support jettisoning the commission if such a move were needed for passage of the bill in the House—he replied, "I haven't changed my mind." That led Senator Allen Ellender of Louisiana to say he was glad that Kennedy was prepared to drop Title VII, and to hope that he might be willing to drop others, too. Two hours later, after reporters asked Kennedy's aides whether he had really meant to say that he was now willing to sacrifice Title VII, the Justice Department was forced to issue a clarification, in which Kennedy said, "I am for Title VII as it stands." Humphrey was even more emphatic. "We are not going to take out Title VII," he said.

And on Sunday, April 19, the pro-civil-rights church groups started their most dramatic lobbying effort yet: teams of Protestant, Catholic, and Jewish seminarians began an around-the-clock prayer vigil at the Lincoln Memorial, vowing to continue the effort until the bill was passed. Students from seventy-five seminaries around the country streamed into Washington to pray in shifts, as the filibuster headed into its seventh week.

In their strategy meeting the next morning, the floor leaders' group reflected the reality that Title VII had always been one of the most controversial parts of the bill—especially because of the way it was included at the last minute as part of the administration's compromise with Bill McCulloch back in October. Stephen Horn correctly surmised that Dirksen's amendments were intended to make the fair employment section palatable to northern businesses. Nick Katzenbach himself acknowledged that northern businesses that did not discriminate might well be put off by Title VII, "because of the records-keeping and the bureaucracy that are created."

But on the floor that same day, Humphrey offered a vigorous defense of Title VII, noting that the Brooklyn Dodgers' hiring of Jackie Robinson had been an economic boon for big league baseball.

"How about the player whom he displaced?" George Smathers demanded.

"He was better than the player whom he displaced," Humphrey replied. "So he earned more money. As a result of the employment of Jackie Robinson the bleachers were filled with more people."

* * *

THE NEXT DAY, TUESDAY, April 21, Dirksen finally unveiled his "eleventh amendment." It was a compromise, aimed at placating Bill McCulloch. Instead of stripping the EEOC of its ability to bring enforcement suits in federal court—a change McCulloch had opposed—it would cede jurisdiction to state agencies for a limited period, giving them three months to resolve allegations of discrimination (or six months, in the case of newly created state agencies), before the federal commission could assert jurisdiction. If these voluntary efforts did not work, an employee could take his case to federal court, and the Justice Department could intervene, at the court's discretion.

"It keeps the local spirit," Dirksen told reporters, insisting that his goal was to strengthen, not weaken, the bill. "It starts back home." But Dirksen acknowledged that his amendment would make the first-blush enforcement of antidiscrimination in employment largely voluntary. For his part, Humphrey said he found the amendment "a bit troublesome," adding, "The more we see of the amendments, the better we like the House bill."

But if the pro-civil-rights forces were discomfited by Dirksen's maneuvering, the southerners were in even worse shape. Indeed, John Stewart would note in his diary, there was an increasing feeling in the Senate that the "southerners know they are in deep trouble on the issue this time. They are increasingly sensitive on the floor and do not appear to be as sharp in terms of parliamentary procedure as one has reason to expect."

There were, in fact, growing internal strains in the southern caucus. Younger senators—men like William Fulbright, George Smathers, even Russell Long and Herman Talmadge—were not dead-enders like Strom Thurmond. The liberal columnist Murray Kempton described the situation as a case "of age resisting youth, and a cause is hardly healthy when the realistic young think of a separate peace and only the principled old think of resistance to the end."

Richard Russell himself had acknowledged on *Meet the Press* on March 1 that even residents of Georgia were not insulated from the changing times. "My people are not immune from brainwashing," he said. "A great many of them have been brainwashed and they have forgotten the first Constitutional principles and have failed to see the dangers of passing legislation on the threat of demonstrations."

Now Russell confided—to Clarence Mitchell, of all unlikely interlocutors—that he had no hope of getting any major compromises on the bill from Johnson, though he believed the southerners could have gained major compromises from John Kennedy. Instead, Russell admitted, "The jig is just about up."

So just hours after Dirksen offered his eleventh amendment—as the Senate talked right past its previous thirty-seven-day record for a civil rights filibuster—the southerners switched tactics and for the first time proposed a real amendment of their own.

The amendment was offered by Russell's fellow Georgian Herman Talmadge, who dragged out that oldest of civil rights hobgoblins—the jury trial. Talmadge proposed to guarantee a jury for defendants in all cases of criminal contempt—that is, for those accused of defying a court order—involving civil rights violations under the bill. He asked that his amendment immediately be made the Senate's pending business.

"The denial of the right of a trial by jury to our forebears in the original Colonies was one of the reasons why our forebears instituted a revolution and made the Declaration of Independence," Talmadge intoned. Asked if he intended to press for a vote that day, Talmadge answered that he did not, and Willis Robertson of Virginia said archly, "I believe the Senate can look forward to a considerable elucidation of what is involved."

In a flash, Humphrey and his civil rights allies were on the defensive. The issue, of course, was that all-white southern juries would be unlikely to uphold prosecutions for contempt of court. But, as had been true in the debate over the 1957 civil rights bill, it was hard for civil rights supporters to explain why anyone should oppose such a seemingly basic right, enshrined in centuries of Anglo-Saxon law. The 1957 bill had allowed nonjury trials for criminal contempt—the defiance of court orders—in cases of voting rights or public accommodations. But it had limited punishment in such cases to a $300 fine or forty-five days in jail. The House-passed version of H.R. 7152 had retained this provision in Titles I and II (voting rights and public accommodations) but had given no jury trial protection for any of the bill's other sections. Talmadge's amendment would extend mandatory jury trials to all cases of criminal contempt.

Russell now took the floor to say that depriving defendants of a jury trial would be to revert to the "ancient practice in England, under the common law which existed at the time of Chaucer," when "men were tried in private and had no rights whatsoever."

As debate over the Talmadge amendment preoccupied the Senate's public discourse, Russell was entitled to believe he had the civil rights forces on the ropes. What he could not hear was the quiet conversation on the floor that same day—"a very interesting talk," John Stewart would call it in his diary—between Hubert Humphrey and Everett Dirksen. Humphrey had approached Dirksen for one of their regular chats, and now, for the first time, the Republican leader confided that he knew that H.R. 7152 was going to pass, and "that he knew it was his duty, or at least his position, whereby he would have to lend his weight and influence to the bill." Dirksen told Humphrey that he believed the southerners "were running to the end of their rope," that there was little more they could say, and that they were convinced the bill would pass largely in its current form, perhaps without even resorting to cloture. When Humphrey insisted that the southerners would demand a cloture vote as political cover for dropping their fight, Dirksen at last agreed to help round up the Republican votes that would be needed to close off debate.

"In short," Stewart concluded, "it appears that Dirksen is beginning to swallow the great man hook and, when it is fully digested, we will have a civil rights bill."

* * *

THE FIRST CONCRETE SIGN of Dirksen's new spirit of cooperation came on Friday, April 24, when he joined with Mike Mansfield to offer a substitute for the Talmadge jury trial amendment, and their "Mansfield-Dirksen Substitute" now became the Senate's pending business. After negotiations with the pro-civil-rights forces and Justice Department lawyers, Dirksen had agreed to a proposal that would allow nonjury trials in cases of criminal contempt but would limit punishment in such cases to a fine of $300 or thirty days in jail. (The administration wanted to keep the forty-five-day sentence from the House-passed bill, while Dirksen wanted ten days, so they split the difference.)

The details of the proposed amendment were less important than the sheer fact that Dirksen was at last working directly with the pro-civil-rights senators to forge a bill. In a meeting of the bipartisan floor leaders' group, Clifford Case of New Jersey put his finger on just what made the southerners' demand for a jury trial amendment so tricky: it was an idea that appealed across the board, to liberals and conservatives alike, and the civil rights forces were not in a strong position to fight it. The best they could hope for was that Dirksen could give them cover to find a more palatable proposal.

"Let's not kid ourselves," Joseph Clark, a staunch liberal from Pennsylvania, told his colleagues. "This has become the Dirksen bill! I deplore it, but that's it."

But the Mansfield-Dirksen jury trial proposal was not enough to attract Russell, who on Monday, April 27, continued to rail against the bill as "violative of all the laws and concepts of justice that free men have had since the dawn of history." Because the Senate has no mechanism for forcing action short of cloture itself, votes can generally occur only with the unanimous consent of the members. And because the pro-civil-rights forces had refused to allow consideration of the Talmadge amendment, the southerners retaliated by refusing to entertain any other amendments, including Dirksen's proposed changes to Title VII.

So the Senate remained paralyzed. At the same time, five thousand religious leaders from around the country streamed into town for their biggest lobbying push yet—a long-planned interfaith convocation at Georgetown University on Tuesday, April 28. "It is your job, as men of God, to reawaken the conscience of your beloved land," Lyndon Johnson told representatives of the group at the White House the next day.

Rafts of clergymen and their lay allies also descended on Capitol Hill to lobby senators directly, much to Dirksen's annoyance. "I fairly scream and hope that I can get some work done," he told Rabbi Irving Rosenbaum of Chicago Loop Synagogue. "You aren't the only delegation, you know." In a meeting in a reception room outside the Senate chamber, one visiting priest told Dirksen, "We want you to make your decisions in terms of your conscience, your concern for the entire country, and the goals of the United States."

"I would make it no other way," Dirksen replied tersely.

When B. Julian Smith, bishop of the Christian Methodist Episcopal

Church of Chicago, allowed that "If you could just paint your face black, like mine, and go with me into the world for two days, I wouldn't have to say a word," a weary Dirksen answered, "Must I do that? After thirty years in Congress, can't I evaluate the importance of legislation? Really, do I have to do that?" Finally, Dirksen told the group, "The best thing you can do is say a prayer for me."

Dirksen was feeling testy, his resentment still simmering that black voters in Illinois—and national black leaders such as Clarence Mitchell and Roy Wilkins—had not adequately recognized what he considered his sympathetic civil rights record over the years, or supported him in his 1962 reelection campaign. But he was also in need of prayerful intercession. For on this same Wednesday, Dirksen would have an even more frustrating encounter—with his old friend Lyndon Johnson, to whom he had gone seeking a deal.

* * *

JOHNSON AND DIRKSEN'S CORDIAL relationship dated back to their days in the House of Representatives, but it deepened when Dirksen became the Senate Republican leader in 1959. As majority leader, Johnson had been thrilled to be the first lawmaker in the capital to acquire a telephone in his official limousine. When Dirksen eventually got one, too, he promptly telephoned Johnson's car to say he was calling from his new mobile line, only to hear Johnson say, "Can you hold on a minute, Ev? My other phone is ringing."

The two men had tangled mightily over the 1957 Civil Rights Act, with Dirksen unsuccessfully opposing Johnson's bargaining with the southerners to weaken it. But their mutual affection was real and unforced. "We were both agreed," Dirksen once recalled, employing a bit of sarcastic indirection, "that the Senate could not be a functioning body unless the ladies got along and understood each other and each other's problems." So he and Johnson came, he added, "to understand each other quite intimately" and were, despite their partisan differences, "the very best of friends."

Ten weeks earlier, when Dirksen had been hospitalized for a bleeding ulcer in the middle of the House debate on H.R. 7152, Johnson called his room at Sibley Hospital to cheer him up. "If you'd quit drinking that damned Sanka and get on a good Scotch whisky once in a while," the president advised, as a groggy and sedated Dirksen replied, "Well, I think you got a point there."

Dirksen was used to Johnson's ready acceptance of his choice of Republican nominees for various federal boards and commissions. "You couldn't name a commission where there wasn't a Dirksen man on it somewhere," Jack Valenti would recall. Just before Christmas, Dirksen had called the president about an ambassadorial appointment for William Macomber, an Eisenhower-era State Department official.

"Do you want him appointed?" Johnson asked.

"Well, he's a damn good guy," Dirsken replied.

"Well, I don't care if he's a good guy," the president rejoined. "There are a million Johnson men that are good guys. But he's a Republican, and if we're going to appoint Republican ambassadors, they better be your Republican ambassadors. I'm not going to be appointing them just out of the skies."

"There are all kinds of Republicans," Johnson concluded. "You're my kind."

So Dirksen was entitled to think that Johnson might be ready for one of his famous compromises, might be willing to strike a grand bargain on H.R. 7152. But the president—his back already up at the protracted Senate debate—was in no mood for wheeling or dealing. On top of everything else, Johnson was irked that Dirksen had told the press that he intended to lobby the president for a deal—and in the process had criticized Johnson's holding one of his beagles up by the ears to pose for White House photographers.

"You say you want the House bill without any change," Dirksen had told reporters, describing his proposed line of argument with the president. "Well, in my humble opinion, you are not going to get it. Now it's your play."

Johnson was having none of that.

"I'm going to tell him that I support a strong civil rights bill," Johnson told Mike Mansfield on the telephone from the White House before Dirksen arrived. "He gave out a long interview of what he was going to tell me today before he comes, which is not like him. I don't know what's happening to him here lately. He's acting like a shit-ass . . . First thing, he said he wouldn't treat his dog like I treated mine . . . And it's none of his damn business how I treat my dog, and I'm a helluva lot better to dogs and humans, too, than he is."

Mansfield told the president that he was reluctantly considering the idea of seeking a cloture vote on the jury trial question, though he said he would much rather hold out for cloture on the whole bill.

"Well, then what I'm going to say to him is this," Johnson replied. "I'm going to say, 'Now, these details can't be decided down here in the White House, legislative-wise. I have the attorney general, and he's in constant contact with Senator Mansfield and Senator Humphrey, and whatever you all work out, I'm sure will be agreeable.'"

"Yes sir," Mansfield replied. "I'll put it back on us and stroke his back."

Dirksen arrived in the Oval Office with a commemorative "Baby Ben" Westclox alarm clock—along with the chief executive of the firm that made them in LaSalle, Illinois—only to learn that there was to be no deal at all. He was in and out of the White House in less than twenty minutes, and was forced to tell the press that he and the president had barely touched on the topic of civil rights.

In fact, the very next day, Thursday, April 30, Johnson called Hubert Humphrey to upbraid him for even seeming to suggest that the president might be amenable to some compromise on the bill. "They would like very, very much to say I weakened the bill and I'm not going to—that's not my position," the president said. "I'm against any amendments. Going to be against them right up until I sign them."

* * *

IN THE WAKE OF the Dirksen-Johnson standoff, a fresh complication now arose. Thruston Morton, a moderate Republican from Kentucky, had huddled with Russell and Sam Ervin and come up with his own jury trial amendment as a "perfecting" amendment—that is, one that offered new language, but not a complete substitution—to Talmadge's original version. Morton was in favor of civil rights, but during a postmortem of the 1960 election, in which he had served as chairman of the Republican

National Committee, he shared Richard Nixon's frustration that the black vote was a "bought vote, and it isn't bought by civil rights," to which Morton added, "The hell with them."

Morton's amendment would compel jury trials under every section of the bill except Title I—the voting rights section—in which judges would still have discretion to order nonjury trials, as they did under the 1957 Act. On Friday, May 1, Morton called up his amendment and asked it be made the pending business. That meant that it would now have precedence over the Mansfield-Dirksen jury trial amendment, as would a similar perfecting amendment by Morton's Kentucky colleague, John Sherman Cooper, which would order automatic jury trials for some sections of the bill but give judges discretion in others.

The pro-civil-rights forces immediately feared that the Morton and Cooper amendments might well pass—and thereby undo the progress they had hoped they were making by working with Dirksen. So it was no surprise that Russell now dropped his objection to consideration of any amendments and agreed with Mansfield and Dirksen that voting on the jury trial amendments could begin the following Wednesday, May 6. "I am sure that we can find some way whereby the Senate can vote," Russell said drily, "even though this vitally important amendment has not been discussed at the length which its importance would justify."

That same day, the emotional symbolism of the jury trial issue boiled over into an angry twenty-minute exchange on the floor between Russell and Jacob Javits, who suggested that white southern juries would be unlikely to administer evenhanded justice in civil rights cases. Russell immediately leaped to his feet, Javits objected to the interruption, and an increasingly bitter colloquy ensued until Russell said that Javits always managed to suggest that there was "something fundamentally evil and sinful about people living in the South," and always made his comments about southern juries with "a little sneer on his face." Russell cited the case of Kitty Genovese, a young Queens woman who had reportedly been attacked and left to die even though nearly forty of her neighbors heard her screams. "I say that couldn't happen in the South, demean it as you may," Russell said. Javits insisted he had intended no offense, and the two men shook hands. But the encounter reflected the increasingly ran-corous mood in the chamber.

The following day, Saturday, May 2, Humphrey wondered aloud on the floor whether his colleagues might be persuaded to allow votes on all pending amendments—and the bill itself—by Memorial Day. "I have no particular holiday in mind, other than the Fourth of July, to which I would like to show some reverence," Humphrey said. "However, if they have a particular day in mind that they wish to honor with a vote, I am sure favorable consideration would be given to such a proposal."

Allen Ellender of Louisiana promptly piped up, "How about Christ-mas?"

Two days later, on Monday, May 4, as George Smathers was inveigh-ing against the defects of Title VII to an almost empty Senate chamber, Kenneth Washington, a twenty-six-year-old black man from Passaic, New Jersey, shouted from the gallery: "How can you say you are protect-ing the black man when there are only five of you here?" It was a fair question, but Washington's breach of decorum landed him in D.C. Gen-eral Hospital for mental observation all the same.

* * *

WITH HIS JURY TRIAL amendments stacked up behind the southerners' alternatives, Ev Dirksen now sought another path. When reporters asked him what he was trying to do, he responded with a bit of wordplay that summed up his challenge: "I'm trying to unscrew the inscrutable." To that end, Dirksen invited Humphrey and Kuchel, along with an extended bipartisan group of senators and aides interested in the bill, to a meeting on Tuesday morning, May 5, in his office just thirty-three paces off the Senate floor. Joined by Bob Kennedy and Nick Katzenbach, they gath-ered around a polished mahogany table under a tinkling crystal chande-lier that had once belonged to Thomas Jefferson.

To general astonishment, Dirksen announced that instead of just one remaining amendment—his long-promised proposal regarding Title II, the public accommodations section—he now had scores of other proposed changes, the result of careful review by his staff lawyers Neal Kennedy,

Clyde Flynn, and Bernard Waters. The amendments were divided into three groups: Track A (technical in nature), Track B (semitechnical), and Track C (substantive). If his colleagues were surprised by Dirksen's switched signals, they should not have been. He had more than once remarked that his one unshakable principle was flexibility, and his son-in-law, the future senator Howard Baker of Tennessee, would later recall that "virtually every idea he held, he held tentatively." In 1950, when Dirksen first ran for the Senate, the *Chicago Sun-Times* published an analysis of his voting record in the House of Representatives, accusing him of switching his position on military preparedness thirty-one times, on isolationism sixty-two times, and on farm policy seventy times during his sixteen years in Congress.

Dirksen had never made any secret of his qualms about H.R. 7152. In the private notebook in which he recorded his running observations about the pending bill, he summed up his questions about Title II, in capital letters for emphasis: "THE PURPORT OF THE LANGUAGE IN THIS TITLE IS simply this," he wrote. "Can Congress destroy FREEDOM OF ASSOCIATION in the case of privately owned and operated businesses?" Dirksen represented the Land of Lincoln, but even in Lincoln's time, Illinois had embraced a wide array of views on civil rights, race, and federal power. "You have to remember that Illinois runs both north and south of the Mason-Dixon line," one of Dirksen's aides would recall. "The Senator grew up seeing both sides of the question. Dirksen is a man without prejudices and believes in equal rights, but he also knows how the local people feel when the federal government shoves something down their throats."

Indeed, just after the House passed H.R. 7152 in February, Dirksen had urged reporters to "do me the justice of putting in whatever you write down that I've always had an open mind and I always feel free to come along with alternatives and substitutes that are infinitely more to my liking, because I still take my freedom straight. I'm like little Johnny when the teacher said to him, 'Johnny, how do you spell straight?' He said, 'S-t-r-a-i-g-h-t.' She said, 'And what does it mean?' He said, 'Without ginger ale.' And that's the way I take my freedom."

Now Dirksen was ready with yet another batch of "alternatives and substitutes," and the crucial action on the bill shifted to his office suite, out of respect for the minority leader's role as the indispensable man.

A key player in the deliberations to come was Neal Kennedy, a forty-three-year-old Yale-educated, Harvard-trained lawyer from Chicago who since 1959 had been Dirksen's lead counsel on the Judiciary Committee's minority staff. Kennedy had been an Army Air Corps weather officer in World War II, leapfrogging across the Pacific in advance of General Douglas MacArthur to provide forecasts for the coming invasion of Japan. In the 1950s, in between work in private practice and a job as an assistant United States attorney in Chicago, he had traveled to such exotic destinations as Pakistan and Afghanistan and had hitchhiked all over Africa, from Cairo to Cape Town and from Nairobi to Timbuktu. He had serious doubts about how the enforcement provisions of H.R. 7152 would work in practice, especially for the sections governing access to public accommodations and discrimination in employment.

"Dirksen and I had the same general approach to everything," Kennedy would recall. "Support the businessman fighting to survive in the capitalist system." In fact, when Dirksen first hired Kennedy, he sent his newest lawyer a brief memo outlining his view of a senator's role in interceding with the federal bureaucracy on behalf of constituents. "I have proceeded on the theory," Dirksen wrote, "that government is at once so labyrinthine, so bewildering, so complex, so big, so baffling, so frustrating, that the average citizen—and this goes for businessmen and others who are normally well informed on governmental operations—that it becomes impossible for the citizen to find his way around in this uncharted wilderness."

Because James Eastland's Judiciary Committee had had no meaningful role in forging the civil rights bill—having first refused to move the Senate version along and then having been shut out of consideration of H.R. 7152 by Mansfield—it now fell to Neal Kennedy to create an informal bipartisan group that could do the work of revising the bill in a way that would win the support of Dirksen and enough of his fellow Republicans to achieve cloture. "This had to be a bipartisan bill," Kennedy would recall, so he reached out to [his] counterpart in Mike Mansfield's office, a young lawyer named Kenneth Teasdale. "I said to him that I thought the first thing we should do is to get the fifteen greatest Senate aides, legislatively speaking, to work with us, and he agreed," Kennedy recalled. "And I told him that he should get 60 percent of them, since that was the basic [partisan] ratio, and I get the others, and he agreed."

Under Kennedy's direction, there now began a process "almost unprecedented in the annals of legislative history," as the journalist Elizabeth Drew would write. "A sort of ad hoc committee of Senators with an interest, senators who were friends of the Senators with an interest, senators' aides, and Justice Department officials took the place of a regular legislative committee."

Like the private negotiations involving Bill McCulloch, John Lindsay, and Nick Katzenbach that had settled the final House version of the bill, the discussions in Dirksen's suite had the advantage of occurring behind closed doors, out of sight of reporters and lobbyists. "True give and take was possible, decisions were neither public nor final, and the need to sustain one's public posture on certain issues was greatly reduced," John Stewart would recall.

"We were all very dear friends," Ken Teasdale would remember. "I mean, we all got along, we all were heading in the same direction."

* * *

But all was not collegial as the Dirksen working group began its negotiations that May 5. If Hubert Humphrey and Bob Kennedy were taken aback by Dirksen's demands for a raft of new amendments, some members of the minority leader's own caucus were equally discomfited by his decision to cooperate with the administration and the pro-civil-rights Democrats. Bourke Hickenlooper, the dyspeptic Iowa conservative who chaired the Senate's Republican Policy Committee, and was thus a rival to Dirksen for his party's ear, blasted Dirksen as a "softie." He stalked out of the meeting, never to return to the group, and later declared that the minority leader "does not speak for the Senator from Iowa." (Indeed, Dirksen did appear to be soft-soaping his conservative colleagues, and the liberal columnist Murray Kempton speculated in print that Dirksen "seems to be moving toward the passage of a strong civil rights bill by telling the conservatives it is weak.")

The Republican liberals were not happy, either. Tom Kuchel told Stephen Horn that he was "pretty disgusted with the Dirksen slowdown."

Lyndon Johnson was pretty disgusted with the sluggish pace, too. At his weekly meeting with the Democratic congressional leadership just before the working group's meeting in Dirksen's office, Johnson undertook to do a little lobbying for cloture. He had already been on the case for weeks. After the second-largest earthquake in recorded seismography devastated Alaska on Good Friday, March 27, Johnson put Air Force Two at the disposal of the state's two Democratic senators, Ernest Gruening and E. K. "Bob" Bartlett, and then worked with Mike Mansfield to arrange for the Senate to pause long enough in the civil rights fight to approve tens of millions of dollars in emergency aid.

Now the president turned his attention to another small-state senator, Carl Hayden of Arizona, the eighty-six-year-old president pro tem of the Senate, who had never once voted for cloture. The issue was especially sensitive for him, because in 1911 the Senate had filibustered to prevent President William Howard Taft and a Republican-controlled House of Representatives from combining the Arizona and New Mexico territories into a single state, which would likely have elected two Republican senators, instead of two states that would likely have elected two Republicans and two Democrats. In that sense, Hayden owed his very office to the power of the filibuster.

But since 1947, as Johnson well knew, Hayden had had another pet cause: the Central Arizona Water Project, an effort to pump much-needed water from California to the rapidly growing areas around Phoenix and Tucson. Now, the president suggested ever so casually, if Hayden would support cloture, he would support the water project. Within days, the president received a memo from Secretary of the Interior Stewart Udall reporting that Hayden's staff believed that Johnson's "gambit on cloture" had been "very persuasive."

And on Wednesday, May 6, Johnson went to work on another surprising target: Bourke Hickenlooper. Mansfield had let the White House know that Hickenlooper was irritated at the administration for rejecting his favored candidate as ambassador to the Philippines, and he suggested that the senator's feelings might be assuaged by consulting him on

Latin American affairs, a subject in which he had a strong interest. And if Hickenlooper voted for cloture he might well bring along such fellow midwestern conservatives as Karl Mundt of South Dakota, James Pearson of Kansas, and Roman Hruska and Carl Curtis of Nebraska. Johnson promptly dispatched Secretary of State Dean Rusk to talk to Hickenlooper.

* * *

BUT NOTHING DEMONSTRATED THE precarious position of the pro-civil-rights forces more dramatically than the vote that same Wednesday on Thruston Morton's jury trial amendment. It was a near disaster that required four separate roll calls to settle, and it revealed the limits of Mike Mansfield's easygoing, decentralized leadership style. The Senate chamber was packed that day for the first real action on H.R. 7152 in six weeks. The first vote on the Morton amendment was a 45 to 45 tie, and western Democrats and conservative Republicans joined with Russell and the southerners amid shouts of "No, no, no!" when the tally was announced. Because the amendment needed a clear majority to pass, it failed. But when Dirksen moved to table—that is, set aside—Mansfield's routine motion to reconsider the amendment, the pro-civil-rights forces themselves failed, by a vote of 44 to 47. (That was partly because Senator Ted Moss, a Utah Democrat who was famous for being perpetually late, had missed the first vote altogether because the Democratic staff had failed to summon him from the cloakroom in time, so he voted against the tabling motion out of spite.) Next came a vote on the motion to reconsider the amendment, giving Morton one more shot. That passed, 46 to 45. Only on the fourth and final vote was the amendment at last defeated for good, and then by only a single vote, 45 to 46. John Sherman Cooper's jury trial amendment was then also defeated.

The *New York Times* called the vote on the Morton measure a "hair-breadth victory" for the pro-civil-rights forces. It was the lowest moment in their cause since the bill reached the Senate floor, and it "shook hell out of them," Larry O'Brien would recall.

John Stewart sounded a glum note in his diary for the day. "It will be somewhat of a minor miracle if the pro-civil rights forces can get themselves back in order and push ahead with some degree of resolution and determination," he wrote.

Emboldened by what had happened on the floor, Russell now announced that he could not allow a vote on the Mansfield-Dirksen jury trial amendment until at least the following week, because several southern senators would be joining President Johnson on a tour of poverty in Appalachia and the South. That same day, at a White House news conference, Johnson threatened to call Congress back into session after the summer political conventions if it had not wrapped up the civil rights debate and moved on to the rest of his pending social welfare agenda. "The people's business must come first," the president said, "and I think that the people of this country are entitled to have a vote on these important measures."

The next morning, Thursday, May 7, Humphrey told the bipartisan floor leaders' group that it would be "terribly important" to get a bigger vote on the Mansfield-Dirksen jury trial amendment than on the Morton amendment, to demonstrate that they might eventually muster the sixty-seven votes needed for cloture. "If the leaders, backed up by their deputies can't produce, then we are in trouble," he said. "If we can produce sixty-four votes, we are okay. But if we only secure forty-nine votes, then we have had it."

For his part, Joe Rauh said that he and the Leadership Conference still opposed direct negotiations with Dirksen. Humphrey responded in exasperation. "Whatever we are doing has but one purpose," he said. "And that is to secure a civil rights bill! Anybody who has an alternative, I'm glad to hear it. It is not pleasant for Tommy Kuchel and myself to have it appear that Dirksen is writing the ticket. I want the bill passed—the House-passed bill." Then Humphrey turned the tables on Rauh. "The Leadership Conference should be out getting votes," he said. "I saw a number of conservative Republicans taking on their own leader in the Republican cloakroom last evening. I'm not getting much help on cloture."

The gloom of the civil rights forces was reflected in a wide-ranging telephone call Lyndon Johnson made to Senator Allen Ellender of Louisiana around this time. "Fifty days you and Dick Russell, fifty days you talked about the same bill, and you voted four times and you're right back where you started!" the president told Ellender. "Y'all are making Humphrey and them look like they don't know any parliamentary rules at all." But Ellender replied that if Mansfield and Humphrey had backed the Morton amendment, instead of barely defeating it, they might have won support for cloture. And he acknowledged the broader reality now facing the southerners. "I believe there's nothing that's going to get this bill . . . I know damn well we can't beat it," Ellender told the president.

* * *

IN FACT, THE DRAFTING sessions in Dirksen's office were making progress. At the morning session of Thursday, May 7, Dirksen wrestled with how to define discrimination that would be punishable under Title II, the public accommodations section. All along, Dirksen had been particularly concerned about how this section would be enforced, and worried that it could be used to harass individual business owners who might refuse to serve blacks with threats of court action, when a less confrontational approach might work just as well. For his part, Neal Kennedy believed there should be no need to prove that a restaurateur or hotel owner intended to discriminate. The discrimination should be self-evident, and the punishment self-enforcing, as with a speed limit. An offender should be easily judged to have exceeded the limit, or not.

"One of my roommates in law school had been a guy from south Georgia," Kennedy would recall. "His father had died when he was very young, and his mother had brought him back to the family plantation to grow up. And at the plantation, of course, his only playmates were the children of the house staff, all black. And I guess they played together very well, except when they would go into Valdosta. He had to walk on one side of the road and they had to walk on the other. It was just custom. That figured a great deal in my thinking on the bill."

The Justice Department lawyers approached the problem from a different perspective. Unless they had the authority to use court orders to force all the businesses in a given geographical area to desegregate (or cease discriminatory hiring practices under Title VII), they feared that there would be "strong competitive advantages for individual firms to hold out as long as possible," as John Stewart would recall. Making a factual determination on a case-by-case basis would be impossibly burdensome. But how best to describe the sort of widespread conduct that would be punishable under the law?

That afternoon—in a meeting of the working group limited to staff members—Ken Teasdale of Mansfield's office suggested using the words "pattern or practice" to describe what would constitute punishable discrimination. Neal Kennedy and his fellow Republicans liked that idea. The appeal of the phrase was that it could encompass varying interpretations.

"The Dirksen lawyers thought it shouldn't be just one instance [of discrimination]," recalled Charles Ferris, another young lawyer on Mansfield's staff who played a key role in the negotiations. "It was obvious they had in mind sequential actions by the same person before the act was violated," instead of prevailing social customs "that in effect generated community support for the actions of individuals." Ferris promptly telephoned Burke Marshall at the Justice Department, who also liked the language. "He thought that sounded great," Ferris recalled, because the Justice Department was hoping for a way to sanction "communities that supported this type of behavior." So the phrase "pattern or practice" was incorporated into both Title II and Title VII, to define the type of discrimination in public accommodations and employment that would be outlawed by the bill (with Dirksen's caveat that employment discrimination would still have to be "willful").

"'Pattern or practice' had a vagueness to it," Ferris recalled. "It meant different things to different people." The very vagueness of the phrase "was the beauty," Ferris added, and it proved to be a crucial breakthrough.

But that was not immediately apparent at the time. That same evening Kuchel went to see Humphrey about the possibility of a cloture vote in a couple of weeks and found the majority whip "pretty discouraged."

"Tommy, I'm talking out of both sides of my mouth," Humphrey admitted, acknowledging that he had floated the idea of a cloture vote simply "to keep the civil rights groups in line." In fact, Kuchel reported to Stephen Horn, Humphrey did not "think that we can secure any action before the first week in June."

* * *

THE NEXT DAY, FRIDAY, May 8, in Atlanta on his southern tour, Lyndon Johnson made his most emphatic plea yet in favor of the civil rights bill. Winning front-page nationwide headlines, and favorable editorial comment, the president told a breakfast meeting of the Georgia State Legislature of his own family's southern roots, but insisted, "My office is not a single trust for a single section or a single state. The people it serves occupy one continent. They are all ruled by one Constitution. As I am president of all the people, you are part of all the people. I speak to you not, therefore, as Georgians this morning, or as southerners, but as Americans."

More than half a million people had lined the president's motorcade route in Atlanta, and he was welcomed enthusiastically there and at a second stop in Gainesville, where forty thousand people filled a public square. Johnson quoted Atticus Haygood, the president of Emory College, who had declared in 1880, "We in the South have no divine call to stand eternal guard by the grave of dead issues." Now, Johnson said, "because the Constitution requires it, because justice demands it, we must protect the constitutional rights of all our citizens regardless of race, religion or the color of their skin. For I would remind you that we are a very small minority, living in a world of three billion people, where we are outnumbered 17 to 1, and no one of us is fully free until all of us are fully free, and the rights of no single American are truly secure, until the rights of all Americans are secure."

The icing on the cake was Lynda Byrd Johnson's tribute to "my beloved friend Dick Russell, who helped raise me." But Russell was not there to hear the praise. He was elsewhere in Atlanta, addressing a gathering of the Junior Chamber of Commerce, saying, "I must, in candor, tell you that we do not have the votes to prevent passage of the bill, and the outcome is uncertain."

Back on Capitol Hill that morning, at the bipartisan floor leaders' meeting, Nick Katzenbach summarized the state of negotiations with the Dirksen working group, predicting, "We will reach either impasse or agreement with Dirksen next week." That afternoon, pro-civil-rights Republicans from both Houses met with Bill McCulloch to talk about whether liberal senators should try to offer strengthening amendments to the bill. As usual, McCulloch's was the crucial voice in the room.

"I don't believe a useful purpose is served to try to make the House-passed bill stronger," he said. "The House-passed bill *is* a strong bill. Four months before it was passed, we could not have passed it." When Jacob Javits asked about extending Title I's voting rights provisions to state elections, and noted the difficulty for his fellow Republicans of allowing Dirksen's amendments to be the only ones considered, McCulloch explained that he had given up on covering state elections in the House bill in the interest of "getting the show on the road." He explained that he was not opposed to all amendments. "We aren't that pig-headed," he insisted. "We are talking that way—talk's big—so we don't have a wide hole in the dike."

But William Copenhaver, the Republican staff counsel to the House Judiciary Committee, explained a more sobering reality. With each passing day, and with continuing civil rights protests around the country—especially Martin Luther King's SCLC campaign in St. Augustine, Florida—Republican support for H.R. 7152 in the House was growing shakier. "There was a time when a package proposal was a possibility," Copenhaver said. "If the House of Representatives had the bill before it today, it could not pass the present bill. Each day the filibuster goes on, we lose support in the House."

By Monday, May 11, as the negotiations with Dirksen dragged on, Nick Katzenbach told his colleagues in the bipartisan floor leaders' group that Dirksen understood that his proposals for revising the public accommodations section were not yet acceptable. Indeed, Katzenbach would recall, the challenge in negotiating with Dirksen was to get his firm agreement to any changes before so much bourbon had been consumed that Dirksen would not remember the following day what he had accepted the evening before. Dirksen often seemed to want changes in language for change's sake, and while Burke Marshall could provide one new draft of wording that would not much change the bill's meaning, it was much harder for him to do it twice.

Praising the virtue of flattery, Dirksen liked to say that "the oil can is mightier than the sword." He was also a firm believer in the lubricating properties of distilled spirits. "You'd be surprised at how chummy" people can get "at a party with a drink in their hands," he once explained. Frank Valeo, then secretary to the Senate majority, insisted that Dirksen "wasn't an alcoholic," but he nevertheless drank almost constantly. Dirksen himself acknowledged, "Champagne is Mrs. Dirksen's favorite vegetable," while "I prefer a fellow by the name of Jonathan Daniels."

In the back of his office suite, Dirksen kept a private retreat, with refrigerator and full bar, known as the Twilight Lodge, or simply "the back room." There was a clock on the wall with each hour showing the numeral 5. "No matter where the hands stood, it was always after 5 o'clock and time for a drink," John Tower, then a freshman Republican senator from Texas, would recall. During one late morning negotiating session on the bill, John Stewart would remember, he reached to pour himself what he thought would be a glass of water from a crystal pitcher filled with ice and clear liquid. "Don't touch that!" an aide cried.

"The senator's picky about his water?" Stewart asked.

"That ain't water, kid," came the answer.

Indeed, it was gin, and Dirksen soon came in and poured himself a large glass before lunch and went back onto the Senate floor. Jack Rosenthal, then a young speechwriter for Bob Kennedy, recalled Dirksen's leaving a meeting late one hot afternoon and greeting reporters waiting outside the door: "Well, here we are," the senator said. "Fake pearls before real swine."

Yet for all the good cheer, the negotiations had yet to produce an agreement. At the Democratic leadership's weekly meeting with President Johnson at the White House on Tuesday, May 12, Mike Mansfield was forced to tell the president that "progress on the bill to date is nil." An infuriated Johnson once again urged round-the-clock sessions, and later that day he warned a meeting of the President's Committee on

Equal Employment Opportunity—the very body he had chaired as vice president—of the dire consequences if H.R. 7152 should fail.

"That bill must be passed," the president said. "That kind of legislation must become the law of the land. We cannot see our democratic system spend sixty days on a bill like that and then fail. But it is going to fail unless the people, in righteous indignation let them know that they do not have that superior feeling and they do require legislation that protects a person because of his particular color. If the Congress does not act on that legislation, we will have some very dark days in this country."

11

It Can't Be Stopped

Just when things looked darkest for the civil rights forces, the crucial breakthrough came. Dirksen had taken pains to let his constituents know that an agreement might be in the offing. He was a pioneer in the Senate at using television to keep in touch with voters back in Illinois, and he sent home weekly filmed chats for broadcast on local television and radio stations in which he explained legislative issues in remarkably detailed and noncondescending fashion. He called his report for the week of May 11 "The 59th Day," and it summed up the state of negotiations on H.R. 7152.

"Sometimes people may say this is an effort to water down the civil rights bill," Dirksen explained. "I assure you it is nothing of the kind. I must say to you as a legislator who takes pride in his own craftsmanship that there are imperfections, there are deficiencies, there are holes in this bill, and what we are trying to do is to develop an area of agreement on these particular proposals and I think we have gone a long ways."

The meeting of Neal Kennedy's bipartisan working group in Dirksen's suite on this morning marked the fifth day of negotiations, and

Dirksen himself began by suggesting that agreement was a foregone conclusion. He spoke of the need to mimeograph copies of his proposed amendments and circulate them to other senators, the necessity for both party caucuses to review the changes, the possibility of voting for cloture title by title. Hubert Humphrey countered that all that would depend on just what the two sides agreed to—and Bob Kennedy got down to cases on the remaining areas of division.

The biggest sticking point was the attorney general's enforcement powers under Titles II and VII—the public accommodations and fair employment sections. Dirksen did not want the Justice Department jumping around the country like an ad hoc legal aid society, getting involved in cases that might better be resolved locally, ideally through voluntary cooperation. He wanted to enumerate the attorney general's enforcement authority in a separate, new Title XII to the bill. But Humphrey pointed out that was impractical, since such a section would be a more inviting target to be struck from the final bill, leaving the underlying public accommodations and fair employment sections toothless. So Dirksen eventually agreed to place the attorney general's powers within the existing titles. And he agreed to let the Justice Department sue in cases where there was a "pattern or practice" of systemic discrimination in access to public places or jobs—the language that had first been hammered out by his and Mansfield's aides. In more isolated cases of discrimination—in keeping with Dirksen's earlier raft of proposals on Title VII—individuals would have to bring their own complaints, either through existing local agencies or through the new Equal Employment Opportunity Commission, or through the Community Relations Service that would also be established by the bill. Once an individual suit had been filed, and if a court permitted, the attorney general could intervene on a plaintiff's behalf.

Dirksen then objected to a provision in Title V that would allow the United States Civil Rights Commission to investigate allegations of voter fraud. Kennedy agreed that it did not belong in the bill but noted that it had been inserted at the insistence of Bill McCulloch and the House Republicans so he was unwilling to take it out. It stayed in. Both sides also easily agreed to a demand from Karl Mundt of South Dakota to exempt jewelry makers on Indian reservations from the provisions of the bill.

The pro-civil-rights forces had lobbied Mundt relentlessly for his support of H.R. 7152, knowing that his would be a crucial vote for cloture. Charles Ferris of Mike Mansfield's staff recalled that it was widely understood that Mundt's wife, Mary, supported the bill, so each morning after the senator had left home, someone from Humphrey's or Mansfield's staff would call to give her the latest updates on the state of the debate. Religious leaders from South Dakota were also enlisted to lobby Mundt, and when he supported the pro-civil-rights forces on a key procedural vote, he was heard to mutter, "I hope that satisfies those two goddamned bishops that called me last night!" The Indian jewelry amendment was part of Mundt's price for supporting cloture. The bill's supporters were moving ever closer to the magic number of sixty-seven votes.

But when Dirksen suggested yet more tinkering with Title VII, Joe Clark of Pennsylvania stormed out of the room in a fit of anger, shouting, "It's a goddamn sellout!" Clark was a tempestuous liberal, but his demonstration had been prearranged by the civil rights supporters, who had decided in their own meeting before the bipartisan negotiating session to take a tougher stand with Dirksen, convinced he now needed them as much as they needed him.

"See what I'm up against?" Humphrey said to Dirksen as Clark bustled out. "I can't concede any more on this point."

All remaining obstacles seemed to evaporate, and Dirksen, Bob Kennedy, and Humphrey met the press.

"We have a good agreement," Dirksen reported.

"This bill is perfectly satisfactory to me," the attorney general said.

"And to me, too," Humphrey chimed in.

Bill McCulloch let Dirksen know that he, too, accepted the agreement. At the heart of Dirksen's package were the substantive changes in Titles II and VII—giving state agencies first crack at enforcing access to public accommodations and employment. Dozens of other technical changes in wording throughout the bill satisfied Dirksen's desire to claim that he had made a large number of alterations, without really changing its substance much. Both sides could claim victory.

"Dirksen was only switching 'ands' and 'buts,'" Joe Rauh would later recall.

Neal Kennedy would remember that it was "just a question of doing the job—writing a good, enforceable bill." The question, he said, was always, "How do we get the policy the country would innately want to have?"

As usual, Bill McCulloch offered the most judicious summation, concluding that Dirksen had written "amendments into the bill which left the bill little changed in force and effect, but which materially assisted passage of the legislation in the Senate."

The full Senate would have to accept the new proposals, of course. And because of Dirksen's dozens of changes, the House of Representatives, too, would have to approve the amended bill before it could become law. But the compromise with Dirksen was a huge step toward both of those goals.

At first, the civil rights groups, who had been kept in the dark through the five days of private talks with Dirksen, were skeptical, announcing that they would reserve judgment until they could review the proposals. When Bob Kennedy telephoned Lyndon Johnson shortly after 4:00 p.m. to tell him of the deal, the president replied, "Wonderful, congratulations," and then asked about the civil rights lobby.

"Yeah, you know, they're not going to be happy," the attorney general replied, "but then, nothing makes them happy, and so we just have to accept that." But after some grumbling, Joe Rauh and the Leadership Conference also joined in praising the new package. "I thought it would be a lot worse," recalled Rauh, who told Humphrey that if the rewritten bill passed the Senate, "it would be a great victory for civil rights."

A few minutes after his call with the attorney general, Johnson called Dirksen to congratulate him, and to ask about the prospects of moving the bill along and getting a vote. Dirksen reported that he had talked to Richard Russell that morning. "He gave me no comfort," Dirksen said, explaining that Russell would not commit to scheduling any votes because the southerners were "going to keep the show going."

"Well," Dirksen told the president, "I said, 'Dick, you're going to have to fish or cut bait, because I think that we've now gone far enough. And I think that we've been fair.'"

Johnson heaped praise on the minority leader, recalling that he had just seen Walt Disney's new "audio animatronic" Lincoln robot in the Illinois pavilion at the recently opened World's Fair in New York. "You're worthy of the Land of Lincoln," Johnson said. "And the man from Illinois is going to pass the bill, and I'll see that you get proper attention and credit."

Later that evening, Johnson reached out to Hubert Humphrey. "Now, can Dirksen get votes for cloture?" the president demanded.

"Yes, sir, he can get twenty-five votes," Humphrey replied. "I had dinner with him last night, and Mr. President, we've got a much better bill than anybody even dreamed possible. We haven't weakened this bill one damned bit . . . in fact, in some places, we've improved it, and that's no lie, we really have."

"That's wonderful," Johnson replied, emphasizing once more how important it was to make the bill bipartisan. "We'll have real revolution in this country when this bill goes into effect," Johnson said, adding that "it doesn't do any good to have a law like the Volstead Act," which had created Prohibition under the Eighteenth Amendment, "if you can't enforce it."

In fact, the tally for cloture was steadily rising. Only the day before, Humphrey had estimated that there would be fifty-five solid votes in favor, plus eight possible others, including Dirksen's. Now Dirksen was committed, and Ernest Gruening of Alaska, who had so benefited from Johnson's push for emergency earthquake aid, told Humphrey, "I am prepared, before long, to vote for cloture."

* * *

BUT H.R. 7152 WAS not the only issue facing the Senate. A totally unrelated matter—a bitter partisan battle over the Bobby Baker affair—would soon threaten the institution's decorum and risk jeopardizing the drive for cloture.

The catalyst for the fight was an effort by Senate Republicans—led by the dogged John Williams of Delaware—to broaden the Senate Rules Committee's investigation of Baker's business dealings to include an inquiry into improper behavior by senators themselves. The committee was on the verge of making its initial report on the subject, and Lyndon Johnson was livid at the thought that the investigation might be prolonged, let alone expanded. In a telephone call to Mike Mansfield the same evening of the deal with Dirksen, he urged the majority to denounce any such move as "lowdown, dirty, cheap politics," and to do his best to block it.

On the Senate floor the next afternoon, Thursday, May 14, Mansfield did just that, saying that the original scope of the inquiry was wide enough to cover any contingencies. He challenged Williams to "name the senator or senators whom you wish interrogated" and to "state your charges or allegations against them."

When Clifford Case of New Jersey, a cosponsor of the effort to expand the investigation, sought to interrupt Mansfield with a point of order, the majority leader refused to yield the floor "for any purpose," and a fifteen-minute shouting match erupted, escalating into what the *New York Times* called "one of the angriest debates in recent congressional history." Ted Kennedy, presiding over the Senate at the time, and by no means yet a master of procedure, ordered a sputtering Case to take his seat.

Mansfield's motion to block the widened investigation ultimately passed by a vote of 42 to 33, but the majority leader's own aides were embarrassed by his uncharacteristic strong-arm tactics, and the Republicans were outraged. John Stewart confided to his diary that he feared that some senators who had been thinking of voting for cloture might now refuse to do so, out of anger at Mansfield's treatment of Case.

It now remained for both parties to present Dirksen's amendments to their respective caucuses, in meetings scheduled for early the next week. On Friday, May 15, Kenneth Keating's counsel Patricia Connell asked Nick Katzenbach what would happen if Dirksen's conservatives refused to accept his package. "Marshall and I will slit our throats," Katzenbach replied. But in the next breath, Katzenbach added, "I can't believe Dirksen would go as far as he did unless he is able to produce the votes."

* * *

AT THE BIPARTISAN FLOOR leaders' meeting on Monday, May 18, there was some grumbling from the liberals about the deal with Dirksen. He had inserted a provision into Title VII limiting the bill's coverage of job discrimination to firms employing workers for at least twenty weeks a year. Joe Rauh feared this would leave migrant farm workers unprotected. Joe Clark was his usual dyspeptic self, declaring, "There are no public cheers from me on any of this. You may find some sullen acquiescence on my part."

On Tuesday, May 19, the parties caucused separately to review the Dirksen package. The Democrats met in the elegant Old Senate Chamber, in the Capitol's original section. The southerners were predictably dour. Dick Russell complained that Dirksen's amendments made the bill "a punitive expedition into the South." John Stennis of Mississippi accurately discerned Dirksen's motives, asserting that "the amendments are designed to make the bill less burdensome to the states in which the proponents can probably pick up a few votes." But liberals like Clark and Philip Hart of Michigan said they could live with it.

The Republicans held their meeting in a large conference room just off the Senate floor, and the conservatives were livid. Bourke Hickenlooper told reporters afterward that he was appalled at the powers the bill granted to the attorney general. "It's a gargantuan thing!" he exclaimed, adding that the amendments "don't go far enough to meet the real evils of the bill." Milward Simpson of Wyoming was equally blunt. "They've just warmed it over like hash to make it more palatable," he said.

Everett Dirksen's showman's instincts told him it was time for a direct appeal to the public. So after the caucus, he summoned reporters to the comfortable leather couches of the Senate press gallery, and when one reporter—not fully aware of Dirksen's long-aborning behind-the-scenes role in working for a bill—asked why he had suddenly become such a champion of civil rights, the minority leader began what he called "a little sermon."

Dirksen summarized the long history of once controversial reforms that had become an accepted part of American life, from laws mandating pure food and drugs, to those barring child labor and governing wages and hours, to the creation of the civil service system and the advent of women's suffrage. Then, paraphrasing Victor Hugo, Dirksen declared, "No army can withstand the strength of an idea whose time has come."

He cited the nearly half million black Americans who had served as he had in the armed forces in World War I, and the nearly two million who had served in World War II, and asked, "What do you think they told their kids about the freedom they experienced wherever they served abroad?" When asked about the criticisms of his proposed amendments, Dirksen responded laconically by citing the story of a young airman on his first bombing mission who had shouted to his commander in panic, "Sarge, they're shooting at us!"

"Yes," the sergeant replied, "they're allowed to."

As to the bill's ultimate fate, Dirksen expressed not a sliver of doubt. "Let editors rave at will and let states fulminate at will," he said, "but the time has come and it can't be stopped."

* * *

THE REPUBLICANS CAUCUSED AGAIN on May 20 and 22 to go over Dirksen's proposed changes, while the southerners continued to rail against the package in speeches on the Senate floor. For weeks, the segregationists had hoped that strong showings by George Wallace in the presidential primaries might help rally public opinion to their side. But now Russell was forced to acknowledge that not even Wallace's 43 percent plurality in the Maryland primary on May 19 would have any real effect on the bill's fate. "The Senate is usually the last place in the government to get the drift of American public opinion," Russell told reporters.

Finally, on Tuesday, May 26, Dirksen formally introduced his package of revisions, cosponsored with Mansfield, as "an amendment in the nature of a substitute," which meant it would replace the existing version of H.R. 7152 in its entirety. As a result of the discussions with his Republican colleagues, he had inserted a provision in Title VII making it explicit that no employer or union could be required to give preferential treatment or establish quotas because of any racial imbalance that might exist in a company or union. He explained that the origins of the compromise stretched back to John Kennedy's proposals of the previous June. "As I look back now upon the time that has been devoted to the bill,

I doubt very much whether in my whole legislative lifetime any measure has received so much meticulous attention," he said. "We have tried to be mindful of every word, of every comma, of the shading of every phrase. We have attempted to be fair in giving everyone an opportunity to present his case."

Mansfield then dared to "hope that it will not be too long before an attempt is made to invoke cloture, because, in my opinion, that is the only way by which we can face the issue, an issue which I sincerely wish had come before my time or afterward. But the issue is here, and it cannot be evaded, dodged or delayed much longer." Hubert Humphrey praised the compromise's "practical, commonsense approach."

But Russell was not ready to give up just yet. "I realize that those who have participated in this historic gathering feel 'it is all over now,' except for counting the votes and sending the messages to the states that are not to be covered by the bill, and sending the emissaries of the FBI to the states that are to be covered by it," he said bitterly. Humphrey jumped up in protest. "Mr. President," he insisted, "those of us who have worked on this measure do not feel that way. We are most respectful of our colleagues."

A few minutes later, Russell concluded, "As one who lives in the South, as one who has never been ashamed of being a Southerner, and as one who believes that the people of the South are as good citizens as people anywhere else in the country, I resent this political foray. It may be that the proponents will be successful in getting this measure through by gagging those associated with me in opposing this bill; but I will always maintain that I do not believe it is consistent with the fundamental principles of fair play to which all American citizens usually subscribe."

* * *

A FORCED LULL FOLLOWED the introduction of the Dirksen substitute. The Memorial Day recess was looming and so were a series of memorial fundraising dinners commemorating what would have been John Kennedy's forty-seventh birthday on May 29. President Johnson used the break to try to round up a few more votes for cloture. On Tuesday, May 26, he lobbied his old friend and protégé Howard Cannon of Nevada. When Cannon, a highly decorated World War II pilot, had come to the

Senate in 1959, Johnson had mentored him, giving him a seat on the Armed Services Committee. Now the president gently raised the question of cloture on H.R. 7152. "It wasn't a sell-type meeting," Cannon would recall. "He didn't push as hard on this as he did on other things." But the running tally for cloture was adding up.

The next day, Mansfield announced that he hoped to be able to hold a cloture vote in early June. "You have to hit bedrock some time and have a showdown," he said. The following Monday, June 1, Dirksen promised to circulate an annotated copy of his proposed changes, to make the differences from the original bill "crystal clear, with brackets and underscoring."

And then, just at the moment when his powers of persuasion were needed most, Dirksen fell seriously ill, with a bad chest cold that kept him at home. For weeks he had been running on fumes, and the hectic pace and unrelenting pressure had taken their toll. "Listen, they forget I'm no spring chicken anymore," he complained. "I get out of this damn place at eight, nine or ten o'clock, drive home, have dinner at eleven and get up in the morning at dawn. My main problem is getting enough restorative sleep."

Russell now seized on this moment to say that he was ready to begin voting on the remaining jury trial amendments right away. But Humphrey and Mansfield knew they did not yet have the last needed votes for cloture lined up. So the pro-civil-rights forces now had to stage a slowdown, holding the floor in what amounted to a kind of counterfilibuster. Because Dirksen was not present to explain the proposed changes from the floor as had been planned, Humphrey did his part on Thursday, June 4, outlining the new package, including the inclusion of the Mansfield-Dirksen jury trial amendment. That same day, Mansfield proposed a tightly limited plan in which senators would vote on the pending jury trial amendments separately and then on the substitute bill. But Russell was unwilling to be so tightly constricted, preferring to have the flexibility to bring up any of the hundreds of potential amendments still pending. "If we go in the basis which the Senator from Georgia has outlined, we shall be here until 1984 and we will still be voting on amendments," Mansfield complained.

In Dirksen's absence, Bourke Hickenlooper's long-simmering frustrations boiled over. As head of the Senate's Republican Policy Committee, the party's agenda-setting group in the Senate, he resented being given short shrift by Dirksen, who was junior to him in service. "Bourke had the feeling that without talking to a number of his older colleagues, like himself, Everett had the tendency to run off and sit down with Hubert and sort of take over as representing the Republicans in the Senate without having done perhaps as much coordination as he might have," Hickenlooper's fellow Iowan Jack Miller would recall. "To the average observer, there was no friction, but in the corridors and cloakroom, there were comments."

Hickenlooper now rallied other conservatives—some of whom had been on the verge of supporting cloture—to hold out for further changes. When Dirksen returned to his office on Friday, June 5, he found a revolt in progress. At a meeting that morning, Hickenlooper led the charge, but Norris Cotton of New Hampshire and Roman Hruska of Nebraska also complained, each of them wanting consideration of amendments of their own. Mansfield had been hoping to hold the cloture vote as early as Tuesday, June 9, but Hickenlooper wanted it postponed until Wednesday, because many senators would be attending the national governors' conference in Cleveland on Monday. That was a reasonable enough request, and Mansfield agreed to set the cloture vote for Wednesday, June 10. Then Hickenlooper sprang a surprise. He asked the Senate's unanimous consent to vote on three amendments on Tuesday: Thruston Morton's jury trial amendment (which had been just slightly revised); another by Norris Cotton restricting the coverage of Title VII's employment discrimination provisions to businesses with one hundred or more employees (instead of twenty-five, as in the House-passed bill); and still another of his own devising, to delete all provisions relating to aid for desegregation of public schools.

There was instant panic, as neither the pro-civil-rights forces nor the southerners knew just how Hickenlooper's proposal might play out or how it would affect each side's advantage in what was now clearly the endgame. If the civil rights forces blocked Hickenlooper's demand, would he retaliate by rallying his conservative allies to oppose cloture? If

Russell blocked him, would he do the opposite? "I fear that if we accept the proposal," Paul Douglas said, "we shall open a Pandora's box." Russell drily noted that Hickenlooper seemed to be having much more success than he had in getting movement on consideration of amendments, noting that Mansfield had met his own proposals with "a grin" and "a very polite declination."

To give both sides time to review the bidding, Russell proposed deferring consideration of Hickenlooper's request until the next day, Saturday, June 6.

Overnight, Hubert Humphrey received commitments from three Republicans—Karl Mundt, Roman Hruska, and Norris Cotton—that in exchange for a vote on the new amendments, they would definitely support cloture. Jack Miller of Iowa, a Catholic and a former law professor at Notre Dame, had already announced that he would agree to cut off debate, having been heavily lobbied by the archbishop of Dubuque. This meant that there were now almost certainly enough Republican votes lined up to assure the sixty-seven votes needed, but Hickenlooper was still a question mark.

As the Senate reconvened on that Saturday morning, Hickenlooper again asked for unanimous consent to debate the three amendments—with four hours allotted for each—on Tuesday, June 9. No objection was heard. When Russell remonstrated with Humphrey for agreeing to Hickenlooper's demands while refusing his own earlier request for votes on amendments, the majority whip was candid. "Well, Dick," he said, "you haven't any votes to give us on cloture and these fellows do."

So Morton's jury trial amendment—the very amendment that just a month earlier had loomed as a potentially lethal threat to the bill because it might unleash a flood of weakening amendments—now became the price the civil rights forces were willing to pay to achieve cloture. It was a small enough price in the end. Justice Department lawyers determined that the amendment—which would allow jury trials in all cases of criminal contempt under the bill (except for voting rights cases under Title I) with maximum penalties of $1,000 or six months in jail—would do no real harm to the bill.

On Monday, June 8, Mike Mansfield rose on the Senate floor,

addressed the presiding officer, his fellow Montanan, Lee Metcalf, and began the process of invoking cloture. "We, the undersigned Senators," he said, "in accordance with the provisions of Rule XXII of the Standing Rules of the Senate, hereby move to bring to a close the debate on the bill." The cloture motion would now be voted on at ten o'clock Wednesday morning, after the Senate waited the required two days. Debate would be limited to one hour.

But first the Senate had to deal with Hickenlooper's demands, which it did on Tuesday. The Morton amendment—once so controversial—passed by a vote of 51 to 48. "Does this jury amendment bother you any?" Lyndon Johnson asked the attorney general after the vote.

"No, I think it makes it much more difficult, but hell, we can live with it," Bob Kennedy replied.

The Hickenlooper amendment to withhold financial aid for desegregation of public schools failed 40 to 56, while Norris Cotton's amendment to exempt businesses with fewer than one hundred employees from Title VII's fair employment provisions failed 34 to 63. Every obstacle to the cloture vote had now been cleared away.

Every obstacle but one, that is. As the day wound down, Mike Mansfield drily warned his colleagues, "It is my understanding that there may be speeches beyond the hour of 12 o'clock midnight tonight." And at 7:38 p.m., the redoubtable Robert Byrd of West Virginia took to the floor with an eight-hundred-page speech, vowing to talk through the night in the filibuster's last gasp. "As I have indicated, and as I repeat, the bill would not create any new civil rights," Byrd declared. "In my judgment, it would impair the civil rights of all Americans. It cannot be justified on any basis—legal, economic, moral or religious." Byrd attacked the bill section by section. He read newspaper articles and editorials criticizing it. At one point, Humphrey interrupted to inquire when Byrd might finish. "I have enough material to carry me, if I proceed to read it carefully and painstakingly, as I am now doing, another twelve or fifteen hours," Byrd replied. "But I shall hardly be able to carry on for that length of time. I assure the amiable and able Senator from Minnesota that I shall indeed complete my recitation no later than 9:59 o'clock a.m., in time to recess in accordance with the previous order." When Humphrey thanked him for his courtesy, Byrd replied with flights of poetry:

> *The roses red upon my neighbor's vine*
> *Are owned by him but they are also mine.*
> *His was the cost, and his the labor, too.*
> *But mine as well as his the joy, their loveliness to view . . .*
> *So why be selfish, when so much that's fine*
> *Is grown for me, upon my Minnesota neighbor's vine . . .*

"I thank the Senator from West Virginia," Humphrey replied with an exaggerated flourish. "He has just reminded me that at my abode and domicile out in Northwest Chevy Chase, there is a fence banked with beautiful red roses. I shall go to them and in the morning, at approximately 9:59 a.m., I shall bring my good friend the Senator from West Virginia some of those beautiful red roses that were so patiently planted and nourished by Mrs. Humphrey, and which are viewed by the neighbors and loved by all."

And with that, Humphrey concluded, "As we say in that fine land of the Scandinavians, '*Buenos noches.*'"

That night, Humphrey told Lyndon Johnson that he was sure of sixty-eight votes for cloture, forty-two of them from Democrats. (J. Howard Edmondson of Oklahoma, whom Johnson had also lobbied, had agreed to vote for cloture because of the adoption of the Morton jury trial amendment.)

"Well, the Republicans are doing a little better than we are, aren't they?" Johnson said. Indeed, in proportional terms, they were. Dirksen felt confident that he had at least twenty-six out of thirty-three Republican votes.

* * *

THE NEXT MORNING, WEDNESDAY, June 10, Dirksen rose early at Heart's Desire and went into his own garden to clip some long-stemmed roses to take in to the office. He had stayed up late the night before with his wife,

Louella, typing his twelve-page speech in the large-font typeface that he used for floor speeches. He arrived just as Byrd was finishing his soliloquy. Fourteen hours and thirteen minutes in all, it was the single longest speech of the whole debate on H.R. 7152.

At 10:00 a.m., the Senate chamber was packed, with 150 standees, including many House members, lining the pale yellow walls. In the overflowing galleries, there were precisely six black spectators, including the faithful Clarence Mitchell and Cecil E. Newman, an old friend of Humphrey's and the editor of the *St. Paul Recorder*, a black newspaper. Nick Katzenbach and Burke Marshall had to sit on the steps in a gallery aisle.

Mike Mansfield rose to begin the hour-long debate on the cloture motion by noting that on the Senate's calendar, it was still the legislative day of March 30, the day the filibuster had begun. "If my memory is correct, we are now in our third month and first legislative day of debate," he said. Mansfield then read a poignant letter he had received from a twenty-nine-year-old Montana woman, a mother of four.

"I was conceived by a pair of good, respectable, hard-working white parents," the woman had written. "I was allowed to grow and mature, to have faith in myself and my future, and when I married and gave birth to my lovely children, to have faith in them and their future . . . This morning, the thought occurred to me, that by that same accident of birth, I could have been conceived by a pair of equally good, respectable, hard-working Negro parents. The process is the same, but what immense differences there would have been in my life and upbringing. How heartbreaking it must be for a child to have to learn that his future is sharply limited even if his intelligence and his ability is not. How confusing it must be for a child to learn that he may not buy an ice cream cone or a Coke in the same shop as a lighter-skinned child, even though his dime has the same value as the other.

"At night, when I kiss my children goodnight, I offer a small prayer of thanks to God for making them so perfect, so healthy, so lovely, and I find myself tempted to thank Him for letting them be born white. Then I am not so proud, either of myself, nor of our society, which forces such a temptation upon us. And that is why I don't feel that this is a southern problem. It is a northern problem, a western problem, an eastern problem. It is an American problem, for all Americans. It is my problem. I am only one person, one woman. I wish there was something I could do in this issue. The only way I know how to start is to educate my children that justice and freedom and ambition are not merely privileges, but their birthrights."

Richard Russell now rose, unmoved by Mansfield's eloquence. "Mr. President, the argument the Senator from Montana made in behalf of this bill has an emotional appeal—but no more emotional appeal than that which could be made for a purely socialistic or communistic system that would divide and distribute among all our people every bit of the property and wealth of the people of these United States." He concluded, "I appeal to the Senate to vote down this gag rule . . . I appeal to Senators to rise above the pressures to which they have been subjected and to reject this legislation that will result in vast changes, not only in our social order but in our very form of government."

Mansfield then yielded two minutes to Hubert Humphrey, who stood, a red rose in his lapel, to declare, "In the Senate, the Constitution of the United States is on trial. The question is whether we will have two types of citizenship in this nation, or first-class citizenship for all. The question is whether there will be two kinds of justice, or equal justice under the law for every American. The question is whether this nation will be divided or, as we are taught in our youth in the Pledge of Allegiance, 'one nation, under God, indivisible, with liberty and justice for all.'

"I say to my colleagues of the Senate that perhaps in your lives you will be able to tell your children's children that you were here for America to make the year 1964 our freedom year."

At last it was Everett Dirksen's turn. He first outlined the final compromise package, now including the Morton jury trial amendment, that would be considered after cloture. He spoke for a quarter hour in soft, even tones. It was obvious to everyone in the chamber that he did not feel well; twice he swallowed pills passed to him by an aide. Speaking from his typed text, he reviewed the long history of H.R. 7152. "Sharp opinions have developed," he said. "Incredible allegations have been made. Extreme views have been asserted. For myself, I have had but one purpose, and that was the enactment of a good, workable, equitable, practical bill having due regard for the progress made in the civil rights field at the state and local level."

"There are many reasons why cloture should be invoked, and a good civil rights bill enacted," the minority leader continued, again paraphrasing Victor Hugo: "Stronger than all the armies is an idea whose time has come."

"The time has come for equality of opportunity in sharing in government, in education and in employment," Dirksen insisted. "It will not be stayed or denied." He cited the example of a learned professor who had developed what he believed was an incontrovertible scientific premise and submitted it to his peers for review. "Quickly they picked it apart," Dirksen said. "In agony he cried out, 'Is nothing eternal?' To this one of his associates replied, 'Nothing is eternal except change.'"

"I appeal to all Senators," he concluded. "We are confronted with a moral issue. Today, let us not be found wanting in whatever it takes by way of moral and spiritual substance to face up to the issue and to vote cloture."

"The time of the Senator from Illinois has expired," the presiding officer, Lee Metcalf, announced. "All time has expired." Metcalf ordered a quorum call, and after it was quickly established that all one hundred senators were indeed present, he admonished the dozens of aides and clerks who were crowding the Senate floor to overflowing that staff members were allowed on the floor only when actually assisting senators in the conduct of their duties. "The Senate is now approaching a vote," Metcalf said. "The present occupant of the chair does not see how clerks and members of the staff can come under the rule of the privilege of the floor. A quorum being present, the chair submits to the Senate, without debate, the question: Is it the sense of the Senate that the debate shall be brought to a close?"

Felton "Skeeter" Johnston, the secretary of the Senate, a taciturn Mississippian who had worked on Capitol Hill for thirty-five years, now called the roll. When he reached the name "Engle," there was silence. Clair Engle, the fifty-two-year-old junior senator from California, a Democrat, was recovering from surgery to remove a brain tumor. He had been brought into the chamber just minutes earlier in a wheelchair, but he was unable to speak. Now, with supreme effort, he lifted his left hand three times and pointed to his eye. "I guess that means 'aye,'" Johnston said softly.

By 11:15, sixty-six votes had been cast for cloture.

"Williams?" Johnston called.

John Williams of Delaware, who spoke so quietly that Senate reporters had nicknamed him "Whispering Willie," quietly answered, "Aye."

Hubert Humphrey raised his arms in silent exultation. It was the sixty-seventh vote.

The ancient Carl Hayden, cane in hand, had been waiting in the cloakroom. He had, in the end, acceded to Lyndon Johnson's importunings, pledging to vote to cut off debate—but only if his was needed as the deciding vote. "It's all right, Carl," Mansfield now assured him. "We're in."

Outside the Capitol, in the one-hundred-degree morning heat, Roger Mudd was broadcasting live on CBS. Since cameras and microphones were barred from the Senate chamber, Mudd had jury-rigged a groundbreaking notification system in which a Senate gallery employee sitting in the chamber would whisper each vote into a telephone. In the radio and television workspace, another Senate employee would repeat the vote aloud to Mudd's producer, who would repeat it into his headset. "We tested it a dozen times and it worked every time," Mudd would recall. "I lagged behind the vote not more than seven or eight seconds."

The final tally was 71 to 29, four votes more than the required two-thirds. Of the seven uncertain Republican votes that Stephen Horn had predicted in June 1963 might be obtainable, Dirksen lost only one, Edwin Mechem of New Mexico, and he picked up three of the eight that Horn had thought beyond reach: Karl Mundt, Norris Cotton, and Carl Curtis.

* * *

HUMPHREY AND HIS TROOPS had not a moment to savor their victory. With cloture now in effect, each senator was limited to an hour's speaking time on the Mansfield-Dirksen substitute. But that still left a hundred hours of potential further debate, and some five hundred amendments—many of them hostile southern ones that could yet be appended to the

Mansfield-Dirksen package to undermine it—stacked up for potential consideration. And because only those amendments that had been presented prior to the cloture vote could be called up after it (except by unanimous consent), there would be no way to rectify an amendment hostile to the bill by a subsequent one; if an amendment passed and was added to the substitute bill, there it would remain. So there was no room for error on the part of the civil rights supporters. It was at this very moment that all their weeks of carefully enforced discipline collapsed in exhaustion and inattention.

The wily Sam Ervin was first on his feet, calling up an amendment to the still pending Talmadge jury trial amendment that would prohibit a person from being subject to a charge of criminal contempt after being acquitted of an actual crime under the bill, and vice versa. The civil rights forces immediately feared that this double jeopardy provision could gut the bill, because someone acquitted of a civil rights violation by a sympathetic state court could not later be charged with a federal offense under the law. "Ervin set forth the proposal in a very garbled and unclear way," John Stewart would recall, and "there was great turmoil in the chamber. Neither the pro-civil-rights forces nor the opposition were at all clear as to what was happening in the chamber, and before anyone knew it, we were having a roll call vote." The initial tally was 47 to 48, and Lee Metcalf announced that the measure had failed. So Herman Talmadge withdrew his own amendment, only to have Metcalf announce that Ervin's measure had in fact passed, 49 to 48. But since the Ervin amendment had been attached to the now withdrawn Talmadge amendment, it was rendered null under the Senate's rules, however bizarre or unfair that might seem.

Mansfield now called up the new Dirksen substitute bill as the pending business of the Senate. Richard Russell immediately moved to amend it by delaying the effective date of Title II, the all-important public accommodations section, to November 15, 1965. "Mr. President, we are confronted with the spirit of not only the mob but of a lynch mob in the Senate of the United States," Russell complained. "Senators are paying no attention to what they are doing." But they paid enough attention to defeat Russell's amendment by a vote of 40 to 59, and Mike Mansfield, reeling from all the activity, asked unanimous consent to recess until three o'clock that afternoon "to regroup, rethink and recollect."

In the courtliest of gestures, Clarence Mitchell walked a dejected Russell back to his office. The weary Georgian praised Humphrey for his fairness throughout the debate, and for letting the southerners have their say, which Russell believed would ultimately make the bill acceptable and enforceable in the South, because the segregationists had given their all to the fight.

When the Senate reconvened that afternoon, Albert Gore of Tennessee moved to strike Title VI, the provision that allowed for the withholding of federal funds from state and local programs that practiced discrimination. Gore was a Democrat and a progressive in most matters, but he was running for reelection in a border state and could not afford to be seen as supporting these provisions. His amendment was easily defeated, and the Senate recessed.

During this period, John Stewart would recall, "Humphrey seemed to be quite distraught and not really in command of the situation." Together with Justice Department officials and representatives of the Leadership Conference on Civil Rights, the majority whip debated how to handle the inevitable flood of forthcoming amendments. One conciliatory move aimed at minimizing ill feelings involved finding a way to make Sam Ervin's double-jeopardy amendment acceptable—since it had passed, after all. In the end, Justice Department lawyers worked up new language for the amendment, making it clear that the provision applied only to federal charges under "the laws of the United States" and not to state prosecutions. The lawyers said that the amendment, as revised, would do no harm, and Ervin accepted the change.

At their daily meeting on Thursday, June 11, the bipartisan floor leaders' group agreed to oppose all future amendments unless they were minor and accepted by the leaders of both parties. In the Senate session that day, the revised Ervin amendment passed by a vote of 80 to 16, but the next eleven southern amendments failed on roll call votes. The next day, Russell proposed yet another temporizing amendment—to submit the bill to a national referendum before it could take effect. This was too much for Dirksen, who ridiculed that idea, declaring, "I am ready to accept my responsibility under the bill and for the bill. I am not going to pass the buck to people back home and say, 'I am rather shaky on the inside. I am thinking now about my party and how it is going to fare. I am thinking about the next election. I would rather get a guideline from you.' Then they should write to me and say, 'Haven't you guts enough to stand up as a legislator and be counted because of the mantle of authority with which you have been clothed by the Constitution?' What a shameful concession to make. I shall never make it." Russell's amendment failed 22 to 67.

On Saturday, June 13, the floor leaders accepted an amendment to Title VII proposed by John Tower of Texas, the sole Republican who had aligned himself consistently with the southerners throughout the debate. Tower's amendment—strongly backed by Dirksen—was a response to the infamous Motorola case, in which an Illinois fair employment hearing officer had ordered the company to hire a black employee who had failed an ability test. Tower's amendment specified that it would not be an illegal employment practice for an employer to administer and act on any ability test so long as the test was not "designed, intended or used" to discriminate on the basis of race or sex. Tower's proposal passed on a voice vote.

By Monday, June 15, Humphrey and Kuchel decided that the only way to expedite the amendment process was not only to battle the southerners but to persuade any liberals who still hoped to offer strengthening amendments to refrain from doing so, and they announced this policy publicly.

For his part, Russell let it be known that he had lost his stomach for the fight, though he still had to contend with the dead-enders in his caucus like Strom Thurmond who were willing to continue offering weakening amendments. As sessions dragged late into the night, with almost all the southern amendments being defeated, senators would resort to breaks for liquid refreshment in their hideaway offices near the Senate floor. One evening, when Russell Long of Louisiana offered an amendment after Dirksen believed he had agreed not to, an obviously well-oiled Dirksen leaped to his feet "gesticulating wildly" and complained, "God damn you, Russell! You've broken our agreement! Why, you've welshed on our deal!"

Mike Mansfield, too, was growing irritated at the southerners' delaying tactics. On Tuesday, June 16, he decided to keep the Senate in session past midnight, and it met for thirteen hours, from 11:00 a.m. Tuesday until 12:01 a.m. Wednesday, racking up thirty-four roll call votes, the most ever recorded in the Senate in a single day.

Later that same Wednesday, Hubert Humphrey was summoned off the floor in midafternoon to take a call from his wife in Minnesota. Their son Bob had noticed a swelling in his neck and gone into the hospital to have it checked out. Doctors now determined that he had a malignant growth and would have to undergo major surgery to clean out his lymphatic system. Humphrey was in agony; he desperately wanted to fly home but felt he could not abandon the fight for H.R. 7152 in its final hours. Clarence Mitchell and Joe Rauh happened to drop by his office, full of happiness at the state of play on the bill, only to join the majority whip in tears. "I had a terrible time pulling myself together to go back to the Senate floor, where I had to be," Humphrey would recall. "Arguments and rhetoric that I might have listened to calmly and without emotion were much harder to take when I should have been at Bob's bedside."

That same day, Sam Ervin and Strom Thurmond both promised to limit the remaining number of amendments that they would call up, which assured that the bill could come to a final vote by Friday, June 19. In the end, of the 117 amendments considered by the Senate after cloture, only eleven minor revisions were adopted. The civil rights forces had protected the Dirksen substitute from any real harm.

Finally, that Wednesday evening, the Senate voted on the Dirksen-Mansfield-Humphrey-Kuchel substitute amendment, as it was now known. It passed overwhelmingly, 76 to 18, with forty-six Democrats and thirty Republicans voting aye. Now all that remained was the final vote on H.R. 7152, as amended. Mansfield announced that final arguments on the bill would take place Thursday and Friday and suggested, "because we have been under quite a strain for some time, that we take it easy and go home and get a good night's sleep," and return at eleven o'clock Thursday morning.

When the Senate convened that morning, Russell still had nineteen of the sixty minutes' time remaining to him under the cloture rule. "Mr.

President," Russell began, addressing Ted Kennedy, who was presiding in the chair, "the moving finger is writing the final act of the longest debate and the greatest tragedy ever played out in the Senate of the United States." Sounding a bit like the florid prologue to the film version of *Gone with the Wind*, Russell declared, "Indeed, Mr. President, history may well record this as the last sustained fight to keep inviolate the federal system with its division of powers between the states and the central government."

"Mr. President, those of us who have been upon this floor day after day for more than three months have used every weapon available," Russell went on. "Until we were gagged, we made no secret of the fact that we were undertaking to speak in detail and at length in an effort to get the message across to the American people. We did not deceive anyone as to our purposes."

At this Ted Kennedy interrupted, "The time of the Senator from Georgia has expired."

Russell was taken aback. His eyes glistened with tears.

"I express the hope that those who are keeping the time will apply the same rules to others which they have applied to me," he complained. Then there was nothing left for him to do but sit down.

Speaking for the Republican leadership, Kuchel declared that the bill "will be an American achievement, for the leaders and the members of both parties helped to fashion the pending bill." He added, "The sham and shame of unequal justice are about to be sheared away, for they have no place in our American system."

Soon enough, though, the Republican who in just a few weeks' time would become his party's presidential nominee was on his feet in the chamber, opposing the bill. Barry Goldwater knew that Kuchel had worked assiduously, but in vain, on behalf of his opponent Nelson Rockefeller in the recent California primary, in a last-ditch effort to deny Goldwater the nomination. Now Goldwater rose to say that while he opposed "discrimination of any sort," he nevertheless would oppose the bill on constitutional grounds, insisting that it would "require the creation of a federal police force of mammoth proportions" and would result in the "development of an 'informer' psychology in great areas of our national life—neighbors spying on neighbors, workers spying on workers, businessmen spying on businessmen—where those citizens for selfish and narrow purposes will have ample inducement to do so."

When the Senate convened again on Friday, June 19, one year to the day since John Kennedy had first submitted H.R. 7152 to Congress, the seventy-sixth and final edition of the civil rights newsletter had appeared. "Joining the legions of other small rural dailies, we cease publication," its staff reported, tongue firmly but proudly in cheek. "Suffice it to say here that the job was done. We have a good bill. We still have a Senate, and we have miles to go before we sleep, and miles to go before we sleep."

The first order of business on the floor was a motion from Albert Gore, who yet again was trying to have it both ways by blocking the bill without actually having to cast a clear vote against it. Unbeknown to Humphrey, Gore had clandestinely received unanimous consent to offer a motion that morning. John Stewart would recall that Humphrey regarded Gore's move as "the highest breach of senatorial ethics." Gore contended that the provision of Title VI that allowed for the cutoff of federal funds for programs that practice discrimination was so onerous that the whole bill should be recommitted to the Judiciary Committee—where it would, of course, be sure to die in Jim Eastland's firm grip. Gore's colleagues rejected his motion after a short debate by a vote of 25 to 74.

Hubert Humphrey then made his final speech in support of the bill. "These have been difficult and demanding days," he declared. "I doubt whether any Senator can recall a bill which so tested our attitudes of justice and equality, our abilities as legislators, our sense of fairness as individuals, and our loyalty to the Senate as an institution of democratic government." He concluded, "I will consent to this measure because for the first time in recent history, the Congress of the United States will say in clear and unmistakable terms, 'There is no room for second-class citizenship in our country.'"

Mike Mansfield then took to the floor to sum up the struggle, full of praise for Everett Dirksen but also for "the insistence of the opposition on prolonged debate."

"It was learned and thorough, and it played an essential role in refining the provisions of the bill," the majority leader said. "But, in my judgment, its most important function was to discourage self-righteousness on the part of the majority. There is no room for unwarranted sentiments of victory if the legislation we have molded is to be given constructive meaning for the nation in the years ahead. If we are about to enter upon a second Reconstruction—as the Senator from Georgia called it—then it must be a reconstruction of the heart, a reconstruction involving, not one section, but all sections of the nation. The dimensions of the problem with which we have been struggling these past months stretch the length and breadth of the nation. An accurate appraisal of them leads, not to a sense of triumph over the passage of this bill, but to a profound humility. No one, let me say, understood this reality better than the late President John Fitzgerald Kennedy. This, indeed, is his moment as well as the Senate's."

The last word was left for Everett Dirksen. He did not disappoint.

"On occasion, a number of the boys up in the gallery have asked me, 'How have you become a crusader in this cause?'" he began. "It is a fair question, and it deserves a fair answer." The answer, he said, lay in the words of the poet John Donne. "He left what I believe is a precious legacy on the parchments of history. He said, 'Any man's death diminishes me, because I am involved in mankind.' I am involved in mankind, and whatever the skin, we are all involved in mankind. Equality of opportunity must prevail if we are to complete the covenant that we have made with the people, and if we are to honor the pledges we made when we held up our hands to take an oath to defend the laws and to carry out the Constitution of the United States." From time to time, Dirksen stared directly at Barry Goldwater, as if to scold him, but he never mentioned the Arizonan by name. Finally, Dirksen declared, "I am prepared for the vote."

Once again, Clair Engle appeared in his wheelchair as the clerk called the roll. Once again, he lifted his hand toward his eye. At 7:40 p.m., the clerk announced that H.R. 7152 had passed, 73 to 27. All but six of the Senate's thirty-three Republicans had voted for it, compared with just forty-six of its sixty-seven Democrats. (Two Republicans who had voted for cloture—Cotton and Hickenlooper—voted against the bill, while two who had voted against cloture—Milton Young of North Dakota and Wallace Bennett of Utah—voted for the bill.)

In San Francisco for a Democratic fundraising dinner where he had received a hero's welcome, Lyndon Johnson hailed the bill's passage by the Senate—and anticipated its final victory in the House of Representatives in the coming days. "No single act of Congress can, by itself, eliminate discrimination and prejudice, hatred and injustice," the president said. "But this bill goes further to invest the rights of man with the protection of law than any legislation in this century." For her part, Lady Bird Johnson wondered in her diary whether "anybody but me" would remember that June 19 had long been a special day in her home state. "Juneteenth was always celebrated by all the Negroes in Texas," she wrote. "Nobody's maid worked on Juneteenth because it was the day the Emancipation Proclamation went into effect in Texas a hundred or so years ago."

Hours later, when Hubert Humphrey and the faithful John Stewart finally left the Senate, hundreds of spectators, who had gathered to await the final vote, were still clustered around the East Front steps of the Senate wing, and they raised a rousing cheer. "Never in my fifteen years in the Senate, nor in the memory of Senators with a far longer period of service than mine," Humphrey would remember, "had there ever been anything like it."

12

The Law of the Land

THURSDAY, JULY 2, 1964

FROM THE MOMENT THE Senate approved the bill, there had been press reports that Johnson wanted to have it on his desk in time to sign it on the Fourth of July. Now, just before 10:30 a.m., with the House of Representatives about to give final passage to the amended Senate version of H.R. 7152, the president received an outraged telephone call from his friend and former congressional colleague Clare Boothe Luce, the Connecticut Republican who was also a playwright and the wife of the founder of the Time-Life publishing empire.

"I heard . . . that you were going to sign the civil rights bill on the Fourth of July and it seemed to be such an *appalling* idea," Luce began.

"No, I never had any thought of doing that," Johnson replied.

"It was in all the papers," she countered.

"I know it, honey," the president rejoined, by now chuckling, "but I don't want to be critical of the press . . . No human being has ever discussed it with me, and I've never given any indication that I would do anything except to sign it the first moment it was available, which would be Thursday" (as it happened, that very day).

Leaving aside the notion that anyone might find it "appalling" to sign a law guaranteeing equal rights for all Americans on the holiday commemorating the idea that "all men are created equal," Luce's phone call was only one among the many considerations and complications that had besieged Johnson since the Senate passed the bill.

Just hours after the final vote on June 19, Ted Kennedy had nearly been killed in a small-plane crash in western Massachusetts as he and Senator Birch Bayh of Indiana were on their way to address the state Democratic convention. They had been delayed in Washington waiting for the vote and then ran into bad weather as their pilot tried to bring the plane in for a night landing. The pilot and a friend of Kennedy's were killed on impact, while the senator himself, dragged from the plane by a dazed Bayh, had three fractured vertebrae, two broken ribs, a bruised kidney, and multiple lacerations. He faced immobilization in a kind of a mesh waffle iron of a bed, plus six months or more of intensive rehabilitation. (In fact, he would never again walk normally.) Johnson had sent four doctors from Walter Reed Army Hospital to the Cooley Dickinson Hospital in Northampton, Massachusetts, to aid in the treatment, and had been especially solicitous of the Kennedy family.

Barely an hour after the call from Clare Boothe Luce, Johnson was on the phone with Robert Kennedy, who was just back from a trip to Warsaw and West Berlin, where he had gone to dedicate John F. Kennedy Platz in memory of the late president's *"Ich bin ein Berliner"* speech of the year before. Kennedy, too, had some pressing concerns about how and when the civil rights bill might be signed.

"If it's signed today," the attorney general warned, "we're going to have a rather difficult weekend, a holiday weekend . . . That Friday and Saturday, with the Fourth of July and firecrackers going off . . . with Negroes running all over the South figuring that they get the day off, that they're going to go into every hotel and motel and every restaurant . . . If it's possible . . . to postpone it till Monday and sign it . . . I don't know whether it's gone so far that you feel it's necessary to sign it today."

In fact, Johnson was certain that it would be better to sign the bill as soon as possible. For one thing, he had promised to sign it as soon as it reached his desk in part to scotch the notion of signing it on July 4—a notion that he blamed Kennedy's Justice Department for helping to float in the first place. Moreover, he had promised Charlie Halleck, who was eager to get his members out of town as soon as possible to prepare for the Republican National Convention in San Francisco on July 13, that he would sign the bill before the long July 4th weekend if at all possible—and he did not want to deprive the Republicans who had been vital to its passage of the chance to be present at this final moment. "Now when it gets to us," the president told Kennedy, "I don't know, but I think it will be late today."

But Johnson's distrust of his attorney general was so complete that he did not give a definitive answer of his own. Instead, he promptly called five other people to air Kennedy's proposal, all the while making clear his own doubts about it.

Roy Wilkins at the NAACP assured Johnson that "signing it as soon as it's available is the correct idea."

"*No, sir,*" said Johnson's press secretary, George Reedy. "I think it'd be very bad if you waited."

Secretary of Commerce Luther Hodges advised, "Mr. President, I don't think you can hold it up," while Hubert Humphrey allowed, "That would be very unfortunate." Larry O'Brien echoed the president's own thinking, "God, we ought to go forward with this, this evening."

Fifty years later, Bob Kennedy's warning seems overblown, if not racist. But in the first week of July 1964, there was already serious racial turmoil throughout the South. In St. Augustine, Florida, Martin Luther King had been besieged (and jailed after trying to eat in a whites-only motel restaurant) when a desegregation march touched off two weeks of violent disturbances. On Sunday, June 21, two days after the Senate passed H.R. 7152, three young voting rights workers—part of an idealistic army bound for "Freedom Summer"—had gone missing outside Philadelphia, Mississippi. The whereabouts of James Chaney, Andrew Goodman, and Michael Schwerner were still unknown as Johnson prepared to sign the bill, though the burned-out husk of the station wagon they had been driving had been found off Highway 21 in Neshoba County, leading J. Edgar Hoover himself to inform the president that he assumed they had been killed. On this same Thursday, Johnson would ask Hoover to "put fifty, a hundred people" on the trail of the Ku Klux Klan and other white supremacist groups in Mississippi lest they cause disruptions in the wake of the bill signing. "I don't want these Klansmen to open their mouth without your knowing what they're saying," Johnson told Hoover.

The president had asked his new in-house intellectual adviser, the Princeton historian Eric F. Goldman (who had succeeded Arthur Schlesinger), to draft a statement for him to deliver upon signing the civil rights bill. "The season of summer is upon us," Goldman wrote in his draft. "Summer means a thousand delights—the gardens full with blossoms, the long, lazy flicker of a trout line in the sunlight, the happy skip-and-jump of our children. But the summer of 1964 is no ordinary season. It brings not only anticipation of delights but deep anxieties. I would be failing in my duty if I did not inform you that responsible observers, white and Negro, warn me of the possibility of serious racial disturbances in the North or South of this country, and possibly in both."

As he flew to Washington to witness the signing of the bill into law, Martin Luther King told reporters that the new statute "will bring a great deal of practical relief to Negroes in many southern communities." In the short term, he noted, the law would raise expectations for further progress, but "it will probably take five years to see the civil rights bill fully implemented in the South." He added, "The scope of direct action this summer will depend on the scope of compliance" with the bill.

* * *

THE AMENDED H.R. 7152 had arrived back in the House at the opening of business on Monday, June 22, when a Senate clerk carried it down the chamber's center aisle and solemnly intoned, "A message from the Senate." The previous Friday, just after the Senate passage, Manny Celler and Bill McCulloch had issued a joint press release urging its swift adoption by the House.

"Not all the amendments are to our liking," the Judiciary Committee chairman and his ranking member said. "However, we believe that none of the amendments do serious violence to the purpose of the bill. We are of a mind that a conference could fatally delay enactment of this measure. We believe that the House membership will take the same position."

All along, the paramount strategy of the civil rights forces had been to avoid a House-Senate conference committee, in which the bill might be amended further, requiring it to go back once more to the Senate, where it would face the threat of yet another filibuster. So Celler and McCulloch now wanted the House to adopt the Dirksen-revised Senate bill unchallenged and unchanged.

But before agreeing to such an unorthodox course, Charlie Halleck had a price: two weeks' vacation for his members, starting July 3. "Now wait a minute, Mr. President," Halleck told Johnson on June 22. "I appreciate your calling me and I don't want to detain you because you're a damn sight more important than I am. But let me just tell you this, my friend. We get your civil rights bill passed, and you can't do it without us, understand? You sign that up July 4. Give us the next two weeks off in the House—"

Johnson argued that the administration had a total of thirty-one measures—including his hotly desired antipoverty program—pending in both houses. But Halleck was insistent.

"Now, goddamn it, Mr. President, I'll do a few of those things, but you ain't going to curry any favor with me, I might as well be blunt about it, making us stay here when we got twenty, thirty guys from the House wanting to go to our convention."

Johnson might be able to finesse Charlie Halleck, but there was no practical way to avoid another trip to Judge Smith's Rules Committee before the bill could get to the House floor. The civil rights forces had briefly considered asking for a suspension of the rules in order to send the bill instead to the Judiciary Committee, where a sympathetic Celler would promptly report it out. But such a procedure would require a two-thirds vote, and it could only be invoked on the first and third Mondays of the month—meaning on July 6 at the earliest. That would run afoul of Charlie Halleck's wishes, so Celler and McCulloch resigned themselves to one more audience with the Rules Committee, whose most progressive members in both parties were willing to play along.

Celler and McCulloch prepared House Resolution 789, to provide for the "concurrence of the House of Representatives to the Senate amendment to H.R. 7152," and Speaker McCormack promptly referred it to the

Rules Committee. Under House rules, any three members of the Rules Committee could request a meeting, and if the chairman failed to comply within seven calendar days, including at least three legislative days, any eight members of the committee could demand a hearing at a time of their choosing. Just as had been the case in the winter, the civil rights supporters on the committee were prepared to force Howard Smith's hand.

On Wednesday, June 24, after waiting the required three days, Dick Bolling of Missouri filed a formal request that Judge Smith hold a hearing on Resolution 789. Smith was no more supportive of the bill than he had ever been, but he also well knew that the rump caucus of his committee had the power to beat him, so he reluctantly scheduled a hearing for the last possible day under the rules—Tuesday, June 30.

On that day, Celler was the committee's lead witness. "These changes are not lethal," he assured his colleagues of the Senate's amendments. It was Bill McCulloch's turn next, and when a contemptuous Howard Smith drawled, "I understand you were one of the architects of the Senate bill," McCulloch replied drily, "I had some consultation with some senators." That same afternoon, the committee, with support from Republican members like the reliable Clarence Brown of Ohio, voted to overrule Judge Smith's wishes to prolong testimony, ending consideration of Resolution 789 that day. The committee then voted to grant the resolution a "closed" rule, allowing a single hour of floor debate in the full House, to be divided evenly between supporters and opponents. And, in a final indignity, Bolling proposed that Ray Madden of Connecticut, a civil rights supporter, and not Judge Smith, be given the privilege of presenting the resolution on the floor. This was too much for Smith's loyal No. 2, Bill Colmer of Mississippi, who declared, "If Martin Luther King were chairman of this committee and I was opposed to his position, I would do nothing to take the chair away from him and slap him in the face." Judge Smith's frustrated members had at last done something awfully close to just that—and, then, in one last rebuke, three times they defeated his proposals to extend floor debate to four, three, or even two hours, from the agreed-upon one.

* * *

ON THURSDAY, JULY 2—ONE year to the day since Burke Marshall's visit to Piqua to seek Bill McCulloch's support for the bill—the House of Representatives convened, with 402 of its 435 members present. Ray Madden spoke first. "I want it to be understood that the members of the Rules Committee in my judgment were displaying no disregard or lack of confidence in the integrity of our chairman," he insisted. "The majority of our members decided that it was time to call a termination to some of the shenanigans and delays to which the progress of this legislation has been a victim."

Then Judge Smith had his last, bitter fifteen-minute say. "The bell has tolled," he said. "In a few minutes, you will vote this monstrous instrument of oppression upon all of the American people. You have sowed the wind. Now an oppressed people are to reap the whirlwind. King, Martin Luther, not satisfied with what will be the law of the land, has announced his purpose, with the backing of the executive department, to begin a series of demonstrations inevitably to be accompanied by mob violence, strife, bitterness and bloodshed. Already, the second invasion of carpetbaggers of the Southland has begun. Hordes of beatniks, misfits and agitators from the North, with the admitted aid of the Communists, are streaming into the Southland on mischief bent, backed and defended by other hordes of Federal marshals, Federal agents and Federal power."

Basil Lee Whitener of North Carolina spoke next for the South. "Forever and a day, July 2, 1964, will be marked as the day on which greater violence was done to the U.S. Constitution than had ever been witnessed by Americans."

But when Bill McCulloch's turn came, he was typically low-key, taking pains to debunk some of the prevailing myths about H.R. 7152, using a fact sheet he had carefully worked up weeks earlier in response to public attacks on the bill. The bill would not, he said, permit the federal government to tell banks to whom they must lend; or to tell any home owner to whom he must sell or rent; or to interfere with the day-to-day operations of business or unions; or to require an employer or union to hire or admit a quota of people from any given minority group; or "to interfere with or destroy the private property rights of individual businessmen."

"No statutory law will or can completely end the discrimination under attack by this legislation," he concluded. "Such discrimination will finally end only when the mind and heart and conscience of everyone of goodwill decrees it." Still, he said, "In the meantime, twenty million Americans can, for the first time, dream some dreams, and in due course see nearly all of them come true."

At this, John Lindsay asked if McCulloch would yield, and when he did, declared that his fellow Republican had worked "with dignity, with courage, with energy, and with great skill in a very difficult time on a very difficult subject." In a rare tribute, the whole House rose in a standing ovation. Modest to the end, McCulloch simply paraphrased Churchill to say, "Never have so many of such ability worked so hard, and so effectively, for which so few received the credit."

Next came Charles Weltner, a freshman Democrat from Atlanta, who had voted against the bill in February. Now, he announced, he was changing his vote. "Change, swift and certain, is upon us, and we in the South face some difficult decisions," he said. "We can offer resistance and defiance, with their harvest of strife and tumult. We can suffer continued demonstrations, with their wake of violence and disorder. Or we can acknowledge this measure as the law of the land. We can accept the verdict of the nation. I will add my voice to those who seek reasoned and conciliatory adjustment to a new reality, and, finally, I would urge that we at home now move on to the unfinished task of building a new South. We must not remain forever bound to another lost cause."

Then Manny Celler swiftly summarized the changes the Senate had made to the House bill. "Further delay, I will say, would be fatal," he said. "Cervantes once said, 'By the street of bye and bye, you reach the house of never.'" Celler concluded with words from the Old Testament. "I hope that we will have an overwhelming vote for this bill: that that vote will reverberate throughout the length and breadth of the land so that it can be said that Congress hearkens unto the voice of Leviticus, 'proclaiming liberty throughout the land, to all the inhabitants thereof.'" Now it was Celler's turn for an ovation, and the first man on his feet to lead the applause was Howard Smith.

At 2:05 p.m., the House majority leader, Carl Albert, called the White House to tell the president where things stood. Johnson was in a Cabinet meeting, so his senior secretary, Juanita Roberts, took the message: "We are voting on the bill. Will be over in about ten minutes—fifteen at the most—we are past the danger point." Moments later, a White House congressional liaison, Claude Desautels, delivered another message to Roberts, and she took a small slip of paper in to the president in the Cabinet Room. He interrupted the meeting to read Roberts's note. "House passed the bill: 289 yeas, 126 nays . . ."

As soon as the Cabinet meeting was over, Johnson called Albert, whose Oklahoma constituents had little fondness for the bill, to congratulate him, adding, "I guess you know that probably you'll get more congratulations up here that you'll get at home." By now, Johnson had already decided to sign the bill in the ceremonial East Room of the White House, and he had left it to Larry O'Brien to organize the details. "Just as long as . . . you're in charge of it," he said, "I'll feel relieved, and I don't want to know."

But being Lyndon Johnson, he could not help sweating the details. Moments after getting off the phone with O'Brien, he was back on it with George Reedy and Bill Moyers to discuss the timing of his speech. The White House had asked for national airtime at 7:00 p.m., but the networks said they would prefer 6:45, when they claimed they would have a larger audience. Johnson was skeptical, as perhaps only a man who had grown rich through the ownership of a local television station could be. "I don't believe that," the president said. "That's cheaper time. Six forty-five is four-forty-five in a good part of our country, George." He added, speaking of the network executives, "They're selfish bastards" who, like his own station manager in Austin, wanted public affairs programming carried in the afternoon because they "don't want to give up that night primary time."

Johnson had also given a great deal of consideration to how he wanted to sign the bill, and what he wanted to say when he did so. On June 16, he had asked the advice of his civil rights adviser, Lee White. "Mr. President, it's so monumental," White replied. "It's equivalent to a . . . signing an emancipation proclamation and it ought to just have all the possible attention that you could focus on it. It's *so* significant."

Eric Goldman, Richard Goodwin, Douglass Cater, and Bill Moyers all had a hand in working up a speech. The early, unused draft that contained Goldman's paean to summer also contained this alliterative passage: "We are a people who believe in law and order. We believe in ballots, not bullets; arguments, not arms; laws and courts, not license and chaos," along with some strong words about the violence in Mississippi. A penciled note on this draft on June 24 from presidential aide Dick Nelson passed on Johnson's views: "Get Doug Cater and Dick Goodwin to start working on this, hard. I like it but I don't want to go this strong on Mississippi at this time."

In the end, there were at least six drafts. As late as July 2 itself, Horace Busby sent a memo to Moyers objecting to having the president say he was signing the bill because "the moral law of a just God forbids" segregation. "The thought must be in the speech," Busby wrote, "but I seriously question this wording. Theologically, it is difficult to support with specifics—at least to the satisfaction of many southern clergymen and laymen (including some Catholics as well as Protestants). Likewise, there is a question of propriety about the presidential usage of a 'just God.' This may seem a small exception to some. But this is the head of a needle on which many, especially in the South, would dance at length, challenging the president 'to cite chapter and verse.' My suggestion would be 'Morality forbids it," or 'The weight of the moral beliefs of our society forbids it.'"

At 4:30 that afternoon, Johnson ducked into the White House barbershop for a prespeech haircut, and then he went to the residence for a celebration of his daughter Luci's seventeenth birthday. By six o'clock, scores of invited guests were gathering in the East Room for the signing ceremony—one year to the day after the organizers of the March on Washington had held their first planning meeting at the Roosevelt Hotel in New York.

* * *

DESPITE LARRY O'BRIEN'S BEST efforts, the signing had been arranged so hastily—final invitations did not go out to most people until after the House vote—that there were bound to be hurt feelings and overlooked names. Marvin Caplan of the Leadership Conference on Civil Rights, who was among the overlooked, would recall a moment marred by "pettiness, self-interest and haste," while Joe Rauh described the scene as "an exciting mishmash," albeit one "with all kinds of people around who had nothing to do with the bill."

In the grand white and gold East Room where Abigail Adams had once hung her washing in the still unfinished White House and where Union troops once bivouacked during the Civil War, the bill's supporters gathered as the president began his speech at 6:45. In the front row sat the bipartisan team that had passed the bill: Humphrey and Dirksen, Celler and McCulloch (the latter two wearing pink carnations in their lapels). A grim-faced Bob Kennedy stared straight ahead, his face blank. Lady Bird Johnson sat hard by J. Edgar Hoover. Scattered in rows near the front were Martin Luther King, Roy Wilkins, Whitney Young, and other civil rights leaders.

At a small table in the center of the room, peering into the television camera from behind his black-rimmed glasses, sat Lyndon Johnson. Reading from a script of half-inch type with grease-penciled underlining on a spool of perforated yellow paper threading its way through the teleprompter, he solemnly invoked the country's founding ideal.

"We believe that all men are created equal," he began in his distinctive Texas twang. "Yet many are denied equal treatment. We believe that all men have certain unalienable rights. Yet many Americans do not enjoy those rights. We believe that all men are entitled to the blessings of liberty. Yet millions are being deprived of those blessings—not because of their own failures, but because of the color of their skin. The reasons are deeply imbedded in history and tradition and the nature of man. We can understand—without rancor or hatred—how this all happened.

"But it cannot continue," he went on. "Our Constitution, the foundation of our Republic, forbids it. The principles of our freedom forbid it. Morality forbids it. And the law I will sign tonight forbids it."

In Vicksburg, Mississippi, student volunteers of Freedom Summer crammed into their headquarters. "He's signing!" someone shouted, and a chorus of "We Shall Overcome," and then "We Have Overcome," rang out.

Johnson continued. Strikingly—but understandably, given the deep divisions at play in the country—the president described the guts of the bill in the most minimalist terms.

"It does not restrict the freedom of any American, so long as he respects the rights of others," he said. "It does not give special treatment to any citizen. It does say the only limit to a man's hope for happiness, and for the future of his children, shall be his own ability. It does say that there are those who are equal before God shall now also be equal in the polling booths, in the classrooms, in the factories, and in hotels, restaurants, movie theaters, and other places that provide service to the public."

The president closed on a note of hope, urging "every public official, every religious leader, every business and professional man, every workingman, every housewife—I urge every American—to join in this effort to bring justice and hope to all our people—and to bring peace to our land."

"My fellow citizens," he concluded, "we have come now to a time of testing. We must not fail. Let us close the springs of racial poison. Let us pray for wise and understanding hearts. Let us lay aside irrelevant differences and make our Nation whole. Let us hasten that day when our unmeasured strength and our unbounded spirit will be free to do the great works ordained for this Nation by the just and wise God who is the Father of us all."

With Larry O'Brien at his side, Johnson began dipping the first of more than seventy pens in an inkwell, using each one to inscribe a small portion of his vigorous, jagged signature—which always looked something like the up-and-down line of a busy EKG monitor. He passed the first pen to Dirksen, the second to Humphrey. After Charlie Halleck, Bill McCulloch, and Manny Celler had their moments, a beaming Martin Luther King eased his way behind the president and happily accepted his pen. "Thank you, sir. Thank you!" he exclaimed, then lingered unhurriedly, enjoying his moment in camera range. (Back in Atlanta, King's wife, Coretta, was not smiling. She had taken her two sons, Martin and Dexter, to have their tonsils removed, and King had promised to call home after the signing. In his excitement, he had forgotten, and Coretta was deeply pained by the lapse.)

"Hello, Roy, so glad to see you all," Johnson said as Roy Wilkins approached. "Has anybody talked to you all about I want to talk to you before you leave? Will you see that the others, I want to talk to 'em when this is over with . . . Cabinet Room."

"Hello, Edgar, good to see you, my man," the president greeted his FBI director, thrusting a fistful of pens his way. "You deserve several of those . . ."

As the others surged forward to collect their pens, Robert Kennedy hung back. Roy Reuther of the United Auto Workers grabbed him by the arm and led him across the floor to the president. Barely looking up, Johnson passed pens over his shoulder. "Mr. Attorney General," he said, "give this one to Katzenbach, and give this one to Burke Marshall, and give this one to John Doar." (In fact, Kennedy had Doar's pen framed and sent it to him with this inscription: "Pen used to sign President Kennedy's civil rights bill.") For the Reverend Walter Fauntroy, the SCLC's District of Columbia representative, the joy of the occasion was "dampened by the sadness that we saw in Bobby's eyes."

In the Cabinet Room, after the signing was complete, the president met with King, Wilkins, Young, Farmer, and the other leaders of civil rights organizations. He told them that there must now be an acknowledgment that the rights they had been seeking were guaranteed by law, making demonstrations unnecessary or even self-defeating. King and the others knew, however, that Johnson had another kind of self-defeat in mind: his own, at the polls that November, just four months away. Indeed, for all the excitement of the bill's passage, Johnson could not shake a sense of foreboding.

In the wake of the Senate passage in June, Lady Bird Johnson had written in her diary: "Now, with victory in sight, everybody's mind turns to the problems that victory will bring in its wake. No solutions yet, not for a decade, or several decades—but tension and trouble and probably bloodshed lie ahead. But it is a path that has to be taken—a step forward long overdue."

The president's immediate impulse was to get home to Texas. Bags had already been packed. Lady Bird was ready with a bite of dinner, and then the Big Bird of Marine One landed on the South Lawn. The chopper took them to Andrews Air Force Base, where a small Lockheed Jetstar would take them directly to the LBJ ranch. (Gerri Whittington and others would join them there.) On the flight down, the president read the papers and then took a nap.

"When he signed the act he was euphoric," Bill Moyers would recall, "but late that very night I found him in a melancholy mood as he lay in bed reading the bulldog edition of the *Washington Post* with headlines celebrating the day. I asked him what was troubling him." Johnson replied to Moyers, "I think we just delivered the South to the Republican Party for a long time to come."

Still, when the Johnsons arrived at the ranch in the wee hours and got a quick briefing on rainfall levels and the state of their cattle and crops, Lady Bird could not contain her satisfaction. "This was one of those rare nights, starry in every way, when one does not think about tomorrow," she wrote, "a wonderful state of euphoria rarely attained."

* * *

THE PRESIDENT SLEPT LATE on the morning of July 3, no doubt done in by his labors. His first call on waking was to his attorney general. Johnson summarized the favorable drift of the White House mail about the bill in Texas-sized, mathematically impossible percentages. "It runs about 70–50," he said, adding: "I don't tell that figure to anybody, but I don't give it out, but just for you." Bob Kennedy informed the president that the unrepentant Governor Paul Johnson of Mississippi had called for noncompliance with the law until it could be tested in court. He suggested that the president might call Governor Johnson—who had been, after all, a strong Kennedy man in 1960—to suggest that he might amend his view to explain that, if and when the courts upheld the law, Mississippi would obey it.

"It's been relatively calm," Kennedy said, "and for the first time in Jackson, Mississippi, they've got some of the Negroes and whites sitting down and talking over some of the problems, some of the people that are down there now. So, you know, there's some promising things."

Later, Johnson talked with Governor John Connally of Texas about how to handle his own obligations under the new law. "Talk about observance," the president told his old friend. "Everybody wants to *observe* the law . . . When you go to *enforcing* something, a man gets his back up." Johnson told Connally that he was pleased with southern reaction to his signing speech. "I didn't cuddle up to them," he said. "But I wasn't . . . I wasn't the least bit critical or vicious or demanding, and I just appealed for us reasoning together."

As if to prove the point, the president soon reached out to Governor Johnson in Mississippi, carefully explaining the advice he had given the civil rights groups the night before. "Let's take this thing slow and easy," he said. "And kind of adjust to it instead of making mass invasions and mass violations and things of that kind." For his part, Governor Johnson replied that he had told Mississippi reporters that "the success of this thing depended upon how fast, you know, some of these big niggers like to move, you know? And they could make it mighty, mighty rough."

"Well, you keep a stiff upper lip, and if you need me, call me," the president advised.

Then Johnson took a call from one of his oldest Texas political friends, C. C. "Charley" McDonald, of Witchita Falls. "You became president yesterday," McDonald said. "That was your most wonderful hour. It only comes to a president about every forty years."

At some point during the long weekend, a restless Lyndon Johnson knocked on the door of Gerri Whittington's guest room in the wee hours of the morning. Without waiting to learn why he was there—and, she later thought, he may simply have wanted to talk—she told him she wasn't feeling well, that it was her "time of the month," and he immediately left. But the experience discomfited her, and when she and the president's party returned to Washington after the holiday, she made a point of avoiding Johnson for a few days. She never again returned to the ranch, and about a year later, she transferred to the State Department, where she went to work for the chief of protocol, Lloyd Hand.

On Independence Day, Johnson again checked in with Bob Kennedy, who told him that the Jackson, Mississippi, Chamber of Commerce had voted to abide by the law, and that the cities of Savannah, Atlanta, Birmingham, and Montgomery had all swiftly followed suit. Johnson

confided that the traveling White House press corps had spent the previous day interviewing the motel proprietors of Johnson City, Texas.

"Oh, really?" Kennedy said.

"They got the right answers, too," the president replied.

As evening came, Johnson touched base with George Reedy. The
president was testy and full of complaints. He informed his press secretary that he did not intend to return to Washington the next day—
Sunday—and would probably not return until Monday, July 6. But he did
not want Reedy to alert the traveling press to these plans.

Then he seized on a quote from Reedy in that day's news reports—that
the president had "been in touch with Martin Luther King continuously."

"No, that's ... that's a mis ... at the time ... mistake," Reedy har-
rumphed.

"I haven't been in touch with him at all," Johnson spat back, "and
don't want to be. You know his record."

"Yeah, I know," a sheepish Reedy replied.

"It's the last thing," Johnson continued, seeming to quote from some
invisible report: "'The President has been in *continual* touch with
Dr. King.'"

"I said, 'From time to time he has seen Martin Luther King,' is what I
said," Reedy explained.

"Well, why do you say that?" Johnson demanded.

"Well," Reedy said, "you saw him at the ceremony."

"Well," Johnson snapped, "I say, *why* do you say it?"

"Because I was asked, and because they'd seen you there," Reedy said.

"I'm sorry he was there," Johnson said. "It was very unfortunate he
was there, and don't you get hung in on it. And then you get it in a tran-
script that he's been in continual touch with him. That's the last thing I
want. They're making an issue on you, and you'll hear from King before
this campaign's over with. And then you go to making an explanation, it
won't do any good. So I'd just say ... that you don't know a damn thing
about who I've seen. And you don't. If they ask you if I've seen him you
tell them you don't know. Don't get in there that I'm in continuous touch
with him."

On the 188th anniversary of the first July 4th, those were the last recorded thoughts of the thirty-sixth president of the United States. And at the moment of Lyndon Johnson's greatest triumph, those angry words were a prescient sign of an unfinished story: the half century of advancement and retreat, of progress and pain, of hope and despair that the brave men and women of both races and both parties who made H.R. 7152—and their sons and daughters—would yet live to see.

Epilogue

For all the storm over the passage of what had now officially become the Civil Rights Act of 1964, acceptance of the new law was swift and widespread. There were stubborn pockets of defiance, though, especially in Mississippi and Alabama. The Robert E. Lee Hotel in Jackson, Mississippi, closed its doors "in despair" on July 6, 1964, rather than accept integration. (It would reopen some months later as a private club before being sold to the state for use as an office building.) Far more typical was the experience of Captain Colin Powell, who in the summer of 1964 went back to the same Georgia drive-in that had refused to serve him just months before and ordered a hamburger without incident.

"All across the South there was this sense of openness, the sense of 'We can do it now,'" John Lewis would recall. In December 1964, the Supreme Court upheld Title II, the bill's public accommodations section, assuring that its eventual enforcement would be in no doubt in every corner of the land. Scores, if not hundreds, of legal challenges to other sections of the bill would follow, but the essence of its constitutional validity had been swiftly upheld.

Meantime, the balance that Dirksen had struck in Title VII in favor of court rulings—not enforcement action by the Equal Employment Opportunity Commission—gave rise to a robust wave of private class action employment discrimination lawsuits that effectively altered the composition of the workforce in ways that an administrative agency alone might not have managed (even if the agency itself did not open its doors for business until a full year after the bill was signed). The federal funds cutoff provision of Title VI revolutionized the enforcement of the *Brown* decision, as school districts around the country scrambled to end discriminatory programs or risk losing education aid from Washington.

The bill inspired and emboldened not only the civil rights cause of black Americans, but also of Hispanic and Native Americans, of the women's movement, and, later, of the gay rights movement as well. Howard Smith's inclusion of the word "sex" in Title VII transformed the legal status of women, even if it did not end stubborn and enduring disparities in pay and respect. On the political fringe, some aspects of the bill continued to spark fierce debate half a century later. In his campaign for the U.S. Senate from Kentucky in 2010, the libertarian Republican Rand Paul seemed to suggest that the Civil Rights Act's ban on discrimination in public accommodations was an unconstitutional overreach of government authority, despite the Supreme Court's definitive ruling. But most Americans long ago subscribed to Richard Russell's verdict when the bill was passed: "These statutes are now on the books and it becomes our duty as good citizens to live with them."

The Civil Rights Act by no means finished the job of assuring equality before the law. Less than a year after its passage, bloody protests in Selma, Alabama, demonstrated the enduring extent of blacks' lack of access to the ballot box, and Lyndon Johnson and most of the same cast of congressmen and senators, chief among them Bill McCulloch and Everett Dirksen, responded with the Voting Rights Act of 1965, which barred states and localities from imposing any "voting qualification or prerequisite to voting," ended poll taxes and literacy tests in every jurisdiction in the country, and required most southern states and some northern counties to receive advance approval from the Justice Department before making any changes in voting laws.

"What happened in Selma is part of a far larger movement which reaches into every section and state of America," Johnson said in proposing the voting rights bill, adopting the rallying cry of the movement itself. "It is the effort of American Negroes to secure for themselves the full blessings of American life. Their cause must be our cause, too. Because it is not just Negroes, but really, it is all of us, who must overcome the crippling legacy of bigotry and injustice. And we *shall* overcome."

Together, the 1964 and 1965 acts were the most important laws of the twentieth century and a high-water mark of shared civic purpose, national unity, and hope that the nation might yet live up to its founding creed. In the ensuing decades, those laws would transform the South, gradually burning away the toxic air that had suffused and stifled the region for generations. By 1987, Mississippi would lead the nation in the total number of black elected officials, and Alabama would have the highest percentage of black officeholders of any state. Cities throughout the South elected black mayors and state legislators, even as blacks struggled to win statewide office in the region and as southern black representation in Congress continued to lag. Not until 2013, after Governor Nikki Haley of South Carolina appointed Representative Tim Scott to fill a vacancy, was there an African American senator from the South since Reconstruction, and even then Scott was but the seventh black senator out of the more than 1,900 in American history. (A few weeks later, Mo Cowan of Massachusetts, also appointed to fill a vacancy, became the eighth, and in October Cory Booker of New Jersey won a special election to become the ninth.)

By the late 1990s, with northern industrial cities crumbling in the wake of lost jobs in a rapidly changing economy, the South saw strong net gains of black migrants from all the other regions of the country, reversing a decades-long trend that had begun with the "Great Migration" from the South in the early twentieth century. Without the scourge of Jim Crow, long-standing cultural and kinship ties once again drew blacks to progressive southern cities like Atlanta and Charlotte.

"Sometime I hear people saying nothing has changed, but for someone to grow up the way I grew up in the cotton fields of Alabama to now be serving in the United States Congress makes me want to tell them, 'Come and walk in my shoes,'" John Lewis, the former leader of SNCC who was elected to the House of Representatives from Georgia in 1986, told thousands of people gathered at the Lincoln Memorial to celebrate the fiftieth anniversary of the March on Washington in 2013. "Fifty years later, we can ride anywhere we want to ride, we can stay where we want to stay. Those signs that said 'white' and 'colored' are gone. And you won't see them any more—except in a museum, in a book, on a video."

But as Lewis was also quick to note, progress has not been unalloyed. In 1963, John Kennedy had soberly explained that "a Negro baby born in America" had just half as much chance of completing high school as a white baby born in the same place on the same day, one-third as much chance of completing college, one-third as much chance of embarking on a professional career, twice as much chance of becoming unemployed, about one-seventh as much chance of earning $10,000 a year, a life expectancy seven years shorter, and the prospect of earning only half as much.

What are such a baby's prospects today?

As of 2010, according to the Department of Education, black high school freshmen graduate at about 80 percent the rate of their white counterparts, while about 50 percent of black students at four-year colleges complete their bachelor's degrees within six years, compared to just over 60 percent of whites. Black life expectancy is now roughly four years shorter than that of whites.

Equality of opportunity has improved markedly, but true equality lags. Black unemployment rates are still roughly twice those for whites, while the average per capita income for blacks is roughly half.

Moreover, a darker, more divisive, more violent era followed the passage of the 1964 and 1965 civil rights laws. Just five days after President Johnson signed the Voting Rights Act, the Watts neighborhood of Los Angeles erupted in a bloody six-day riot, a portent of widespread unrest to come as the decade unfolded.

Never again would the national consensus on civil rights be so strong, as controversies over affirmative action, busing, and black power splintered the movement and the broader society. Even as a new wave of state voter identification laws and other measures clearly aimed at suppressing minority voting turnout took effect around the country in the twenty-first century, the Supreme Court in 2013 rejected as outdated the formula in the Voting Rights Act that mandated advance approval for changes in voting laws in states with a history of discrimination. Partisan divisions in Congress were so sharp that no appropriate revision of the law seemed likely to pass. It was left to a new wave of lawsuits and intervention by the Justice Department in Washington to address the problem.

Nor would mainstream religious groups ever again join in a crusade like the ones that made the 1964 and 1965 laws possible, though the religious right would later take a page from their playbook on the questions of abortion rights, gay rights, and other social issues that have divided the nation from the 1970s and 1980s on.

* * *

FOR MOST OF THOSE individuals who made the 1964 Civil Rights Act possible, the high hopes of that summer evening in the East Room would not last long. Exactly a month after the bill signing ceremony, on August 2, 1964, the destroyer USS *Maddox* engaged three North Vietnamese torpedo boats in the Gulf of Tonkin, and five days later Lyndon Johnson won passage of an open-ended congressional resolution allowing the United States to come to the aid of any Southeast Asian nation threatened by Communist aggression. The path was laid for the "bitch of a war" that would destroy his presidency.

Less than four years later, Martin Luther King and Robert Kennedy would both be dead by assassins' bullets, both long since estranged from Johnson. Though Justice Department guidelines called for a periodic review of the department's authority for the wiretap on King, Kennedy apparently never conducted one, and the taps continued for years. In October 1964, King was awarded the Nobel Peace Prize for his civil rights work. He accepted the honor in Oslo two months later "on behalf of a civil rights movement which is moving with determination and a majestic scorn for risk and danger to establish a reign of freedom and a rule of justice." J. Edgar Hoover's reaction was to brand King "the most notorious liar in the country."

Bob Kennedy learned of King's death on April 4, 1968, just as he was about to address a large street rally in the heart of a black neighborhood in Indianapolis. Despite warnings from the police that they could not protect him if violence broke out, Kennedy spoke anyway, his journey to the side of the black cause now complete. "What we need in the United States," he said, "is not division; what we need in the United States is not hatred; what we need in the United States is not violence and lawlessness, but love and wisdom and compassion toward one another, and a feeling of justice towards those who still suffer within our country, whether they be white or whether they be black." America's task, he continued, was to "dedicate ourselves to what the Greeks wrote so many years ago: to tame the savageness of man and make gentle the life of this world." The crowd broke up quietly into the night, but barely two months later, Kennedy himself was murdered hours after winning the California presidential primary.

In January 1965, Charles Halleck, his reputation with his Republican caucus never quite restored, was deposed as House minority leader by Gerald Ford of Michigan, in the first loss of his electoral career. He retired four years later and died in 1986.

Hubert Humphrey's son Robert recovered completely from his cancerous tumor. Humphrey himself was not so lucky. He won the vice presidency alongside Lyndon Johnson in 1964 and was to have been the Johnson administration's point man in coordinating civil rights programs. But White House infighting and Lyndon Johnson's ego made that impossible. Four years later, Humphrey's failure to make a clear break with Johnson over the increasingly divisive Vietnam War made the man who was once seen as so far ahead of his time on issues like civil rights seem a tired establishment has-been by the time of his own 1968 presidential campaign. "Dump the Hump!" angry crowds cried all over the country. (When Humphrey's press secretary, Norman Sherman, noticed his candidate smiling after a particularly brutal encounter with a group of protesters, Humphrey, ever the happy warrior, exulted, "I got one in the balls with my briefcase!") After his defeat at the polls, he returned to the Senate, ran unsuccessfully for the Democratic presidential nomination in 1972, flirted with the same idea in 1976, and died of bladder cancer in 1978.

Everett Dirksen, whose role in passing the Civil Rights Act helped him to supplant Richard Russell as the single most influential senator of the 1960s, became a kind of folk hero. His spoken-word album, *Gallant Men*, in which he recited a collection of patriotic poems, songs, and stories, reached No. 16 on the *Billboard* charts and won a Grammy Award as Best Documentary Recording in 1968. On a 1967 episode of the television game show *What's My Line?*, a blindfolded Tony Randall tried to guess the identity of Judy Garland, who had explained her bona fides with a tinkling bell and a disguised voice. "You sing, you dance, you're funny, you've been around a long time," Randall said, before guessing, "Senator Dirksen?" But the years of heavy smoking and drinking took their toll on Dirksen's health, and he died of complications from lung cancer in 1969, just nine months after Richard Nixon's election to the presidency ended Dirksen's long run as the most important Republican in Washington. His fellow Republican senator Margaret Chase Smith of Maine, who had long battled Dirksen's nominee for national flower with her own candidate— the rose—placed a single long-stemmed marigold on his desk in the Senate chamber. Dirksen is remembered today for the marble Senate office building that was renamed for him in 1972 (as is Richard Russell, whose name is on the building next door). But schoolchildren do not think of Dirksen in the same breath with Lincoln, as Lyndon Johnson had insisted they would.

Russell's own friendship with Johnson survived their disputes on civil rights but foundered irrevocably in a disagreement over a nominee for a federal judgeship. Russell died of complications from emphysema in 1971.

Despite his decades-long support for civil rights and liberal causes, the aging Emanuel Celler was defeated in a primary for reelection in 1972 by Elizabeth Holtzman, in part because of his failure to keep pace with the times, as exemplified by his implacable opposition to the Equal Rights Amendment for women. He died in 1981 and is anything but a household name, even in Brooklyn.

Clarence Mitchell remained a dogged crusader for civil rights all through the 1960s and 1970s, enduring the frustrations of the Nixon years and continuing well into the administration of Jimmy Carter, who awarded him the Presidential Medal of Freedom. But his departure from the NAACP in 1978 was unhappy. Passed over to succeed the retiring Roy Wilkins as executive director, he went into private law practice and wrote a weekly column for the Baltimore *Sun*. When he died in 1984 in the midst of a presidential campaign, all the Democratic candidates in the race attended his funeral, where the eulogists included Lyndon Johnson's daughter Lynda Robb.

Gerri Whittington continued her career as a government secretary, even working briefly in the Nixon White House for Robert J. Brown, a special presidential assistant who was black and wanted an experienced hand to show him the ropes. But in 1970, at the age of thirty-eight, she suffered a massive and debilitating stroke from which she never fully recovered. She died in 1993, on the same day as the retired Supreme Court justice Thurgood Marshall.

Representative Charles Weltner, the young Georgian who had changed his initial vote against H.R. 7152 to support its final passage in the House, won reelection in 1964 but declined to seek a third term in 1966, because the Georgia Democratic Party would have required him to sign a loyalty oath pledging to support the segregationist gubernatorial candidate Lester Maddox. "I love the Congress," Weltner said, "but I will give up my office before I give up my principles." He went on to a distinguished legal career, serving for more than a decade on the Georgia Supreme Court, winding up as its chief justice, the very job Richard Russell's father had held sixty years before. In 1991, he became the second recipient of the John F. Kennedy Library's "Profile in Courage" award, and he died the following year.

And Lyndon Johnson, that sprawling riddle wrapped in an enigma, a president of unmatched achievements shrouded in pathologically outsize flaws? In the popular myth, he has come to be seen as almost single-handedly responsible for the passage of the Civil Rights Act. The truth is more complex but no less admirable, especially given the discipline it must have required for such an impulsive, impassioned man to so strategically limit his own role in Congress's consideration of the bill. Johnson did indeed help round up crucial votes for cloture, and he was always "the shotgun behind the door," as John Stewart put it. But Johnson's biggest contribution was that he never wavered in his public or private support for the strongest possible bill, while letting Humphrey, Mansfield, and Dirksen determine just what that would be.

Johnson died on January 22, 1973, almost exactly four years after leaving office. His last public appearance was at a civil rights symposium at his presidential library in Austin in December 1972. He was unwell and suffered a visibly agonizing attack of angina during his speech, slipping a nitroglycerin tablet from his pocket into his mouth to ease the pain. He told the crowd that the cache of documents just released by the library, including those on civil rights, "holds most of myself and holds for me the most intimate meaning." He said he was ashamed that he had not been able to do more for the cause in five years in office and insisted that civil rights should remain the entire country's concern.

"To be black," he said, "is to be proud, is to be worthy, is to be honorable. But to be black in a white society is not to stand on level and equal ground." He added: "Whites stand on history's mountain, and blacks stand in history's hollow." The challenge, he concluded, was to "get down to the business of trying to stand black and white on level ground."

* * *

IT IS A POIGNANT paradox that the man whom no less a judge than Nick Katzenbach considered the single most important influence in passing the bill—Bill McCulloch—is the least remembered of all. That is as much a testament to McCulloch's unwavering modesty as it is to history's fickle eye. After the passage of the Civil Rights Act, McCulloch kept up his quiet fight for justice, again playing a crucial role in the Voting Rights Act of 1965 and the Fair Housing Act of 1968, while also maintaining his staunch fiscal conservatism. It was no surprise that Johnson named him (together with John Lindsay, by then mayor of New York City) to the National Advisory Commission on Civil Disorders, chaired by Governor Otto Kerner of Illinois and charged with investigating the riots that swept American cities in 1967. The most famous line from the commission's report belied the promise of H.R. 7152: "Our nation is moving toward two societies, one black, one white—separate and unequal."

In a 1967 essay, McCulloch envisioned a central role for his beloved party in the civil rights struggles yet to come. "The old battles have been won," he said. "The Republican Party, however, is not content with the past. For all the dreams have not come true. There is work to be done. History shows that the Republican Party will be the party which, in large part, will see that these dreams come true." He would not live long enough to see how far off the mark he was.

In May 1970, McCulloch slipped and fell on a newly waxed floor at his home in Washington. He suffered a concussion—undiagnosed at first—and was in and out of hospitals for a year. Though he lived on until 1980, he was never again in robust health. He announced that he would not run for reelection in 1972, prompting an extraordinary three-page hand-written letter from one close observer of the battles of 1963, who remembered with aching clarity all that he had done. "Please forgive the emotional tone of this letter," Jacqueline Kennedy Onassis wrote from aboard the yacht *Christina* on June 24, 1971, "but I want you to know how much your example means to me."

"I know that you, more than anyone, were responsible for the civil rights legislation of the 1960s," the former First Lady wrote. "You made a personal commitment to President Kennedy in October 1963, against all the interests of your district. When he was gone, your personal integrity and character were such that you held to that commitment despite enormous pressure and political temptations not to do so. There were so many opportunities to sabotage the bill, without appearing to do so, but you never took them. On the contrary, you brought everyone else along with you.

"And as for my dear Jack, it is a precious thought to me that in the last month of his life, when he had so many problems that seemed insoluble, he had the shining gift of your nobility, to give him the hope and faith he needed to carry on. May I thank you with all my heart, and may God bless you."

* * *

IN THE SHORT TERM, neither side of the bipartisan coalition that had made the Civil Rights Act possible reaped much political benefit from the bill. Barry Goldwater, the Republican nominee in the 1964 election, was, after all, one of the six Senate Republicans who had voted against it, and for better or worse his candidacy set the Party of Lincoln on a course that turned it into the party of white backlash, as he carried Louisiana, Mississippi, Alabama, Georgia, and South Carolina. Lyndon Johnson won election in his own right in a national landslide, but his gloomy presentiment that he had delivered the South to the Republicans for a generation proved correct. Even a brave, 1,628-mile whistle-stop tour of southern states by Lady Bird Johnson could not make up for the electoral damage the civil rights bill had done. In the 1968 election, Richard Nixon and George Wallace between them won all the states of the Old Confederacy, except Johnson's own state of Texas, and four years later, Nixon's "Southern strategy" made it a clean sweep. Only Nixon's resignation and the advent of a southerner, Jimmy Carter, put the South back in play for the Democrats in 1976, before Ronald Reagan recaptured it in 1980. More than a decade would pass until Bill Clinton, yet another southerner, again made the South competitive.

Over the decades, Republican dominance of the South continued and grew, especially in Congress, where the region wielded disproportionate power under its new party label just as the southern Democrats had in the past, fueled by white resentment and, later, by the rise of the Tea Party movement. At the same time, the Republican Party as exemplified by the South became increasingly isolated and marginalized from the rest of the country in ways that hurt its national standing, particularly with the new waves of Hispanic voters that were coming to the fore. By 2008, the legal changes begun by the Civil Rights Act, and the demographic changes wrought by shifting populations, made it not only possible for a black Democratic candidate to win presidential primaries throughout the South, but almost certain that he would—and that he could go on to carry such once unimaginable states as Virginia and North Carolina in the general election. That candidate was a freshman senator from Illinois, who, as it happened, held Everett Dirksen's old seat. His name was Barack Obama.

In his tense meeting with black intellectuals in 1963, Robert Kennedy had reflected on the prejudice that his immigrant Irish ancestors had faced, only to have a son of the old sod in the White House just over a century later. There was every reason to believe, Kennedy continued, that there could be a "Negro president" in forty years.

He was wrong, of course. But only by five years.

Notes

The following abbreviations are used in the notes:

CAHP   Papers of Charles A. Halleck, Lilly Library, Indiana University, Bloomington, Indiana

CR   *Congressional Record*

CQ   *Congressional Quarterly*

EMDP   Papers of Everett McKinley Dirksen, Dirksen Congressional Center, Pekin, Illinois

HHHP   Papers of Hubert H. Humphrey, Minnesota State Historical Society, St. Paul, Minnesota

JFKL   John F. Kennedy Library, Boston, Massachusetts

LBJL   Lyndon B. Johnson Library, Austin, Texas

LCCR   Leadership Conference on Civil Rights

LOC   Library of Congress

OH   Oral History

PPP   *Public Papers of the Presidents*

TPR   *The Presidential Recordings*, University of Virginia Miller Center, published by W. W. Norton

WMMP   William Moore McCulloch Papers, Ohio State University Archives, Columbus, Ohio

Prologue

1   "Your brother," Riedel began: Roger Mudd, *The Place to Be* (New York: Public-Affairs, 2008), pp. 126–29; Richard Langham Riedel, *Halls of the Mighty: My 47 Years*

at the Senate (Washington: Robert B. Luce, 1969), p. 183; William Manchester, *The Death of a President* (New York: Penguin Books, 1977), pp. 197–98.

2   A few blocks down: Hubert H. Humphrey, *The Education of a Public Man* (Minneapolis: University of Minnesota Press, 1991), pp. 190–93.

2   The attorney general struggled: Manchester, *Death of a President*, pp. 195–96.

2   In Atlanta, Martin Luther King: David J. Garrow, *Bearing the Cross: Martin Luther King and the Southern Christian Leadership Conference* (New York: HarperCollins Perennial Classics, 2004), p. 307.

3   "The president's dead": Manchester, *Death of a President*, pp. 256–57.

3   "For most of us who gathered there": Humphrey, *Education of a Public Man*, p. 192.

4   "Only someone suffering": *New York Times,* Nov. 22, 1963.

4   As the bulletins came in from Dallas: Mudd, *Place to Be*, p. 127.

4   The crusty House Republican leader: Statement by Charles A. Halleck, Nov. 23, 1963, CAHP.

4   "This is what's going to happen to me": Coretta Scott King, *My Life with Martin Luther King, Jr.* (New York: Puffin Books, 1993), p. 227.

5   "a tragic death": *CR*, 88th Congress, 1st Session, Dec. 5, 1963, p. 23469.

5   Now, King thought: Garrow, *Bearing the Cross*, p. 307.

5   "consistent commitment to and espousal of basic human rights": *New York Times*, Nov. 23, 1963.

5   "He didn't even have the satisfaction": Manchester, *Death of a President*, p. 407.

7   "Well, Mr. President, you may well do that": Jack Valenti, *This Time, This Place: My Life in War, the White House and Hollywood* (New York: Three Rivers Press, 2007), p. 41.

1: A Century's Unfinished Business

12   "The best commemoration lies not": *PPP*, John F. Kennedy, 1962, p. 702.

12   Rockefeller urged the nation to rededicate: http://www.nysm.nysed.gov/staffpubs /docs/20491.pdf.

13   Kennedy's principal personal reaction: Richard Reeves, *President Kennedy: Profile of Power* (New York: Simon and Schuster, 1993), p. 464.

13   The Davises' presence: Lee C. White OH, JFKL.

13   "a freedom more fictional than real": Reeves, *President Kennedy*, p. 464.

14   "The most cynical view holds": Nick Bryant, *The Bystander: John F. Kennedy and the Struggle for Black Equality* (New York: Basic Books, 2006), p. 373.

14   The Supreme Court had outlawed segregation: Frank H. Mackaman, *The Long Hard Furrow: Everett Dirksen's Part in the Civil Rights Act of 1964* (Pekin, Ill.: Dirksen Congressional Center, 2006), p. 3.

15   One black Army captain: Colin Powell, *My American Journey* (New York: Random House, 1995), p. 108.

15   "I am not enthusiastic about the amendment": Robert Mann, *The Walls of Jericho: Lyndon Johnson, Hubert Humphrey, Richard Russell, and the Struggle for Civil Rights* (San Diego: Harcourt Brace, 1997), p. 321.

17   A similarly weak bill was passed by Congress: Mackaman, *Long Hard Furrow*, pp. 3–4.

18 In fact, Richard Russell: Harris Wofford, *Of Kennedys and Kings: Making Sense of the Sixties* (Pittsburgh: University of Pittsburgh Press, 1992), pp. 58–59.

19 "When my administration takes office": Harold Brayman, *The President Speaks Off the Record* (Princeton, N.J.: Dow Jones Books, 1976), p. 637.

19 "Toward the end of '61 and '62": White OH.

20 "Tell these ambassadors": Bryant, *Bystander*, p. 221.

20 Yet another case loomed: Ibid., p. 254.

21 The attorney general's ringing tone: Edwin Guthman, *We Band of Brothers: A Memoir of Robert F. Kennedy* (New York: Harper and Row, 1971), p. 162.

21 "My belief does not matter": Bryant, *Bystander*, p. 258.

21 CORE's press release announcing the rides: Guthman, *We Band of Brothers*, p. 166.

22 Attorney General Kennedy sent a top aide: Reeves, *President Kennedy*, pp. 122–25.

22 Seigenthaler received assurances: Guthman, *We Band of Brothers*, p. 170.

22 "I knew, suddenly, betrayal": "Freedom Riders: A Film by Stanley Nelson," *American Experience* (PBS), 2011.

22 "I grabbed her by the wrist": Ibid.

23 Seigenthaler was beaten unconscious: Guthman, *We Band of Brothers*, p. 171.

23 "Now, Reverend, don't tell me that": Ibid., p. 178; Reeves, *President Kennedy*, p. 131; Bryant, *Bystander*, pp. 270–73. The expression "dead as Kelsey's nuts" refers neither to legumes nor to gonads, but to John Kelsey, a pioneering automobile wheel manufacturer. Kelsey's wheels were attached with nuts and bolts that were reputed to be "dead" tight, and thus highly safe.

23 Neither man would ever talk to Governor Patterson again: Gerald S. and Deborah H. Strober, *Let Us Begin Anew: An Oral History of the Kennedy Administration* (New York: HarperCollins, 1993), p. 272.

23 "That was the attitude the Kennedys had": Ibid., p. 280.

24 "What we did was to outline": Robert F. Kennedy, *Robert F. Kennedy in His Own Words: The Unpublished Recollections of the Kennedy Years* (New York: Bantam, 1988), p. 100.

24 "What in the world does he think I should do?": Wofford, *Of Kennedys and Kings*, p. 126.

24 Furious that the new president had not: Bryant, *Bystander*, p. 331.

25 After a long legal battle: Ibid.

25 "But he *likes* Ole Miss": Guthman, *We Band of Brothers*, p. 191.

25 Kennedy ordered his aides: Reeves, *President Kennedy*, p. 356.

26 Even as the president prepared: Ibid., p. 362.

26 "Where's the Army?": Philip Zelikow et al., eds., *The Presidential Recordings: John F. Kennedy*, vol. 2 (New York: W. W. Norton, 2001), p. 280; Bryant, *Bystander*, p. 350.

27 With the crisis over: Edwin Guthman papers, Box 1, JFKL.

27 Days later, the president's pollster: Reeves, *President Kennedy*, p. 364.

28 In January 1963: White House staff files, Lee White papers, Box 22, JFKL.

28 "Let it be clear": *PPP*, John F. Kennedy, 1963, p. 222.

29 he insisted that the time was not ripe: Reeves, *President Kennedy*, p. 468.

29 There, on scraps of paper: Martin Luther King Jr., *Why We Can't Wait* (New York: Signet Classics, 2000), p. 91.

30   He expressed special disappointment: Ibid., p. 97.

30   "Look at those niggers run!": Bryant, *Bystander*, p. 386.

30   The next afternoon: Oval Office Meetings, Tape #85, JFKL.

32   "This has a lot of Oxford in it": Jonathan Rosenberg and Zachary Karabell, *Kennedy, Johnson, and the Quest for Justice: The Civil Rights Tapes* (New York: W. W. Norton, 2003), p. 101.

2: A Great Change Is at Hand

34   "awfully damn nervous": White OH, JFKL.

35   "For in the final analysis": *PPP*, John F. Kennedy, 1963, p. 464.

36   "quietly going frantic": White OH.

36   Together, the brothers scratched notes: President's Office Files, Speech Files, Box 45, JFKL.

36   "The monitor is all right": Hugh Sidey, *John F. Kennedy: President* (New York: Atheneum, 1964), p. 334.

36   At the beginning of his Senate career: Theodore C. Sorensen, *Kennedy* (New York: Harper and Row, 1965), p. 460.

36   His civil rights adviser: Wofford, *Of Kennedys and Kings*, p. 177.

37   By May 17, on a flight to Asheville: Kennedy, *Robert F. Kennedy in His Own Words*, p. 172.

37   "They can stand at the lunch counters": Rosenberg and Karabell, *Kennedy, Johnson, and the Quest for Justice*, p. 120.

38   Still, Larry O'Brien: Ibid., p. 121.

38   "The trouble with King is": Ibid., p. 125; Reeves, *President Kennedy*, p. 501.

38   When a former policeman kicked: Reeves, *President Kennedy*, p. 501.

38   "I think it's absolutely essential": Oval Office Meetings, Tape #90, JFKL.

38   (A statement drafted that same day): President's Office Files, Speech Files, Box 45, JFKL.

39   "I haven't read the bill": Oval Office Meetings, Tape #90, JFKL.

39   In fact, Johnson had much more specific advice in mind: Office Files, George Reedy, Edison Dictaphone Recording, Box 1, LBJL.

40   "Doctor, I don't know five people": Bryant, *Bystander*, pp. 23–25.

40   "this marvelous expression": Chris Matthews, *Jack Kennedy: Elusive Hero* (New York: Simon and Schuster, 2011), p. 231.

40   "I don't know any Negroes": Strober and Strober, *Let Us Begin Anew*, p. 278.

40   "We had bigger houses, more servants": Robert Dallek, *An Unfinished Life: John F. Kennedy, 1917–1963* (Boston: Little, Brown, 2003), p. 31.

40   As president, he would tell: Reeves, *President Kennedy*, p. 62; Laurence Leamer, *The Kennedy Men, 1901–1963* (New York: Harper Perennial, 2001), p. 100.

40   They might banter: Bryant, *Bystander*, p. 24; Leamer, *Kennedy Men*, p. 94.

41   The signers were thrown in the brig: Doris Kearns Goodwin, *No Ordinary Time: Franklin and Eleanor Roosevelt; The Home Front in World War II* (New York: Simon and Schuster, 1994), p. 166.

41   After the war: Reeves, *President Kennedy*, p. 62.

41   That didn't spare Thomas: Benjamin C. Bradlee, *Conversations with Kennedy* (New York: W. W. Norton, 1975), p. 223.

42 "Can you believe that such people": Matthews, *Jack Kennedy*, p. 230.

42 Kennedy once countermanded: Thurston Clarke, *JFK's Last 100 Days: The Transformation of a Man and the Emergence of a Great President* (New York: Penguin Press, 2013), p. 134.

42 Another friend, the artist William Walton: Dallek, *Unfinished Life*, p. 72.

43 Kennedy's reply was dismissive: Bryant, *Bystander*, p. 17.

43 As a freshman in the House: Ibid., pp. 27–28.

44 Yet Kennedy also kept his distance: Sorensen, *Kennedy*, p. 471.

44 Kennedy took the issue seriously enough: Bryant, *Bystander*, p. 36.

45 More immediately: Ibid., p. 38.

45 The Senate of that day: William S. White, *The Citadel: The Story of the U.S. Senate* (New York: Harper and Brothers, 1956), p. 72.

45 That July . . . on *Meet the Press*: Bryant, *Bystander*, p. 55.

46 "I'll be singing Dixie": Ibid., p. 60.

46 In his 1956 book: John F. Kennedy, *Profiles in Courage* (New York: Harper and Brothers, 1956), p. 153.

47 Once more, he paid a price: Bryant, *Bystander*, p. 78.

47 "This is one of the saddest days": Robert A. Caro, *Master of the Senate: The Years of Lyndon Johnson* (New York: Alfred A. Knopf, 2002), p. 988.

48 Wilkins's answer was direct: Dallek, *Unfinished Life*, p. 217.

48 After a speech in Jackson: Bryant, *Bystander*, pp. 86–88.

48 he became the first member of Congress: Ibid., p. 94.

49 King didn't even bother to reply: Ibid., pp. 105, 111.

49 "Now, in five minutes, tick off ten things": Wofford, *Of Kennedys and Kings*, p. 58.

50 "It is in the American tradition to stand up": Ibid., p. 62.

50 "This is a moral question": Ibid., p. 63.

51 "Do you know that this election may be razor close": Ibid., p. 19.

51 Kennedy's Republican opponent, Richard Nixon, had considered: Arnold Rampersad, *Jackie Robinson: A Biography* (New York: Alfred A. Knopf, 1997), p. 351. William Safire, then a Nixon aide, would report that Robinson left a meeting with the candidate with "tears of frustration in his eyes."

51 a pamphlet for distribution in black neighborhoods: Bryant, *Bystander*, p. 186.

51 "Did you see what Martin's father said?": Wofford, *Of Kennedys and Kings*, p. 28.

52 That summer, the Coast Guard Academy: Richard N. Goodwin, *Remembering America: A Voice from the Sixties* (Boston: Little, Brown, 1988), p. 4.

52 Those few words had the effect: Author interview with Wofford, 2010.

52 But Kennedy did *not* adopt: Robert F. Kennedy preadministration political files, General Subject, Box 52, JFKL.

53 "and I'm hopeful that we will shortly conclude": *PPP*, John F. Kennedy, 1961, p. 33.

53 "there was going to be plenty of time to fight": White OH, JFKL.

54 It was also news to Wofford: Wofford, *Of Kennedys and Kings*, p. 132.

54 "Jesus Christ!" Kennedy exclaimed: Reeves, *President Kennedy*, p. 517.

55 "We're still talking about that": Ibid., p. 518.

57 But if Kennedy's words were ringing: President's Office Files, Speech Files, Box 45, JFKL.

58 "ran out of runway": Author telephone conversation with White, Oct. 17, 2012.

58 Barely a minute after Kennedy went off the air: http://www.jfklibrary.org/Asset-Viewer/fXbXxZHwaUmJqbxW_5IrQg.aspx, JFKL.

58 Four hours later, in Jackson: Reeves, *President Kennedy*, p. 523.

3: The Heart of the Problem

62 "I'm not going to admit I'm straddling the fence": Scrapbook, 1963–1964, Box 129, CAHP.

62 "The legal remedies I have proposed": Charles and Barbara Whalen, *The Longest Debate: A Legislative History of the 1964 Civil Rights Act* (Cabin John, Md.: Seven Locks Press, 1985), p. 1.

62 But on Capitol Hill, the southern bulls bellowed: Bryant, *Bystander*, p. 28.

62 Most insisted that the bill did not: *New York Times*, June 20, 1963.

63 "The time is long past": Justice Department Online Archives, http://www.jfklibrary.org/Asset-Viewer/fXbXxZHwaUmJqbxW_5IrQg.aspx.

63 "Oh, it was awful": June 12 conversation, Dictation Belt 22A.2, JFKL.

64 "seemed alarmed over the pace": Arthur M. Schlesinger Jr., *Journals, 1952–2000* (New York: Penguin Press, 2007), p. 199.

64 "A patent compromise": LCCR Files, Box 117; Folder Civil Rights Act 1963, LOC.

64 "Any individual can come here and get a job": *New York Times*, June 15, 1963.

64 "The fact that I was Attorney General": Kennedy, *Robert F. Kennedy in His Own Words*, p. 75.

65 The very name Bobby: Evan Thomas, *Robert F. Kennedy: His Life* (New York: Simon and Schuster, 2000), p. 249.

65 "His obvious characteristics are energy": Arthur M. Schlesinger Jr., *Robert Kennedy and His Times*, vol. 2 (Boston: Houghton Mifflin, 1978), p. 620.

66 "What you had to do when the meeting was over": Strober and Strober, *Let Us Begin Anew*, p. 281.

66 "He would ask me every four days": Kennedy, *Robert F. Kennedy in His Own Words*, p. 179.

66 "For the last two and a half years": Meeting, June 17, 1963, Lee White office files, Box 23, JFKL.

66 "didn't lie awake nights worrying": Kennedy, *Robert F. Kennedy in His Own Words*, pp. 66, 72.

67 "I didn't give a shit about civil rights": C. David Heymann, *RFK: A Candid Biography of Robert F. Kennedy* (New York: Dutton, 1998), p. 278.

67 "Who really knew Bob Kennedy?": Warren Rogers, *When I Think of Bobby* (New York: HarperCollins, 1993), p. 187.

67 he briefly had a paper route: Heymann, *RFK*, p. 23.

67 caught up in a cheating scandal: Thomas, *Robert F. Kennedy*, p. 36.

67 After the war, he earned C's and D's: Ibid., p. 55.

67 "Mr. Kennedy, the Dinosaur Is Dead": Ibid.

68 the only one of the Kennedy boys: Ibid., p. 45.

68 "What we did grow up with": Kennedy, *Robert F. Kennedy in His Own Words*, pp. 66–67.

68   Bunche became the first speaker: Thomas, *Robert F. Kennedy*, p. 56; Kennedy, *Robert F. Kennedy in His Own Words*, p. 68.

69   "Every adjective ever applied to his father": David Nasaw, *The Patriarch: The Remarkable Life and Turbulent Times of Joseph P. Kennedy* (New York: Penguin Press, 2012), p. 664.

69   "In that event, we will want to have him": Ibid., pp. 671–72.

70   In 1955, he undertook a fact-finding tour: Ibid., p. 689.

70   "The more I thought about the injustice of it": Thomas, *Robert F. Kennedy*, pp. 102–3; Kennedy, *Robert F. Kennedy in His Own Words*, pp. 70–71.

70   "Sure I'm glad": Thomas, *Robert F. Kennedy*, p. 104.

71   "You weren't making fun of yourself": Ibid., p. 111; Brayman, *President Speaks Off the Record*, p. 632.

71   "Clearly, Bobby was not qualified": Nicholas deB. Katzenbach, *Some of It Was Fun: Working with RFK and LBJ* (New York: W. W. Norton, 2008), p. 22.

72   he chose Burke Marshall: Bryant, *Bystander*, p. 247.

72   "Our training as soldiers or sailors": *New York Times*, obituary of Guthman, Sept. 2, 2008.

72   at his confirmation hearings: Bryant, *Bystander*, p. 245.

73   Nick Katzenbach would remember: Katzenbach, *Some of It Was Fun*, p. 31.

73   "One of the hallmarks of the Kennedys": Arthur M. Schlesinger Jr., *Robert Kennedy and His Times*, vol. 1 (Boston: Houghton Mifflin, 1978), pp. 249–51.

73   "Don't tell me what I can't do": Ibid., p. 254.

73   At his first staff meeting: Ibid., p. 302.

73   To his formal, walnut-paneled office: Author conversation with Eric Holder, 2013.

74   From the start of Kennedy's tenure: Guthman Papers, Box 1, JFKL.

74   Bob Kennedy told *Look* magazine: Bryant, *Bystander*, pp. 245–46.

75   As if reflecting the emotional divide: Lena Horne and Richard Schickel, *Lena* (Garden City, N.Y.: Doubleday, 1965), p. 229.

77   On and on it went: Harry Belafonte with Michael Shnayerson, *My Song* (New York: Alfred A. Knopf, 2011), pp. 266–69; Schlesinger, *Robert Kennedy and His Times*, vol. 1, pp. 344–48; Thomas, *Robert F. Kennedy*, pp. 244–45.

77   "I think that Bobby also sensed": Strober and Strober, *Let Us Begin Anew*, p. 191.

77   To Arthur Schlesinger the attorney general complained: Schlesinger, *Robert Kennedy and His Times*, vol. 1, p. 348.

77   But just days later: Thomas, *Robert F. Kennedy*, p. 245.

77   "He resented the experience, but it pierced him": Schlesinger, *Robert Kennedy and His Times*, vol. 1, p. 348.

78   "What my father said about businessmen": Kennedy, *Robert F. Kennedy in His Own Words*, p. 204.

78   "For the first time, people were concerned enough": Ibid., p. 173.

78   The attorney general began his opening statement: Whalen and Whalen, *Longest Debate*, pp. 5–6; Department of Justice Online Archives, prepared testimony for June 26, 1963, http://www.justice.gov/ag/rfkspeeches/1963/06-26-1963.pdf.

79   "Today, business enterprises are regulated": DOJ online archives testimony, June 26.

80   "I want this legislation to pass": Whalen and Whalen, *Longest Debate*, p. 7.

80 "Frankly, it would be extremely difficult": Ibid., p. 9.

80 On the Senate side of Capitol Hill: Mann, *Walls of Jericho*, p. 368.

81 The first time Kennedy appeared before the committee: *CR*, Judiciary Committee Hearings, Civil Rights: The President's Program, July 16, 17, 18, 24, 25, 30, 31, August 1, 8, 23, and September 11. All the material in this section comes from the transcripts of those hearings.

81 "Isn't it true, if we pass this bill": *CR*, Judiciary Committee Hearings, July 17.

83 The grilling was so exhausting: Thomas, *Robert F. Kennedy*, p. 260.

4: Tell 'Em About the Dream!

87 They had been met at the North Portico: Preston Bruce, *From the Door of the White House* (New York: Lothrop, Lee and Shepard, 1984), p. 95.

87 "the best meeting I attended": Arthur M. Schlesinger Jr., *A Thousand Days: John F. Kennedy in the White House* (Boston: Houghton Mifflin, 1965), p. 968.

87 When someone asked why no Negroes: Reeves, *President Kennedy*, p. 529.

87 "We want success in Congress": Schlesinger, *Thousand Days*, p. 969.

89 "a good many programs I care about": Ibid., p. 971.

89 "I assume you know": Reeves, *President Kennedy*, p. 530.

90 "If they shoot you down": Garrow, *Bearing the Cross*, p. 273.

90 the FBI had known since the early 1950s: David J. Garrow, "The FBI and Martin Luther King," *Atlantic Monthly*, July 2002.

91 What Hoover never told the president: Ibid.

91 Because of the existing tap: Robert Kennedy's suspicions of King would influence his whole family. In 1964, in interviews not made public for half a century, Jacqueline Kennedy told Arthur M. Schlesinger Jr. that King was "really a tricky person" and said she could not see a picture of him "without thinking, you know, that man's terrible." See Jacqueline Kennedy: *Historic Conversations on Life with John F. Kennedy* (New York: Hyperion, 2011), p. 260.

92 (The FBI could never confirm): Sally Bedell Smith, *Grace and Power: The Private World of the Kennedy White House* (New York: Random House, 2004), p. 386.

93 known to his friends as Tweedie: Taylor Branch, *Parting the Waters: America in the King Years* (New York: Simon and Schuster, 1988), pp. 55–56.

93 "Cogitating with the cosmic universe": Marshall Frady, *Martin Luther King Jr.: A Life* (New York: Penguin, 2006), p. 13.

94 "I was determined to hate every white person": Garrow, *Bearing the Cross*, p. 35.

94 King's spiritual awakening: Branch, *Parting the Waters*, p. 60.

94 He also fell deeply and painfully in love: Ibid., pp. 90–91; Frady, *Martin Luther King Jr.*, pp. 20–22.

95 The very night of Rosa Parks's arrest: Frady, *Martin Luther King Jr.*, p. 26.

96 "You know, my friends, there comes a *time*": Ibid., p. 34.

96 "Lord, I'm down here trying": Ibid., p. 46.

97 "It ends with me getting killed": Ibid., p. 51.

97 "I think I should choose the time and place": Ibid., p. 73.

98 The president responded with politesse: Bryant, *Bystander*, p. 294.

98 "I am in Birmingham because injustice is here": King, *Why We Can't Wait*, p. 86.

98 "the moral passion is missing": Wofford, *Of Kennedys and Kings*, pp. 128–29.

99 "That little baby does not belong to me": Branch, *Parting the Waters*, p. 841.

99 "Well," King had replied: Ibid., p. 849.

99 Wilkins still favored "quiet, patient lobbying tactics": Roy Wilkins, *Standing Fast: The Autobiography of Roy Wilkins* (New York: Da Capo Press, 1994), p. 291.

100 Only when Franklin D. Roosevelt agreed: Goodwin, *No Ordinary Time*, p. 252.

100 ("an old black fairy"): Thomas, *Robert F. Kennedy*, p. 263.

100 Rustin was an organizational genius: Garrow, *Bearing the Cross*, pp. 277–78.

101 "we cawn't have any disorganized pissing": John Lewis, *Walking with the Wind: A Memoir of the Movement* (New York: Simon and Schuster, 1998), p. 215.

102 "The attitudes began to change": Author interview with James Hamilton, 2013; James F. Findlay Jr., *Church People in the Struggle: The National Council of Churches and the Black Freedom Struggle, 1950–1970* (Oxford: Oxford University Press, 1993), pp. 50–55.

102 "Well, I'll run it then": John Douglas OH #3, JFKL.

102 "that's in the great tradition": PPP, John F. Kennedy, 1963, pp. 572–73.

103 "Only those citizens who are committed to non-violence": Robert F. Kennedy, Attorney General Correspondence, Box 11, JFKL.

103 Burke Marshall would later recall: Henry Hampton and Steve Fayer, *Voices of Freedom: An Oral History of the Civil Rights Movement from the 1950s through the 1980s* (New York: Bantam, 1981), p. 161.

103 "I do not intend to be disturbed": Civil Rights 1963–65, Folder 3, EMDP.

103 Charles Halleck . . . noted that there were strict rules and regulations: Civil rights statement, July 1963, EMDP.

103 "They're not going to bluff me": Whalen and Whalen, *Longest Debate*, p. 24.

103 no detail was too small: John Reilly papers, Department of Justice Files, Series #195, Box 1, JFKL.

104 *no dogs*: Douglas OH #3, JFKL.

104 "All this arranging and orchestrating": Lewis, *Walking with the Wind*, p. 213.

104 an old enemy of Stan Levison's: Garrow, *Bearing the Cross*, p. 285.

104 Reilly even suggested: John Reilly papers, JFKL.

105 the press and public knew next to nothing: John Douglas OH #3, JFKL.

105 "I thought you would be interested": Garrow, *Bearing the Cross*, p. 280; Branch, *Parting the Waters*, p. 861.

105 the streets of the city were eerily empty: John Douglas OH #3, JFKL.

105 with thousands more troops on standby alert: Whalen and Whalen, *Longest Debate*, p. 24.

106 "When I saw the number of people": Author conversation with Eleanor Holmes Norton, *The Daily Rundown*, MSNBC, August 23, 2013.

106 Bayard Rustin's elaborate sound system: John Reilly papers, JFKL.

106 a documentary about the day: Author interview with George Stevens Jr., Jan. 25, 2012.

107 News organizations feared the worst: Author email with Philip Kopper, Jan. 17, 2013.

107 The *New York Times* went even further: Author email with Russell Baker, Dec. 16, 2011.

107 Shortly before 11:00 a.m.: Author interview with Gregory B. Craig, Jan. 2012.

108 "he doesn't get what we're yelling": Ibid.

108 he had debated up to the last minute: Edward M. Kennedy, *True Compass: A Memoir* (New York: Twelve, 2009), p. 201.

108 He went to the mansion's third-floor solarium: Bruce, *From the Door of the White House*, p. 97; Clarke, *JFK's Last Hundred Days*, p. 108.

108 The night before, an advance copy: Garrow, *Bearing the Cross*, p. 282.

109 Lewis and his fellow activists: http://www.crmvet.org/tim/timhome.htm.

109 "John, we've come this far together": Lewis, *Walking with the Wind*, p. 223.

109 "Wake up, America": Clarence B. Jones, *Behind the Dream: The Making of the Speech That Transformed a Nation* (New York: Palgrave Macmillan, 2011), p. 65.

110 with the help of Clarence Jones: Ibid., pp. 76–77.

110 "Tell 'em about the dream, Martin!": Ibid., p. 112.

111 "Today you were smokin'!": Ibid., p. 125.

111 "He's damned good": Reeves, *President Kennedy*, p. 585; Branch, *Parting the Waters*, p. 883.

111 "We cannot *defend* freedom in Berlin": Branch, *Parting the Waters*, p. 883.

112 as usual, the president was pessimistic: Meetings: Tape 108/A43, Civil Rights, Aug. 28, 1963, JFKL.

112 "Grab the nigger vote": Lee C. White papers, Box 23, JFKL.

112 "we must mark him now": Tim Weiner, *Enemies: A History of the FBI* (New York: Random House, 2012), p. 235.

112 "of all the places to be": Craig interview.

113 John Lewis found himself disappointed: Lewis, *Walking with the Wind*, p. 226.

113 "that means there's going to be a civil rights bill": Author interview with Kenneth Teasdale, May 2013.

113 A Gallup poll that July: Stephan and Abigail Thernstrom, *America in Black and White* (New York: Touchstone, 1999), p. 139.

113 "I would like to think": Katzenbach, *Some of It Was Fun*, p. 126.

5: A Compromise Between Polar Positions

117 "Bill had an engagement": Interview of David Carver by Adam Clymer, May 13, 2008.

118 "Your representative owes you": Ibid.

118 "There is no such thing as easy money from Washington": *Dayton Daily News*, Oct. 20, 1948.

118 he preferred the term "equal rights": Folder SC389, McCulloch Papers, Public Library, Piqua, Ohio, "Bill McCulloch and Civil Rights Act of 1964," Bill Milligan address to YMCA, Apr. 8, 1987; also interview of Ann Carver by Adam Clymer, Apr. 7, 2008.

118 "The Constitution doesn't say": Whalen and Whalen, *Longest Debate*, p. 105.

119 "Reality is what we live by": Ibid., p. 13.

119 As the spring wore on: Ibid., p. 34.

120 William Moore McCulloch was born in 1901: James Oda submission, Piqua Historian and Librarian, Clymer papers. Author possession.

121 "I have never spent nearly as much": McCulloch letter, Aug. 20, 1964, Folder C, Public Library, Piqua, Ohio.

121 "His constituents were very conservative": Clymer interview of Joe Metz, May 15, 2008.

122 Throughout that summer and into the fall: Whalen and Whalen, *Longest Debate*, p. 33.

123 "This is a reasonable, moderate bill": Author interview of David Filvaroff, June 19, 2013.

123 "Bill McCulloch became the conscience of the bill": Author interview of Robert Kimball, Feb. 27, 2013.

124 By Friday, August 2: Whalen and Whalen, *Longest Debate*, p. 22. See also House Judiciary Committee Hearings, Subcommittee No. 5, Parts 1–3, Jan. 1, 1963–Aug. 2, 1963.

124 "When we ask for one half of a loaf": Whalen and Whalen, *Longest Debate*, p. 36.

125 "It may be the feeling in Birmingham": Rosenberg and Karabell, *Kennedy, Johnson, and the Quest for Justice*, pp. 143–63.

126 "This is wholly confidential": Guthman papers, Box 1, JFKL.

126 By the end of the month, still more liberal amendments: Whalen and Whalen, *Longest Debate*, pp. 34–35.

128 "I'll go as far as I can go": Rosenberg and Karabell, *Kennedy, Johnson, and the Quest for Justice*, p. 179.

130 "There would have been no living with the Bureau": Thomas, *Robert F. Kennedy*, p. 264.

130 "just left of King George III": Eric F. Goldman, *The Tragedy of Lyndon Johnson* (New York: Dell, 1969), p. 33.

131 "The Ev and Charlie Show": Henry Z. Scheele, *Charlie Halleck: A Political Biography* (New York: Exposition Press, 1966), p. 207.

131 Halleck held court in a hideaway office: James Peter Carroll, "Charlie Halleck's Capitol Clinic," *American Spectator*, Dec. 1991.

131 "every time I talk to him, he's drinking": TPR, Lyndon B. Johnson, vol. 8, p. 209.

132 Among the hostile communiqués: Subject file Civil Rights, Box 109, CAHP.

132 Halleck was under assault that summer: Correspondence, Box 72, CAHP.

132 Halleck's delicate situation: Ibid.

133 Celler was not happy: Kennedy, *Robert Kennedy in His Own Words*, pp. 217–18.

134 Bob Kennedy now summed up his views on these changes: Testimony of Robert F. Kennedy, Oct. 15, 1963, Department of Justice online archives, http://www.justice.gov/ag/rfkspeeches/1963/10-15-1963.pdf.

134 "What I want is a bill, not an issue": Whalen and Whalen, *Longest Debate*, p. 45. See also House Judiciary Committee Hearings, Subcommittee No. 5, Part 4, Oct. 15–16, 1963.

135 the civil rights groups hit the ceiling: Bryant, *Bystander*, p. 449.

135 the attorney general approved additional electronic surveillance: Kennedy, *Robert Kennedy in His Own Words*, p. 145; Weiner, *Enemies*, p. 235.

136 "Lib, where are we at here, anyway?": *Time*, Nov. 1, 1963.

137 "The committee chairman was forced to label the subcommittee bill": Whalen and Whalen, *Longest Debate*, pp. 47–49.

138 "You're in a damn sight better position": Rosenberg and Karabell, *Kennedy, Johnson, and the Quest for Justice*, pp. 184–92.

138 In the end, Kennedy proposed a compromise: Whalen and Whalen, *Longest Debate*, p. 52.

139 "like trying to pick up a greased pig": Bradlee, *Conversations with Kennedy*, p. 222.

139 "the president's personal prestige": Kennedy, *Robert Kennedy in His Own Words*, p. 216.

139 The meeting broke up without any definitive result: Whalen and Whalen, *Longest Debate*, pp. 52–53.

139 "I've got you the votes": Lawrence F. O'Brien, *No Final Victories: A Life in Politics from John F. Kennedy to Watergate* (New York: Ballantine, 1976), p. 148.

140 they went through the bill section by section: Whalen and Whalen, *Longest Debate*, pp. 55–56.

140 Katzenbach had an inspiration: Katzenbach, *Some of It Was Fun*, p. 127.

142 the president needed at least five more votes: Whalen and Whalen, *Longest Debate*, pp. 58–61.

142 "He'll vote for any goddamned thing you want!": Oval Office Conversation, Oct. 28, 1963, Dictabelt #28A, JFKL.

143 "You know my concern about FEPC": Whalen and Whalen, *Longest Debate*, p. 63; Oval Office Meetings, Tape #118, Oct. 29, 1963, JFKL.

144 Celler then ordered a vote on the new bill: Whalen and Whalen, *Longest Debate*, pp. 64–66.

144 The president called the bill "comprehensive and fair": PPP, John F. Kennedy, 1963, p. 820.

144 The biggest loser was probably Roland Libonati: Whalen and Whalen, *Longest Debate*, p. 66.

145 "I got a little trouble on my side": Dictabelt #28A, JFKL.

145 "violated the compact with the southerners": *New Republic*, Nov. 9, 1963.

145 The *Washington Post* editorialized: *Washington Post*, Nov. 13, 1963.

145 someone placed a furled umbrella: *Washington Post*, Nov. 11, 1963, clipped in CAHP; Whalen and Whalen, *Longest Debate*, p. 67.

145 "Halleck has been warned": *Dayton Journal Herald*, Nov. 1, 1963.

145 "We had Kennedy locked in a box": Ibid.

145 "THE HAIRY APE OF THE PARTY": CAHP, Correspondence, Box 74.

146 puzzlement about just why Halleck had agreed: Whalen and Whalen, *Longest Debate*, p. 54.

146 "If the senior Republican on a committee": Author interview of Nicholas Katzenbach, 2012.

146 "My purpose is to remove this bill": *Dayton Journal Herald*, Nov. 8, 1963.

146 "one of the poorest receptions": *New York Times*, Oct. 31, 1963.

147 "I think it is unfortunate": PPP, John F. Kennedy, 1963, p. 846; Whalen and Whalen, *Longest Debate*, p. 69.

147 Charlie Halleck refused to shoulder any blame: Joint Senate-House Republican Leadership, Nov. 21, EMDP.

147 "Possibly I can get in touch with him": Correspondence, Box 75, CAHP.

6: A Good Man in a Tight Spot

148 He drew a small notepad from the desk: Robert A. Caro, *The Passage of Power: The Years of Lyndon Johnson* (New York: Alfred A. Knopf, 2012), p. 358.

149 "is that bipartisan leadership?": *TPR*, Lyndon B. Johnson, vol. 1, pp. 44–45.

149 "I was a man in trouble": Lyndon Baines Johnson, *The Vantage Point: Perspectives of the Presidency* (New York: Holt, Rinehart and Winston, 1971), pp. 12, 18.

149 Johnson once told his biographer: Doris Kearns Goodwin, *Lyndon Johnson and the American Dream* (New York: St. Martin's Press, 1991), p. 164.

149 Johnson had spent just ten hours: Caro, *Passage of Power*, p. 225.

149 "Who is Lyndon Johnson?": Robert Dallek, *Flawed Giant: Lyndon Johnson and His Times* (Oxford: Oxford University Press, 1998), p. 44.

150 "Whatever Happened to Lyndon Johnson?": Caro, *Passage of Power*, p. 226.

150 "it must have been a tremendous frustration": Dallek, *Flawed Giant*, p. 44.

150 "They don't listen to me": Whalen and Whalen, *Longest Debate*, p. 74.

150 "we weren't drinking, of course": Caro, *Passage of Power*, p. 672.

150 Barely two hours later: Ibid., p. 369.

151 "He put his arm around me": Manchester, *Death of a President*, p. 406.

151 he praised the Senate minority leader: *TPR*, Lyndon B. Johnson, vol. 1, p. 83.

151 "I would have bet on it": Jack Valenti, *This Time, This Place*, p. 31.

152 "It's going to be a long day tomorrow": Caro, *Passage of Power*, p. 372.

152 now Eisenhower was in the White House complex: Johnson, *Vantage Point*, p. 32.

152 "I believe it'd be *reassuring*": *TPR*, Lyndon B. Johnson, vol. 1, p. 102.

153 Smathers informed Johnson that he had cut a deal: Ibid., p. 112.

153 "*most* interesting visit": Ibid., pp. 109–10.

153 "I couldn't let that happen": Goodwin, *Lyndon Johnson and the American Dream*, p. 191.

154 "you are going to be judged on merit": Caro, *Passage of Power*, pp. 420, 486, 677.

154 "it's just an *impossible* period": *TPR*, Lyndon B. Johnson, vol. 1, pp. 161–62.

155 "Let us put an end to the teaching": *PPP*, Lyndon B. Johnson, 1963, p. 10.

155 "a man of too many paradoxes": Reedy OH, LBJL.

155 "he went through the walls": Dallek, *Flawed Giant*, p. 4.

156 "an animal sense of weakness in other men": Bill Moyers, *Moyers on America: A Journalist and His Times* (New York: Anchor Books, 2005), pp. 189–90.

156 "My ancestors were teachers and lawyers": Charles Peters, *Lyndon B. Johnson* (New York: Times Books, 2010), p. 2.

156 "the inexplicable power of his will": Goodwin, *Lyndon Johnson and the American Dream*, p. 22.

156 From his earliest days: Ibid., p. 25.

157 ("He could look busy doing nothing"): Peters, *Lyndon B. Johnson*, p. 6.

157 "His greatest forte": Goodwin, *Lyndon Johnson and the American Dream*, p. 53.

157 "You never forget what poverty and hatred can do": Peters, *Lyndon B. Johnson*, p. 8.

158 "Texas is a part of the South": Johnson, *Vantage Point*, p. 155.

158 "We are not speaking against the Negro race": Caro, *Master of the Senate*, p. 213.

159 Johnson's motives . . . were "highly mixed": Reedy OH, LBJL.

159 (His feet were the same size as Johnson's): Michael L. Gillette, *Lady Bird Johnson: An Oral History* (New York: Oxford University Press, 2012), p. 256.

159 "Well, Senator, it's tough enough": Johnson, *Vantage Point*, pp. 154–55.

160 "I always wanted the ham and egg": Caro, *Passage of Power*, p. 486.

160 The crowd waved placards: Ibid., p. 150.

161 "there was genuine feeling": Wilkins, *Standing Fast*, p. 298.

161 "happier than he had been for months": Caro, *Passage of Power*, p. 253.

161 "The hours are short": Ibid., p. 255.

161 "the Negro remains in bondage": Dallek, *Flawed Giant*, p. 36.

162 "felt that if he said something, they'd leak it to the *New York Times*": Baker OH, Senate Historian's Office, p. 91.

162 "I think he's got to have his bill": Sorensen Dictabelt recording, p. 14, LBJL.

162 "Don't try to kill the snake": George Reedy, *Lyndon B. Johnson: A Memoir* (New York: Andrews and McMeel, 1982). p. xv.

162 "It is my thought that you might wish me": Central Subject Files Civil Rights Box 2, LBJL. Cross's memo is filed under the subject of civil rights at the Johnson Library, but in a brief telephone interview with the author on August 26, 2013, Cross, who retired as a brigadier general in 1971, said he no longer remembered just what he had in mind when he composed it. Speaking from his home in Texas, Cross, then eighty-eight years old, also said he could not remember whether the crew of Air Force One was integrated in that era, though he noted that he had personally served with integrated crews.

163 "I want that bill *passed*": Wilkins, *Standing Fast*, p. 296.

164 "If we fail on this, then we'll fail on everything": *TPR*, Lyndon B. Johnson, vol. 1, pp. 263–65.

164 "the only lever we've really got": *TPR*, Lyndon B. Johnson, vol. 2, p. 73.

165 "some evidence of a dramatic impact": Caro, *Passage of Power*, p. 494.

165 "words can never be put in his mouth": Scrapbooks, 1963–1964, Box 129, CAHP.

165 "I am the only president you have": *PPP*, Lyndon B. Johnson, 1963, p. 24.

165 A discharge petition was, indeed, a drastic step: Legislative Series, Box 6, Folder 18, WMMP.

165 "This move for a petition is irritating some people": Scrapbooks, Box 15, January 1964 Roscoe Drummond newspaper column, WMMP.

166 "I don't want to run over you, Judge": Whalen and Whalen, *Longest Debate*, pp. 85–87.

167 a solemn promise from the president: Caro, *Passage of Power*, p. 470.

167 "you've got to learn to handle a gun": Dallek, *Flawed Giant*, p. 33.

168 "Chamberlain umbrella man": Caro, *Passage of Power*, p. 230.

168 "If only John Glenn were a Negro!": Reeves, *President Kennedy*, p. 286.

170 "You can't let your people talk about me": Jeff Shesol, *Mutual Contempt: Lyndon Johnson, Robert Kennedy, and the Feud That Defined a Decade* (New York: W. W. Norton, 1997), p. 123.

170 "what we can do about Bobby": *TPR*, Lyndon B. Johnson, vol. 2, p. 319.

170 "an animal in many ways": Kennedy, *Robert Kennedy in His Own Words*, p. 417.

170 "You help me, though, get that bill out": *TPR*, Lyndon B. Johnson, vol. 2, p. 384.

171 "Bird, let's have Congress over tonight!": Whalen and Whalen, *Longest Debate*, p. 88.

171 "I don't care if only twenty come": *TPR*, Lyndon B. Johnson, vol. 2, pp. 709, 719.

172 "We're Americans first": *CQ Weekly*, 1963, p. 2243; Whalen and Whalen, *Longest Debate*, p. 89.

172 "power . . . began flowing back to the White House": Johnson, *Vantage Point*, p. 40.

172 support for the civil rights bill stood at 62 percent: Whalen and Whalen, *Longest Debate*, pp. 89–90.

172 "we can't pay you much else": *TPR*, Lyndon B. Johnson, vol. 2, p. 689.

172 "She's got to have about a bale cut off": Ibid., p. 737.

173 "Gerri, where are you?": Ibid., pp. 764–65.

174 "She's got good character?": Ibid., p. 776.

174 "Come in, honey": Ibid., pp. 786–88.

174 he upended his newest secretary's plans: Simeon Booker (with Carol McCabe Booker), *Shocking the Conscience: A Reporter's Account of the Civil Rights Movement* (Jackson: University of Mississippi Press, 2013), pp. 243–44; author interview with Carol McCabe Booker, 2013.

175 "Yes, sir": E. Ernest Goldstein, "How LBJ Took the Bull by the Horns," *Amherst Magazine*, Winter 1985, pp. 12–17.

7: A Great Big Vote

176 a rapprochement so striking: Marvin Caplan, *Farther Along: A Civil Rights Memoir* (Baton Rouge: Louisiana State University Press, 1999), pp. 213–14.

176 "we're going to work together": Joseph L. Rauh OH, LBJL.

177 "Clarence Mitchell was the leading civil rights lobbyist": Ibid.

177 Mitchell was essentially a conservative: Denton L. Watson, *Lion in the Lobby: Clarence Mitchell, Jr.'s Struggle for the Passage of Civil Rights Laws* (Lanham, Md.: University Press of America, 2002), p. xxii.

177 "I don't care how long it takes": Whalen and Whalen, *Longest Debate*, p. 97.

178 "the movement cannot be stayed": *CQ Weekly*, week ending Jan. 24, 1964, p. 157.

178 "He was a fox": Author interview with John Dingell, 2012.

178 "He thought he was too old": Author interview with Robert Kimball.

179 "Because of my receding red hair": Whalen and Whalen, *Longest Debate*, p. 93.

179 "*New occasions teach new duties*": *New York Times*, Feb. 16, 1964.

180 "If he's not satisfied": *TPR*, Lyndon B. Johnson, vol. 3, pp. 622–23.

180 "I can implement it on an installment basis": Ibid., pp. 694–95.

180 "I am opposed to the speedup": Caro, *Passage of Power*, p. 560; *New York Times*, Jan. 24, 1964.

180 a lesson he had learned the hard way: Watson, *Lion in the Lobby*, p. 604.

182 "you don't need to add any touches of horror": Maryland State Archives online, http://msa.maryland.gov/megafile/msa/speccol/sc3500/sc3520/013700/013750/html/13750bio.html; Watson, *Lion in the Lobby*, p. 12.

182 "periods of great financial difficulties": Watson, *Lion in the Lobby*, p. xv.

182 "He was a very busy guy": Ibid., p. xvi.

183 "He sure kept you honest": Author telephone interview with John Stewart, Mar. 7, 2013.

183 Mitchell endured regular indignities: Watson, *Lion in the Lobby*, p. xix.

183 his own conduct was above reproach: Ibid., p. xviii.

183 "He had the patience of Job": Ibid., p. xxii.

183 "I resent being treated like a fool": Caplan, *Farther Along*, pp. 209–10.

184 ("Howard Smith's got his foot on Lincoln's neck"): *TPR*, Lyndon B. Johnson, vol. 3, p. 879.

184 members began streaming into the chamber: Whalen and Whalen, *Longest Debate*, pp. 100–101.

185 "almost identical with the platforms": *CQ Weekly*, week ending Feb. 7, 1964, p. 250.

185 "one of the great debates of modern American history": Ibid.

185 "is all this done out of fear?": Whalen and Whalen, *Longest Debate*, p. 102.

185 "our Constitution shall apply to all people": Ibid., p. 104.

186 "hedged about with . . . safeguards": *CQ Weekly*, week ending Feb. 7, 1964, p. 250.

186 "the most drastic and far-reaching proposal": Ibid.

187 "as patient and as kindly as could be": Author interview with Jane O'Grady, 2013.

187 Thompson also supplied "a great deal of liquor": Author interview with Nicholas Katzenbach, 2012.

187 "It was nuts, but I didn't know that then": O'Grady interview.

187 "By the third or fourth day": Caplan, *Farther Along*, p. 218.

188 "The chair would designate 'tellers'": Ibid., pp. 216, 217.

188 "This really aroused a lot of concern": Robert Loevy interview with Mitchell, Collection 151, EMDP.

188 "vultures in the spectators galleries": Caplan, *Farther Along*, p. 216.

189 "monstrosity of unknown origin": *CQ Weekly*, week ending Feb. 7, 1964, p. 250.

189 "yes, I do expect a filibuster": *PPP*, Lyndon B. Johnson, 1963–64, p. 259.

189 Another amendment, by Bill Cramer of Florida: Whalen and Whalen, *Longest Debate*, p. 109; *CQ Weekly*, week ending Feb. 7, 1964, p. 251.

190 But over the next two days: *CQ Weekly*, week ending Feb. 7, 1964, p. 251.

190 In response, Charles Goodell: Ibid., p. 251.

191 "If I were cutting corns": Whalen and Whalen, *Longest Debate*, p. 108.

191 "See if you can vote against it": Ibid., p. 110.

192 McCulloch gently upbraided his colleague: *CQ Weekly*, week ending Feb. 7, 1964, p. 251.

192 "There is just no teeth in this amendment": Whalen and Whalen, *Longest Debate*, p. 111.

192 "I disagree with you, but I respect you": Ibid., p. 110.

192 "He was waging a terrific battle just to stand erect": Watson, *Lion in the Lobby*, p. 613.

193 "I am interested in getting this bill passed": Whalen and Whalen, *Longest Debate*, p. 112.

193 McCulloch was more concerned: Kimball interview.

193 he let the amendment pass on a voice vote: *CQ Weekly*, week ending Feb. 14, 1964, p. 295; Whalen and Whalen, *Longest Debate*, pp. 112–13.

193 A much more serious drama: *New York Times*, Feb. 8, 1963.

194 "I am appalled that this is being supported": *CQ Weekly*, week ending Feb. 14, 1964, p. 293; Kimball interview.

195 "If we pick up this old provision from the bill": Whalen and Whalen, *Longest Debate*, p. 114; *CR*, p. 2492.

195 "After the word 'religion' insert 'sex'": Bruce J. Dierenfield, *Keeper of the Rules: Howard W. Smith of Virginia* (Charlottesville: University Press of Virginia, 1987), p. 195.

196 In 1956, during the initial debate: Jo Freeman, *We Will Be Heard: Women's Struggles for Political Power in the United States* (Lanham, Md.: Rowman and Littlefield, 2008), p. 177.

197 "I might do that," the judge replied: Ibid., p. 180.

197 Now, at the eleventh hour: Dierenfield, *Keeper of the Rules*, p. 194.

197 Smith's amendment "could doom the bill": Caplan, *Farther Along*, p. 218; Watson, *Lion in the Lobby*, p. 613.

197 "We are entitled to this little crumb of equality: Whalen and Whalen, *Longest Debate*, p. 117.

198 "We made it!": Dierenfield, *Keeper of the Rules*, p. 195.

198 "There is no need for your amendment": Whalen and Whalen, *Longest Debate*, p. 118.

198 The ninth and final day: *CQ Weekly*, week ending Feb. 14, 1964, p. 296.

198 Rauh ducked out to a pay phone: Rauh OH, LBJL.

198 "No lobbyist could ever outdo Lyndon": Wilkins, *Standing Fast*, p. 301.

199 The last substantive amendment: Whalen and Whalen, *Longest Debate*, p. 120.

199 One by one, the members answered: *CQ Weekly*, week ending Feb. 14, 1964, p. 293.

199 "It was sort of a source of great pride": Dingell interview.

200 "well over a thousand persons from every state": *CQ Weekly*, week ending Feb. 21, 1964, p. 366.

200 diligent gallery-watching efforts paid off: Whalen and Whalen, *Longest Debate*, p. 121; *CQ Weekly*, week ending Feb. 14, 1964, p. 293.

200 lobbying by the church groups . . . bore fruit, too: Findlay, *Church People in the Struggle*, p. 54.

200 In gratitude to the members and aides: O'Grady interview.

200 At the White House, President Johnson: *TPR*, Lyndon B. Johnson, vol. 4, pp. 441–43.

201 "By golly, we got this thing back of us": Ibid., p. 437.

201 When Halleck went home: Speech and clipping files, CAHP.

201 "We were all happy": Watson, *Lion in the Lobby*, p. 614.

201 Less than an hour after the final vote: *TPR*, Lyndon B. Johnson, vol. 4, pp. 451–52.

202 Johnson and Kennedy had barely seen each other: Guthman, *We Band of Brothers*, p. 251.

203 "Don't ever do a favor for me again!": Ibid., p. 254; Shesol, *Mutual Contempt*, pp. 184–87; Goodwin, *Remembering America*, pp. 247–48; Caro, *Passage of Power*, pp. 583–84; *TPR*, Lyndon B. Johnson, vol. 4, pp. 468–76; Kennedy, *Robert F. Kennedy in His Own Words*, pp. 406–7.

204 "What do you think of President Johnson?": http://www.pophistorydig.com/?tag=beatles-in-1964.

8: You Listen to Dirksen!

208 "into the bright sunshine of human rights!": Charles L. Garrettson, *Hubert H. Humphrey: The Politics of Joy* (New Brunswick, N.J.: Transaction, 1993), p. 5; Carl Solberg, *Hubert Humphrey: A Biography* (Minneapolis: Borealis Books, 2003), p. 18.

209 "Call me whenever there's trouble": Hubert H. Humphrey, *The Education of a Public Man: My Life in Politics* (Minneapolis: University of Minnesota Press, 1991), p. 204. It is not clear on precisely which date this conversation took place. Some accounts place it on March 8, 1964, after Humphrey's appearance on *Meet the Press*. But Johnson's telephone call to him on that occasion was not tape-recorded, and Humphrey himself later recalled being approached by Johnson on this topic just after being named floor manager. So I have concluded that the weight of available evidence suggests the talk took place on or about February 18. The substance of Johnson's repeated message to Humphrey about Dirksen in this period is not in any doubt.

209 Katzenbach . . . retained a vivid impression: Katzenbach, *Some of It Was Fun*, p. 142.

209 Carl Hayden . . . had never voted for cloture: Whalen and Whalen, *Longest Debate*, p. 126.

210 "Talking voting details": Katzenbach, *Some of It Was Fun*, pp. 139–40.

210 "The bill can't pass unless you get Ev Dirksen": Humphrey OH, LBJL.

211 Dirksen was the single most flamboyant senator: Louella Dirksen, *The Honorable Mr. Marigold: My Life with Everett Dirksen* (Garden City, N.Y.: Doubleday, 1972), p. 222; Nick Kotz, *Judgment Days: Lyndon Baines Johnson, Martin Luther King, Jr., and the Laws That Changed America* (Boston: Houghton Mifflin, 2005), p. 155.

211 "Ev's up!": *New York Times*, obituary of Dirksen, Sept. 9, 1969.

211 "the inimitable and euphonious sockdolager": Neil MacNeil and Richard A. Baker, *The American Senate: An Insider's History* (Oxford: Oxford University Press, 2013), p. 293.

212 "speak to the folks in the back rows": Neil MacNeil, *Dirksen: Portrait of a Public Man* (New York: World, 1970), p. 33.

212 "the little violations of liberty": Civil Rights files, Box 1963–65, EMDP.

213 "If it's made of dough": Byron C. Hulsey, *Everett Dirksen and His Presidents* (Lawrence: University Press of Kansas, 2000), p. 14.

213 "this is terrible country": Mackaman, *Long Hard Furrow*, p. 51.

214 "foot or finger in every possible camp": Hulsey, *Everett Dirksen and His Presidents*, p. 61.

214 Among Dirksen's policy differences with Eisenhower: Ibid., p. 89.

215 "the heavens will not be rent asunder": Ibid., p. 100.

215 "thus retained more flexibility": Ibid., p. 102.

215 Of the Senate's thirty-three Republicans: Whalen and Whalen, *Longest Debate*, p. 160.

216 "we would organize": Mann, *Walls of Jericho*, p. 394; MacNeil, *Dirksen*, p. 204.

216 "I had to make up my mind": Humphrey recollection, quoted in Robert D. Loevy, ed., *The Civil Rights Act of 1964: The Passage of the Law That Ended Racial Segregation* (Albany: State University of New York Press, 1997), pp. 81, 86.

217 "The time is now": Whalen and Whalen, *Longest Debate*, p. 132.

217 "We are not operating a pit": Mann, *Walls of Jericho*, p. 394.

217 Mansfield would immediately share them with Dirksen: Author interview with Charles Ferris, May 15, 2013.

217 "those qualities had to be preserved": Author interview with John Stewart, April 2012.

217 "Oh, that god-damned, no-good outfit": TPR, Lyndon B. Johnson, vol. 4, p. 621.

218 "She's just a troublemaker": Ibid., p. 659.

218 Humphrey quickly welcomed Kuchel: Humphrey manuscript, cited in Loevy, ed., *Civil Rights Act of 1964*, p. 84.

219 "I'm taking the full responsibility": TPR, Lyndon B. Johnson, vol. 4, pp. 712–13.

219 Lee Metcalf . . . overruled Russell: John Stewart manuscript, cited in Loevy, ed., *Civil Rights Act of 1964*, p. 215.

220 "We would make a great mistake": Whalen and Whalen, *Longest Debate*, p. 135.

220 "extraordinary, but legal, means": Stewart manuscript, cited in Loevy, ed., *Civil Rights Act of 1964*, p. 215.

220 the immediate effect of his gesture was to alienate: Stephen Horn log, p. 27, EMDP.

220 "He would use time": Author interview with Walter F. Mondale, June 2012.

221 "more solutions than we have problems": Gilbert C. Fite, *Richard B. Russell, Jr.: Senator from Georgia* (Chapel Hill: University of North Carolina Press, 1991), p. 420.

221 "Stay out of bed as long as you can": Humphrey, *Education of a Public Man*, pp. 8–9.

221 "I sometimes wonder": Ibid., p. 17.

221 "just fade away and go broke": Ibid., p. 23.

222 "you felt it less": Ibid., p. 28.

222 "Why haven't I a chance?": Ibid., p. 32.

222 "a most difficult and impecunious time": Ibid., p. 39.

223 "Why, it's uneconomic": Ibid., p. 42.

223 (he thought it looked pompous): Stewart interview.

223 won by more than thirty thousand votes: Humphrey, *Education of a Public Man*, p. 50.

223 "newspapers in Minnesota": Ibid., p. 73.

224 "a glib, jaunty spellbinder": Solberg, *Hubert Humphrey*, p. 133.

224 "the Senate's gabbiest freshman": Mann, *Walls of Jericho*, p. 99.

224 Humphrey . . . could always tell when Young was suffering an attack: Mondale interview.

224 "He always believed . . . that you could solve anything": Mann, *Walls of Jericho*, p. 94.

225 "he is one of us!": Humphrey, *Education of a Public Man*, p. 171.

225 "He doesn't want us to get bear": Horn log, pp. 24–26, EMDP.

226 only too happy to compromise in the end: Mann, *Walls of Jericho*, p. 393.

227 "And if you just hold out long enough": Stewart interview.

227 "we stand on the House bill": PPP, Lyndon B. Johnson, 1963–64, p. 328.

228 "You be sure that you explain to him": TPR, Lyndon B. Johnson, vol. 4, p. 945.

228 "so I never learned to swim": Michael Beschloss, *Taking Charge: Lyndon Johnson's Secret White House Tapes* (New York: Simon and Schuster, 1997), p. 268.

228 "President Kennedy could have lost this bill": Whalen and Whalen, *Longest Debate*, p. 139.

9: We Shall Now Begin to Fight

230 "I believe the Senate is prepared now": *PPP*, Lyndon B. Johnson, 1963–64, p. 343.

230 Dirksen's openly voiced doubts: MacNeil, *Dirksen*, p. 205.

231 "There will be no wheels and no deals": Whalen and Whalen, *Longest Debate*, p. 140.

231 "The secret of passing this bill": Horn log, pp. 29–30, EMDP.

231 Organized religion had played a key role: Findlay, *Church People in the Struggle*, p. 57.

231 Newspaper accounts of the debate: *Charlotte Observer*, Aug. 25, 1963.

232 THE CRUCIAL SENATE FIGHT: Mann, *Walls of Jericho*, p. 398.

232 Because the Senate did not have the usual option: John G. Stewart, *Witness to the Promised Land: Observations on Congress and the Presidency from the Pages of "Christianity and Crisis"* (Santa Ana, Calif.: Seven Locks Press, 2005), p. 22.

233 Richard Russell was first on his feet: Whalen and Whalen, *Longest Debate*, p. 141.

233 "It is much more drastic than any bill": Ibid., pp. 142–43.

233 "This is such a moment": Loevy, ed., *Civil Rights Act of 1964*, p. 218.

233 Humphrey and Kuchel and their troops: Horn log, p. 34, EMDP; author interview with Peter Smith, June 19, 2013.

234 Such diligence impressed even Lyndon Johnson: *TPR*, Lyndon B. Johnson, vol. 5, p. 151.

234 "better fluid than frozen": Horn log, p. 37, EMDP.

235 Indeed, Humphrey was proving that it was possible: John G. Stewart manuscript, quoted in Loevy, ed., *Civil Rights Act of 1964*, p. 221.

235 "The Negro was freed of his chains": *TPR*, Lyndon B. Johnson, vol. 5, p. 198.

236 "the heaviest cost of all": Bipartisan Civil Rights Newsletter, Mar. 16, 1964, Burke Marshall papers, Box 27, JFKL.

236 That same day, Robert Kimball: Horn log, p. 43, EMDP.

236 By this point, the strain: Bipartisan Civil Rights Newsletter, Mar. 17, 1964, Marshall Papers, Box 27, JFKL.

236 no idea seemed too far-fetched: Legislative Files, Civil Rights, Box 241, HHHP; author email exchange with William Connell.

237 "If fifty Negroes came": Horn log, p. 54, EMDP.

237 By this point, the southerners were dragging: Ibid., pp. 54, 61b.

237 At a meeting with the floor leaders' group: Ibid., p. 63.

238 "There is a feeling that Martin Luther King should stay out": Ibid., p. 67.

238 "We shall now begin to fight the war": Whalen and Whalen, *Longest Debate*, p. 147.

239 "I cannot overemphasize the historic importance": *CR*, 88th Congress, 2nd Session, p. 6529.

239 "This issue should not be a partisan fight": Ibid., p. 6553.

239 Johnson telephoned Ted Kennedy: *TPR*, Lyndon B. Johnson, vol. 5, p. 580.

240 Even as the Senate opened debate: *New York Times*, Mar. 31, 1964.

240 The mood of the Senate: Author interview with Daniel K. Inouye, June 2012.

240 For all the presumed drama: Mudd, *Place to Be*, p. 144.

240 "Let there be extended debate": *CR*, p. 6574.

241 "It may take some time": Ibid., pp. 6606–7, 6637.

241 Soon enough, Russell's bumptious colleague: Ibid., p. 6651.

242 But Thurmond was having none of this: Ibid., p. 6662.

242 "Baseball fan. Roman bearing": Mudd, *Place to Be*, p. 148.

242 Indeed, by this stage: Fite, *Richard B. Russell, Jr.*, p. 1; Caro, *Master of the Senate*, p. 209.

243 "incomparably the truest current Senate type": Fite, *Richard B. Russell, Jr.*, p. 126.

244 Russell eschewed the crude populist racism: Caro, *Master of the Senate*, pp. 185–86.

244 he was fighting a losing battle: Fite, *Richard B. Russell, Jr.*, pp. 337–42.

245 in occasional public flashes: Caro, *Master of the Senate*, p. 191.

245 "I do not think much of him": Ibid., p. 194.

245 "I don't like to say too much": Zephyr Wright OH, LBJL.

246 State Senator Lamar Plunkett: Mann, *Walls of Jericho*, p. 402.

246 "no case in history of a mongrel race": Ibid.

246 In truth, for all his erudition: Caro, *Master of the Senate*, pp. 470–71.

246 "We knew there was no way in hell": Herman E. Talmadge, *Talmadge: A Political Legacy, a Politician's Life* (Atlanta: Peachtree Publishers, 1987), p. 195.

247 "Dirksen asked us to take a look at the bill": Loevy interview with Flynn, Collection 151, EMDP.

247 "We met with him literally fourteen hours a day": Mackaman, *Long Hard Furrow*, p. 77.

247 "it will be one great headache": Ibid., p. 73.

247 Dirksen's concern was also fueled: Robert Samuel Smith, *Race, Labor, and Civil Rights* (Baton Rouge: Louisiana State University Press, 2008), p. 26.

248 They persuaded him to hold off: Mackaman, *Long Hard Furrow*, p. 78.

248 If the Senate lacks a quorum: CR, p. 6863.

249 An embarrassed Humphrey explained: *New York Times*, Apr. 5, 1964.

249 "My position is no amendments": Horn log, p. 79, EMDP.

250 few new arguments to be made: CR, p. 7032.

250 "No Southerner has been elected President": Ibid., p. 7035.

250 The segregationists suggested: Ibid., p. 7098.

250 "In spite of the protestations": Ibid., p. 6820.

251 Sometimes, the southerners simply told lies: Ibid., p. 8346.

252 The exchanges were not without humor: Ibid., p. 7418.

252 But no amount of levity could mask: Ibid., p. 8052.

253 "charm never covered up a running sore": Ibid., pp. 8062–64.

253 Humphrey was now quick to dismiss Wallace's performance: TPR, Lyndon B. Johnson, vol. 5, p. 751.

253 "The principle requires no argument": CR, p. 7064.

253 "a carte blanche bill": Ibid., p. 5074.

253 That afternoon, Stephen Horn: Horn log, p. 82, EMDP.

254 Meantime, Everett Dirksen kept noodling: Mackaman, *Long Hard Furrow*, p. 79.

255 "Then we've got him": Horn log, p. 84, EMDP.

255 "Do you think that's true?": TPR, Lyndon B. Johnson, vol. 5, pp. 891–92.

255 "We have not suffered from this effort": CR, p. 7380.

256 No Republicans were present: Adam Clymer, *Edward M. Kennedy: A Biography* (New York: William Morrow, 1999), pp. 57–58.

256 John Stewart was lobbied fiercely by Betty Friedan: Stewart interview.

256 there was widespread concern among civil rights supporters: Mackaman, *Long Hard Furrow*, p. 80.

257 "I wouldn't leave Dick Russell": *TPR*, Lyndon B. Johnson, vol. 5, p. 959.

10: Alternatives and Substitutes

258 "Don't you break out in a sweat": Horn log, p. 87, EMDP.

259 "You can't give people blood tests": Ibid., p. 103.

259 "There are enough groups and interests": John Stewart manuscript, quoted in Loevy, ed., *Civil Rights Act of 1964*, pp. 96–97.

259 shortly before midnight: *CR*, p. 7799.

261 At this point, the bells: Horn log, p. 94, EMDP.

261 Dirksen at long last introduced his fair employment amendments: *CR*, p. 8192.

261 Dirksen's proposals would: *New York Times*, Apr. 17, 1964.

262 Dirksen also announced: Mackaman, *Long Hard Furrow*, p. 85.

263 That evening, Humphrey and Kuchel's staff analysis: Horn log, pp. 97–98, EMDP.

263 "we've lost our virginity": Ibid., p. 102.

264 "We are not going to take out Title VII": *New York Times*, Apr. 19, 1964.

264 Katzenbach himself acknowledged: Horn log, p. 106, EMDP.

264 "He was better than the player": *CR*, p. 8451.

265 "It keeps the local spirit": Mackaman, *Long Hard Furrow*, p. 87.

265 "The more we see of the amendments": Stewart manuscript, cited in Loevy, ed., *Civil Rights Act of 1964*, p. 252.

265 "southerners know they are in deep trouble": Ibid., p. 102.

265 a case "of age resisting youth": Mann, *Walls of Jericho*, p. 401.

265 Richard Russell himself had acknowledged: Ibid., pp. 401–2.

266 "The jig is just about up": Stewart manuscript, quoted in Loevy, ed., *Civil Rights Act of 1964*, pp. 95–96.

266 Talmadge proposed to guarantee a jury: *CR*, p. 8650.

266 "I believe the Senate can look forward": Whalen and Whalen, *Longest Debate*, p. 167.

266 Russell now took the floor: *CR*, p. 8666.

267 "In short," Stewart concluded: Stewart manuscript, quoted in Loevy, ed., *Civil Rights Act of 1966*, pp. 94–95.

268 "Let's not kid ourselves": Horn log, p. 129, EMDP.

268 not enough to attract Russell: *CR*, p. 9135.

269 "Must I do that?": Mackaman, *Long Hard Furrow*, p. 96.

269 "My other phone is ringing": Robert Dallek, "Lyndon B. Johnson," in Robert A. Wilson, ed., *Character Above All* (New York: Simon and Schuster, 1995), p. 109.

269 "the very best of friends": Dirksen letter to Richard Okamoto, Apr. 3, 1964, EMDP.

270 "I think you got a point there": *TPR*, Lyndon B. Johnson, vol. 4, p. 101.

270 "You couldn't name a commission": Hulsey, *Everett Dirksen and His Presidents*, p. 186.

270 "Do you want him appointed?": *TPR*, Lyndon B. Johnson, vol. 2, pp. 523–24.

270 "You say you want the House bill": Whalen and Whalen, *Longest Debate*, p. 171.

270 Johnson was having none of that: *TPR*, Lyndon B. Johnson, vol. 6, p. 326.

271 "I'm against any amendments": Ibid., p. 360.

272 "The hell with them": Jeffrey Frank, *Ike and Dick: Portrait of a Strange Political Marriage* (New York: Simon and Schuster, 2013), p. 220.

272 The pro-civil-rights forces immediately feared: *CR*, p. 9810.

272 "I say that couldn't happen in the South": *New York Times*, May 2, 1964.

273 "How about Christmas?": *CR*, p. 9854.

273 for mental observation: Mudd, *Place to Be*, p. 146.

273 "I'm trying to unscrew the inscrutable": MacNeil, *Dirksen*, p. 234.

274 "virtually every idea he held": Everett McKinley Dirksen, *The Education of a Senator* (Urbana: University of Illinois Press, 1998), p. 8.

274 In 1950, when Dirksen first ran: MacNeil, *Dirksen*, p. 129.

274 Dirksen had never made any secret of his qualms: Mackaman, *Long Hard Furrow*, p. 102.

274 "The Senator grew up seeing both sides": Elizabeth Drew, "The Politics of Cloture," *The Reporter*, July 16, 1964, p. 21.

274 "how do you spell straight?": Civil Rights File, EMDP.

275 "Dirksen and I had the same general approach": Loevy interviews, Collection 151, EMDP.

275 "so labyrinthine, so bewildering": EMD, Alpha, 1959, Kennedy, EMDP.

275 "This had to be a bipartisan bill": Author interview with Cornelius Kennedy, June 2013.

276 "A sort of ad hoc committee": *The Reporter*, July 16, 1964, p. 20.

276 "True give and take was possible": Stewart manuscript, cited in Loevy, ed., *Civil Rights Act of 1964*, p. 260.

276 "We were all very dear friends": Author interview with Kenneth Teasdale, May 2013.

276 But all was not collegial: Whalen and Whalen, *Longest Debate*, p. 176.

276 He stalked out of the meeting: Loevy, ed., *Civil Rights Act of 1964*, p. 256.

276 (Indeed, Dirksen did appear): Mary McGrory, "Rights Bill Rests with 2 Men," *Washington Star*, May 6, 1964.

277 The Republican liberals were not happy, either: Horn log, p. 159, EMDP.

277 Johnson's "gambit on cloture": Whalen and Whalen, *Longest Debate*, pp. 174, 178.

278 "shook hell out of them": *TPR*, Lyndon B. Johnson, vol. 6, p. 528.

278 "somewhat of a minor miracle": Stewart manuscript, cited in Loevy, ed., *Civil Rights Act of 1964*, p. 116.

279 "The people's business must come first": *PPP*, Lyndon B. Johnson, 1963–64, p. 618.

279 "I'm not getting much help on cloture": Horn log, p. 161, EMDP.

280 "I know damn well we can't beat it": *TPR*, Lyndon B. Johnson, vol. 6, pp. 511–12.

280 "One of my roommates in law school": Kennedy interview.

281 "hold out as long as possible": Stewart manuscript, quoted in Loevy, ed., *Civil Rights Act of 1964*, p. 257.

281 "'Pattern or practice' had a vagueness to it": Author interviews with Teasdale and Ferris; Ferris OH, U.S. Senate Historian's Office.

281 "I'm talking out of both sides of my mouth": Horn log, p. 168, EMDP.

282 "My office is not a single trust": *PPP*, Lyndon B. Johnson, 1963–64, p. 330.

282 "we do not have the votes to prevent passage": Whalen and Whalen, *Longest Debate*, p. 178.

284 "You'd be surprised at how chummy": Hulsey, *Everett Dirksen and His Presidents*, p. 148.

284 drank almost constantly: Valeo OH, U.S. Senate Historian's Office.

284 "Champagne is Mrs. Dirksen's favorite vegetable": Combined sources, cited in Hulsey, *Everett Dirksen and His Presidents*, p. 148.

284 "No matter where the hands stood": John G. Tower, *Consequences: A Personal and Political Memoir* (Boston: Little, Brown, 1991), p. 56.

284 "That ain't water, kid": Author interview with John Stewart.

284 "Fake pearls before real swine": Author interview with Jack Rosenthal.

284 "progress on the bill to date is nil": *TPR*, Lyndon B. Johnson, vol. 6, p. 954.

285 "some very dark days in this country": *PPP*, Lyndon B. Johnson, 1963–64, p. 684.

11: It Can't Be Stopped

286 "we have gone a long ways": Mackaman, *Long Hard Furrow*, p. 105.

288 The pro-civil-rights forces had lobbied Mundt: Author interview with Ferris.

288 "those two goddamned bishops": Mann, *Walls of Jericho*, p. 413.

288 "See what I'm up against?": Whalen and Whalen, *Longest Debate*, p. 183.

288 "And to me, too": Ibid., p. 183; Mackaman, *Long Hard Furrow*, p. 106.

289 "just a question of doing the job": Loevy interviews with Rauh and Kennedy, Collection 151, EMDP.

289 McCulloch offered the most judicious summation: "Man Was Born to Be Free," Box 1, Folder 2, WMMP.

289 "they're not going to be happy": *TPR*, Lyndon B. Johnson, vol. 6, p. 652.

289 "it would be a great victory for civil rights": Whalen and Whalen, *Longest Debate*, p. 183.

290 "worthy of the Land of Lincoln": *TPR*, Lyndon B. Johnson, vol. 6, p. 662.

290 "We'll have real revolution in this country": Ibid., p. 697.

291 "lowdown, dirty, cheap politics": Ibid., p. 690.

291 "Marshall and I will slit our throats": Horn log, p. 197, EMDP.

292 "There are no public cheers from me": Ibid., p. 198.

292 "to make the bill less burdensome": *CR*, p. 11288.

292 But liberals like Clark . . . said they could live with it: Whalen and Whalen, *Longest Debate*, p. 184.

292 "It's a gargantuan thing!": Ibid., p. 185; *CQ*, week ending May 22, 1964, p. 987.

293 "No army can withstand": *New York Times*, May 20, 1964. Dirksen claimed that Hugo had written such a sentiment in his diary on the night he died; no such diary has ever surfaced. The quotation seems most likely to have come from Hugo's short story "Histoire d'un Crime," where it was rendered as "A stand can be made against invasion by an army; no stand can be made against invasion by an idea." See Mann, *Walls of Jericho*, p. 422.

293 "they're allowed to": MacNeil, *Dirksen*, p. 235.

293 he had inserted a provision: Smith, *Race, Labor, and Civil Rights*, p. 28.

294 "We have attempted to be fair": *CR*, p. 11935.

294 "But the issue is here, and it cannot be evaded": Ibid., p. 11936.

294 Humphrey praised the compromise's "practical, commonsense approach": Ibid., p. 11937.

294 "As one who lives in the South": Ibid., p. 11943.

295 "It wasn't a sell-type meeting": Whalen and Whalen, *Longest Debate*, p. 187.

295 "crystal clear, with brackets and underscoring": *CR*, p. 12275.

295 "Listen, they forget I'm no spring chicken anymore": MacNeil, *Dirksen*, p. 236.

295 "we shall be here until 1984": *CR*, p. 12642.

296 "Bourke had the feeling": Whalen and Whalen, *Longest Debate*, p. 191.

296 There was instant panic: *CR*, p. 12847.

297 Russell drily noted: Ibid.

297 Overnight, Hubert Humphrey received commitments: Whalen and Whalen, *Longest Debate*, pp. 190–92.

297 "Well, Dick," he said, "you haven't any votes": Hubert H. Humphrey memo, cited in Loevy, ed., *Civil Rights Act of 1964*, p. 91. John Stewart would recall that claiming credit for gaining Hickenlooper's support for cloture became a kind of Senate parlor game, with multiple sources believing their own influence had been crucial. For example, Frank Valeo, the secretary of the Senate, would recall that when he told Hickenlooper that Lyndon Johnson had reportedly said that getting Hickenlooper's vote would be as tough as getting Strom Thurmond's, Hickenlooper took umbrage at being compared to such a segregationist and insisted, "I've got nothing against civil rights, it's just that the goddamn bill is no good." Valeo said that Mike Mansfield had then urged the bipartisan lawyers' group working on the bill to listen to Hickenlooper's complaints, thus softening Hickenlooper's opposition. See Valeo OH, Senate Historian's Office.

298 "We, the undersigned Senators": Whalen and Whalen, *Longest Debate*, p. 194.

298 "I think it makes it much more difficult": *TPR*, Lyndon B. Johnson, vol. 7, p. 149.

298 "there may be speeches beyond the hour of 12 o'clock": *CR*, p. 13098.

298 "it would impair the civil rights of all Americans": Ibid., p. 13133.

299 And with that, Humphrey concluded: Ibid., p. 13175.

299 He had stayed up late the night before: Remarks and Releases, June 10, 1964, EMDP.

300 the Senate chamber was packed: Whalen and Whalen, *Longest Debate*, p. 197.

300 Nick Katzenbach and Burke Marshall had to sit on the steps: Smith interview.

300 "I was conceived by a pair of good": Ibid., p. 13308.

301 "I appeal to the Senate to vote down this gag rule": Ibid., pp. 13308–9.

301 "to make the year 1964 our freedom year": Ibid., p. 13310.

302 "Nothing is eternal except change": Ibid., p. 13319.

303 "It's all right, Carl," Mansfield now assured him: Whalen and Whalen, *Longest Debate*, p. 199.

303 Roger Mudd was broadcasting live on CBS: Mudd, *Place to Be*, p. 154.

304 "Ervin set forth the proposal": Stewart manuscript, cited in Loevy, ed., *Civil Rights Act of 1964*, p. 137.

305 "to regroup, rethink and recollect": *CR*, p. 13330.

305 The weary Georgian praised Humphrey: Humphrey, *Education of a Public Man*, p. 211.

305 The lawyers said that the amendment, as revised, would do no harm: Stewart manuscript, cited in Loevy, ed., *Civil Rights Act of 1964*, p. 139; Whalen and Whalen, *Longest Debate*, p. 207; *CQ Weekly*, week ending June 12, 1964, p. 1171.

306 floor leaders accepted an amendment: Smith, *Race, Labor, and Civil Rights*, p. 29.

306 Tower's proposal passed on a voice vote: EMD, Alpha, 1964, Piper, EMDP.

306 "God damn you, Russell": Stewart interview.

307 Later that same Wednesday: MacNeil, *Dirksen*, p. 212.

307 "because we have been under quite a strain": *CR*, p. 14239.

307 When the Senate convened that morning: Whalen and Whalen, *Longest Debate*, p. 213. In Texas, a forty-year-old oil company executive who was the Republican candidate for the U.S. Senate embraced Goldwater's position. His name was George Herbert Walker Bush, and his stance would dog him uncomfortably for the rest of his political life.

309 "Joining the legions of other small rural dailies": Ibid., p. 217.

309 "the highest breach of senatorial ethics": Stewart manuscript, cited in Loevy, ed., *Civil Rights Act of 1964*, p. 146.

309 "There is no room for second-class citizenship in our country": Whalen and Whalen, *Longest Debate*, p. 214.

310 "This, indeed, is his moment as well as the Senate's": *CR*, p. 14509.

310 "I am prepared for the vote": Dirksen, *The Honorable Mr. Marigold*, p. 193; *CR*, p. 14511.

311 "No single act of Congress": *PPP*, Lyndon B. Johnson, 1963–64, p. 787.

311 "Nobody's maid worked on Juneteenth": Russell, *Lady Bird*, p. 244.

311 "Never in my fifteen years in the Senate": Whalen and Whalen, *Longest Debate*, p, 216.

12: The Law of the Land

312 From the moment the Senate approved the bill: *TPR*, Lyndon B. Johnson, vol. 8, pp. 350–51.

314 "signing it as soon as it's available is the correct idea": Ibid., p. 359.

314 "I think it'd be very bad if you waited": Ibid., p. 362.

314 "I don't think you can hold it up": Ibid., p. 365.

314 "That would be very unfortunate": Ibid., p. 374.

314 "we ought to go forward with this": Ibid., p. 382.

315 "Summer means a thousand delights": Statements of LBJ, Box 112, LBJL.

316 "Now, goddamn it, Mr. President": *TPR*, Lyndon B. Johnson, vol. 8, p. 539.

317 "If Martin Luther King were chairman of this committee": Whalen and Whalen, *Longest Debate*, p. 222.

318 "The bell has tolled": *CR*, p. 15870.

318 "Forever and a day": Ibid., p. 15871.

319 "Never have so many of such ability": Ibid., p. 15894.

319 he was changing his vote: Ibid.

319 "an overwhelming vote for this bill": Ibid., p. 15896.

320 "House passed the bill": President's Daily Diary, LBJL.

320 "I'll feel relieved": *TPR*, Lyndon B. Johnson, vol. 8, p. 379.

320 "They're selfish bastards": Ibid., p. 384.

320 "Mr. President, it's so monumental": Ibid., p. 374.

321 "Get Doug Cater and Dick Goodwin": Bill Moyers Files, Box 125, LBJL.

321 "The thought must be in the speech": Ibid.

322 "with all kinds of people around": Caplan, *Farther Along*, pp. 230–31.

322 "He's signing!" someone shouted: Bruce Watson, *Freedom Summer* (New York: Penguin Books, 2010), p. 132.

324 "the sadness that we saw in Bobby's eyes": Schlesinger, *Robert F. Kennedy and His Times,* vol. 2, p. 674.

325 "we just delivered the South to the Republican Party": Moyers, *Moyers on America*, p. 197.

325 "I don't tell that figure to anybody": *TPR*, Lyndon B. Johnson, vol. 8, p. 400.

325 "It's been relatively calm": Ibid., p. 401.

326 "a man gets his back up": Ibid., p. 417.

326 She never again returned to the ranch: Booker, *Shocking the Conscience*, p. 246.

327 "They got the right answers, too": *TPR*, Lyndon B. Johnson, vol. 8, p. 446.

327 "I'm sorry he was there": Ibid., p. 454.

Epilogue

329 "All across the South": John Lewis, interview with Adam Clymer, May 8, 2008.

330 "These statutes are now on the books": Mann, *Walls of Jericho*, p. 430.

331 By 1987, Mississippi would lead the nation: *Southern Changes*, vol. 9, no. 5 (1987), p. 25.

332 "Fifty years later, we can ride anywhere": *Washington Post*, Aug. 28, 2013.

336 Gerri Whittington continued her career: Booker, *Shocking the Conscience*, pp. 246–47.

337 "The old battles have been won": *Man Was Born to Be Free*, Box 1, Folder 2, WMMP.

338 "Please forgive the emotional tone of this letter": Correspondence files, 1971, WMMP.

339 a "Negro president" in forty years: Schlesinger, *Robert F. Kennedy and His Times,* vol. 1, p. 346.

Bibliography

Abernathy, Ralph David. *And the Walls Came Tumbling Down: An Autobiography*. New York: Harper and Row, 1989.

Baker, Bobby. *Wheeling and Dealing: Confessions of a Capitol Hill Operator*. New York: W. W. Norton, 1978.

Belafonte, Harry, with Michael Shnayerson. *My Song*. New York: Alfred A. Knopf, 2011.

Beschloss, Michael. *Reaching for Glory: Lyndon Johnson's Secret White House Tapes, 1964–1965*. New York: Simon and Schuster, 2001.

———. *Taking Charge: The Johnson White House Tapes, 1963–1964*. New York: Simon and Schuster, 1997.

Black, Earl, and Merle Black. *Politics and Society in the South*. Cambridge, Mass.: Harvard University Press, 1987.

Blaine, Gerald, and Lisa McCubbin. *The Kennedy Detail*. New York: Gallery Books, 2010.

Bogle, Donald. *Heat Wave: The Life and Career of Ethel Waters*. New York: Harper, 2011.

Bolden, Abraham. *The Echo from Dealey Plaza: The True Story of the First African American on the White House Secret Service Detail*. New York: Harmony Books, 2008.

Booker, Simeon, with Carol McCabe Booker. *Shocking the Conscience: A Reporter's Account of the Civil Rights Movement*. Jackson: University of Mississippi Press, 2013.

Bradlee, Benjamin C. *Conversations with Kennedy*. New York: W. W. Norton, 1975.

Branch, Taylor. *The King Years: Historic Moments in the Civil Rights Movement*. New York: Simon and Schuster, 2013.

———. *Parting the Waters: America in the King Years, 1954–63*. New York: Simon and Schuster, 1988.

———. *Pillar of Fire: America in the King Years, 1963–65*. New York: Simon and Schuster, 1987.

Brauer, Carl M. *John F. Kennedy and the Second Reconstruction*. New York: Columbia University Press, 1977.

Brayman, Harold. *The President Speaks Off the Record*. Princeton, N.J.: Dow Jones Books, 1976.

Brennan, Mary C. *Turning Right in the Sixties: The Conservative Capture of the GOP*. Chapel Hill: University of North Carolina Press, 1995.

Bruce, Preston. *From the Door of the White House*. New York: William Morrow, 1984.

Bryant, Nick. *The Bystander: John F. Kennedy and the Struggle for Black Equality*. New York: Basic Books, 2006.

Byrne, Jeb. *Out Front: Preparing the Way for JFK and LBJ*. Albany, N.Y.: Excelsior Editions, 2010.

Caplan, Marvin. *Farther Along: A Civil Rights Memoir*. Baton Rouge: Louisiana State University Press, 1999.

Caro, Robert A. *Master of the Senate: The Years of Lyndon Johnson*. New York: Alfred A. Knopf, 2002.

———. *Means of Ascent: The Years of Lyndon Johnson*. New York: Alfred A. Knopf, 1990.

———. *The Passage of Power: The Years of Lyndon Johnson*. New York: Alfred A. Knopf, 2012.

———. *The Path to Power: The Years of Lyndon Johnson*. New York: Vintage, 1983.

Civil Rights Act of 1964, The. Washington, D.C.: Operations Manual, BNA Incorporated, 1964.

Clymer, Adam. *Edward M. Kennedy: A Biography*. New York: William Morrow, 1999.

Cobb, Charles E., Jr. *On the Road to Freedom: A Guided Tour of the Civil Rights Trail*. Chapel Hill, N.C.: Algonquin Books, 2008.

Connelly, Michael. *The President's Team: The 1963 Army-Navy Game and the Assassination of JFK*. Minneapolis: MVP Books, 2009.

Cowger, Thomas W., and Sherwin J. Markman, eds. *Lyndon Johnson Remembered: An Intimate Portrait of a Presidency*. Lanham, Md.: Rowman and Littlefield, 2003.

Cross, James U. *Around the World with LBJ: My Wild Ride as Air Force One Pilot, White House Aide, and Personal Confidant*. Austin: University of Texas Press, 2008.

Dallek, Robert. *Flawed Giant: Lyndon Johnson and His Times*. Oxford: Oxford University Press, 1998.

———. *An Unfinished Life: John F. Kennedy, 1917–1963*. Boston: Little, Brown, 2003.

Daschle, Tom, and Charles Robbins. *The United States Senate*. New York: St. Martin's Press, 2013.

Dierenfield, Bruce J. *The Civil Rights Movement*. Harlow, UK: Pearson Education Limited, 2008.

———. *Keeper of the Rules: Congressman Howard W. Smith of Virginia*. Charlottesville: University Press of Virginia, 1987.

Dirksen, Everett McKinley. *The Education of a Senator*. Urbana: University of Illinois Press, 1998.

———, with H. Paul Jeffers. *Gallant Men: Stories of American Adventure*. New York: McGraw-Hill, 1967.

Dirksen, Louella. *The Honorable Mr. Marigold: My Life with Everett Dirksen*. Garden City, N.Y.: Doubleday, 1972.

Dudziak, Mary L. *Cold War Civil Rights: Race and the Image of American Democracy.* Princeton, N.J.: Princeton University Press, 2000.

Durham, Michael S. *Powerful Days: The Civil Rights Photography of Charles Moore.* New York: Stewart, Tabori and Chang, 1991.

Euchner, Charles. *Nobody Turn Me Around: A People's History of the 1963 March on Washington.* Boston: Beacon Press, 2010.

Farmer, James. *Lay Bare the Heart: An Autobiography of the Civil Rights Movement.* New York: Arbor House, 1985.

Findlay, James F., Jr. *Church People in the Struggle: The National Council of Churches and the Black Freedom Struggle, 1950–1970.* Oxford: Oxford University Press, 1993.

Fite, Gilbert C. *Richard B. Russell, Jr.: Senator from Georgia.* Chapel Hill: University of North Carolina Press, 1991.

Frady, Marshall. *Martin Luther King, Jr.: A Life.* New York: Penguin, 2006.

Frank, Jeffrey. *Ike and Dick: Portrait of a Strange Political Marriage.* New York: Simon and Schuster, 2013.

Freeman, Jo. *We Will Be Heard: Women's Struggles for Political Power in the United States.* Lanham, Md.: Rowman and Littlefield, 2008.

Friedly, Michael, and David Gallen. *Martin Luther King, Jr.: The FBI File.* New York: Carroll and Graf, 1993.

Garner, James, and Jon Winokur. *The Garner Files.* New York: Simon and Schuster, 2011.

Garrettson, Charles L., III. *Hubert H. Humphrey: The Politics of Joy.* New Brunswick, N.J.: Transaction, 1993.

Garrow, David J. *Bearing the Cross: Martin Luther King, Jr., and the Southern Christian Leadership Conference.* New York: HarperCollins/Perennial Classics, 2004.

Gentry, Curt. *J. Edgar Hoover: The Man and the Secrets.* New York: W. W. Norton, 1991.

Gillette, Michael L. *Lady Bird Johnson: An Oral History.* Oxford: Oxford University Press, 2012.

Gillon, Stephen M. *The Kennedy Assassination, 24 Hours After: Lyndon B. Johnson's Pivotal First Day as President.* New York: Basic Books, 2009.

Golden, Harry. *Mr. Kennedy and the Negroes.* New York: World, 1964.

Goldman, Eric F. *The Tragedy of Lyndon Johnson.* New York: Dell, 1969.

Golway, Terry, and Les Krantz. *JFK: Day by Day.* Philadelphia: Running Press, 2010.

Goodwin, Doris Kearns. *Lyndon Johnson and the American Dream.* New York: St. Martin's Press, 1991.

———. *No Ordinary Time: Franklin and Eleanor Roosevelt; The Home Front in World War II.* New York: Simon and Schuster, 1994.

Goodwin, Richard N. *Remembering America: A Voice from the Sixties.* Boston: Little, Brown, 1988.

Guthman, Edwin. *We Band of Brothers: A Memoir of Robert F. Kennedy.* New York: Harper and Row, 1971.

Hamilton, Nigel. *JFK: Reckless Youth.* New York: Random House, 1992.

Hampton, Henry, and Steve Fayer. *Voices of Freedom: An Oral History of the Civil Rights Movement from the 1950s Through the 1980s.* New York: Bantam, 1991.

Hansen, Drew D. *The Dream: Martin Luther King, Jr., and the Speech that Inspired a Nation.* New York: HarperCollins, 2003.

Hardemann, D. B., and Donald C. Bacon. *Rayburn: A Biography*. Austin: Texas Monthly Press, 1987.

Heymann, C. David. *RFK: A Candid Biography of Robert F. Kennedy*. New York: Dutton, 1998.

Hill, Clint. *Mrs. Kennedy and Me*. New York: Gallery Books, 2012.

Horne, Lena, and Richard Schickel. *Lena*. Garden City, N.Y.: Doubleday, 1965.

Hulsey, Byron C. *Everett Dirksen and His Presidents*. Lawrence: University Press of Kansas, 2000.

Humphrey, Hubert H. *The Education of a Public Man: My Life and Politics*. Minneapolis: University of Minnesota Press, 1991.

Johnson, Lady Bird. *A White House Diary*. Austin: University of Texas Press, 2007.

Johnson, Lyndon Baines. *Public Papers of the Presidents, 1963–64,* vols. 1 and 2. Washington, D.C.: United States Government Printing Office, 1965.

———. *The Vantage Point: Perspectives of the Presidency, 1963–1969*. New York: Holt, Rinehart and Winston, 1971.

Jones, Clarence B., and Stuart Connelly. *Behind the Dream: The Making of the Speech That Transformed a Nation*. New York: Palgrave Macmillan, 2011.

Katzenbach, Nicholas deB. *Some of It Was Fun: Working with RFK and LBJ*. New York: W. W. Norton, 2008.

Kennedy, Edward M. *True Compass: A Memoir*. New York: Twelve, 2009.

Kennedy, Jacqueline. *Historic Conversations on Life with John F. Kennedy*. New York: Hyperion, 2011.

Kennedy, John F. *Profiles in Courage*. New York: Harper and Brothers, 1956.

———. *Public Papers of the Presidents; 1961–63,* vols. 1–3. Washington, D.C.: United States Government Printing Office, 1962–64.

Kennedy, Robert F. Edited by Edwin O. Guthman and C. Richard Allen. *Collected Speeches*. New York: Viking, 1993.

———. *Robert Kennedy in His Own Words*. New York: Bantam, 1988.

———. *To Seek a Newer World*. Garden City, N.Y.: Doubleday, 1967.

Kennedy, Rose Fitzgerald. *Times to Remember*. New York: Doubleday, 1995.

King, Coretta Scott. *My Life with Martin Luther King, Jr.* New York: Puffin Books, 1993.

King, Martin Luther, Jr. *Why We Can't Wait*. New York: Signet Classics, 2000.

Kotz, Nick. *Judgment Days: Lyndon Baines Johnson, Martin Luther King, Jr., and the Laws That Changed America*. Boston: Houghton Mifflin, 2005.

Leamer, Laurence. *The Kennedy Men, 1901–1963*. New York: Harper Perennial, 2001.

Lewis, John. *Walking with the Wind: A Memoir of the Movement*. New York: Simon and Schuster, 1998.

Loevy, Robert D., ed. *The Civil Rights Act of 1964: The Passage of the Law That Ended Racial Segregation*. Albany: State University of New York Press, 1997.

———. *To End All Segregation: The Politics of the Passage of the Civil Rights Act of 1964*. Lanham, Md.: University Press of America, 1990.

Mackaman, Frank H. *The Long Hard Furrow: Everett Dirksen's Part in the Civil Rights Act of 1964*. Pekin, Ill.: Dirksen Congressional Center, 2006.

MacNeil, Neil. *Dirksen: Portrait of a Public Man*. New York: World, 1970.

———. *Forge of Democracy: The House of Representatives*. New York: David McKay, 1963.

————, and Richard A. Baker. *The American Senate: An Insider's History.* Oxford: Oxford University Press, 2013.

Manchester, William. *The Death of a President.* New York: Penguin Books, 1977.

Mann, Robert. *The Walls of Jericho: Lyndon Johnson, Hubert Humphrey, Richard Russell, and the Struggle for Civil Rights.* San Diego: Harcourt Brace, 1997.

Martin, Ralph G. *A Hero for Our Time: An Intimate Story of the Kennedy Years.* New York: Macmillan, 1983.

Matthews, Chris. *Jack Kennedy: Elusive Hero.* New York: Simon and Schuster, 2011.

McCarthy, Abigail. *Private Faces, Public Places.* New York: Curtis Books, 1972.

McPherson, Harry. *A Political Education: A Washington Memoir.* Austin: University of Texas Press, 1995.

McWhorter, Diane. *Carry Me Home: Birmingham, Alabama, the Climactic Struggle of the Civil Rights Revolution.* New York: Touchstone, 2002.

Middleton, Harry. *LBJ: The White House Years.* New York: Harry N. Abrams, 1990.

Miller, Merle. *Lyndon: An Oral Biography.* New York: Ballantine, 1981.

Moyers, Bill. *Moyers on America: A Journalist and His Times.* New York: Anchor Books, 2005.

Mudd, Roger. *The Place to Be: Washington, CBS, and the Glory Days of Television News.* New York: PublicAffairs, 2008.

Nasaw, David. *The Patriarch: The Remarkable Life and Turbulent Times of Joseph P. Kennedy.* New York: Penguin Press, 2012.

O'Brien, Lawrence F. *No Final Victories: A Life in Politics, from John F. Kennedy to Watergate.* New York: Ballantine, 1976.

Pach, Chester. *The Johnson Years.* New York: Facts on File, 2006.

Perry, Barbara A. *Rose Kennedy: The Life and Times of a Political Matriarch.* New York: W. W. Norton, 2013.

Peters, Charles. *Lyndon B. Johnson.* New York: Times Books, 2010.

Powell, Colin. *My American Journey.* New York: Random House, 1995.

Rampersad, Arnold. *Jackie Robinson: A Biography.* New York: Alfred A. Knopf, 1997.

Reedy, George B. *Lyndon B. Johnson: A Memoir.* New York: Andrews and McMeel, 1982.

Reeves, Richard. *President Kennedy: Profile of Power.* New York: Simon and Schuster, 1993.

Reporting Civil Rights, Part Two, 1963–1973. New York: Library of America, 2003.

Riedel, Richard Langham. *Halls of the Mighty: My 47 Years at the Senate.* Washington, D.C.: Robert B. Luce, 1969.

Ritchie, Donald A. *Reporting from Washington: The History of the Washington Press Corps.* Oxford: Oxford University Press, 2005.

Rogers, Warren. *When I Think of Bobby.* New York: HarperCollins, 1993.

Rosenberg, Jonathan, and Zachary Karabell. *Kennedy, Johnson, and the Quest for Justice: The Civil Rights Tapes.* New York: W. W. Norton, 2003.

Rowan, Carl T. *Breaking Barriers: A Memoir.* Boston: Little, Brown, 1991.

Rubel, David. *The Coming Free: The Struggle for African-American Equality.* London: DK Publishing, 2005.

Russell, Jan Jarboe. *Lady Bird: A Biography of Mrs. Johnson.* Lanham, Md.: Taylor Trade Publishing, 2004.

Schapsmeier, Edward L., and Frederick H. Schapsmeier. *Dirksen of Illinois: Senatorial Statesman.* Urbana: University of Illinois Press, 1985.

Scheele, Henry Z. *Charlie Halleck: A Political Biography.* New York: Exposition Press, 1966.

Schlesinger, Arthur M., Jr. *Journals, 1952–2000.* New York: Penguin Press, 2007.

———. *Robert Kennedy and His Times.* 2 vols. Boston: Houghton Mifflin, 1978.

———. *A Thousand Days: John F. Kennedy in the White House.* Boston: Houghton Mifflin, 1965.

Seeger, Pete, and Bob Reiser. *Everybody Says Freedom: A History of the Civil Rights Movement in Song and Pictures.* New York: W. W. Norton, 1989.

Sevareid, Eric, ed. *Candidates 1960.* New York: Basic Books, 1959.

Shesol, Jeff. *Mutual Contempt: Lyndon Johnson, Robert Kennedy, and the Feud That Defined a Decade.* New York: W. W. Norton, 1997.

Sides, Hampton. *Hellhound on His Trail: The Electrifying Account of the Largest Manhunt in American History.* New York: Anchor Books, 2011.

Sidey, Hugh. *John F. Kennedy, President.* New York: Atheneum, 1964.

Siracusa, Joseph M., ed. *The Kennedy Years.* New York: Facts on File, 2004.

Skrentny, John D. *The Minority Rights Revolution.* Cambridge, Mass.: Belknap Press of Harvard University Press, 2002.

Smith, Robert Samuel. *Race, Labor, and Civil Rights: Griggs versus Duke Power and the Struggle for Equal Employment Opportunity.* Baton Rouge: Louisiana State University Press, 2008.

Smith, Sally Bedell. *Grace and Power: The Private World of the Kennedy White House.* New York: Random House, 2004.

Solberg, Carl. *Hubert Humphrey: A Biography.* Minneapolis: Borealis Books, 2003.

Sorensen, Ted. *Counselor: A Life at the Edge of History.* New York: Harper, 2008.

Sorensen, Theodore C. *Kennedy.* New York: Harper and Row, 1965.

Stern, Mark. *Calculating Visions: Kennedy, Johnson and Civil Rights.* New Brunswick, N.J.: Rutgers University Press, 1992.

Stewart, John G. *Witness to the Promised Land: Observations on Congress and the Presidency from the Pages of "Christianity and Crisis."* Santa Ana, Calif.: Seven Locks Press, 2005.

Stossel, Scott. *Sarge: The Life and Times of Sargent Shriver.* Washington, D.C.: Smithsonian Books, 2004.

Strober, Gerald S., and Deborah H. Strober. *Let Us Begin Anew: An Oral History of the Kennedy Presidency.* New York: HarperCollins, 1993.

Talmadge, Herman E. *Talmadge: A Political Legacy, a Politician's Life.* Atlanta: Peachtree Publishers, 1987.

Theoharis, Jeanne. *The Rebellious Life of Mrs. Rosa Parks.* Boston: Beacon Press, 2013.

Thomas, Evan. *Robert F. Kennedy: His Life.* New York: Simon and Schuster, 2000.

Tower, John G. *Consequences: A Personal and Political Memoir.* Boston: Little, Brown, 1991.

United States Capitol Historical Society. *We the People: The Story of the United States Capitol, Its Past and Its Promise.* Washington, D.C.: United States Capitol Historical Society, 1963.

Updegrove, Mark K. *Indomitable Will: LBJ in the Presidency.* New York: Crown, 2012.

Valenti, Jack. *This Time, This Place: My Life in War, the White House, and Hollywood.* New York: Three Rivers Press, 2007.

———. *A Very Human President.* New York: Pocket Books, 1977.

Van Dyk, Ted. *Heroes, Hacks, and Fools: Memoirs from the Political Inside.* Seattle: University of Washington Press, 2007.

Vivian, Octavia. *Coretta: The Story of Coretta Scott King.* Minneapolis: Fortress Press, 2006.

Watson, Bruce. *Freedom Summer.* New York: Penguin Books, 2010.

Watson, Denton L. *Lion in the Lobby: Clarence Mitchell, Jr.'s Struggle for the Passage of Civil Rights Laws.* Lanham, Md.: University Press of America, 2002.

Weiner, Tim. *Enemies: A History of the FBI.* New York: Random House, 2012.

Weiss, Nancy J. *Whitney M. Young, Jr., and the Struggle for Civil Rights.* Princeton, N.J.: Princeton University Press, 1989.

Whalen, Charles, and Barbara Whalen. *The Longest Debate: A Legislative History of the 1964 Civil Rights Act.* Cabin John, Md.: Seven Locks Press, 1985.

White, Lee C. *Government of the People: Reflections of a White House Counsel to Presidents Kennedy and Johnson.* Lanham, Md.: Hamilton Books, 2008.

White, William S. *The Citadel: The Story of the U.S. Senate.* New York: Harper and Brothers, 1956.

Widmer, Ted, ed. *Listening In: The Secret White House Recordings of John F. Kennedy.* New York: Hyperion, 2012.

Wilkerson, Isabel. *The Warmth of Other Suns: The Epic Story of America's Great Migration.* New York: Vintage, 2011.

Wilkins, Roy, with Tom Mathews. *Standing Fast: The Autobiography of Roy Wilkins.* New York: Da Capo Press, 1994.

Williams, Juan. *Thurgood Marshall: American Revolutionary.* New York: Three Rivers Press, 1998.

Wilson, Sondra Kathryn, ed. *In Search of Democracy: The NAACP Writings of James Weldon Johnson, Walter White, and Roy Wilkins (1920–1977).* New York: Oxford University Press, 1999.

Wofford, Harris. *Of Kennedys and Kings: Making Sense of the Sixties.* Pittsburgh: University of Pittsburgh Press, 1992.

Woods, Randall B. *LBJ: Architect of American Ambition.* New York: Free Press, 2006.

Zelikow, Philip, et al., eds. *The Presidential Recordings: John F. Kennedy,* vols. 1–3. New York: W. W. Norton, 2001.

———. *The Presidential Recordings: Lyndon B. Johnson,* vols. 1–8. New York: W. W. Norton, 2005–2011.

Acknowledgments

I owe this book to Cullen Murphy, editor nonpareil. For a long time, he urged me to find such a project, and in 2011, anticipating the anniversary of the Civil Rights Act, he came up with this one. I thank him for his wise counsel at *Vanity Fair*, and not least for the invaluable suggestions he offered after a careful reading of a near-final draft of this manuscript. He is a valiant prince, a true friend, and a good writer.

Paul Golob at Henry Holt and Company (backed by the generous support of Holt's publisher, Steve Rubin) bought the proposal and then made the book a reality, with keen intelligence and critical support at every step. Having worked with Paul on another book a decade ago, I understood his amazing skills—his seemingly bottomless font of general knowledge, and his swift and sure way with a pencil. It was, nevertheless, a pleasure to be reminded what a haimish guy he is, the Steve Allen of editors. He makes hard work feel fun, and he has my enduring gratitude. My lawyer, Bob Barnett, made the project feasible in a way that would have done his fellow Waukeganite Jack Benny proud. He knows how much I owe him, and tells me, with good humor, by the billable hour. Graydon Carter and Chris Garrett have given me unstinting support at

Vanity Fair, and indulged me for what amounted to a six-month hiatus. John Harris and Jim VandeHei at *Politico* took a chance on an aging player, and offered me a new foothold in the daily news game.

Emma Hurt, a Washington neighbor and undergraduate at Rice University, spent weeks reviewing the *Congressional Record*'s account of the Senate debate on the bill, producing elegant, accurate, accessible summaries of high-blown oratory and low-down dealings. I simply could not have written this book without her help.

My old friend and *New York Times* colleague Adam Clymer bequeathed me a singular gift early on: reams of his own research from an abandoned book project on the bill, including priceless interviews with colleagues and family members of Congressman William McCulloch, the unsung hero of the tale. Adam's generosity was not surprising, but it was stunning all the same, and he went on to scrub the manuscript with the eye of the veteran congressional correspondent he is, catching errors and infelicities too numerous and embarrassing to mention. David Shribman kindly shared other McCulloch materials. Gwen Ifill, another fond friend from *Times* days, did me the great honor of reviewing the manuscript, and with her shrewd and discerning eye brought essential perspective. Karen Avrich, author and researcher extraordinaire, checked the facts—and so much more. To say that Karen is the class of her field is to say that Everest is a hill. I labor in her shadow, and all the mistakes are mine. Barclay Walsh gave key early research aid.

Melissa Goldstein, one of the nation's premier photo researchers, found indelible images that brought the book's characters to life. The design team at Holt—Rick Pracher, who conceived the striking cover, and Meryl Levavi, who designed the elegant, readable text—made the book look great. Emi Ikkanda crossed all the t's with grace and good cheer, and Maggie Richards in marketing and Pat Eisemann in publicity always knew what to do, and when to urge an armchair flack to step back. The production editor, Rita Quintas, and copy editor, Emily DeHuff, eased the process of putting the pages between covers.

Anyone who would presume to write about the Civil Rights Act of 1964 stands in incalculable debt to the late Representative Charles Whalen of Ohio, and his wife, Barbara, who wrote the pioneering one-volume account of H.R. 7152's passage. Congressman Whalen not only knew Bill McCulloch, but interviewed many of the participants in the fight for the bill who have long since died, preserving their priceless firsthand recollections. The scholarship of Robert D. Loevy, Robert Mann, and Nick Kotz—each of whom has written or edited important works dealing with the bill—blazed the trail I followed. Mick Caouette, whose documentary on Hubert Humphrey recorded precious voices, generously shared interview transcripts. The journalist Nick Bryant uncovered riveting, little-known details about John Kennedy's early record on civil rights in his book, *The Bystander: John F. Kennedy and the Struggle for Black Equality.*

Two indefatigable diarists, one from each party, kept the most important contemporary accounts of Senate action on the bill: the late Stephen Horn, legislative assistant to Senator Thomas Kuchel of California, and John Stewart, who played the same role for Hubert Humphrey. Horn's meticulous daily log and Stewart's episodic but equally insightful diary entries were my constant companions in re-creating the long days of the filibuster. Horn, who went on from the Senate to become a university administrator and congressman from California, died in 2011. But John Stewart and his accomplished wife, Nancy, are very much alive. They not only answered endless questions and read the manuscript in draft, but also welcomed me as an overnight guest at their home and offered the gift of unexpected friendship.

I am grateful beyond words to the many other House, Senate, White House, and Justice Department staff members, and to the veterans of the labor and ecumenical movements, who took the time to share their memories, answer my queries, and check my work, including Bill Connell, Richard Donohue, Nancy Dutton, Charles Ferris, David Filvaroff, James Hamilton, Lloyd Hand, Neal Kennedy, Robert Kimball, Jane O'Grady, Jack Rosenthal, Norman Sherman, Peter Smith, James Symington, Kenneth Teasdale, Ted Van Dyk, and [the late] Lee C. White. I owe a special debt to my fellow Princetonian Nicholas deB. Katzenbach, who took the time to speak to me even as he was dying. The sharp mind and sense of humor that must have helped so much in passing the bill were palpably intact, even as his body failed him. Two of the last surviving members of the Senate that passed the bill—Birch Bayh and the late

Daniel Inouye—likewise took time to recall a signal moment in the life of the institution they loved. Former vice president Walter F. Mondale shared warm insights about his friend and colleague Hubert Humphrey and about the Senate they served. Representative John Dingell of Michigan, the "Dean of the House," was equally generous with his time. Among contemporary journalists, Roger Mudd of CBS News and the late E. W. Kenworthy of the *New York Times* provided conspicuously trenchant and helpful accounts of the bill's creation.

Family members of many figures involved in the history of the bill offered support, beginning with Caroline Kennedy, whose encouragement was unflagging. I am also grateful to Jean Kennedy Smith, Catie Marshall, Anne Talbot Kennedy, Ann McCulloch Carver, and Nancy McCulloch, and to Peter Douglas and Kate Douglas Torrey for working to unseal the oral history of their late father, John Douglas, at the John F. Kennedy Library after four decades.

Karen Adler Abramson, the Kennedy Library's chief archivist, supported my request to open the Douglas files, and her colleague Stephen Plotkin tirelessly answered many questions and pointed me in the right direction in reviewing the civil rights–related papers of both John and Robert Kennedy. At the Lyndon B. Johnson Library in Austin, Texas, I received enthusiastic backing from its director, Mark K. Updegrove, and eagle-eyed help from archivist Allen Fisher, who specializes in the library's civil rights collection. Frank Mackaman at the Dirksen Congressional Center in Pekin, Illinois, is a peerless one-man band, a veteran archival librarian and the reigning expert in all things Ev. His monograph on Dirksen's role in the bill was never far from my side, and I am everlastingly grateful for his help, including his willingness to read the final manuscript. Jeffrey Thomas and Laura Kissel at the Ohio State University Archives in Columbus were my wise guides to the papers of Bill McCulloch, and James Oda and his colleagues Gary Meek and Roger Hartley played the same role at the Piqua Public Library. David K. Frasier at the Lilly Library at Indiana University eased my journey into the world of Charlie Halleck, as the "Minnesota nice" staff of the Minnesota State Historical Society in St. Paul did with my trip to the world of Hubert Humphrey. Ted Widmer, director of the John Carter Brown Library at Brown

University, and the editor of *Listening In: The Secret White House Recordings of John F. Kennedy*, answered more than one pesky question.

The tireless team at the University of Virginia's Miller Center of Public Affairs, including Timothy Naftali, Philip Zelikow, Ernest May, Jonathan Rosenberg, Zachary Karabell, Robert David Johnson, David Shreve, Kent B. Germany, Max Holland, Guian A. McKee, and David C. Carter, are the guardians of purest historical gold. Their exquisitely edited, carefully annotated, lovingly compiled transcripts of the secret White House tape recordings of John Kennedy and Lyndon Johnson, published in conjunction with W. W. Norton & Company and now numbering eleven volumes and counting, are the single most vivid record of those two vivid presidencies.

I am indebted to my friend Charles Johnson III, retired parliamentarian of the House of Representatives, for his patient help with technical questions of House procedure, and for showing me the annotated copy of H.R. 7152 that appears on the cover of this book. I thank, as well, his colleague in the "other body," Peter Robinson, senior assistant parliamentarian of the Senate, for the same. The Senate historian, Donald A. Ritchie, was generous enough to read the portions of the manuscript involving the Senate debate, and to point me toward the remarkable series of oral history interviews that he conducted with Bobby Baker. Ken Keto, associate historian of the House of Representatives, offered a trenchant critique of the chapters involving the People's House, and his colleague Farar Elliott, the House's curator, helped me re-create the look and feel of hearing rooms on Capitol Hill circa 1963–64. Walter Oleszek of the Congressional Research Service provided a crucial early tutorial on such arcane topics as the Senate's morning hour, the concept of the "legislative day," and the differences between recessing and adjourning.

I am lucky enough to count myself not only a devoted reader but a friendly acquaintance of the leading popular historians of the Kennedy-Johnson era: Michael Beschloss, Robert Dallek, Doris Kearns Goodwin, Richard Reeves, and Sally Bedell Smith. The footnotes show the debt I owe to them, and to the indefatigable Robert A. Caro, whom I have never met but whose work I have read with avid appreciation for forty years, since the first serialization of *The Power Broker* in the *New Yorker*.

I am also lucky beyond measure to have come to the coverage of Washington and national politics for the *New York Times* just in time to know, interview—and, in many happy cases, dine and drink with—so many of the journalistic and political veterans of the New Frontier and Great Society, and this book reflects, if only by osmosis, scores of their recollections, impressions, and anecdotes. Happily still among us are Russell Baker, Harry Belafonte, Benjamin C. Bradlee, John Doar, Elizabeth Drew, Max Frankel, Marianne Means, Newton N. Minow, George Stevens Jr., Sander Vanocur, Harris Wofford, and Rosalind Wyman. Treasured in memory are R. W. Apple Jr., Letitia Baldrige, David S. Broder, Robert J. Donovan, Edwin O. Guthman, Haynes Johnson, James J. Kilpatrick, Fletcher Knebel, Anthony Lewis, Harry MacPherson, Mary McGrory, Burke Marshall, Robert Novak, George Reedy, John Reilly, Arthur M. Schlesinger Jr., Theodore C. Sorensen, Godfrey Sperling Jr., and Helen Thomas. It is not an overstatement to say that they—and my colleagues and editors on the *Times*—taught me everything I know.

To my parents, Connie and the late Jerry Purdum, I owe life itself, along with a love of books, music, and politics—and an expensive education that has enriched that life. My sister Edie and my brother Steve always have my back, and they helped combine research trips to Indiana and Minnesota with family gatherings. The dedication of this book only hints at the role that Dee Dee Myers has played, for nearly two decades now, as partner, first line of defense, and last voice in the ear—in my life and work. She has been all that and more, for better—and yes, for worse. I hope she has some small sense of what no words can tell her. I can only keep trying to make sure that she does. Our children, Kate and Stephen, make us ever mindful of the gift they are growing up with, one their mother and I did not share in our own childhoods, when the turmoil of the civil rights movement swirled around us without our understanding it. They are children of the twenty-first century, and their generation—black and white alike—lives in a better world because our brothers and sisters, living and dead, heard freedom's song and marched into the sunshine.

Index

About the Author

TODD S. PURDUM is a contributing editor at *Vanity Fair* and senior writer at *Politico*. He previously spent more than twenty years at the *New York Times*, where he served as diplomatic correspondent, White House correspondent, and Los Angeles bureau chief. A graduate of Princeton University, he lives in Washington, D.C., with his wife, Dee Dee Myers, the political commentator and former White House press secretary, and their two children.